NATIONALIZING GOVERNMENT

Public Policies in America

Theodore J. Lowi
Alan Stone

editors

 SAGE PUBLICATIONS   *Beverly Hills / London*

For information address:

SAGE PUBLICATIONS, INC.
275 South Beverly Drive
Beverly Hills, California 90212

SAGE PUBLICATIONS LTD
28 Banner Street
London ECIY 8QE

Printed in the United States of America

Library of Congress Cataloging in Publication Data
Main entry under title:
Nationalizing government.
    Includes bibliographical references and index.
    1. United States—Politics and government—1945—Addresses, essays, lectures. 2. Policy sciences—Addresses, essays, lectures. I. Lowi, Theodore J. II. Stone, Alan, 1931-
JK271.N38   309.1'73'092   78-19848
ISBN 0-8039-0707-9
ISBN 0-8039-0708-7 pbk.

FIRST PRINTING

CONTENTS

FOREWORD

This book represents a landmark in the policy studies literature. Previous books in the field have emphasized (1) methods or process, rather than substance, (2) readings or unintegrated symposia rather than integrated text, and (3) policy formation or evaluation rather than an analysis of the policies themselves. This book, however, focuses on ten of the most important specific policy problems in America by arranging to have commissioned experts analyze the key policies in those ten problem areas. As such it does emphasize substance, text, and the policies themselves. It is thus also likely to be widely used in public policy courses and widely referred to in public policy research.

The book could not have been so easily written 10 years ago when political scientists were much more concerned with the process of government than the outputs. Within recent years, however, the public policy or policy studies field has grown tremendously as indicated by the increasing list of relevant journals, organizations, articles, books, book series, convention papers, conference themes, courses, schools, academic positions, government jobs, foundation grants, summer institutes, curricula, and other indicators of academic and practitioner activity. Policy studies in this context can be defined as research that relates to the nature, causes, or effects of alternative public policies. This book concentrates on the nature of public policies, but the chapters also refer to causes and effects. By public policies are meant governmental decisions with regard to ways of handling various problems that are generally considered to require collective rather than individual or private action.

The recent growth of the policy studies field reflects some of the broader social forces relating to the general public's concern for civil rights, the war on poverty, peace, women's liberation, environmental protection, and other social problems. The growth of the interest of government in the scientific evaluation of alternative public policies is a reflection of the recent growth in government, especially the permanent establishment of a national presence. Social problems are increasingly being considered as requiring collective or governmental action that nationalization or centralization is one of the underlying themes of the chapters in this book.

Explaining that shift toward increased government involvement is virtually the same as explaining governmental growth which can be done largely in terms of three types of factors. First, there are socioeconomic forces such as (1) the increasing severity of wars, (2) the growing importance of education, (3) the growth of big business—especially interstate big business, (4) the growth of big labor and other pressure groups that seek aid and require regulation, (5) increased urbanization and the resulting loss of self-sufficiency, (6) increasing severity of periods of inflation and recession, (7) competition with foreign ideologies, and (8) the fact that regulation and governmental activity generates more regulation and activity. Second, there are certain enabling factors such as (1) expanded sources of government revenue necessary for carrying on increased government programs, (2) improved managerial techniques for handling large-scale government operations, and (3) changing constitutional interpretations. Third is the ideological shift from a prevailing attitude favoring least government toward the attitude that the government has many positive responsibilities. These factors have particularly resulted in an increased role for the federal government mainly because the socioeconomic forces referred to are often too big for state and local governments to handle given the geographical spread of the problems, the volume of money needed, and the possibly less aggressive personnel at the state and local levels.

Though the book has many authors, there are some continuities of concern, among which three seem to stand out. The first of these common concerns or themes is nationalization. Without any question, the authors document and assess the significance of the displacement of state and local options with attempts at national direction—attempts that only occasionally succeed. A second theme is bureaucratization. For all its problems, it is ubiquitous because it is efficient. Within the federal government, there has been increasing delegation of its problem-solving activities to administrative agencies because such agencies generally have greater specialized expertise, time, and flexibility to cope with the problems than Congress has. That is also true of relations between state legislatures and state executive agencies.

Another shared concern is the presence of the need for political and legal restraints. Political restraints manifest themselves in the American two-party system, the countervailing role of interest groups, and the periodic electoral process. Legal restraints manifest themselves in judicial review of executive and legislative acts, separation of powers whereby legislatures can restrain administrators, and federalism whereby local authorities can often frustrate the implementation of federal mandates.

Another underlying theme involves capitalism or private ownership as the prevailing relation between the government and the economy. That relation shapes many of the public policies in the 10 specific problem areas analyzed. It clearly influences the options available and chosen with regard to the policy problems discussed concerning the business cycle, consumer protection, agriculture, energy, environmental protection, urban policy, natural resources, health, civil rights, crime, civil liberties, and foreign policy, although more so in some problems than others. One general effect of a private ownership system is to decrease the ability of the government to develop systematic comprehensive long-term planning in spite of the centralization trends mentioned above. All these underlying themes are further integrated and clarified by the opening chapter of Theodore Lowi and the concluding chapter of Alan Stone.

This volume was originally planned for the Sage Yearbooks in Politics and Public Policy of which I am the series editor. The Yearbooks are published in cooperation with the Policy Studies Organization. Volumes in the series generally consist of the best papers organized around a coherent theme presented in the previous year at the annual meetings of the American Political Science Association, the regional political science associations, and other policy-relevant gatherings. Theodore Lowi was the coordinator for a set of public policy panels at the 1976 APSA meeting. In attempting to bring together a good set of papers, Lowi and Stone exceeded their high original goals by starting from scratch and commissioning a new set of experts in the 10 public policy fields covered. This resulting volume goes beyond the Yearbook series in its size, procedures, and in covering virtually all the substance of American public policy. It is hoped that public policy teachers, researchers, students, practitioners, interested laymen, and others will find much of value here in obtaining a better understanding of public policies in America and the centralization of public policy making.

—*Stuart S. Nagel*
University of Illinois
at Urbana-Champaign

PREFACE

The development of this volume is a representation of its own subject—response to a perceived need, improvisation, adoption of a plan after the fact, and good luck. We had committed ourselves as editors to a Sage-PSO Yearbook in Politics and Public Policy based upon papers presented at the 1976 APSA Meetings. Immediately we confronted the fact that policy analysis in political science remains a very diffuse field. The attractive papers were too far away from completion, and many of the papers in final draft form were too superficial or too specialized, or both, for the kind of book we wanted to edit. We could not get the desired coverage from the chance presentations at the annual professional meeting, and it became equally clear that through this method we would not get papers that would address themselves equally to practitioners and students as well as academicians. Our alternatives ran a very narrow gamut between abandonment, selection of unrelated papers that would appear to be little more than a special issue of somebody's journal, or commissioning *de novo* our own set of papers according to criteria we would lay down in advance. We are very happy to have chosen the third alternative, although it was far the most difficult, the most time-consuming, and the least predictable.

If we are immodest in our claims and hopes for this book, it is because our contribution as editors was our good taste in authors. Beyond that, we kept our instructions to a minimum and our editorial role primarily to matters of style and consistency. Each chapter is a highly professional statement by an expert in the field, each attempts to analyze and to account for the policies and patterns in the subject area covered, yet each chapter manages to provide a tremendous amount of the instruction that the general lay public, including students, rarely get in public policy. The two of us, as editors, have tried to highlight certain important issues in the book in our opening and closing chapters.

Although we do commend the book as an unusually successful combination of professional analysis and textbook instruction, we make no claim to coverage of all important policy areas, nor do we claim exhaustive treatment of those areas selected. We claim only that the selected policy areas are of fundamental importance to the future of the United States, that each area will remain of fundamental importance for many years to come, and that no grasp of what our government is attempting to do will be secure without the materials each author has provided in this volume. Other than our constant concern for the relevance of each chapter and for presentation of the essentials of each policy area, there is no continuous theme running throughout the book—

unless it is this: that we Americans have committed ourselves to a large, modern state, that in so doing we have tied the fate of our democracy to the performance of our government, and that we can no longer look at policies in isolation from the political system itself because the legitimacy of the political system is now based upon the successful performance of government. This is a new and unprecedented moment in American history. We have, as a consequence of the development of a modern state, taken the famous slack out of our system. And we have no choice but to advance, for the risks of going back to a smaller ideal are even greater.

The record of government performance, as shown in this volume, is too spotty for the comfort of anyone who supports democratic government; but the story is not one of consistent failure or of inevitable defeat. Many failures have been absolute, real, and undeniable; but far more frequently, we have probably defined partial success as failure because of the high-flown rhetoric of our politicians. Although rhetoric is, of course, part of performance, good analysis and criticism of real policies may help sober up the rhetoric.

Somewhere in the relationship between political demands, policy responses, rhetoric about those responses, and the long-range legitimacy of the political system, there is a role for political science in policy analysis. This volume is part of a continuing effort by our authors and by our colleagues in the Policy Studies Organization to bring about some kind of balance, through responsible criticism, between government efforts, claims about these efforts, and the ultimate success of the nation's experiment with democracy. Now that the United States has become a modern state, in which the legitimacy of politics rests heavily upon the performance of the state, criticism of government becomes a fundamental political act, even when it is based upon disinterested scholarship. We insist further that policy analysis, independent of government, producing sustained criticism of that government, must become an essential phase of the democratic process. We hope this volume will make a substantial contribution to the lifting of political discourse toward a politics of policy analysis. If we leave this job to technocrats, we will have delegated to them the right to govern us as well as to administer us.

—Theodore J. Lowi
Alan Stone

ACKNOWLEDGMENTS

We are especially grateful to Ruth Sorelle for her role as copy editor and general assistant. It had to be a labor of devotion; the payment was too paltry to have defined it as a contractual relation. We also want to express our thanks to Stuart Nagel. His vigorous support of this special project outside the Series is merely one more example of the vital role he plays in the Policy Studies Organization. There are times when we feel Stu *is* the PSO. And, though it may be an unprecedented gesturre, each of us wants to thank the other in print for a delightful, instructive, and, we hope, productive editorship. Neither of us is sorry it's over, but we are, as a consequence of this endeavor as well as our long friendship, not likely to shun other opportunities to collaborate.

—*Theodore J. Lowi*
Alan Stone

1.

EUROPEANIZATION OF AMERICA?

FROM UNITED STATES TO UNITED STATE

THEODORE J. LOWI

Cornell University

Among the large nation-states of the 20th century, the United States is the oldest constitutional republic and has the youngest consolidated national government. The modern, positive national state in the United States is a product of the years since 1933. Our institutions of government are still adapting themselves to their new functions and new relationships. Even the vocabulary of analysis has been adjusting itself to the state and related concepts, which had once been rejected as too abstract, formalistic, legalistic, and European to have any precision or utility in the American context. Once we were unique as a large nation where government was almost a matter of politics. In the 1960s and 1970s, government became the central presence and politics a peripheral, occasionally significant, collection of activities oriented toward influencing the government—i.e., the apparatus of the state.

Between 1789 and the 1930s the national government was not such a significant force in the economic or social life of the citizens of the United States. The most important principle in the Constitution of 1787 was Federalism, and for well over a century, despite the Civil War and abolition, Federalism was one of the dominating realities. Given their intimate knowledge of European political theory and experience, the Founders certainly must have selected the term "state" as the name for our lower units of governement in order to indicate where most sovereignty was expected to reside. Comparison of national and state legislative activities in any year after 1800 will show that the states did almost all the governing in the United States. The domestic policies of the federal government were almost entirely concerned with subsidies, bounties, and claims. Land grants were piled upon land sales at low prices, and these were piled upon still additional land grants until the frontier ran out. Subsidies in the form of money and privilege were granted to the coastal trade, the railroads, and other common carriers. Tariffs were handed out to virtually any manufacturer or producer who could gain effective representation in Congress. The federal government was spending about 99 percent of its domestic effort husbanding commerce. In the meantime, the states were held responsible for the entire use of the "police power," which referred to the authority and obligation of governments to provide for the health, safety, and morals of the community. Through the police power the state governments provided for all of the property laws, the estate and family laws, the commerce laws, (including ownership and exchange), family laws (including morals), public health laws, occupation and professions laws, construction codes, water and mineral resources laws, electoral laws, banking and credit laws, insurance laws, most of the criminal laws—in sum, virtually all of the legal and governmental framework for civil society.

It is no paradox at all, as some would like us to believe, that the national political system of the United States was so stable despite the instability and dynamism of the society and the economy during all the formative years of the Republic. The fact of the matter is that all the fundamental social choices involving the coercive powers of government were being made at levels of government far below the national. The Constitution, quite deliberately, had delegated the fundamental social choices to the lower level and therefore had delegated or surpressed or diffused political conflict. We had not, for lack of a feudal system to overthrow, merely lucked up on political peace, class harmony, and intergroup consensus. We had really designed a means by which the opposites of peace, harmony, and consensus could be institutionally dispersed. Federalist 10, understood in the context of constitutional federalism and the actual comparative functions of government, was the most successful planning document in the history of the world.

Liberal historians are nevertheless correct insisting that the United States was never free of government and that our economy was never for an instant laissez-faire. Our economy was free, but only within an elaborate and stable framework of government. Moreover, it was not merely a government-as-umpire, although the use of government positively to enforce contracts was absolutely essential. Government during the era of our liberal economy was far more positive than this, and any images to the contrary are pure mythology. However, it would be equally mythological to argue that the role of government today is the same as the role of government in the 19th century. In a very important sense the New Deal was a "Roosevelt Revolution," as Mario Einaudi put it in the title of a very important analysis from a European perspective of the 20th century American experience with government. And the New Deal is significant far beyond its contribution to the size and scale of the national government, measured in budgetary terms. Although it is true that federal domestic expenditures increased from .8 percent of GNP in 1929 to 4.9 percent in 1939, the factor of far greater significance is the change during the New Deal in the *functions* of the federal government. Subsidy policies continued to be enacted by Congress; in fact, growth in subsidy programs accounts for a large portion of the general budgetary growth. However, the federal government was adopting two new kinds of functions, new at least for the federal government. These two new functions are *regulation* and *redistribution.* With the adoption of a very large number of important regulatory policies the federal government discovered the "police power." The second function is usually recognized as fiscal and monetary policies, but these bland labels mask the true significance of the new redistrubutive function.

Regulatory and redistributive functions and their respective policies are different from each other in a number of important respects. However, they have one very important thing in common which distinguishes the two of them from almost everything the federal government was doing prior to the 1930s. *They require the direct and coercive use of power over citizens.* With the adoption of such policies on a large scale, it was no longer possible for the federal government or its professional observers to hide from themselves the fact that "policy" and "police" have common roots. This is what is fundamentally new in the new, positive national state. There are, of course, well known precedents for both of these new kinds of policy, but the New Deal is the transition into the new state because of a number of such policies adopted at that time and because of the establishment once and for all of the constitutional right of the federal government to take on these new functions.

The New Deal was at most a transition, however, because a very large proportion of the policies adopted at that time were justified by the emergency conditions and might well have been repealed or weakened after the emergency had passed. After all, probably a minority of 1930s Democrats were intensely positive toward all the new interventions. Signs of permanent acceptance of the entire apparatus were few in the postwar years. The Employment Act of 1946 is the most significant sign that attitudes toward large positive national government had changed, but these signs were balanced by many negative signs, such as the softening of the Wagner Act by Taft-Hartley, and the softening of public housing with the much more private-sector oriented urban redevelopment. Attacks on TVA, welfare, and the alphabetocracy of the regulatory commissions were common throughout the 1946-1960 era. One can say therefore, that the new national state was not forever ensconced until the 1960s.

The return of the Democrats in 1961 brought with it far more than a commitment to the completion of the unfinished New Deal and Fair Deal programs. Of far greater significance was the new attitude they brought with them. Whereas the rhetoric of the 1930s had conceded that the new interventions were departures from tradition, and whereas even the New Deal Democrats attempted to justify many new programs as necessary evils, the leadership of the New Frontier accepted the positive national state and its programs as a positive virtue, as something desirable for its own sake and patently necessary for the society. There was great optimism about the ability of the national government to set the world to rights. There was optimism that the interests of all groups and classes were basically in harmony and that conflicts among these interests were never so far apart that they could not be adjusted by systematic, noncoercive governmental interventions. There was optimism about the ability of professionals and technocrats to define society's basic problems and to identify or invent the mechanisms appropriate for their solution.

Out of these attitudes grew the extremely optimistic and positive role of the national government we now accept as a commonplace fact about the Kennedy and Johnson Administrations. What is less well appreciated is the continuity between those Administrations and the Nixon-Ford Administrations. The accompanying tables and figures are a good overview of the policies and problems dealt with in this volume. But they are significant beyond that because they indicate that the positive national state is no longer simply a Democratic program. The national state is no longer a partisan matter at all. Republicans represent a different set of interests; Republicans may be stingy where Democrats are generous; Republicans may favor one mechanism and Democrats another. But there is no longer any variation between the two parties in their willingness to turn to the positive state, to expand it and to use it with vigor, whenever society's problems seem pressing and whenever governmental inaction may jeopardize electoral opportunities.

Table 1 is a listing, not necessarily exhaustive, of the important federal regulatory laws enacted by Congress since 1970. This looks more like a binge than a Republican retrenchment. Granted, some of these were pushed upon a reluctant President by a Democratic Congress. On the

Table 1.1. Federal Regulatory Laws and Programs Enacted Since 1970

Year Enacted	Title of Statute
1969-1970	Child Protection and Toy Safety Act
	Clear Air Amendments
	Egg Products Inspection Act
	Economic Stabilization Act
	Fair Credit Reporting Act
	Occupational Safety and Health Act
	Poison Prevention Packaging Act
	Securities Investor Protection Act
1971	Economic Stabilization Act Amendments
	Federal Boat Safety Act
	Lead-Based Paint Elimination Act
	Wholesome Fish and Fisheries Act
1972	Consumer Product Safety Act
	Equal Employment Opportunity Act
	Federal Election Campaign Act
	Federal Environmental Pesticide Control Act
	Federal Water Pollution Control Act Amendments
	Motor Vehicle Information and Cost Savings Act
	Noise Control Act
	Ports and Waterways Safety Act
1973	Agriculture and Consumer Protection Act
	Economic Stabilization Act Amendments
	Emergency Petroleum Allocation Act
	Flood Disaster Protection Act
1974	Atomic Energy Act
	Commodity Futures Trading Commission Act
	Consumer Product Warranties Act
	Council on Wage and Price Stability Act
	Employee Retirement Income Security Act
	Federal Energy Administration Act
	Hazardous Materials Transportation Act
	Housing and Community Development Act
	Pension Reform Act
	Privacy Act
	Safe Drinking Water Act
1975	Energy Policy and Conservation Act
	Equal Credit Opportunity Act
1976	Consumer Leasing Act
	Medical Device Safety Act
	Toxic Substances Control Act

other hand, these did not require passage over a Presidential veto. Moreover, the most significant regulatory program of that decade, and one of the most significant in American history, was the Economic Stabilization Act of 1970, which, although passed over Presidential objections and signed into law accompanied by expressions of presidential misgivings, was used elaborately and vigorously by President Nixon as soon as the rate of "stagflation" began to threaten the economy and the 1972 election.

Although people disagree intensely in their interpretations of the motives and significance of the Republican efforts in the field of redistribution, especially welfare policy, no one can deny the fact that Nixon was a very active President in the welfare area and that the net effect of his effort was a rather significant increase in the positive national state. One book-length account of Nixon's welfare policy activities opens with the following sentence: "Anyone who had predicted that Richard Nixon would be the first President to propose a guaranteed income for families coupled with wage supplements for poor fathers, would have been dismissed as mad."[1] Thus, although the increases shown on Table 1.2 were mainly mandated by commitments made prior to the 1970s— loosened eligibility rules, increased rates, inflation clauses, and so on— the Republicans were making their own contributions to further growth of welfare and would have expanded it even further, had the Democratic Congress been more cooperative.[2] Congress rejected Nixon's Family Assistance Plan by an unusual coalition of liberals, who, always suspicious of Nixon, felt the Plan did not go far enough and conservatives who feared the Plan would go far beyond the existing welfare structure, which was already far beyond the acceptable conservative limits. But Democrats and Republicans accepted the second most important Nixon proposal in the field of redistributive policy when they enacted General Revenue Sharing and then on top of that accepted several of Nixon's requests for "Special Revenue Sharing" to consolidate a large number of existing categoric grant-in-aid programs. From the fiscal standpoint, General Revenue Sharing is not all that significant. It committed the federal government to $30 billion over the first five years of operation and has never contributed more than 5% to the operating budgets of any local government. Special revenue-sharing proposals were not greeted with cheers by the Democratic majority in Congress, but eventually two of the seven requests were adopted. These were the Comprehensive Education and Manpower Act of 1973 and the Housing and Community Development Act of 1974. The first of these collapsed the existing 10,000 federal manpower contracts into 50 state and 350 large city "bloc grants." The second replaced seven major categoric grant programs with a single Community Development program grant.

Table 1.2. Federal Social Welfare Expenditures* (in Millions)

	FY 1965	FY 1970	FY 1976
Social Insurance	21,806	42,245	120,809
Public Aid	3,593	9,648	33,244
Health and Medical Programs	2,780	4,775	9,353
Veteran's Programs	6,010	8,901	18,790
Education	2,469	5,875	9,168
Housing	238	581	2,427
Other Social Welfare	812	2,258	4,534
(Vocational rehabilitation, child nutrition,			
OEO and ACTION) TOTAL	37,708	77,433	196,325

*Source: *Social Security Bulletin* (Washington, D.C., Government Printing Office, January, 1977): 5-7. For a more discriminating statement of Federal social welfare expenditures, see Lawrence A. Lynn, "A Decade of Policy Developments in the Income Maintenance System," in Robert Haveman *A Decade of Federal Anti-Poverty Programs* (Madison: Institute for Research on Poverty, 1977).

A good argument can be made that the motivation back of this special revenue-sharing approach was not merely to consolidate the many categoric grant-in-aid programs, but also to mask a net reduction in the total federal support for local governments. Nevertheless, there is a profound continuity between Democrats and Republicans which outweighs the minor difference in degree of generosity. The fact is, the Republicans were not opposing positive national government at all; quite the contrary. *Despite any reductions in the total amount of money they were willing to make available, they were actually tying the local governments closer to the national government than they had ever been tied before.* How is this possible? They did it by making the federal government more discretionary than it had been before. Under traditional grant-in-aid programs, there is a moderate limitation to discretion inherent in the fact that each grant-in-aid program was tied to a particular subject matter category. This is why we came to call them "categoric aid" to distinguish them from general bloc grants. Under General and Special Revenue Sharing, the Republicans took what little discretion there was in the categories and eliminated that almost entirely. This means that each of the 39 thousand communities eligible for revenue sharing can take whatever grants they get and decide for themselves whether the money should go to tax relief, to new public works, or to the purchase of General Sherman tanks. From the other side, this means that the federal government is all that much more able to use grant-in-aid appropriations on a patronage basis to buy the support of mayors, governors, and urban lobbies. In the very short run, this increased discretion, which increases the opportunities to use federal monies as patronage, will produce "clientele relationships" between the national center and the 39,000 local principalities. This changed or intensified relationship is far more important than marginal increases and decreases in the total amount of money available. In this sense, the national presence has been extended, and the direct national-local relationship has been cemented. Thereby our positive national state has been perpetuated in virtually the same manner as earlier national states cemented and eventually perpetuated the relationship between the central prince *(primes inter pares)* and all of the other feudal lords.

Although it would be impossible to overlook the growing power and presence of the national government through the conventional fiscal and monetary policies, one aspect of this has generally been overlooked: investment guarantees and insurance. The so-called Lockheed loan of 1975 is a good illustration of this kind of a national power, precisely because it was not a loan but was widely understood to be a loan. Lockheed, on the brink of actual bankruptcy, was neither allowed to disolve nor saved by a direct subsidy. The government took positive steps, but it spent no money, granted no loan, made no direct transfers at all. The government action was merely a signature by a representative of the Emergency Loan Guarantee Board on a document which stated that the federal government would guarantee up to $250 million that Lockheed could borrow from private sources. With that guarantee—and it was no more than a signature by a public official on a slip of paper— Lockheed could go to private banks and get money at relatively low interest rates or money that was not otherwise forthcoming at all. The authority of the Board, established by statute in 1970, was as follows:

> The Board, on such terms and conditions as it deems appropriate, may guarantee, or make commitments to guarantee, lenders against loss of principal or interest on loans that meet the requirements of this Act.

The so-called requirements in that passage were simply that the Board must find that in their opinion the economy would be seriously affected if the applicant was not able to continue operation.

Table 1.3 gives a quick sketch of the scale and variety of this particular policy activity in the 1970s. And stress should be put upon the fact that this is a listing only of the discretionary investment guarentee activities. The table does not include other programs of investment guarantees and insurance that are nondiscretionary.[3]

Figure 1.1 shows a striking growth of the accumulated commitments of all the agencies on Table 1.3. Note should be taken especially of the accelerated growth of this kind of national commitment since 1970. Obviously this is a technique of national government which the Repub-

Table 1.3. Discretionary Fiscal Policy: Federal Investment Guarantee Activity, 1976*

Program	New Guarantees (in millions)	Total Guarantees Outstanding (in millions)
International	$1,412	$ 2,502
Farmers Home Administration	4,391	17,847
Rural Electrification Administration	860	1,114
Maritime Administration	1,169	3,431
Economic Development Assistance	1	160
Defense-Tanker charters		180
HEW		
—Health	215	1,061
—Education	1,397	6,849
HUD		
—Low Rent	7,660	13,607
—FHA	8,316	88,988
—Communities	210	2,799
—GNMA	8,999	25,610
—Other credit	0	549
Interior		
—Indian Programs	29	29
Transportation		
—Railroads	264	670
—WMATA (DC Transit)	0	997
—Aircraft	78	100
Treasury	1,260	0
General Services Administration	24	956
Veterans Administration–Housing	10,250	64,116
Emergency Loan Guarantee Board (Lockheed)	0	185
Export-Import Bank	5,147	5,273
FDIC	0	1,144
Small Business Administration	1,768	4,979
Other agencies	13	68
TOTAL	53,463	243,213*

Source: Special Analyses, Budget of the U.S., FY1978, Sec. E.

*Several agencies, including the Government National Mortgage Association (GNMA), the Federal Financing Bank (FFB) and several federally sponsored private enterprises, including the Federal National Mortgage Assn. (FNMA), formerly a public agency, actually buy up many guaranteed loans from the banks, converting them essentially into direct government loans. In 1976, $25 billion, nearly half, of the loan guarantees were so converted; and enough conversions take place to reduce the accumulated figure from the $243.2 billion on the Table to $169.8 billion. Budgetary policy at OMB prefers the lower figures, arguing that otherwise there is double counting. But I prefer the larger figure because (1) it indicates the scale of this activity and (2) because all of it, converted or not, is discretionary and "off-budget." These intermediary or secondary institutions are a form of "backdoor" credit.

licans prefer,while the Democrats seem to prefer direct regulatory involvements or conventional fiscal and monetary policy. But for neither party is it any longer a question of *whether* the national government should maintain and expand its presence in the economy and the society. Both are regularly using government vigorously and positively, and both parties prefer a discretionary approach to these things, even in fiscal and monetary fields where we have had a great deal of experience and success in constructing clear and detailed nondiscretionary programs called "automatic stabilizers." Why this preference for discretion as well as scale and positiveness? One does not have to pierce the inner thought processes of elites to appreciate the advantages inherent in discretionary programs—to be crassly brief, how much more intimately this ties the prospective recipients to the dispensing government. The discretionary element of these investment guarantee programs, therefore, adds a particularly important element of leverage to the size of this sector as measured by the figures on Table 1.3 and Figure 1.1. In the case of investment guarantees and insurance, the ties are to corporations and organizations in the private sector rather than to local governments. But here is another extremely important dimension of the national presence and how it is being established, perpetuated, and institutionalized.[4]

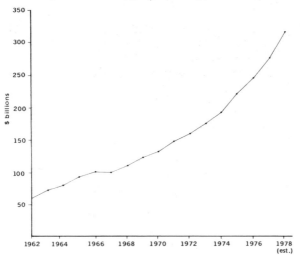

Source: Special Analyses, Budget of the U.S., Sec. F., 1967–1978.

Figure 1.1. Growth of Federal Investment Guarantee Activities, 1962–1978

There is no room left for doubt that a large, positive, interventionist, national state is finally and forever the central feature of the American political system. It is also becoming clear that the emergence of such a state will be accompanied by the decline and eventual disappearance of some familiar patterns and conditions, which are being replaced by some already familiar but not fully appreciated patterns. For example, the emergence of the large, positive state has been the major contributor to the permanent changes in the relationship between President and Congress. In a generation we have moved from a Congress-centered national government to an executive-centered national government, and the most recent decade or so, we have moved from an executive-centered to a White House-centered national government. Because of the close association between the Executive branch and the positive state, those who have favored the latter have been eager to foster the development of the former. In fact, there has been a considerable rewriting of American democratic theory in order to show that the President is the manifestation of the Real Majority. A related feature of this is the development of a Presidential constituency separate from all other constituencies. We now have a mass, plebicitary relationship between the President and the public, and this shows up consistently in the national electoral process and in the fluctuations and responsiveness of national opinion polls to Presidential activity. Still other recent constitutional developments can have probably been attributed to the emergence of the large, national state apparatus. And why not? Something as large and demanding as the establishment and maintenance of a national presence in a nation as large and highly developed as our own must call forth a tremendous amount of energy organized in forms appropriate to the new needs.

But among all of the changes we can recognize, and among all of the changes we can attribute to the emergence of the new national state, probably the most important is the changed perspective of the federal executive branch toward its responsibilities. We may have here the most important case study of Karl Mannheim's theory of "bureaucratic conservatism." According to Mannheim, bureaucratization has a fundamental effect on the political theory developed by and for bureaucrats. A central element of this political theory is the view or hypothesis that all unpredictable features of the agency environment are irrational and therefore a threat to the responsibilities and the mission of the agency. Put in broader terms, politics itself is irrational.

This is an operatiing perspective held not merely by bureau chiefs with a job to do and too few resources with which to do it. This is a view held in one form or another by the responsible elites of the executive branch and reinforced in a variety of ways by academic analysis. It was the view expressed eloquently by John F. Kennedy as he was trying to advance and justify the central position of the Presidency:[5]

> Old sweeping issues have largely disappeared. The central domestic problems of our time are more subtle and less simple. They relate not to basic clashes of philosophy or ideology, but to ways and means of reaching common goals—to research for sophisticated solutions to complex and obstinate issues. (Yale Commencement Address, 1962)

Thus, on the very eve of one of the most ideological periods in American history, President Kennedy and the very thoughtful persons around him were expressing the view that groups and classes in our society were basically in harmony with one another and that their conflicts could be dealt with more than adequately if we would just stop and adequately research them. It was also a view expressed literally in the behavior as well as the rhetoric of those who were building participatory democracy into a variety of important national programs in the mid-1960s. It is an extraordinary expression of bureaucratic optimism (as well as conservatism) that the mission of a national agency can be made compatible with and furthered by the absorption on a formalized and large scale of the participation of locally organized and highly antagonistic groups. Those who refused to participate or by their antagonism to the system obstructed the processes would simply be counting themselves out of dispensations of federal largesse and privilege. The perspective of the national state might best be synthesized as the "myth of the apocalypse." By that I simply mean that the leaders of the executive branch, both the top career people and the political appointees in and around the Presidency, have come to feel that society is so dependent upon the national government that it would fall apart if the national government were unresponsive to organized demands and that the society would even more surely fall apart if the national government were unprepared to intervene at the first sign of community disorder. It is distressing how many self-identified liberals have come to be preoccupied about disorder during the past 20 years.

It is possible to be very concrete about these perspectives. Just as preparedness to intervene in the economy is no longer limited to liberal Democrats, so is preparedness to infringe, through government, on civil liberties no longer limited to conservative Republicans. The government apparatus has grown so large, and society appears to be so dependent upon it, that Democrats have become conservatives about political dissidence as well as community disorder. For example, during the 20 years between September, 1945, and August, 1965, the federal government called up the National Guard and other military personnel 83 times, using 44,927 troops. During the three and one-half years between August, 1965, and December, 1968, there were 179 call-ups involving 184,133 federal and National Guard troops. In both periods there were more instances of intervention and the use of more federal troops in local disorders than during the entire previous history of the United States.[6]

During those same turbulent 1960s, at least 100,000 civilians were placed under surveillance by the U.S. Army—an illegal and impeachable act. And political dissidents were being surpressed also through strategic use of conspiracy trials. The advantage to a conspiracy trial is that the government can keep the defendant under very severe court supervision and restraint for the weeks or months of the trial even if the defendant is eventually aquitted. Virtually all the conspiracy trials instituted by the Justice Department during the entire Vietnam war were under Johnson and his liberal Attorney General, Ramsey Clark. Shoring up all crime-fighting units of local governments became a major program of the Johnson Administration. Recently released government materials reveal that the FBI spent more than $1.6 million to hire 300 informants to infiltrate and spy upon the Trotskyist Socialist Workers Party, although it was composed of only 2,500 members by the FBI's own generous count. Moreover, this does not include other possible informants of the CIA and other agencies who may have infiltrated the same party. All this is to indicate that every possible source of disorder was being watched from Washington with considerable care. During this period the FBI almost surely became a dreaded national police force.[7]

One response to these illustrations and examples is that the era in question was a very special time and that national involvements with local disorder and dissidence were corespondingly unusual. But out of special times arise precedents that bind normal times, if indeed there ever are normal times in the United States. And the point of more pressing importance is that during this period we had nationalized local disorders. The national presence had extended itself throughout the length, breadth, and depth of the land. How it will express itself will certainly depend upon whatever is special to each era. But there is no longer any doubt about the national presence and the fact that it will express itself.

Sayre's Law (after the late Wallace Sayre of Columbia University) holds that the gains of any change are immediate and the costs are cumulative. Review of the many programs in this volume suggests that it is high time we start evaluating long-run costs along with short-run benefits and cost. The long-run costs may be directly empirical in their nature, but they also may require certain philosophic posture. Nevertheless, we must somehow approach them, because the welfare of the entire society may be at stake. We have become Europeanized at least to the extent that the United States has become a united state, and we are going to have to prepare ourselves for the consequences. Louis Hartz was only half right in his famous thesis that the liberal tradition in America arose out of the good fortune of not having a feudal system to overthrow. The other half of that thesis is that we were also blessed with not having a large and positive state to defend the basic interests of the ancient regime. Since we cannot reenact our history and give ourselves a feudal order to overthrow, we may be safe to that extent from the loss of our liberal tradition. But we can still lose that liberal tradition if the large and unified national state we have now created is allowed to fail either through falling too short of its promises or through allowing itself to be captured by any combination of elite and corporate interests. Such a state will so confirm the most antagonistic theories of the liberal society that it may produce not an anti-state movement but an anti-liberal revolutionary movement that will simply attempt to free the state from one set of interests and enslave the state with another set. We as citizens would then have exchanged one set of masters for another. In its most fundamental meaning the liberal tradition is worth defending. To what extent is it endangered by the very state that modern liberals have produced? Though we must approach this kind of issue philosophically, we cannot deal with it unless we have concrete empirical materials about the behavior of the modern state, the policies of the modern state, and their consequences. It is our expectation that this volume will contribute to such an analysis; and it is our hope that through such an analysis an appropriate and effective philosophical position will emerge.

NOTES

1. J. Vincent and Vee Burke, *Nixon's Good Deed* (New York: Columbia University Press, 1974): 1.

2. The sentence immediately following was: "He would have been doubly mad if the prophet had also forecast that during the heat of the 1972 campaign Nixon's Democratic rival for the Presidency would delete help for the working poor from his own welfare platform."

3. For example, the Federal Deposit Insurance Corporation (FDIC) insures deposits up to $40,000 in the member banks of the Federal Reserve, and the Federal Savings and Loan Insurance Corporation (FSLIC) performs the same function for its member banks. In 1975 insured deposits were in the neighborhood of $520,300,000,000 and $278,774,000,000 respectively. Many of the Social Security titles are also nondiscretionary, while the other titles are discretionary but are not insurance. The latter titles are particularly important in the present context because, even though they are not as large, fiscally, as the other Social Security titles, they contribute with the other programs on Table 1.3 to the ability of the federal government to cement its ties to still another segment of the society—in this case the poor and dependent.

4. There is one other very important aspect of investment guarantee policies which is relegated to a note only because it is tangential to the present argument. Investment guarantees are completely "out-budget." Since there is no direct transfer of funds, there is no Treasury, OMB, or Congressional clearance. Once Congress has set up the authorizing legislation, including a ceiling on the total commitments the insuring agency can extend, there is no further clearance activity until there are defaults to be liquidated. But this comes later, long after the initial commitment. Thus, an investment guarantee is "out-budget" at the beginning and "mandatory at the end."

5. Yale Commencement Address, Yale University, 1962.

6. Adam Yarmolinsky, *The Military Establishment* (New York: Harper & Row, 1971): 154, 162-163.

7. Cf.,Victor Navasky, *Kennedy Justice* (New York: Atheneum, 1971).

Part I

THE ECONOMIC STRUCTURE

DO NATIONAL POLICIES REGULATE IT? REINFORCE IT? UNDERMINE IT?

2.

MACROECONOMIC POLICY
IN CAPITALIST AMERICA

HOWARD SHERMAN

University of California, Riverside

Macroeconomic policy in the United States is a creature of the capitalist state. Necessarily, this essay begins with a very brief restatement of the Marxist theory of the state. Then it proceeds to examine—again very briefly—the income distribution policies of the U.S. government, both because existing income distribution is an important determinant of macroeconomic behavior, and because these policies are closely tied to macroeconomic stabilization policies. The bulk of the paper is devoted to a study of macroeconomic policy in the Nixon-Ford administration. There is, finally, a brief epilogue on what to expect of the Carter Administration.

THE MARXIST VIEW OF THE CAPITALIST STATE

Many contemporary radical political economists are strongly influenced by the view of political sociology first enunciated by Karl Marx. Marx himself had a very sophisticated and complex view of political sociology.[1] It is a view quite different from some of the vulgarized versions that often pass for Marxism. Where vulgar Marxists usually speak of only two classes fighting for political power, every one of Marx's own analyses—including detailed political studies of France, England, Germany, and the United States—specified numerous sub-classes, remnants of classes, in-between or middle classes, and strife between factions of a single class. Where vulgar Marxists assume that capitalist governments bear a one-to-one relation to the economic interests of "the capitalist class," Marx shows that governments do have a certain limited autonomy from the dominant class, and that politics represent a tangled skein of long-run and short-run interests of a wide variety of different classes and different factions within classes.

To begin with, Marx argues that there are two sides to the origin and functioning of the state. Marx uses the term, "the state," to mean all of the power structures of government (everything from the police functions to the propaganda functions of "public relations" personnel). Marx states that *one* source of the origin of state power was the need for control of some common functions in the interest of the whole community; for example, in ancient Egypt it was necessary to control the Nile and irrigation. A *second* source of the origin of state power was the need by the ruling class, as in ancient Egypt, to hold down and repress the slave class in order to exploit the slave's labor. All U.S. government functions today still have these two aspects: common functions for the community and class functions for the ruling class. For example, the building of highways serves the whole community; but the question of which highways and how many highways is largely determined by the profit goals of the automobile industry and the construction industry (both of which maintain huge lobbies at the federal and state levels).

Marx was also very critical of theorists who insist that there always has been and always will be an elite of rulers and an oppressed mass of ruled. Marx and Engels were among the first to take seriously the findings of anthropology that many primitive societies are built around the extended family or clan, have no government in the modern sense, and certainly no police or other repressive forces. Marx said that this absence of a repressive state was due to the fact that there was no class division. People were elected for temporary leadership of community functions, but there was no need for repression because there was no exploited class.

The goal of Marxists is a communist society in which there will again be no classes, no ruling elite, voluntary cooperation by all, and no repressive state machinery. As the first step in this direction, Marx advocated socialism as the only consistent form of democracy. Marx pointed out that capitalist states have the forms of democracy in the political sphere, but that the dictatorship of a small number of capitalists in the economic sphere extends their power in substance to the political sphere as well. Socialism means a society of democracy in substance as well as form because the democratically elected government will own and control the economy. This direction over the lives of the people is taken away from a few capitalists and exercised by all of the people (that is, the working class).

Vulgar Marxists argue as if the capitalist class directly runs the government of capitalist countries. Marx, on the contrary, emphasized that the actual day-to-day running of the government is usually left to a specialized group (politicians, employed like engineers are employed) and that capitalist control is indirect. Nor is the control exercised by a conspiracy, but by the built-in features of the whole system and its institutions. Marx emphasized in his writings a long list of means by which capitalists and the capitalist state exercise control over the masses of the working class. These means are mostly indirect and mostly accomplished by peaceful propaganda and economic means. Thus, Marx pointed out that the capitalist class largely controls (though not without dissent and a continuing struggle) and uses to spread its ideology: (1) religious organizations; (2) the media, radio, television, newspapers, and all forms of advertising; (3) the educational system; and (4) the legal system and the courts. Capitalists also utilize (5) the control of jobs and co-option of many potentially dissident workers into top positions to pressure and condition people into a pro-business frame of mind. Under capitalism (6), the family transmits the need for "discipline" and "respect" in order to get ahead in the work world. Through all of these channels are pushed ideologies that divide and weaken the working class, including (7) racism, (8) sexism, (9) nationalism, and a more general (10) ideology that individualism is a good thing and elitism is necessary or inevitable in any society. The capitalist institutions, particularly the media, also push mind-deadening and apolitical distractions such as (11) sports mania (e.g., baseball and football) and Roman circuses of violence (e.g., enormous coverage of terrorist activities, murders, fires, earthquakes, and so on).

According to Marx, the capitalist class, through its representatives in the state, sometimes gives (12) reforms as a necessary sop to workers. For example, the many reforms of Roosevelt's New Deal, were certainly pro-labor, but they were designed to save capitalism. Only the most vulgar Marxists think that no reforms can be wrested from the capitalist state. On the contrary, Marx emphasized that reforms may be won by working class pressure or by one faction of the capitalist class to gain popular support, or by the government apparatus acting somewhat autonomously. Marx shows that the capitalist government sometimes is far-sighted enough to pass reforms in the interest of the whole capitalist class in the long run, even though many capitalists vociferously oppose the reform from the viewpoint of their immediate interests. A modern example might be the ending of the Vietnam war even though this seemed against the immediate interests of the capitalists supplying military commodities.

Another means of influence mentioned by Marx is (13) the direct use of corruption and bribery by the capitalist class. For example, during elections in the United States big business routinely gives millions of dollars to the Republicans and Democrats to assure the success of their candidates. Big business also routinely spends millions of dollars on lobbying. And the Watergate scandal exposed all kinds of links and illegal payoffs between business and the President. Yet Marx notes that such illegal means are always quite secondary compared with the systemic, institutionalized modes of control of propaganda and ideological control over the masses.

Finally, only when all other means have failed does the capitalist state resort to (14) repression, as it did during the era of Joe McCarthy and the House Un-American Activities Committee. Only then does the capitalist state resort to (15) the ultimate use of force and violence, such as setting police against students or strikers or armies against national liberation movements; protecting property by sending workers, mostly minorities, to prison; or suppressing radicals by use of the FBI or CIA (or the Gestapo as in Hitler Germany). Such means are inconvenient, expensive, and sure to stimulate reactions against them. The capitalist state avoids these means *whenever possible*—they are weapons of last resort.

U.S. GOVERNMENT AND INCOME DISTRIBUTION

On the basis of all the pressures of the capitalist system, most working class people are convinced to some degree of its virtues (or that it is impossible to fight it), so they vote for the pro-capitalist Republican or Democratic parties. The resulting Congress, executive, and judicial branches are largely white, Anglo, male, not working class, and certainly not poor. For example, the U.S. Senate has 22 millionaires in its 100 members. The Supreme Court is composed of nine old men.

It is no wonder that such a government is pro-capitalist to a large extent in all its activities. There is a reciprocal or feedback mechanism whereby capitalists use their power (over propaganda as well as money) to elect friendly governments, and these friendly governments then act so as to increase capitalist power and wealth. As one friendly U.S. Senator, Boise Penrose, said to a meeting of businessmen (back in 1900, when such things were said more frankly): "I believe in a division of labor. You send us to Congress; we pass laws under . . . which you make money; . . . and out of your profits you further contribute to our campaign funds to send us back again to pass more laws to enable you to make more money."[2] The main function pursued by such a government is the preservation of "law and order," which translates into the preservation of private property. Specifically, this means that the police, courts, and prisons are all used to protect capitalist ownership and to control land, factories, and vast fortunes.

Yet liberals maintain that this same U.S. government reduces inequality by higher tax rates on the rich, welfare payments to the poor, subsidies to the poor farmer, public education for the poor, and break-up of monopoly by anti-trust laws. This naive conception of government becomes more suspect when we discover that several recent studies have found very little change in the distribution of income between 1910 and 1970.[3] Moreover, detailed inspection of each of these programs finds them far more favorable to the rich and far less favorable to the poor than the law would seem to indicate at first glance.

The tax system is most notable for its loopholes, which allowed the wealthy to escape taxes on about $77 billion in 1971 along![4] Although the law says that those with incomes over $1 million must pay 70 percent in federal income tax, this group actually paid only 20 percent in 1969. Major loopholes include the lenient treatment of capital gains, no taxes at all on municipal bonds, oil depletion allowances, and investment tax credits. So the federal tax has very little effect on income distribution. State and local taxes actually take more *proportionately* from the poor than the rich. The net result is that the rich pay a *lower* percentage of their income in *all* taxes (federal, state, and local) than do the poor. Thus in 1967, families with less than $3,000 income paid 34 percent of it in all taxes (federal, state, and local), but families with incomes over $25,000 paid only 28 percent of their income in all taxes.

It is asserted that government welfare payments are an enormous payment by the rich to the poor. In fact, all welfare payments—including unemployment compensation, workmen's compensation, and educational aid to low-income students—constitute a small and diminishing part of income. In 1938, welfare payments rose to 6.7 percent of personal income; but welfare payments have fallen since then to only 3.8 percent of personal income.[5] Moreover, even the poor on welfare pay considerable taxes, so this reduces the net amount from government still further.

Not only do the poor receive a very small sum in total, but *welfare payments to business* are much larger. For example, the late nineteenth century is considered a period of little or no government relations with business. Yet, between 1850 and 1871, the U.S. government gave a free gift to the railroads of 130 million acres of land, an area as large as all of New England plus Pennsylvania and New York! During the same period, state governments gave the railroads another 49 million acres. Today, the government still gives immensely valuable loan guarantees to Lockheed (but not to New York City), and billions in welfare payments (called subsidies) to the merchant marine and several other industries in the interest of "national security."

Another business welfare rip-off is the farm subsidy program. Originally, it got through Congress on the argument that farm workers have the lowest incomes of all occupational groups and that small farm owners are very poor, with hundreds of thousands going bankrupt every year. But farm *workers* get *no* subsidies, and small farm owners get very little. Most farm subsidies go to the richest farmers, mostly corporate-owned farms. For example, in 1963 the richest 20 percent of farms received 51 percent of all farm income before subsidies. In addition, this richest 20 percent received the lion's share of farm subsidies (even more than their percentage of income before subsidies): 83 percent in sugar cane, 69 percent in cotton; 65 percent in rice, 62 percent in wheat, 56 percent in feed grains, 57 percent in peanuts (including a good amount to Jimmy Carter), 53 percent in tobacco, and 51 percent in sugar beets.[6] Thus farm subsidies went mostly to the giant farms and actually increased inequality of farm incomes.

Education is said to be open to everyone, so everyone can gain an equal income status through education. In reality, most individuals from high-income families are able to get far more schooling in the United States than most individuals from low-income families. Children from richer families can be supported through higher education; and these richer families can afford not only the tuitions and support needed in the public universities, but also the very high tuitions in some private universities that will admit students even with low grades. Students from richer families also have the advantage of greater access to formal culture in the home and the tremendous advantage of going to much richer elementary school districts. For example, in 1967 only 20 percent of students graduating high school came from families earning less than $3,000 entered college. Yet in the same year, an amazing 87 percent of students graduating high school came from families earning over $15,000 entered college![7] Thus, the educational system seems to transmit inequality from one generation to the next.

Finally, the anti-trust laws—passed in 1890, 1914, and 1950—are supposed to prevent or break-up monopoly power. Yet there were major waves of corporate mergers *after* each of these laws were passed. In fact, from 1890 to 1914, the anti-trust laws were used mainly to break labor strikes and to put union leaders in jail. The anti-trust laws—and many other regulating laws—appear mainly to provide a vehicle for the government to arbitrate disputes *between* corporations. There is no evidence that the anti-trust laws have slowed the trend toward ever increasing concentration of economic power. Thus, the 200 largest corporations in manufacturing now own about two-thirds of all assets in manufacturing; while the 1,300 largest corporations in the whole economy own 60 percent of all corporate assets.[8] The anti-trust laws are written with enormous legislative loopholes, not enforced by the Justice Department, and leniently interpreted by the courts. As one indication, for many years the budget of the whole Anti-Trust Division of the Justice Department was smaller than the budget of the House Un-American Activities Committee—yet the corporations could afford to use hundreds of lawyers to defend the suits because this activity is tax deductible.

FISCAL POLICY

The economic role of government that most directly influences the level of output, income, and employment is its taxing and spending of money, or *fiscal policy*. During most of American history, the federal government has based its taxing and spending decisions on the political value of the project on which the money was to be spent. The effects of fiscal policy on output, income, and employment were ignored until the depression of the 1930s.

The prevailing economic philosophy was that taxes should be used only to finance necessary government expenditures. It was thought to be an unsound financial practice for governments to borrow money. If a balanced budget, in which expenditures equaled taxes, could not be achieved, it was thought to be preferable to have taxes exceed expenditures so that any debts incurred in the past could be retired. Only the Great Depression and the World War II experience forced a change in this policy. Since that time, government spending has often risen much more rapidly than taxes.

Federal government spending in the United States in 1921-1929 was only 1 percent of GNP. In 1930-1940, as the New Deal responded to the Depression, it had increased to 4 percent of GNP. With World War II, government spending rose to the incredible height of 41 percent of GNP in 1943 and 1944. After the war, it fell somewhat, but it bounced up again in the Korean War, so federal spending averaged 11 percent of GNP in 1945-1959. In 1960-1970, partly owing to the Vietnam War, federal spending averaged 13 percent of GNP—about two-thirds or more being military.[9] Total government spending—including state and local as well as federal—rose to 31 percent of GNP in 1970.

Since World War II, the U.S. economy has entered a new stage of government-with-business. Since the 1890s, the economy has been dominated by the giant monopoly corporations; now the economy is dominated by these same corporations working intimately with a government that strongly affects the economy and is itself a major part of the economy.

How does the U.S. government affect the aggregate demand for goods? Leaving aside international relations, we can say:

$ consumption + $ investment + $ government spending
= $ demand

Aggregate demand is increased by more government spending and decreased by more taxes. If there is unemployment because of deficient demand, then the government can increase demand in one of two ways. It can directly increase government spending, which is a component of demand. It can also decrease taxes, which increases the income available to be spent on consumer or investor demand.

On the other hand, if there is inflation because demand is at too high a level (perhaps because of vast government military spending), then the government can reduce demand in one of two ways. First, it may lower the level of government spending. Second, it may raise taxes, which reduces the amount people have left over for consumer or investor spending. These are the simple mechanics of fiscal policy. We will now proceed to its problems.

AUTOMATIC STABILIZERS

Excessive or deficient demand can be combated in two ways: with *automatic* fiscal devices and with *discretionary* fiscal policies. Automatic fiscal policy is built into the present structure of governmental taxing and spending to react automatically to inflation or depression. Discretionary fiscal policies are changes in the fiscal structure made by current and conscious government decisions. Since World War II, the government has placed more reliance on automatic than on discretionary fiscal measures. The fiscal structure is supposed automatically to expand net government demand in depressions and to decrease net government demand in inflations. An automatic stabilizer is a government device built into the fiscal system that automatically increases or decreases government flows to or from the rest of the economy in response to changes in economic conditions.

In a depression, when the GNP tends to drop, the stabilizers should automatically increase government money flows to businesses and households and/or decrease money flows from businesses and households to the government. This will prevent disposable personal income from dropping as rapidly as otherwise, and thus investment and consumption expenditures can be maintained at a higher level. Similarly, in an inflation, the automatic stabilizers are supposed to decrease the amount given and increase the amount taken away from businesses and households, thus decreasing the total amount of consumer and investor spending. In either case, the net changes in government flows should have a multiple effect.

Now what are the magic devices by which the government is supposed to keep the economy automatically stable? On the spending side of the ledger, the government makes many types of welfare payments that automatically increase in depression and automatically decrease in expansions. For example, as full employment is approached, there will be very little unemployment compensation. But in a depression, with growing unemployment, this may become a significant source of buying power.

On the taxation side, the total amounts of federal income tax collected had declined in most recessions faster than personal income, so it usually left people with more to spend. The federal income tax acted this way because the individual automatically pays a lower tax rate if his income declines. Therefore, the federal tax system was an important automatic stabilizer.

Unfortunately, the depression of 1973-1975 was in a continued price inflation. Therefore, personal income rose in the depression in money terms, though it fell in terms of purchasing power. Thus the percentage of taxes rose in the 1973-1975 depression. For middle-income taxpayers, with an intermediate income by government standards, in 1974 personal income taxes went up 27 percent and Social Security taxes went up 22 percent over 1973.[10] As a result of the inflation, this was the first depression in American history in which the burden of personal income taxes actually increased. Instead of being the most important automatic stabilizer, the federal income tax operated as a major automatic destabilizer!

DISCRETIONARY FISCAL POLICIES AND SOCIAL PRIORITIES

Because the automatic devices have failed to stabilize the economy, liberal Keynesian economists maintain that discretionary fiscal measures are necessary to eliminate depression and inflation. They contend that the legislature merely needs to increase spending and lower taxes in depression, and lower spending and increase taxes in inflation. But these measures also are subject to political and economic complications.

There are three different policy views of what government discretionary fiscal policy ought to be. The most conservative economists, such as

Adam Smith or the contemporary American Milton Friedman, argue that no discretionary fiscal measures are needed. The government should stay out of the economy. Friedman agrees with Adam Smith that the less government the better. He attributes many of our economic problems to too much government interference with private enterprise, which would otherwise automatically adjust to all situations in a near-perfect manner. To the extent that conservatives admit any need for government policy, they say that only monetary measures are necessary. Conservatives favor measures affecting the money supply (via interest rates, for example) rather than any fiscal measures of spending or taxation because they feel that monetary measures do not directly interfere with business. They view an adequate money supply merely as one of the prerequisites for a private enterprise economy. Other prerequisites which they believe government should provide include police and armies to maintain "law and order," primarily to protect private property from its domestic and foreign enemies.

The second, the liberal, view is that of such economists as John M. Keynes or the contemporary American Paul Samuelson. Liberals admit that capitalism has real problems, such as general unemployment and inflation. Liberal Keynesians argue that adequate government measures of increased or decreased spending and increased or decreased taxation are necessary to correct these problems. Finally, they used to maintain that such measures can *always successfully bring about full employment* with stable prices. Some of them now, however, define full employment as "only" 5 or 6 percent unemployment and stable prices as "only" 3 or 4 percent inflation per year. Others, including Samuelson, simply admit that ending inflation *and* getting full employment at the same time is one little thing not yet solved by establishment economists: "Experts do not yet know . . . an incomes policy that will permit us to have *simultaneously* . . . full employment and price stability."[11]

The radical view is expressed by Karl Marx or the contemporary American Paul Sweezy. Radicals argue that problems such as periodic unemployment are deeply rooted in the capitalist system and cannot be cured by any amount of monetary or fiscal measures. They contend that the *U.S. economy has reached full employment only during major wars.* In normal peacetime years, they believe unemployment and/or inflation is the usual state of capitalism. They argue that the necessary drastic fiscal measures cannot be taken by capitalist governments because powerful vested interests oppose each such step, aside from military spending.

Suppose we accept the liberal Keynesian argument that government intervention can prevent large-scale unemployment or runaway inflation.

The basic fiscal formula, to which may be added certain monetary measures, is to raise taxes and lower spending during inflations, while lowering taxes and raising spending during depressions. Moreover, corporate executives and congressmen alike are by now well aware of and receptive to these techniques. But that by no means settles the issue (even aside from the problem of simultaneous unemployment and inflation).

The problem remains: Which spending? Whose taxes? Suppose we agree to spend the large amounts of money necessary to maintain full employment. Many outlets that would be socially beneficial conflict with the vested interests of large corporations or wealthy individuals. Larger welfare payments tend to raise the wage level; government investment in industrial ventures or in public utilities tends to erode monopolistic privileges. The issue is the political constraints to economic policies.

In the years immediately after World War II, the problem was to spend $15-20 billion annually. This might have been a very agonizing social and political issue except for the advent of the Cold War.

Dollars for Cold War armaments did not violate any vested interests. Military spending is considered an ideal antidepression policy by big business for three reasons. First, such expenditures have the same short-run effect on employment and profits as would expenditures on more socially useful projects. Second, military spending means big and stable profits, whereas welfare spending may shift income from rich taxpayers to poor recipients. Third, the long-run effect is even more favorable because no new productive equipment is created to compete with existing facilities. During the past 25 years, the main change has been that the necessary addition to the income stream has risen to at least $70-80 billion a year. *If it were politically possible, the whole amount could be spent on useful public commodities,* such as housing or health or education, rather than on military waste. These useful types of public spending are *not* politically feasible in such large amounts, however, as long as the U.S. government is dominated by big business.

One popular cure for depression is reduction of taxes to allow more money to flow into private spending. Given the composition of the U.S. government, however, tax cuts always end up benefiting mainly the rich and the corporations. Even in the liberal Kennedy administration, the taxes of the poor were reduced very little. The taxes of the rich were reduced very much, resulting in a redistribution of income to the deserving members of the wealthy class. However, the wealthy will not spend their increased income, especially in a depression. The consumption of the wealthy remains at adequate levels even in a depression, and they have no desire to invest in the face of probable losses. Hence, the political restriction as to *who* gets the tax cuts makes this policy economically ineffective.

Similarly, all economists (and even most businessmen) may see a need for more and more vast government spending under capitalism. The prime political question, however, is spending on what, for it is here that vested interests come into play. Thus, even small vital expenditures on medical care have sometimes been defeated by the American Medical Association. Powerful vested interests oppose almost every item in the civilian budget as soon as expansion proceeds beyond the necessary minimum. What kind of interests must be defeated to have the necessary spending to fill a $70-80 billion deficiency in demand? Constructive projects such as the Missouri Valley Authority could develop dams, irrigation, and cheap power, but these have been fought tooth and nail by the private power interests (and, indeed, might lower private investment by direct competition). There could be large-scale public housing, but private contractors have long kept such programs to a minimum.

There might be other welfare spending—for example, on hospitals and schools. The rich, however, see these as subsidies to the poor for things that the rich can buy for themselves out of their own pockets. Proposals to increase unemployment compensation or lower taxes paid by the poor encounter even greater resistance because they would transfer income from the rich to the poor. Likewise, billions could usefully be spent in aid and loans to the less developed world, where poverty and human suffering is so widespread. That, however, could be passed on a massive scale only over the bodies of hundreds of Congressmen, who well represent the wishes of their self-interested constituents and have no concept of the long-run gain to world trade and world peace. If any of these measures is to some extent allowed, it is only after a long political fight and certainly not promptly enough to head off a developing depression.

In every area of possible constructive government spending, powerful vested interests stand in opposition to the satisfaction of some of the nation's most basic social needs. These interests will not tolerate government competition with private enterprise, measures that undermine the privileges of the wealthy or policies that significantly alter the relative distribution of income. They therefore tend to oppose all government nonmilitary spending—except business subsidies. The only major exception to this generalization is government spending on highways, which is actively promoted by the largest and most lucrative single industry after defense: the automobile producers.

MILITARY SPENDING VERSUS WELFARE SPENDING

From all of the facts just given, it must be concluded that welfare or constructive spending on a large scale is opposed by too many special interests to be politically feasible. My hypothesis is that *only large-scale military spending brought the United States out of the Great depression of the 1930s, and only large-scale military spending has kept the United States out of a major depression.* Liberals such as Samuelson are much more complacent. Speaking about mass unemployment and galloping inflations, he says they are things of the past. He asserts that there are ancient problems that are solvable and have been solved: "For example, however true it might have been in the turn-of-the-century era of Lenin ... it is definitely no longer the case in the age after Keynes that prosperity of a mixed economy (i.e., capitalism plus government) depends on cold-war expenditures and imperialistic ventures."[12]

It is a fact, however, that our economy has boomed by spending immense sums of money to kill the people of Vietnam. How would Samuelson replace that crutch to the economy? He says: "Does building missiles and warheads create jobs? ... Then so too will building new factories, better roads and schools, cleaning up our rivers, and providing minimum income-supplements for our aged and handicapped."[13] Certainly it is true that jobs could be created in all these constructive ways rather than the destructive ways of warfare. *But*—and it is a big *but*—we are talking about *government spending,* so we must remember that vested interests will obstruct programs that might harm them. For the government to build new factories means direct competition with private industry. For the government to build schools means taking money from rich taxpayers and transfering it to the education of poorer citizens. To clean up the rivers means both using more tax money and forcing private industry to spend money on purifying its wastes. Giving to the aged and handicapped means again adding taxes and shifting income to the poor.

The political reality is that vested interests oppose each of these programs with violent rhetoric and successful political pressure. Thus Congress does not even talk about building government factories for peaceful use. In fact, government atomic energy plants have been given away free to private capitalists. Presidents Nixon and Ford, both of whom were supported primarily by big business, vetoed a large number of liberal Keynesian bills to stimulate employment by more public jobs or by more spending for health, education, or welfare. President Carter is committed to some Keynesian type spending to stimulate the economy. Yet he also has many ties to business, has many conservative economic advisors, and says he is a "fiscal conservative." Therefore, it is safe to predict that he will *not* launch constructive projects on the massive magnitude needed to approach full employment, but will continue to allow a relatively high level of unemployment. It is also easy to predict that, in spite of his explicit promise to cut military spending, he will *raise* military spending during his term of office.

Paul Samuelson says that radicals have asked: "Politically, will there be as much urgency to spend what is needed for useful, peacetime full-employment programs as there is urgency and willingness to spend for hot- and cold-war purposes?" And he answers: "It was proper to ask this question back in the 1950s. But . . . experience since then has shown that modern electorates have become very sensitive to levels of unemployment that would have been considered moderate back in the good old days. And they do put effective pressure at the polls on their government."[14] But in the first place, the pressure is only to get jobs—not necessarily to get welfare rather than warfare jobs. So both Republican and Democratic administrations continue military spending to avoid unemployment—and do not do large amounts of constructive spending.

In the second place, Samuelson just assumes that "the people" make our governmental decisions. But the dominant power in governmental decision making in the United States is big business. It would have been nice to test what the liberal McGovern would have done in power. Perhaps he would have been able (with much popular support to overcome business pressure) to substitute a little more welfare for a little less warfare. But that has not been the record of previous liberal administrations. The Kennedy administration vastly increased military spending, invaded Cuba, and expanded the Vietnam War; and the Johnson administration further expanded the Vietnam War on a vast scale.

Keynesian liberals fail to see the political constraints that make military spending the only allowable solution to unemployment. The political nature of the problem has become even more apparent in the inflationary situation of the past 20 years. The Korean and Vietnam wars caused so much government demand for military supplies that inflation resulted, with prices rising especially in 1950-1953 and 1967-1974. To cure inflation, the simple Keynesian prescription is to increase taxes and reduce spending.

But whose taxes, which spending? Major increases in taxes on the wealthy are not easily passed by our government. And there is not that much room for further taxes on the poor and the middle class without provoking rising discontent. So it is easier to reduce government spending. But not military spending; politicians and spokesmen for industry and the military continue to convince the nation that this is *absolutely* necessary. Thus welfare spending is cut. Already a tiny percentage of the American government budget, welfare has nevertheless been cut further as a tool to fight inflation. Hence, the burden of inflation has fallen on the common man and woman in the forms of rising prices, rising taxes, and falling welfare spending—all at the same time.

The question of social and political priorities often boils down to a conflict between the genuine needs of the majority and the desires of the tiny minority that possesses immense economic and political power. Most Americans need more education, health, and welfare; but a powerful minority favors military spending.

THE MILITARY ECONOMY

To measure the full extent of the military impact on the economy, we must recall that the U.S. Department of Defense is the largest planned economy in the world today outside the USSR. It spends more than the net income of all U.S. corporations. By 1969, it had 470 major and 6,000 lesser installations, owned 39 million acres of land, spent over $80 billion a year, used 22,000 primary contractors and 100,000 subcontractors—thus directly employing in the armed forces and military production about 10 percent of the U.S. labor force.[15] Some key areas of the economy are especially affected. As early as 1963, before U.S. entry into the Vietnam War, studies show that 36 percent of the output of producers' durable goods were purchased directly or indirectly by the federal government, mostly for military use.

How did the U.S. economy come to have such an enormous military sector?[16] In World War II, of course, the United States had an enormous military production. It was assumed by every policy maker, including economists, businessmen, and political leaders, that the United States would mostly disarm after the war. It was also assumed that this would lead to a depression: therefore every possible solution was considered, with most analyses leading to the sole suggestion of renewed military spending. It was in this atmosphere that the Cold War was born; it provided every possible increase in military spending. In fact, since the United States had a monopoly of atomic bombs, the USSR was very unlikely to be aggressive. Moreover, Soviet foreign policy was mostly very cautious and conservative (so much so that revolutionaries in other countries accused them of betrayal for *not* supplying arms). In reality, the USSR had its sphere of influence—Eastern Europe—which the United States has not invaded, while the United States has spheres of influence and imperial power in much of Latin America, Africa, and Asia, which the USSR has never invaded. Thus, despite the Cold War rhetoric, the two major powers have never clashed militarily (except by indirectly supporting others).

Therefore, armaments spending justified by Cold War rhetoric was not militarily necessary. It was not only utilized, as in Southeast Asia, to protect U.S. investments abroad, but also in large part to support the U.S.

economy at home. Thus, we find in both world wars that the industrialists dictated to the government exactly how the procurement process should be run, completely dominated the Department of Defense, and made enormous rates of profit. This condition has continued ever since.

How big is U.S. military spending? It certainly includes all Department of Defense spending, but it goes considerably beyond that. How far is controversial, but the most careful study to date (by James Cypher) includes half of all "international affairs" spending, veterans benefits, atomic energy and space appropriations (all military-related), and 75 percent of the interest on the public debt (since at least 75 percent of the debt was used to pay for wars). Other things that are too hard to get exact data on are major parts of the budget for research and development, the CIA, and other intelligence agencies—and of course the deaths, wounds, and alienation of young Americans. For the five quantifiable items in military spending, Cypher adds up the grand total of $1.7 *trillion* from 1947 through 1971—enough to buy our entire gross national product for 1969 *and* 1970.

Yet this amount of direct military spending (even if it included the things we can't quantify) still underestimates the impact of military spending on the U.S. economy. There is a very large indirect or secondary effect on (1) additional consumer goods from the spending of those who receive military dollars and (2) additional investment in plant, equipment, and business inventories by military industries. Economists measure the secondary effects of military spending by the government multiplier which measures the ratio of the total increase in all spending to every dollar of increase in government spending. Estimates of the multiplier from military spending range from about $1.85 to $3.50 of total spending for every dollar of military spending.

The most important measure of military spending is as a percentage of our whole gross national product (GNP). From 1947 to 1971 it ranged from a low of 10.1 percent of GNP in 1948 to a high of 21.9 percent in the Korean War year of 1952. It was at 13.5 percent and 13.2 percent in 1967 and 1968, during the Vietnam War peak, and slowly fell to 12.6 percent in 1969, 11.6 percent in 1970, and 11.1 percent in 1971 (with another major rise in 1972). For the whole 1947-1971 period, direct military spending averaged 13.2 percent of GNP. Now if we are quite conservative and assume a multiplier of only 2, it is apparent that direct and indirect military spending accounted for the demand for 26.4 percent of GNP. This means that if military spending and its indirect effects had not been present in this whole period and all other things had been the same (which is very unlikely), we would have had a depression greater than that in the 1930s—when unemployment was 24.3 percent. Of course, if the military multiplier is actually 3, then total demand for GNP would fall by 39.6 percent, if we ended all military spending—always assuming we did nothing else. Actually we have seen that the U.S. government might increase welfare spending a little, but it is not politically feasible on the scale required.

It is worth noting just how military spending has affected the U.S. economy at various times. As late as 1939, it had very little effect, being only 2.6 percent of GNP. In World War II, it rose to about 40 percent of GNP, which brought full employment (and even a shortage of labor). After World War II, there were several times when the drop in military spending seems to have been the main catalyst in setting off a recession. Thus, in 1948, it fell by 11 percent, followed by a recession in 1949. In 1953, it fell by 17 percent and in 1954 by 30 percent; and there was a recession in 1954. In 1957, military spending grew only 2.6 percent, followed by a recession in 1958. In 1960, it fell 3 percent, followed by recession in 1961. In 1969, it grew by only 3 percent, and it fell by 2 percent in 1970, followed by the recession of 1971. All this suggests that military spending must keep rising at a considerable rate to prevent recessions and that when it falters, it sets off a recession.

Obviously, this is no simple case of cause and effect. In the first place, it holds true only when the economy does not have other sources of major new demands (but that has not occurred ever since the first rush of consumer spending after World War II). And there is still an underlying private cyclical mechanism that makes the economy react as it does. Moreover, it can be offset by other policies on the required scale. Thus, in addition to the years mentioned, there is one other time when military spending faltered but did not set off a recession. In 1965, military spending did not change at all, but this lack was offset by the massive tax cut of 1964-1965, which did stimulate some private spending.

On the other side, it should also be noted that military spending seems to have increased each time the U.S. economy needed to get out of recessions. Thus, in the recession of 1949, military spending was immediately increased by 7.6 percent; in the recession of 1958, it was increased by 8.1 percent; and in the recession of 1961, it was increased by 6.6 percent. It was also increased by 7.6 percent in 1955, which may have helped us out of the 1954 recession. In 1971, wage-price controls were used in the new unemployment-inflation situation, but it appears that military spending did take another jump upward in 1972 to help with the continuing unemployment.

Thus, our automatic and inherent pattern of business cycles has now been overlaid with a more politically motivated business cycle. When there is an all-out boom, business influence gets government to reduce military spending. This reduction is desired (1) to avoid inflation and (2) to avoid full employment, which means "uppity" workers and higher wages. Since, however, it is hard to time the military spending reductions exactly, so that they take effect when desired and very hard to estimate exactly how much is needed, this always seems to do more than just limit the boom. It almost always seems to turn into a full-scale recession. Indeed, the capitalist economy never stands still but always has cumulative forces pushing it rapidly up or down once it gets going. Thus, when vested interests reduce military spending a bit—in order to limit the boom—this action may set off a recession. As the recession gets worse and profits decline, the same political-economic power is used to start increasing military spending again, which may set off another boom. This, of course, is much too sketchy and rigid a schema to encompass all the many factors affecting current economic history, but it is an important framework for understanding.

Finally, we must note why big business is so happy with a normally high level of military spending. On the aggregate level, we saw that it is used to protect U.S. investments abroad, to get the economy out of recessions, and to prevent a major depression; but there is an additional incentive for the individual defense contractor. This incentive is based on the fact that the rate of profit is very high in military production and that most of these profits go to a few very large firms. Almost all military contracts go to some 205 of the top 500 corporations, and just 100 of them get 85 percent of all military contracts.

There are some studies of military profits, but all of them understate the profit rates. In reporting to the government, the military firms overstate their costs—and since they do not operate under competition but in a cozy relationship with the Pentagon, they probably overstate costs more than most firms. Thus, they allocate costs of other parts of their business to military contracts and add in all sorts of other unrelated costs. Some have even tossed in the costs of call girls to influence government inspectors (called "entertainment" in their accounts). They also make many hidden profits through the use of complex subcontracting procedures to subsidiaries, unauthorized use of government-owned property, and getting patents on research done for the government.

Still, a study by the General Accounting Office (GAO) of the U.S. government had definitely spelled out their high profit rates.[17] First, the GAO asked 81 large military contractors by questionnaire what their profit rates were for 1966 through 1969. The replies, which were limited by self-interest, still admitted an average profit rate of 24.8 percent— much higher than nonmilitary profits in the same industries. But spot checks showed that these profit rates were still very much underreported.

So the GAO did its own audit of the books of 146 main military contractors. The study found that the profit rate of these merchants of death was a fantastic 56.1 percent rate of return on invested capital!

GOVERNMENT POLICY IN STAGFLATION

Since World War II, the American economy has experienced a first in the nation's history: simultaneous unemployment and inflation. This situation appears impossible, according to elementary Keynesian analysis, because inflation implies an excess of demand over supply, while unemployment implies an excess of supply over demand. The answer to the riddle, as demonstrated elsewhere by this author, lies in the monopoly power of American capitalism. In spite of a certain amount of unemployment, the largest corporations actually still have the power to continue to raise their prices, which might be called *profit-push* inflation.

No aggregate monetary or fiscal policy can remedy or prevent both inflation and unemployment in these circumstances. To end unemployment by increasing aggregate demand sufficiently to affect output in all sectors allows the monopoly sector to set off another inflation spiral. To end inflation by reducing aggregate demand sufficiently to affect monopoly prices causes catastrophic unemployment in the whole economy. The capitalist governments of America and Europe have generally chosen to combat inflation at the expense of more unemployment. Yet even high levels of unemployment have failed to end inflation; only truly catastrophic levels of unemployment would end inflation given the present monopoly structure of the economy.

WAGE-PRICE CONTROLS

Since neither monetary nor fiscal policy is much good against stagflation, even the conservative Nixon administration was forced to try the drastic solution of direct wage-price controls. On August 15, 1971, Nixon announced a new economic policy designed to save America and increase corporate profits.

Phase 1 ran for 90 days from August to November 1971. All wages, prices, and rents were frozen. Profits were not frozen. In actuality, all wage increases were prevented, but some prices continued to creep upward. Nixon explained that the controls were necessary because we had combined inflation and unemployment, and all other monetary and fiscal policies had failed.

Phase 2 lasted from November 1971 until January 1973. The freeze was ended, but there were mandatory controls of wages, prices, and rents, though not of profits. Under this system, inflation continued, though at a reduced rate of "only" about 4 percent per year. Unemployment fell from its highest level (in the official data) of about 6 percent in the 1971 recession down to about 5 percent. When one realizes that the official data leave out many people and do not even try to count part-time unemployment, this is still a very high level. Wages were successfully kept to a very, very slow increase in this period, but profits rose spectacularly (as we shall see in detail).

Phase 3 was supposed to "phase out the economic stabilization program back to the free market, since the price target was being achieved," according to administration spokesmen. It removed all controls over prices in all industries except food, health, and construction, and substituted voluntary controls. The voluntary controls were no controls at all because they had no enforcement procedure. Therefore business paid no attention to them, so prices skyrocketed, rising at about 8 percent a year. In the end, even the administration admitted failure in holding down prices and had to institute a new freeze. Phase 3 lasted only from January to June 1973. A striking feature of it was the pressure kept on the unions to abide by voluntary controls and the extent to which the unions did restrain workers from asking for wage raises. As a result, there was a very, very slight rise in money wages, and the earning power of workers declined. Again there were no controls on profits, which continued to soar.

Phase 3½ was a second freeze. All prices were frozen, but there were no controls on unprocessed food or on rents. Neither wages nor profits were frozen, but wages remained under Phase 3 controls. This phase lasted only 60 days, from June to August 1973.

Phase 4 began in August 1973 and ended in April 1974. It was again a mandatory system of controls over prices, wages, and rents, but not over profits. It was very effective in holding down wages, but prices continued to rise at about 10 percent per year. The lack of enforcement on the price side was apparent in the case of the oil industry. The Cost of Living Council allowed the price of "old oil" (from existing wells, averaging less than $1 to produce) to rise from $4.25 to $5.25 a barrel. The council allowed the price of "new oil" (which costs no more than $2 a barrel to produce) to rise to $10.50. Then during the (phony) shortage winter of 1974, the Federal Energy Office allowed the retailers' profit margin to rise from 7.25 cents a gallon to 11 cents—and this increase was not rescinded in the later period of surplus.[18]

In all of 1973, the actual buying power of workers declined by 4 percent, while profits rose rapidly. In the first half of 1974, unemployment rose to 6 percent, real gross national product declined, and the rate of inflation rose to 12 percent. According to the usual definitions, the U.S. economy was in a recession in the midst of an unprecedented inflation. Nixon, however, denied it was a recession, preferring to call it a slight readjustment. Much later, President Ford finally admitted it was a recession, but not a depression, even though unemployment was over 9 percent. Ford still resisted any attempts to cure unemployment until late 1974; even in October 1974, he was still talking about *raising* taxes.

We have seen that 1975 was a year of depression, high unemployment, and declining real wages due to inflation. In late 1975 and 1976, the economy recovered somewhat, corporate profits rose, *but* unemployment continued very high, while inflation also continued at a slower pace. Because of the wage-price controls and the continued inflation and unemployment, the actual buying power of workers (real wages in constant 1967 dollars) reached a peak in 1972 and has been declining ever since. Thus, the real weekly wages of an urban worker with three dependents (after adjustment for higher prices and after Federal Income taxes) were $96.64 in 1972, $95.73 in 1973, $90.97 in 1974, $90.53 in 1975 and $90.36 in April 1976.[19] This 1976 level of real wages was actually *below* the 1965 level (which was $91.32)!

CONTROLS, INEFFICIENCY, AND CORRUPTION

Economists of all ideological views criticized the controls, but for different reasons. The conservatives, such as Milton Friedman, were horrified at the violation of the First Commandment of laissez-faire economics: Thou shalt not interfere with the market process of setting wages and prices.[20] They have always argued that resources, including capital and labor, cannot be efficiently allocated if prices are not set by competition in the market. If the government arbitrarily sets prices, how can a businessman calculate most efficiently what to produce or what technology to use? If a businessman does follow the arbitrary prices set by the government, then he will not produce what consumers desire, nor will he produce it in the cheapest possible way. It will not be produced as cheaply as possible because those prices do not correctly reflect the true scarcities of resources, and it will not be the combination of goods that consumers desire because those prices do not correctly reflect true consumer preferences. Thus, wage-price controls doom a capitalist economy to inefficiency.

Radicals agree with the truth of this insight. Radicals—and some conservatives—go further along these lines to point out that a huge bureaucracy would be needed to really enforce these controls. Not only would that bureaucracy have enormous repressive power, but it would also be wide open to corruption. After all, if a businessman cannot freely raise his prices when opportunity arises, then he is better off spending his time and money bribing a bureaucrat to raise his prices than worrying about producing a better quality product. At the same time, the controls do not end the money-grabbing aspect of capitalism. If capitalists cannot freely raise prices, then they will either bribe the bureaucrats as described or else evade the controls by selling illegally (that is, on a black market, the way much gasoline was sold during the crisis). In this sense, comprehensive wage-price controls in a capitalist system combine the worst aspects of capitalism and Soviet-style socialism: a huge and inefficient bureaucracy plus private greed.

CONTROLS AND INCOME DISTRIBUTION

When the conservatives, such as Friedman, argued against the controls, their own solution was an unregulated private capitalism. The liberals, such as Paul Samuelson, pointed out politely that Nixon had already tried that solution, and that it was private capitalism that had resulted in our present unpleasant mixture of inflation and unemployment.[21] Moreover, they pointed out that even the usual monetary and fiscal policies could not cope with inflation and unemployment at the same time. In fact, it was the liberals who first advocated the controls; they expected controls to hold down prices, while welfare spending would increase demand to eliminate unemployment. At first, the liberals applauded Nixon's controls. Even in their naivete, though, their reactions were a little doubtful on two points: Would Nixon actually hold down prices or just wages? And would he actually spend enough on welfare programs to end unemployment?

They were right to worry and wrong to applaud at all. Nixon actually (1) held down wages, (2) allowed prices to continue to rise, and (3) did nothing to cure unemployment, except some military spending. The important thing to understand is that this was not accidental, nor would Nixon be the only president to do such a thing. It was shown above that all U.S. governments have been strongly pro-business, for the very good reason among many others that business money elects them. Any wage-price controls under a business-dominated government can be expected to favor business.

The only difference with Nixon is that there was a great deal of evidence in his case that he accepted business bribes (such as those of ITT and the dairy industry) beyond the usual legal election campaign contributions, and he was much more blunt about his pro-business biases than most presidents have been. For example, in his speech announcing the wage-price controls, Nixon said: "All Americans will benefit from more profits. More profits fuel the expansion. . . . More profits mean more investment. . . . And more profits mean there will be more tax revenues. . . . That's why higher profits in the American economy would be good for every person in America."[22] Vice President Agnew repeated the theory, saying: "Rising corporate profits are needed more than ever by the poor."[23] Can you think of some things the poor might need more than rising corporate profits?

Nixon and Agnew were really telling the truth this time. They succeeded quite well in their objectives of limiting wages and raising profits. Thus, in all of Phase 1 and Phase 3½, wages didn't rise at all. During the longer Phases 2 and 3, average hourly earnings rose only 5.9 percent a year. At the same time the cost of living rose by about 4 percent yearly in Phase 2, and 8 percent yearly in Phase 3, and about 10 percent yearly in Phase 4. Since the cost of living rose faster than wages in 1973, for the first time on record in a year of economic expansion, the buying power of workers declined. In 1973, during Phases 3 and 4, wages rose by about 5 percent and retail prices by about 9 percent, so real wages (that is, what the worker can buy) declined by 4 percent.

One way Nixon achieved these results was by appointing a pro-business Pay Board to make wage decisions. The big unions first joined it, hoping to salvage some crumbs, then withdrew when they found they were to be allowed nothing. The AFL-CIO said: "We joined the Pay Board in good faith, desiring—despite our misgivings—to give it a fair chance. . . . The so-called public members are neither neutral nor independent. They are tools of the Administration, and imbued with its viewpoint that all of the nation's economic ills are caused by high wages. As a result, the Pay Board has been completely dominated and run, from the very start, by a coalition of the business and so-called public members. . . . The trade union movement's representatives on the board have been treated as outsiders—merely as a facade to maintain the pretense of a tripartite body."[24]

While real wages were declining in Phases 3 and 4, profit rates were actually climbing. Profit rates on investor's equity (before taxes) in all of manufacturing were "only" 16.5 percent in 1971, but rose to 18.4 percent in 1972; then—under Phase 3—rose to 21.6 percent in 1973; then—under Phase 4—rose to 23.4 percent in 1974 in the first year of the depression.[25] A strange depression!

Finally, in the first quarter of 1975, the profit rate fell to 15.0 percent (not seasonally adjusted). When this fall in the profit rate occurred, Congress and President Ford took immediate action to stimulate the economy by lower taxes, and the profit rate jumped back up to 19.2 percent in the second quarter of 1975.

One must conclude that the inevitable results of wage-price controls under a capitalist government are additional corruption and inefficiency, as well as shift in income distribution away from wages and toward profits. The meaning of the political business cycle is also clarified. At the peak expansion, when workers are pushing for higher wages, the U.S. government talks about inflation; and it uses restrictive monetary or fiscal or direct controls to lower wages and even promote a little unemployment. At the bottom of the depression, the U.S. government is moved by corporate pleas to stimulate the economy. The capitalist system would generate boom and bust cycles without government interference, but the government does reinforce them and may often serve as the catalyst setting off the downswing as well as the upswing (at such times when the economy was ripe for a change in direction anyway).

CARTER AND AFTER

It is a safe bet that both unemployment and inflation will continue to plague the U.S. economy for many, many years. The unemployment is mainly traceable to limited demand for goods and services, which is based on the highly unequal U.S. income distribution. As capitalism causes poverty and lack of monetary demand, it must continue to suffer cyclical depressions. Because capitalist competition leads to ever greater economic concentration, it must continue to suffer the price inflation, which is mainly caused by the exercise of monopoly power.

It is also a safe bet that the Carter administration and other Democratic or Republican administrations—all operating within the constraints of the interests of big business—will never be able to cope with both unemployment and inflation. This article has demonstrated that monetary and fiscal policy *may* stimulate the economy *if* unemployment is the only problem, and monetary-fiscal policy *may* deflate prices *if* inflation is the only problem. No known combination of monetary-fiscal policy can deal with both unemployment and inflation at the same time.

It is also a safe bet that the Carter administration will "fight inflation" by continuing to allow a very high level of unemployment. Truly full employment is anathema to big business and to the governments whose policies it dominates, because it gives workers the power to demand and obtain a decent wage. Thus, the Carter advisors, like the Ford-Nixon advisors, talk about 5 percent (or 5.5 percent) *unemployment* as full employment. Surely, Alice in Wonderland would have appreicated that concept of full employment (especially when it includes 4 or 5 million "discouraged" workers who have been unemployed so long that they have given up—so they are *not* counted as unemployed).

Richard Nixon was the first President to use wage-price controls in peacetime—not because he favors government interference with business as an ideology—but because he saw no other way out of an extreme dilemma. He increased employment by raising government (military) spending, and held down inflation by direct controls. Of course, his controls were mainly on wages, with very little control of prices. Nevertheless, for a short period, such controls will hold down the rate of inflation; the fact that they also redistributed income from workers to capitalists was viewed as an added advantage by Nixon and his financial backers.

If unemployment and inflation both become very severe again, then the Carter administration also will not hesitate to use the Nixon tactics Already, Carter has broken his promise to lower military spending dollars. There is, therefore, little doubt that he will meet large increases in unemployment partly by increased military spending and a smoke screen of other small job programs. There is also little doubt that an accompanying rapid rise of inflation will be met by Carter by wage-price controls, all his present protestations notwithstanding. If the capitalist business cycle follows its usual pattern, we can expect the next depression (with inflation) by 1979 or 1980, if not sooner. Then Carter will be forced to these tactics, but these tactics may create a Left Democratic opposition that may change all of the rules of the game.

WHAT IS TO BE DONE?

The only road to full employment, without inflation, is public ownership of all the monopoly enterprises. These monopolies are the top 1,300 corporations that *average* over a billion dollars in assets each, that hold over 60 percent of all assets, and more than that percentage of all sales and all profits. To avoid alienation, workers in the enterprises should be given 49 percent of the directors; the other 51 percent should be appointed by Congress and the President. Such boards of directors would be responsive to the public rather than the needs of private profit making. They could therefore hold down prices to their present levels, while increasing jobs (and wages) to provide greater amounts of energy, housing, hospitals, schools, cleaning up the environment, and many other necessary and constructive social tasks. There is *no* reason, other than our present economic system, for tolerating immense unemployment and rapid price inflation. A democratic and socialist America will tolerate neither one.

NOTES

1. The best single contemporary Marxist exposition is Ralph Miliband, *The State in Capitalist Society* (New York: Basic Books, 1969). Unfortunately, Miliband's data is on England; for similar U.S. data, see G. William Domhoff, *Who Rules America?* (Englewood Cliffs, N.J.: Prentice-Hall, 1967). The most recent and most thorough study of the evolution of Marx's own political thought is Hal Draper, *Karl Marx's Theory of Revolution* (New York: Monthly Review Press, 1977). Also very useful is Shlomo Avineri, *The Social and Political Thought of Karl Marx* (Cambridge, U.K.: Cambridge University Press, 1968).

2. Quoted in Mark Green, James Fallows, and David Zurick, *Who Runs Congress?* (New York: Bantam, 1972, the Ralph Nader Congress Project): 7-8.

3. See, for example, Gabriel Kolko, *Wealth and Power in America* (New York: Praeger, 1962).

4. See J. Pechman and B. Okner, "Individual Income Tax Erosion," U.S. Congress, Joint Economic Committee, *Economics of Federal Subsidy Programs* (Washington, D.C.: Government Printing Office, 1972): 13-40.

5. See Richard Edwards, "Who Fares Well in the Welfare State," in R. Edwards, M. Reich, and T. Weisskopf, editors, *The Capitalist System* (Englewood Cliffs, N.J.: Prentice-Hall, 1972): 244.

6. See James Bonnen, "The Effect of Taxes and Government Spending on Inequality," in *The Capitalist System* op. cit.: 235-243.

7. See F. Ackerman et al., "Income Distribution in the United States," *Review of Radical Political Economics* (Summer, 1971): 25.

8. See U.S. Internal Revenue Service, *Statistics of Income, Corporate Tax Returns* (Washington, D.C.: Government Printing Office, 1976).

9. See James Cypher, *Military Expenditures* (Ph.D. dissertation, University of California, Riverside, 1973): chapter 6.

10. Joint Economic Committee, U.S. Congress, reported in "Income Taxes Rise in Recession," *Riverside Press-Enterprise* (February 8, 1975): 1.

11. Paul Samuelson, *Economics,* 9th ed. (New York: McGraw-Hill, 1973, 1973): 823.

12. Ibid., 823.

13. Ibid., 824.

14. Ibid., 824-825.

15. These data come from U.S. Defense Department documents that are reported in Seymour Melman, *Pentagon Capitalism* (New York: McGraw-Hill, 1970).

16. Most of the analysis and all of the facts in the rest of this section come from James Cypher, *Military Expenditures and the Performance of the Post-war Economy, 1947-1971,* (Ph.D. dissertation, University of California, Riverside). This dissertation is a gold mine of information and the best discussion now available of military spending.

17. Fully discussed in Cypher, chapter 5.

18. See Bennet Harison, "Inflation by Oligopoly," *The Nation* (August 30, 1975): 147.

19. U.S. Labor Department data, reported in Fred Burton, "The Economic Squeeze on the Worker, 1976," *AFL-CIO American Federationist* (June, 1976): 1.

20. See Milton Friedman, *Newsweek* (August 30, 1971): 45.

21. See Paul Samuelson, *Newsweek* (August 30, 1971): 46.

22. President Richard Nixon, in TV speech, August 15, 1971.

23. Vice President Agnew, at National Governors' Conference, 1971.

24. AFL-CIO Executive Committee, in *The National Economy* (AFL-CIO, 1973): 7.

25. Federal Trade Commission, *Quarterly Financial Report for Manufacturing Corporations* (1st Quarter 1974 and 1st Quarter 1975): 12-16.

3

ECONOMIC REGULATORY AND CONSUMER PROTECTION POLICIES

JAMES E. ANDERSON

University of Houston

The regulation of private economic activities is one of the major functions of government in the United States. Essentially, regulation involves the governmental control, direction, or limitation of private economic behavior; its ultimate effect being to limit the discretion of action of the regulated persons, groups, or organizations. Desired actions may be required, or undesired actions may be prohibited. For example, a minimum wage law limits the discretion of employers by prohibiting the payment of wages below the prescribed minimum. It also limits the discretion of persons to work for less than the minimum wage, but most employees seem undisturbed by this.

Regulation takes a variety of forms: price and rate controls; allocation of goods and services; standard setting; licensing; manipulation of the economic environment, as in the case of monetary policy; taxation; the requirement of particular action, e.g., reports and the accurate labeling of products; and persuasion and "jawboning," to name a few. Regulations may be enforced or implemented by such means as judicial action, as in the case of the Sherman Antitrust Act; agency rule-making and adjudication; inspection and policing; the issuance of orders and prohibitions; the imposition of financial or other penalties; and informal settlements and

AUTHOR'S NOTE: I wish to thank Alan Stone and Michael Levy for their helpful and constructive comments on an earlier version of this article.

agreements, e.g., Federal Trade Commission consent orders. The implementation of regulatory programs may be handled by bureaus in the executive departments, independent regulatory commissions, independent agencies, or government corporations. (See Table 1) The first two

Table 3.1. National Regulatory Agencies (1977)
INDEPENDENT REGULATORY COMMISSIONS

Interstate Commerce Commission
Federal Reserve Board
Federal Trade Commission
Federal Power Commission (Now Federal Energy Regulatory Commission)
National Labor Relations Board
Securities and Exchange Commission
Federal Communications Commission
Civil Aeronautics Board
Federal Maritime Commission
Consumer Products Safety Commission
Nuclear Regulatory Commission
Commodity Futures Trading Commission

INDEPENDENT AGENCIES

Environmental Protection Agency
Equal Employment Opportunity Commission
Federal Deposit Insurance Corporation
Federal Home Loan Bank Board
Federal Mediation and Conciliation Service
Federal Energy Administration
National Transportation Safety Board

BUREAUS IN EXECUTIVE DEPARTMENTS

Packers and Stockyards Administration (USDA)
Agricultural Stabilization and Conservation Service (USDA)
Agricultural Marketing Service (USDA)
Animal and Plant Health Inspection Service (USDA)
Food and Drug Administration (HEW)
Mining Enforcement and Safety Administration (Int.)
Antitrust Division (Justice)
Wage and Hour Division (DOL)
Office of Federal Contract Compliance (DOL)
Occupational Safety and Health Administration (DOL)
Federal Aviation Administration (DOT)
Federal Railroad Administration (DOT)
National Highway Traffic Safety Administration (DOT)
Office of the Comptroller of the Currency (Treas.)
U.S. Customs Service (Treas.)
Bureau of Alcohol, Tobacco and Firearms (Treas.)
Office of Interstate Land Sales Registration (HUD)
Labor-Management Services Administration (DoD)
Army Corps of Engineers (DoD)

are the most frequently used forms. It is difficult to indicate the scope and variety of regulatory activity in a brief statement, but these comments should be suggestive.

It is often difficult to distinguish regulation from the promotion of private economic activity, which is another major activity of government. Promotion involves government action designed to assist, stimulate, or facilitate the conduct of private economic activity. Examples include financial grants and subsidies, provision of services and information, the issuance of corporate charters, protection of property, and the enforcement of contracts. Promotion has a control element as when a particular action is taken to obtain or to avoid losing a subsidy. Regulation, in turn, may have a promotional aspect, depending upon the perspective from which it is viewed. Thus, a minimum wage law is promotional from the standpoint of workers if it enables them to obtain higher wages than they would otherwise receive. The point is, then, that what constitutes regulation can not always be neatly categorized.

Regulation may involve either prescription of the "rules of the game" or direct involvement in the management of private businesses. Examples of regulatory programs setting rules of the game are antitrust laws, regulation of labor-management relations, and truth in lending and wage and hour legislation. Within the framework of rules individuals are left free to exercise their discretion. In the area of labor relations, for example, the government prohibits various unfair labor and management practices, but then it is left up to the parties involved in a given situation to bargain and to agree or disagree. Regulation of the sort applied to railroads, commercial airlines, packers and stockyards, electric and gas utilities, commodity exchanges, and petroleum production prices goes beyond the rules of the game and involves the government in the detailed and operating decisions of business enterprises. In its fullest extent, this can entail control of entry into the business, financial practices, accounting procedures, quality of service, and rates of charge and return. Although such regulation has been applied mostly to enterprises thought of as public utilities, and hence can also be called public utility type regulation, it has been applied to other concerns, e.g., the petroleum industry, under Department of Administration regulations, and most businesses under the Nixon Administration's price and wage controls during the 1971-1974 period.

In a somewhat different manner, regulation may also be classified as "social regulation" or "economic regulation." Social regulation is designed to protect interests or values that would not be adequately cared for by the operation of the market economy. Industrial health and safety, environmental quality, conservation of natural resources, and consumer safety are illustrative. Economic regulation, on the other hand, is intended to eliminate obstacles to the operation of the market, as in the case of anti-trust, or to protect the public interest when the market is adequate, as in the instance of natural monopolies. Regulation which falls in the direct management and economic categories seems to have received the most attention from the advocates of deregulation.

There have been critics of regulation as long as there have been regulatory programs. In recent years, however, the real or alleged shortcomings of economic regulatory programs have been the focus of increased attention, commentary, and controversy. Journalists, academicians, public officials, business spokespeople, and polemicists (the categories are not necessarily mutually exclusive) have generated a substantial volume of literature and commentary. The critics come from both the left and right sides of the political spectrum—liberal Democrats and conservative Republicans, Nader's Raiders and the National Association of Manufacturers, Gabriel Kolko and Milton Friedman. Although their foci may vary and their interests and values may differ, all have found something wrong with the regulatory state. Some of their criticisms and complaints will be treated later.

THE GROWTH OF REGULATION

Since the inception of government under the Constitution, there has always been government regulation of economic activity in the United States. One of the first statutes enacted by the new Congress provided for a protective tariff. That there has never existed a "golden age of laissez faire" seems sufficiently proven as not to require another effort.[1] Nonetheless, regulatory programs at both the national and state levels were comparatively limited in number and significance until toward the end of the nineteenth century. Indeed, Steiner has remarked that "It is probably defensible to observe that up to the 1930s despite some significant exceptions, Federal economic controls were within the scope of a liberal interpretation of the limited-government doctrine."[2]

The first major modern regulatory statutes enacted by Congress were the Interstate Commerce Act (1887) and the Sherman Antitrust Act (1890). In the twentieth century, there have been three major waves of regulatory legislation. These, occurring during the Progressive Era, saw the expansion of railroad and antitrust regulation, the development of meat and food and drug inspection programs, and the creation of the Federal Reserve Systems. A wide varity of matters were brought under regulation during the New Deal—motor carriers, airlines, stock markets and exchanges, labor-management relations, wages and hours of work, agricultural production, and interstate communications. Legislation also dealt further with such matters as railroad, food and drug, and trade regulation. By the end of the 1930s, it was clear that in practice, the nation had abandoned the laissez-faire state, although it lived on in the minds and hearts of various of its citizens. In the 1960s and 1970s, a variety of regulatory statutes were adopted which focused on protecting or improving the quality of life. Some dealt with problems of consumer protection while others, such as the Occupational Safety and Health Act of 1970, dealt with health and safety conditions in the workplace. Major regulatory proposals before Congress in 1977 involved energy use and pricing, the creation of an agency for consumer advocacy, labor law reform, and an increase in the minimum wage level.

Although the trend in the twentieth century has been for the volume of regulation to expand continually, albeit more rapidly at some times than at others, it should be kept in mind that the economy and the totality of opportunities for private economic decisions have also been expanding Much discretion remains under the control of private economic decision-makers. This is not to deny that there is a substantial amount of regulation and that government is rather deeply involved in and intertwined with the private economy.

Why has government regulation of economic activity increased? What are the underlying causes? The explanation can not be explained by such sweeping and vastly oversimplified explanations as the march of social-ism, the grasping of bureaucrats for ever more power, or a "new passion for government regulation."[3] Although some may find these ideologically satisfying, their explanatory power is quite low. The following listing of causes seems more useful.

First, the transformation of the United States from a rural agrarian society into a complex, urban industrial society as a consequence of technological development, economic growth, and urbanization provides the basic framework for the expansion of regulatory activity. As a society becomes more complex, urban, and industrial, the conflicts, needs, and demands which give rise to government action multiply. Where once informal social controls were adequate, formal controls become necessary to deal with public problems. In a society in which most people produce most of their own food and clothing, and in which most goods sold in the market are relatively simple, the rule of *caveat emptor* may suffice. In modern society, such a rule becomes impossible. It leaves the door open to fraud, duplicity, and chincanery in economic interchange. Purchasers of many products are simply unable to determine the products' quality, effectiveness, or safety in use. Consequently, a substantial body of legislation has been enacted to help protect the economic and physical well-being of consumers. (See the section titled "Criticisms of Regulation.") "Consumerism" has become part of our political language. Again, the technical aspects of radio and television broadcasting require some authoritative agency to allocate frequencies among potential users. Whether such regulation should take the form of current Federal Communications Commission policy is open to question.

Many of the assumptions of classical or free market economics have been undermined by the transformation of the American economy. Monopolistic and oligopolistic conditions often exist rather than competitive conditions. Labor and capital often lack mobility. The pursuit of individual self-interest frequently leads to conflict rather than economic harmony, and the market mechanism does not always satisfactorily resolve group conflict. Individuals often lack the information and means necessary to know and pursue their self-interest in the marketplace. The market mechanism, moreover, does not guarantee economic security for those who are industrious and willing to work hard. Resources are often misallocated because groups possess market power. That is, through their domination of product or labor markets, they may be able to set prices or wages at levels above those which would prevail under competitive conditions.

As a consequence of such factors, people have become less and less inclined to rely upon the market mechanism as the sole determiner of their economic condition. Moreover, even if the market in many instances still does a pretty good job of promoting economic efficiency, there may be other social and economic values—equity, for example—which are not adequately cared for by the market. In short, "market failures," as they have come to be called, often serve as a rationale for regulation. Government action becomes necessary to help maintain competition and prevent monopoly, to prevent the waste of natural resources, to regulate natural monopolies such as electric and gas utilities, and to protect industrial health and safety.

The market mechanism is also inadequate to deal with costs and benefits in the form of *externalities* which involve the interests of third parties. Environmental pollution is an example. The costs of pollution are usually not met by the person doing the polluting; the benefits of controlling pollution are not gained solely or even primarily by a person who engages in pollution control measures. Disposal of waste by dumping it in a stream becomes a cheap form of disposal for the dumper. The market thus encourages this activity as it permits the dumper to hold down his operating or capital costs, even though the social costs may be substantial. Government action is necessary if the costs and benefits of externalities are to be more properly allocated than they would be by the market. Private law suits could be used for this purpose, but they are often an awkward, slow, and after-the-fact remedy. The basic purpose of government action here is to prevent pollution rather than to punish polluters. Preventive action can best be supplied through the administrative process.

The need for government to resolve and adjust group conflicts has also contributed to regulatory expansion. With growing complexity and specialization, the number and diversity of economic groups increases and conflicts among groups become more frequent and more intense. Conflicts between labor and management, large and small businesses, automobile manufacturers and dealers, railroads and motor carriers, farmers and the purchasers of farm commodities have given rise to a variety of regulatory programs with attempt to resolve conflicts and often to alter the relative economic power of the involved groups. At the same time, wide acceptance of such values as "fair play" and humaneness and a belief in social justice have helped produce government actions designed to protect the economically weak against the economically strong, as through workmen's compensation, wage and hour, and child labor laws.

Another significant cause of regulation has been the desire and ability of various groups to shift some of their economic risks or costs to government and thereby "socialize" them. Protective tariffs, agricultural price support and production control programs, resale price maintenance (now defunct at the national level), bank deposit insurance, petroleum-production prorationing, many occupational licensing laws, and restrictions on entry into businesses such as banking, motor carrier transport, and commercial airline service are illustrative. Groups whose economic interests are threatened or disadvantaged by the operation of the market are not at all adverse to seeking governmental protection, whether in the name of the protection of "infant industry," the public interest, national defense, or some other worthy purpose. If the discussion were expanded to include promotional and subsidy programs, the illustrations would be legion. Few important economic groups have not secured some sort of governmental aid or protection.

Finally, attitudes concerning the use of governmental power to promote economic interests have changed. The notion that freedom is the absence of governmental restraint has withered. Corporations, unions, and other economic aggregations are recognized as possessing power that can be used for coercive purposes. Governmental power can be used to limit private power and to increase, not decrease, the freedom of citizens generally. By acting to equalize opportunity and by removing economic and social barriers to the exercise of individual faculties and capacities, government can increase the freedom of most individuals. The change in attitudes toward the use of government is also indicated by the breakdown of the traditional distinctions between liberals and conservatives, as noted by Professor Lowi.[4] Until the 1930s, liberals favored the use of governmental power to produce deliberate social change while conservatives were in opposition to this. Now they differ not so much over the use of governmental power as over the groups in whose behalf it should be used. Thus, while liberals tend to favor the regulation of large businesses, but not necessarily their breakup, conservatives display considerable enthusiasm for the control of labor unions. Some of the stanchest supporters of agricultural price support programs are drawn from among the ranks of conservative southern congressmen, who have also come to favor restrictions on international trade to protect southern industries such as textiles.

These various factors should not be assumed to justify as necessary or meritorious all of the regulatory programs that exist. Nor do they indicate why particular programs have the form and substance that they do. That depends, of course, upon the particular political and governmental processes that produce particular programs, whether antitrust, equal employment opportunity, or meat and poultry inspection.

On the whole, the regulatory state has not developed in accordance with any particular theory or design. Rather, individual regulatory programs have emerged in response to particular problems and felt needs, as practical solutions for problems developed by practical men. Not surprisingly, some programs have outlived their usefulness; others have never accomplished their intended purposes; yet others have come into conflict with one another (e.g., antitrust and some of the industry regulatory programs).

CONSUMER PROTECTION LEGISLATION

Change is a basic characteristic of the regulatory arena. Existing policies are constantly being altered or elaborated by legislative, administrative, and judicial action. New statutes are continually being adopted to expand or strengthen, and sometimes weaken or limit, current regulatory programs. No area of regulation, however, surpasses consumer protection in the expansion of legislative and administrative activity during the past decade and a half. Table 2 lists the various national consumer protection laws, all regulatory in nature, which have been enacted since 1960.

Consumer protection legislation can be generally defined as intended to protect the interests and well-being of the ultimate retail purchasers and users of goods and services, when we buy meat or drugs, seek credit, or purchase an automobile. Consumer protection legislation is essentially a twentieth century phenomenon. While some refer to the Interstate

Table 3.2. Consumer Protection Legislation, 1960–1976

Federal Hazardous Substances Labeling Act (1960)
Color Additives Amendments (1960)
Drug Amendments of 1962
Federal Cigarette Labeling and Advertising Act (1965)
National Traffic and Motor Vehicle Safety Act (1966)
Fair Packaging and Labeling Act (1966)
Child Protection Act (1966)
Wholesome Meat Act (1967)
Flammable Fabrics Amendments (1967)
Consumer Credit Protection Act (1968) (includes Truth-in-Lending)
Natural Gas Pipeline Safety Act (1968)
Housing and Urban Development Act (1968) (includes regulation of Interstate
    Land Sales)
Radiation Control for Health and Safety Act (1968)
Mail Fraud Legislation (PL90-590, 1968)
Deceptive Sales Act (1968)
Wholesome Poultry Products Act (1968)
Child Protection and Toy Safety Act (1969)
Fair Credit Reporting Act (1970)
Poison Prevention Packaging Act (1970)
Egg Products Inspection Act (1970)
Lead-Based Paint Poisoning Prevention Act (1970)
Wholesome Fish and Fisheries Products Act (1971)
Consumer Product Safety Act (1972)
Motor Vehicle Information and Cost Savings Act (1972)
Consumer Product Warranties Act (1974)
Equal Credit Opportunity Act (1975)
Medical Device Safety Act (1976)
Consumer Leasing Act (1976)
Toxic Substances Control Act (1976)

Commerce Act of 1887 as the first consumer law, this seems inaccurate as it was designed primarily to protect the interests of shippers—farmers and businessmen—and other railroad users. The first major consumer statutes were the Food and Drug Act and the Meat Inspection Act, both passed by Congress in 1906. Considerable struggle attended their enactment, which was also true of major consumer legislation enacted subsequently, such as the Food, Drug, and Cosmetic Act of 1938 and the Drug Amendments of 1962. (The latter statute required drugs to be certified as effective as well as safe before being marketed.) Some sort of crisis, such as the death of nearly a hundred people because of the use of an unsafe patent medicine called "Elixir Sulfanilimide," which contributed to enactment of the 1938 law, seemed necessary before consumer protection legislation could be passed.

This changed in the 1960s. The development of more effective advocates for consumers, such as Ralph Nader and the Consumer

Federation; growing concern about the quality of life; the Johnson Administration's strong support for consumer protection; and the popularity of consumer protection in Congress all contributed to the outpouring of consumer legislation indicated by Table 2.[5] This volume of legislation falls into two general categories. Some of it, such as the Consumer Credit Protection Act (especially the "Truth-in-lending" provisions), is intended to provide consumers with accurate information on the products or services being purchased so that they can (if they so choose) make rational, informed decisions. The second category involves legislation designed to prevent the sale of unsafe or unwholesome products. Illustrative are the Consumer Product Safety Act and the Wholesome Meat Act.

The consumer protection movement has now lost some of its momentum, partly because of its success in securing legislation. There are not too many matters of consumer importance that have not been dealt with by the legislation. To be effective, of course, legislation must be adequately enforced, and it is here that the consumer movement falters. Agencies such as the Food and Drug Administration, the Federal Trade Commission, and the Consumer Product Safety Commission, do not appear very effective in implementing the laws under their jurisdiction. As students of regulation know, it is not uncommon for legislative victories to erode during the administrative phase of the policy process.

Currently, the major issue involving new legislation concerns the establishment of an "Agency for Consumer Advocacy." As proposed in 1977, this agency would be empowered to represent consumer interests in regulatory proceedings conducted by other agencies, such as the Civil Aeronautics Board or the Department of Agriculture. It would have no substantive duties, no power to legally compel anyone or any agency to do anything. Proponents believe, however, that its articulation and representation of consumer interests would make it more difficult for agencies to ignore them in their decision-making. Opponents contend, among other things, that such an agency is unnecessary and that it would be another bureaucracy too many.

One of the thrusts in the current movement for regulatory reform involves efforts and proposals to improve or enlarge public participation in regulatory agency proceedings. The "Agency for Consumer Advocacy" proposal is in line with this. Another thrust calls for deregulation, for the abandonment of some regulatory programs. Deregulation will be examined in a later section of this chapter, but it can be noted here that the proponents of deregulation have generally devoted little of their attention to consumer protection programs. They would likely not be a popular target. If the consumer it not sovereign, neither is the consumer "fair game."

CRITICISMS OF REGULATION

It seems that almost everyone at the present time is in favor of some sort of deregulation. Regulation is a "failure." The regulatory commissions are the "captives" of their business constituencies. Such are the contentions that we encounter with a few cases, illustrations, or anecdotes being offered as supporting evidence. But what, for example, would "regulatory failure" consist of? Would it mean that a program accomplishes nothing? Or that it accomplishes less than is possible or expected? Or does it mean that the program is doing something other than what the critic, given his interests and values, would prefer? The only definition of regulatory failure that I have encountered in the literature states: "Agencies would be said to fail when they reach substantive policy decisions (including decisions not to act) that do not coincide with what the politically accountable branches of government would have done had they possessed the time, the information, and the will to make such decisions."[6] The authors of this definition themselves indicate that only rarely could it be determined what the President and Congress would have done, which admission really destroys the operational value of their definition.

Regulation, as such, is neither inherently good nor obviously evil. Whether particular regulatory program is socially beneficial or harmful is something best determined by an examination of its causes, costs, benefits, and consequences rather than by sweeping reference to "first principles" or the notion that there is too much regulation and we ought to get rid of some of it. Here, however, given limitations of time, space, and ability, I cannot engage in this sort of systematic evaluation of particular regulatory programs. Rather, I shall content myself with an examination of some of the general complaints levied against regulation. Some of these relate to the *substance* of regulation, others to the *process* of regulation.

Irving Kristol states that the deregulation movement was conceived a couple of decades ago by the Department of Economics at the University of Chicago, which is noted for its orientation toward a free market economy.[7] Many other economists have also become advocates of deregulation. The basic argument of the economist critics is that regulation often distorts or disrupts the operation of the market and consequently results in higher prices, inequities, and the misallocation of resources. Thus, it is argued that the regulation of natural gas prices by the Federal Power Commission has kept prices below market clearing levels, thereby encouraging consumption while discouraging the exploration for and production of natural gas. A natural gas shortage has resulted, the solution for which (from this perspective) is the deregulation of gas prices. The natural gas industry, as one might suspect, has been strongly in favor of this alternative. Indeed, this has been the industry position for over two decades. Given this, one may wonder whether self-interest or philosophic concerns for a free market is the primary motivation of the industry.

A second economic argument is that regulation often impedes the operation of competition. Although competitive failure is often cited as a cause of regulation, there are certainly instances in which regulation limits competition, as in the control of entry into businesses such as motor carrier transport, commercial air transport, and banking. Again, price competition is limited by the Civil Aeronautics Board and the Interstate Commerce Commission. Economists and others have long complained that the Robinson-Patman Act contributed to "soft competition" in retail distribution as a consequence of its attempt to protect small businesses from price discrimination by their larger, more efficient competitors.

A third economic criticism is that regulation may impede technological development. A familiar illustration is the fact that it took the Southern Railway four years to get the approval of the ICC to use its "Big John" grain car, which would permit it to haul profitably more grain and lower rates. The Federal Communications Commission has been noted for slow action on such matters as UHF, color, and cable television.

A fourth economic criticism concerns "cross-subsidization." The CAB has set air fairs on high service and long-distance routes at levels substantially above costs, with the excess revenue being used to subsidize service to small cities with little traffic. This, state the critics, is wrong. If such traffic must be subsidized it should be done directly rather than indirectly as a charge on high-profit route passengers. Or as a second example, take this argument: "Product safety regulation subsidizes those people who would have been injured by negligent manufacturers and would not have received compensation for their injuries. This subsidy occurs at the expense of the far larger number who would have been compensated for injury or escaped it entirely."[8] This second example indicates the absurd level to which an argument can be pushed. One will not find many government programs that do not have a differential effect. Few if any government programs benefit all equally. Should the costs of government programs, regulatory or otherwise, be met only by the direct and immediate beneficiaries?

As was indicated earlier, the market is often an effective mechanism for promoting economic efficiency; that is, the most production at the least cost. Moreover, it seems clear that considerable inefficiencies are often associated with regulatory programs.[9] This seems especially the case for some of the "regulated industries," such as rail, motor, and air transport, where regulation is of the public utility type. Efficiency, however, is obviously not the only decision criterion used in regulatory decision-making. Equity, equality of opportunity, and market stabilization are other values which may underlie regulatory action and which may conflict with concern for efficiency.[10]

There are also a variety of political and administrative criticisms of economic regulation. We will begin with the complaint that regulatory agencies, especially the independent regulatory commissions, are often the captives of the regulated industries.[11] Usually, little evidence is offered in support of this contention, as it has apparently achieved the status of conventional wisdom. The ICC, FCC, and CAB are most frequently trotted out as examples of captives. Would anyone argue that the FPC was really the captive of the natural gas industry? And who are the potential captors of the Federal Trade Commission and the Consumer Product Safety Commission, let alone the Equal Employment Opportunity Commission? James Q. Wilson suggests that the capture theory "reflects a simplistic view of the politics of regulation." He goes on to explain:[12]

> Though there have been few good studies of agency politics, what probably happens is this: An agency is established, sometimes with industry support and sometimes over industry objections, and then gradually creates a regulatory climate that acquires a life of its own. Certain firms will be helped by some of the specific regulatory decisions making up this climate, others will be hurt. But the industry as a whole will adjust to the climate and decide that the costs of shifting from the known hazards of regulation to the unknown ones of competition are too great; it will thus come to defend the system. The agencies themselves will become preoccupied with the details of regulation and the minutiae of cases in whatever form they first inherit them, trying by the slow manipulation of details to achieve various particular effects that happen to commend themselves from time to time to various agency members.

In some cases, as Wilson also suggests, industries may be the captives of the regulating agencies. Regulatory agencies have been established to regulate, they have a bias in favor of regulation, and regulate they do. There may indeed be, as Kharsach has contended, an institutional imperative.[13]

The capture theory currently seems especially popular with those on the political left. If regulatory agencies are in fact captured by the regulated businesses (read "big businesses"), and if regulation is bent to serve their interests, then regulation becomes a sort of business-government conspiracy against the public interest. In a neat turnaround, deregulation becomes an anti-business position for those who find such ideologically attractive.

Suffice it to say, I am skeptical of the validity of the capture theory except in carefully defined circumstances. Solid empirical evidence that supports the general theory is lacking. However, the capture theory may be descriptive of the relationship between various state occupational or professional licensing boards and their clientele, where board members are drawn primarily or exclusively from the licensed group and the boards often operate with little public awareness of their actions. Even here, though, the licensing board is not so much captured by the licensed group as handed over to it by the state legislature. In such situations, "conflict of interest" becomes a basic principle of public policy.

Apart from the capture argument, regulatory commissions have been subject to considerable criticism for their operating methods or style, at least since 1937 when the President's Committee on Administrative Management described them as a "headless fourth branch of govern-ment."[14] Criticisms of the commissions include their failure to ade-quately develop policy; excessive reliance on excessively formal and judicialized procedures; slowness in decision-making; and the frequent lack of high caliber personnel on the commissions. Many of these criticisms were accepted by the Ash Council which, in its 1971 report on the regulatory commissions, concluded that commission regulation was a failure.[15] Little empirical support, however, was provided in support of this conclusion. Indeed, we should note that solid, empirical studies of regulation and the regulatory process, which view them as the political phenomena which they are, are scarce.

Various critics of the regulatory commissions have contended that the commissions could be improved by converting them into singly headed agencies directly responsible to the President. This was the general stance of the Ash Council. There is, however, really no empirical basis for concluding that singly headed agencies, such as the Environmental Protection Administration, Food and Drug Administration, or Packers and Stockyards Administration are more effective regulators than the independent regulatory commissions. About all that closer supervision from the White House, on behalf of the President, would guarantee is that some commission decisions would be more closely geared to the political interests of the President. One thing that we should have learned in recent years is that what is good for the President is not necessarily good for the country.

Another criticism pertains to the nature of the statutory mandates under which regulatory agencies operate. Congress often delegates power to agencies in broad terms. Many statutes are essentially general statements of objectives or policy, and authorizations to agencies to effectuate these goals. Thus, the Securities and Exchange Commission is empowered to make certain rules "as it deems necessary in the public interest or for the protection of investors"; the Federal Communications Commission is directed to license radio and television broadcasters for "the public interest, convenience, or necessity"; and the Federal Power Commission (now the Federal Energy Regulatory Commission) is told to set "just and reasonable" rates for natural gas. The Economic Stabilization Act of 1970 granted the Executive Branch an almost blank check to impose price and wage controls to control inflation. The authorization was "to issue such orders and regulations as he may deem appropriate to stabilize prices, rents, wages, and salaries at levels not less than those prevailing on May 25, 1970." This was the basis for Phase I through IV of the Nixon Administration's price-wage controls. Here clearly is support for Lowi's contention that government action often involves policy without law.[16]

According to Noll, regulatory problems stemming from the vagueness of statutory mandates include "unequal treatment of like cases; additional uncertainty introduced by regulatory inconsistency; elaborate legal procedures, since each case is, in essence, a new law; and a much heavier case load, since a prior adverse decision on an issue is not a sufficient deterrent to raising the issue again."[17]

The Ash Council in its report noted that agency proceedings tend to emphasize legal perspectives "to the detriment of economic, financial, technical, and social perspectives." Administrative procedures in some agencies are so complicated that only legal specialists seem likely to understand them. the effect of procedure often seems to delay or frustrate action rather than facilitate the making of fair, sound, and expeditious decisions. Does the protection of the interests of corporations require procedural guarantees which rival if they do not exceed those guaranteed to real persons accused of crimes? Should they have a constitutionally protected right of freedom of speech?

In recent years, considerable emphasis has been given to the financial costs and burdens, direct and indirect, imposed by regulation upon regulated business and society. Some contend that regulation has been a major contributing factor to the inflation that has afflicted the American economy in the 1970s.[18] Also, attention is often given to some of the trivial or nonsensical rules or actions of regulating agencies. The Consumer Products Safety Commission and the Occupational Safety and Health Administration (OSHA) especially attract attention.

Finally, and simply, a lot of people do not like particular agencies or regulatory programs because they interfere with their pursuit of self-interest, run counter to their notions of proper public policy, or offend their ideological sensitivities, or some combination thereof. A person, however, is likely to be viewed as crass or greedy if he boldly states, "I do not like regulation X because it interferes with my profit seeking." A more socially acceptable rationale for opposition is needed, and the various criticisms sketched above will often fulfill this requirement.

THE MOVEMENT FOR DEREGULATION

Deregulation has now achieved a place on the national policy agenda. President Gerald Ford was a strong advocate of deregulation; and in 1975, his administration sponsored a White House Conference on Regulatory Reform. This was followed by a series of proposals to Congress for deregulation. The Carter Administration has also been strongly in favor of deregulation. Various studies in Congress on regulation and regulatory reform have been undertaken.[19] A variety of bills providing for regulatory reform or deregulation has been introduced. Senators Muskie (Dem., Maine) and Roth (Rep., Del.), for example, have introduced one of the more sweeping proposals. Their bill would require the reauthorization of most federal programs and activities every four years, following a zero-based review and evaluation of them, or else they would expire.[20]

Notwithstanding the popularity of deregulation as a general issue, the likelihood is not strong that much deregulation will actually occur. After several years of effort, by the fall of 1978 the only statute directly generated by the deregulation movement was the Railroad Reform and Revitalization Act of 1975. It permitted some flexibility in rate-setting by railroads. The Democrats, who have controlled Congress continuously since 1955, have not jumped on the overall deregulation bandwagon. They tend to have a bias in favor of regulation (with the exception of some southern Democrats) and, moreover, were disinclined to do the Ford Administration any favors. Nor have they been much more helpful to the Carter Administration. Studies of deregulation and regulatory reform in Congress do not guarantee action; indeed, they are often a substitute for positive action. Moreover, the businesses subject to regulation often favor retention of regulation, with which they have learned to live and which they often find acceptable or beneficial to their interests. The railroad, motor carrier, commercial airline, and broadcasting industries have been sharply critical of the Ford and Carter Administration proposals applicable to them. They suggest that any sharp changes in regulatory policies could cause severe economic dislocations. Thus, trucking companies contend that deregulation of the motor carrier industry, as by removing the control of routes of service and rates, would cause transport costs to rise and service to smaller communities to decline.

What we have is a situation in which the activities being regulated are many and diverse; the same is true for those who seek change or reform. There is agreement that all is not well in the regulatory state, but there is agreement neither on the problems, their causes, nor their remedies. As a Ford Administration economist stated: "Somebody should have explained to the President that regulatory reform to too many people means, 'Get rid of the regulations I don't like but keep the regulations I do like.' "[21] Given such circumstances, the prospects for some kind of systematic or comprehensive deregulation or regulatory reform (and the two are not necessarily identical) seem less than bright.

To say this, however, is not to argue that there has been or will be no change. Change has been occurring in the regulatory state, but it is limited and piecemeal in nature. Some recent events can be briefly commented upon. In late 1975, the national legislation providing an antitrust exemption for state resale price maintenance, or "fair trade" laws, was repealed by Congress. At one time, such laws had existed in 45 of the states; by the time of national repeal, they remained operative in only 21 states. Part of the effort of the 1930s to protect small retail businesses against their larger, more efficient competitors, such as chain stores and department stores, these laws had lost much support. In essence, they were abandoned more because of their own weaknesses and ineffectiveness than because of the opposition to them.

Changing economic conditions, especially increased international demand for American agricultural commodities, and pressure from the Nixon and Ford Administrations for a more market-oriented farm policy, resulted temporarily (at least) in a reduction of controls on agricultural production. Target prices were substituted for traditional price supports. Since for a time market prices were higher than target prices, the cost of the farm program fell substantially. However, by 1977 foreign agricultural production had increased substantially. Demand for American commodities fell and so did prices, causing considerable economic distress in the farming community. The ultimate result was the enactment of legislation in 1977 providing more income support for farmers and the reinstitution of some of the controls on production. The point to be noted here is that in the early 1970s, policy change followed an important structural change in the world economy. Where that change proved to be temporary, the policy change which it had helped produce was modified. Parenthetically, we should note that the development of "stagflation" seems to underlie much of the current desire of industries and groups to escape from regulations which they find uncomfortable.

The Robinson-Patman Act, which prohibits price discrimination, has long been criticized as anticompetitive in nature. The Antitrust Division of the Division of the Department of Justice and the Federal Trade Commission share enforcement jurisdiction. The Antitrust Division, which has a strong procompetitive orientation, has never completed a proceeding based solely on the act. The FTC, which has often depicted itself as the defender of small business, has completed several hundred Robinson-Patman cases. In the mid-1970s, however, the FTC too has almost entirely ceased to enforce the act, which is in accord with the substantive recommendations of various antitrust study commissions and which should also be pleasing to the statute's critics. What we have here, in essence, is deregulation by administrative action. It must be asked, however, whether this is a *proper* exercise of administrative discretion. Should agencies be permitted to substitute their policy judgments for those of Congress? What becomes of the principle of the rule of law in such a situation?

In December 1975, Congress passed a bill which would have permitted construction unions to engage in what is called common situs picketing (i.e., picketing of an entire construction project rather than a designated portal). Such common picketing had been held by the Supreme Court to be included in the Taft-Hartley Act's ban on secondary boycotts. The effect of the bill, then, was to deregulate this union activity. Under strong business and conservative pressure, President Ford reversed his stand and vetoed the bill, thereby sending one effort at deregulation down the tube. Depending upon one's position and interests, some deregulation is better than other deregulation.

Any deregulation which occurs in the future will likely be piecemeal, limited in quantity, and hard won, as the Carter Administration has discovered in its efforts to secure some deregulation in airline and motor carrier regulation.

ALTERNATIVES TO REGULATION

There are a number of alternatives to regulation as means for the control or direction of economic activity in the public interest. Although any definition of the public interest is open to argument and quibbling (an activity at which many academics are quite skillful), it can be taken to include such values as public health and safety, the maintenance of peaceful and orderly relationships in society, and an equitable distribution of income (including "reasonable" profits for business).

Competition and the market mechanism are often presented as the best alternative to regulation.[22] Such diverse sources as the Chicago school of economists and the Antitrust Division are strong advocates of competition as a mode of economic control. We cannot assume, obviously, that competition will exist in the absence of regulation. Nor does competition maintain itself, although there are those who would argue that in the absence of governmental support, monopoly will not endure. Although there would not seem to be a need to "atomize" the economy in order for workable competition to exist, the application of antitrust to prevent collusive action and prevent or break up monopolistic market structures would appear quite necessary. However, some of those who oppose regulation in the name of "free enterprise" and the like manifest little support for government action to maintain competitive conditions. Even with more competition, and granted competition is an an effective means of promoting economic efficiency, there will still be a need for regulation. Competition did not cause the automobile companies to become concerned about passenger safety, or industry generally to focus attention on the control of environmental pollution. Regulation is needed to help prevent abuses by those who control and wield private economic power.

The use of taxation as a regulatory device has gained some popularity, if not much use, in recent years. What this really involves is some governmental manipulation of the market to achieve a policy goal. Thus, in 1911 a tax was levied on white phosphorus matches in order to drive them out of existence. Although the manufacture of such matches was unhealthy for the workers, they were cheaper than other varieties and hence their manufacture was continued. Given the "dictates of the market," did the manufacturers have any other choice? Collectively, they obviously did; although any individual manufacturer who switched to the safer and more expensive variety of matches would have been put at a competitive disadvantage. Once the tax was levied, the manufacture of white phosphorus matches became uneconomical, and they ceased to be produced. How, in essence, does this really differ from a regulatory prohibition?

In a study of national pollution legislation, Kneese and Schultze conclude that efforts to prevent pollution by the regulatory approach have been ineffective.[23] They recommend the use instead of effluent charges (or taxes) which they say would give firms a positive incentive to reduce pollution, as well as discretion in how to achieve this result. Once the charges are fixed, however, they will not enforce themselves. Monitoring and control will likely be necessary to insure compliance. Nor would such actions as the setting of charges and the measurement of waste loads be without difficulty or controversy. It seems that what you really do here is substitute one form of regulation for another. Some would probably disagree.

The Ford Administration's 1975 energy policy package featured higher prices for petroleum and natural gas. Price controls were to be removed. An import tariff and excise tax of $2 a barrel on petroleum and an excise tax of $.37 per mcf on natural gas were to be imposed. Short-term profit increases would be taken by windfall profits tax. According to three economists: "The administration's approach is basically that of the free market . . ."[24] Clearly, all economists do not lack a sense of humor. More to the point, though, it seems difficult to call this kind of manipulation a free market approach, especially since the "market price" of oil is really determined by the Organization of Petroleum Exporting Countries (OPEC) cartel rather than the unrestrained interaction of supply and demand.

A third alternative is government ownership. The philosophy of state socialism (government ownership and operation of the principal means of production, distribution, and exchange) has never had wide appeal in this country. Socialist political parties have ceased to have meaningful electoral significance. Privately owned enterprise has had much attraction for and support from Americans. Nonetheless, there are a substantial variety of public enterprises in the United States—education, medical care, and recreational facilities; power production and distribution systems; the postal system; and housing, insurance, and loan programs.[25] The list is not complete. Enterprises have been established on a pragmatic, piecemeal basis rather than according to doctrinal prescription. For example, after the repeal of national prohibition in 1933, some states choose to continue prohibition within their boundaries; others permitted private businesses to sell liquor under government regulation; yet others choose to establish state liquor stores to handle retail distribution. Differing social and political factors produced a variety of responses to the "liquor problem" in the American states. Extensive reliance upon government ownership as a means for dealing with economic problems seems unlikely in the foreseeable future. If one compares the Tennessee Valley Authority and the Penn Central, government enterprise comes off rather well; it is less the case in a comparison of the Postal Service and the Bell System. Government ownership does not appear as a panacea for our problems.

Yet another alternative is self-regulation, by which the members of a group, industry, or profession regulate themselves. Rules are adopted by agreement and submitted to a public agency for approval. When approved, they have legal status and are enforced primarily by the group itself, although the government may also become involved. The most notable experience in this country with self-regulation was under the National Industrial Recovery Act and its industry "codes of fair competition" during the 1933-1935 period.[26] Wilcox passed the following judgment on this venture:[27]

The NRA did serve one useful purpose. It provided the country with a demonstration of the character and consequences of cartelization. It showed that industry, when given the power of "self-government," could not be trusted to exercise it in the public interest; that enterprise would be handicapped and vested interest protected, progress obstructed, and stagnation assured. It showed that businessmen, if given a blank check to be filled out, would proceed to commit economic suicide, pricing themselves out of the market and encouraging consumers to turn to substitutes; to oil when the price of coal was boosted and to mechanical refrigeration when the price of ice was raised. It showed, moreover, that enforcement of limitations on competition required a greater degree of regimentation than business was prepared to take, and that supervision adequate to protect the public interest would require an enormous organization, to be supported at heavy cost.

Wilcox leaves no doubt as to his position on self-regulation, at least when it takes the form of cartelization.

Self-regulation did not disappear with the Blue Eagle, however. Current examples include milk marketing agreements, railroad rate bureaus, and some self-regulation in the securities business.[28] There is also a considerable aura of self-regulation in the area of occupational licensing, given the usual domination of licensing agencies by members of the licensed group. Self-regulation does not seem an alternative to regulation that is going to get much use in the future. What, for instance, would be the chance for enactment of legislation permitting the petroleum industry, drug manufacturers, or loan sharks to regulate themselves?

This brief review of some of the alternatives to regulation does not do justice to all of their nuances and complexities. Each may appear as a better alternative than regulation in particular situations. Individually or collectively, however, they are unlikely to replace government regulation as our dominant method for dealing with economic problems.

CONCLUSION

The indications are that the totality of economic regulations will increase in the future. Some regulatory programs may be eliminated or reduced in scope, but others will be added and probably at a faster rate. Reliance on the alternatives discussed in the preceding section will most likely be limited. The best bet in this regard seems for some public ownership in the railroad industry. We have a cultural bias in favor of regulation, as something between a kind of laissez-faire free enterprise on the one hand and public ownership on the other. Regulation is seen as a means for controlling or eliminating the abuses and problems generated by the private economy while avoiding the burdens of government ownership and, perhaps, the risks of too much centralization of power. The Marxist, of course, will not find regulation really appealing as it leaves the "locus of power undisturbed." Power is left in private hands subject to governmental control, which it is contended, serves the same economic power. The advocates of "free enterprise" will also be displeased, but they really weaken their case by their inconsistency. Thus in 1976, the chairman of American Telephone and Telegraph declared that he was "a free enterpriser from my socks to my hat" while strongly supporting proposed legislation called the "Consumer Communications Reform Act of 1976."[29] The legislation was intended to prevent some nonoperating companies from competing with AT&T in the sale of some telephone products and services.

The question that confronts us is not one of regulation or no regulation. Rather the question is one of how and where there is going to be regulation, and how to improve the quality of regulation. And it will not hurt to be somewhat skeptical of proposals for new regulation. As Russell Train has commented:[30]

> Surely, we can reduce and cut out some government programs; we can improve the efficiency of others; we can streamline, simplify, and otherwise improve regulation. . . . But these are very different things from simply "getting rid of regulation"; these are ways of making regulation work.
>
> It seems to me that increasing regulation is an inevitable if perhaps unfortunate by-product of our high technology and high economic growth society associated with high and rising densities of human populations. If we really wish to maintain our commitment to an increasingly complex economic, technological, and social system, it is illusory to think we are going to get away from big government. Major government programs and widespread regulation are *inherent* in that kind of society, which is the kind of society we apparently want.

To conclude, the regulatory state is here to stay. What we need to do, rather than bemoan or adore its existence, is to develop a better understanding of regulation. What, really, are its costs and benefits? What functional consequences does it have for the economy and society? How effective are regulatory programs in accomplishing the goals that can be identified? While we need both more empirical studies of regulatory programs and more systematic evaluations of them, we could also use some better theories of regulation.

NOTES

1. See Emmette S. Redford, *American Government and the Economy* (New York: Macmillan, 1965), chapters 1, 4; and Louis Hartz, *Economic Policy and Democratic Thought: Pennsylvania, 1776-1860* (Cambridge, Mass.: Harvard University Press, 1948).

2. George A. Steiner, *Government's Role in Economic Life* (New York: McGraw-Hill, 1953): 87.

3. See, for example, materials reprinted in the *Congressional Record* (July 21, 1975): S13222-S13225 (daily edition).

4. Theodore J. Lowi, *The End of Liberalism* (New York: W.W. Norton, 1969): chapter 3.

5. Cf. Mark V. Nadel, *The Politics of Consumer Protection* (Indianapolis: Bobbs Merrill, 1971), which is the best treatment of this topic.

6. Lloyd N. Cutler and David R. Johnson, "Regulation and the Political Process," *Yale Law Journal,* 84 (June, 1975): 1399.

7. Irving Kristol, "Some Doubts About De-Regulation," *Wall Street Journal* (October 20, 1975): 8.

8. Peter H. Schuck, "Why Regulation Fails," *Harper's Magazine,* 251 (September, 1975): 24.

9. This is the general thrust of the studies in Almarin Phillips, ed., *Promoting Competition in Regulated Markets* (Washington, D.C.: The Brookings Institution, 1975).

10. Arthur N. Okun, *Equality and Efficiency* (Washington, D.C.: The Brookings Institution, 1975) provides an insightful discussion of the conflict between equality and efficiency in government programs.

11. Examples include, Mark Green and Ralph Nader, "Economic Regulation vs. Competition: Uncle Sam the Monopoly Man," *Yale Law Journal,* 82 (April, 1973): 876; and Schuck, op. cit.: 28.

12. James Q. Wilson, "The Dead Hand of Regulation," *The Public Interest,* 25 (Fall, 1971): 47.

13. Robert N. Kharsach, *The Institutional Imperative: How to Understand the United States Government and Other Bulky Objects* (New York: Charterhouse Books, 1973).

14. Many of the studies and reports are ably discussed in Norman C. Thomas, "Politics, Structure, and Personnel in Administrative Regulation," *Virginia Law Review,* 57 (September, 1971): 1033-1068.

15. The President's Advisory Council on Executive Organization, *A New Regulatory Framework* (Washington, D.C.: 1971).

16. Lowi, op. cit.

17. Roger G. Noll, *Reforming Regulation* (Washington, D.C.: The Brookings Institution, 1971): 38.

18. Murray L. Weidenbaum, *Government-Mandated Price Increases* (Washington, D.C.: American Enterprise Institute for Public Policy Research, 1975) illustrates this viewpoint.

19. *Regulatory Reform-1975,* Hearings before the Senate Committee on Government Operations, 94th Congress, 2nd Session, 1975; Senate Committee on Governmental Affairs, *Study on Federal Regulation,* 95th Congress, 4 vols., 1975-1976. (Two more volumes are forthcoming.)

20. Some commentaries on this proposal can be found in *Congressional Record* (April 28, 1976): S6089-S6096 (daily edition).

21. Quoted in *Wall Street Journal* (November 25, 1975): 1.

22. Milton Friedman, *Capitalism and Freedom* (Chicago: University of Chicago Press, 1962), and Henry C. Wallich, *The Cost of Freedom* (New York: Collier Books, 1960) are two able statements of this viewpoint.

23. Allen V. Kneese and Charles L. Schultze, *Pollution, Prices and Public Policy* (Washington, D.C.: The Brookings Institution, 1975): 19.

24. Barry M. Bleckman, Edward M. Gramlich, and Roger W. Hartman, *Setting National Priorities: The 1976 Budget* (Washington, D.C.: The Brookings Institution, 1975): 19.

25. Redford, op. cit., chapter 26.

26. Bernard Bellush, *The Failure of the NRA* (New York: W.W. Norton, 1975), provides a good, brief history of the NIRA experience.

27. Clair Wilcox, *Public Policies Toward Business* (Homewood, Ill.: Richard D. Irwin, 3rd ed., 1966): 687.

28. On the last item, see William L. Cary, *Politics and the Regulatory Agencies* (New York: McGraw-Hill, 1967). Also Michael E. Parrish, *Securities Regulation and the New Deal* (New Haven, Conn.: Yale University Press, 1970).

29. *National Journal,* 8 (July 17, 1976): 1011.

30. Speech by Russell E. Train, "Making Regulation Work." Reprinted in *Congressional Record* (June 1, 1976): E2991-E2993 (daily edition). Train was director of the Environmental Protection Agency.

4.

AGRICULTURE POLICY

DON F. HADWIGER

Iowa State University

The agriculture policy process was once fairly discrete, of interest to scholars, because it was notably a subsystem politics with definable features, and to a specific clientele consisting of commercial farmers and the public agencies and agribusinesses that served them.

Now "farm policy" has become "food policy," with impacts upon the rate of inflation, citizen health and nutrition, the U.S. trade balance, relationships with other world powers, and third world agricultural development. And some policies, which are not of subsystem origin, have important impact on the agricultural economy. These include health and safety regulations, regulations governing toxic chemicals, and the U.S.-U.S.S.R. long-term grain agreement of 1976.

There are now many new, effective participants in decisions once monopolized by the agricultural system. Within government, the number of departments or executive office agencies formally involved in agricultural decision-making has grown from three under President Lyndon Johnson (Department of Agriculture, Council of Economic Advisors, Office of Management and Budget) to 12 under Ford.[1] The posture of new "outside" groups is not always one of establishment confrontation. Emergent consumer groups decided that higher farm prices result in lower food prices over the long run. Therefore, these consumer elites helped to lobby for higher farm price supports in the Emergency Farm Bill of 1975 (which was opposed by Secretary of Agriculture Earl Butz and was vetoed by President Ford). Support from consumer groups gained a response in President Carter's USDA, with the resulting selection of consumer leader Carole Foreman as an Assistant Secretary of Agriculture. The coopting of consumer groups encourages the subsystem to be responsive to other new participants, whose support could reverse the decline in agricultural research budgets, prevent restrictions on agricultural exports, reserve sufficient energy and capital for agriculture, and permit effective strategies for chemical pest control, for increasing water resources, and for conserving the soil. For the subsystem to invite or to tolerate broader participation in agricultrual policy-making, however, requires some assumption that "outside" participants, as they become knowledgeable about the agricultural subsystem, will appreciate its success in producing abundant food and fiber at a reasonable price and therefore, will be willing to reconcile subsystem goals with those which they postulate as important national goals.

Confidence in expanded participation in agricultural decision-making was the theme of a recent report by the "young executives" within the Deparment of Agriculture. The young executives recommended that: "The primary clientele of the Department should be broadened to effectively incorporate the interests of low income persons, consumers in general, and other groups of society significantly affected by functions within the purview of the Department."[2] The report posed the following scenario:

> "Agricultural policy," "foreign food policy," and "domestic food policy" now overlap and decisions in one area may significantly impact another. It seems only a matter of time until there is full recognition of the advantages to be gained by combining these distinct areas. The Department, with strong political leadership drawing upon the full resources and expertise of its professional staff, is in a position to demonstrate public spirited leadership in initiating development of at least a rudimentary framework for a national food policy.

Such an integrated policy process may emerge. But at present, there are often two competing—usually hostile—processes. One is oriented to the interests of producer clientele and is monopolized by the agricultural subsystem. This is the "agricultural policy process" which has been described in previous political science literature. The other process is concerned with alleviating the adverse effects of our revolutionized agricultural system, including:

(1) environmental insults, including chemical pollution of the environment and increased erosion of topsoil;

(2) neglect of small farmers, farmworkers, racial minorities, and rural towns;
(3) food products which, in at least a few instances, are less tasty, less nutritious, and even damaging to consumer health;
(4) the export to developing nations of inappropriate technology which exacerbates their food and employment dilemmas.

This second process, and the influence of its concerns, was acknowledged in 1975 by the USDA's Director of Agricultural Economics, Don Paarlberg, who said that the agricultural establishment had lost control of its agenda and, indeed, that a "new agenda"had been imposed upon it by outsiders.[4]

This second process, which features outsiders who use a different set of institutions and strategies, has already interacted with the subsystem to produce major policies such as the expanded food stamp program and to reform regulations on the use of agricultural chemicals.

This "outside" process has not been well examined, though there is reference to it in Emmette Redford's discussion of the macropolitical system. Redford was of the opinion that subsystem changes must be imposed from the outside. "Substantial changes in the balances among interests served by subsystems can be expected to occur only through macropolitical intervention that modifies the rules and roles operating in the systems."[5]

Redford also conceded that a first step toward macro-intervention might be "a journalistic exposure by an Ida Tarbell or a Ralph Nader . . . ."[6]

The agricultural subsystem has endured much journalistic exposure during the development of its "new agenda" and has experienced confrontations with many outside groups, including some that were media-oriented and allied with macro-political institutions.

The expansion of participation in agriculture decision-making means that more people think it is important. Political scientists, too, who had in the past produced good studies of the agricultural policy process, are returning to the subject. Agricultural economists, who have been constant students of agricultural policy,have recognized that research on political questions which are usually "exogenous" to their own models is needed in order to explain policy.

THE AGRICULTURAL SUBSYSTEM

The impressive characteristics of the agricultural subsystem have been aggregated from several formative eras.

(1) The subsystem is a subculture with a well developed socialization process and well defined norms. Most actors were reared on commercial

farms, attended land grant colleges, and later experienced continuing interaction with other actors through the universities, the marketplace, the media, and political agencies. Indeed, one of the problems of the subsystem's information system is that its function of reinforcing group loyalties hampers its other function of exploring the reality to which the subsystem must adjust. Philip Olson offered, as an example, sociological research which, although intended to help rural people shape their futures, inadvertently reinforced the myths that separated them from current trends.[7] Jim Hightower and Susan DeMarco, in explaining the neglect of the rural poor, were looking for a conspiracy of agribusiness, big farmers, and university officials. Instead, they found a network of "good old boys" whose cooperation was based on friendship and shared values.[8]

(2) The subsystem has key goals—productivity and efficiency— which have been achieved in superlative degree over the short run. As John Brewster said, the system has maintained Jefferson's commitment to a scientific agriculture, linking this for a time with the goal of opportunity to farm.[9] Ultimately, the two goals could not be reconciled, and the "proficient family farm" put other farmers out of business.

(3) The subsystem provides supports, in both material returns and status rewards, to individuals who contribute to subsystem goals. This has been important because agricultural pursuits were not highly regarded by our national society (except in a romantic sense); nor were the sciences, professions, and businesses which have served agriculture. The subsystem increasingly differentiated, however, between the larger commercial farmers who were given status and material benefits, and small farmers and farmworkers to whom these benefits were denied.

(4) The subsystem includes an integrated economy with mechanisms for communicating market information and for the development of services to commercial agriculture. The agricultural economy is served by a distinct academic discipline—agricultural economics.

(5) The agriculture subsystem has possessed remarkable mechanisms for its pursuit of exclusive economic and political power. These include:

(a.) a coalition of groups representing major commodities, coordinated within the Congressional agricultural committees.[10]
(b) a cooperative bureaucracy which included the bureaus of the Department of Agriculture[11] and the land-grant colleges.[12]
(c) a rural electorate, whose large swing votes (outside the South) were noticeably responsive to current prices of principal commodities.[13]
(d) client organizations which exercised grass roots control over the relevant federal bureaucracies[14] while using these bureaucracies as a vehicle for

developing their membership.[15] Lowi called the subsystem "the new feudalism" because each ten agricultural bureaucracies was run by its own clientele.[16]

(e) off-farm agricultural activity (agribusiness) which flowered within the subculture and much of which is located within the commercial farming regions; thus, the subsystem has an industrial sector.

This was by no means a stable system. The general farm organizations competed for power and suffered occasional internal conflicts. Programs for the various commodities were often hard to reconcile. After World War II, the subsystem was divided along party lines on the important issue of commodity price programs. The Congressional coalition which passed price support programs has usually included organized labor and has usually been opposed by the largest farm organization—the Farm Bureau.[17] During the Administration of Secretary of Agriculture Ezra Benson, who sided with Farm Bureau, the subsystem reached an impasse on major commodity programs.[18]

The program mechanisms enacted by the farmer-labor coalition were helpful in stabilizing farm incomes, especially in high-risk farming areas. But agriculture was locked into rapid technology innovation which continually increased productivity and thereby made stabilization very expensive. Furthermore, in terms of equity, the farm programs exemplified interest group liberalism at its worst[19] (serving only the politically influential groups); the terms of coalition between commercial farmers and labor ignored small farmers, rural laborers, and farm townspeople who, in fact, bore the heaviest costs of agricultural change. Their massive outmigration impacted heavily on both rural and urban America. One can argue, especially now that this rural-urban migration has reversed, that a more equitable policy would have served all interests better, and, indeed that such a policy is still needed.[20]

Under the commodity programs, the federal government became burdened with huge commodity surpluses, which in turn provided program opportunities for rural liberals. For example, Hubert Humphrey and George McGovern were leaders in developing Food-for-Peace and in overcoming subsystem opposition to an expanded food stamp program.

It was never to be seriously doubted that the food stamp program provided economic benefits to the subsystem by expanding markets. When it also became clear that an expanded food stamp program could win urban votes for farm programs, subsystem conservatives who had previously prevented the development of the program[21] became reconciled to seeking political advantage from its "welfare" effects.[22]

But if the subsystem has become more flexible in forming coalitions, this does not mean it is more ready to take initiatives in serving "outside" interests. To determine whether this is so, we must look to changes in its values, structure, and actual behavior. On one hand, for example, one can point out that members of the House Agriculture Committee are now younger and more urban, and more open in their deliberations.[23] On the other hand, however, Jim Hightower was correct in the assertion that the USDA agencies are attuned to a narrowing clientele of larger farmers and agri-business firms.[24] As an example of value changes (without clear implications), Michael Lewis-Beck has found that those who remain in farming are more highly participatory than are those in any other occupation group, but that they are also a very conservative group.[25]

THE AGENDA(S)

It should be emphasized that the policy agenda items which the subsystem takes most seriously (and to which agricultural economists devote most of their effort) are the familiar ones relating to farm prices and commercial farm income. This is clear, for example, from the papers of distinguished agriculture policy economists presented at a conference last year[26] and from the testimony presented at agriculture committee hearings on farm and food policy.

Yet there are major new concerns. Most of these as Don Paarlberg said, "have been placed on the agenda over the protests of the agricultural establishment."[27] Paarlberg's list of new agenda, and their sponsors when indicated, is as follows:

Food prices—sponsored by consumers; food programs—by the hunger lobby; ecological questions—by environmentalist; rural development—by non-farmers in rural areas; land use; civil rights; collective bargaining for farm labor—by organized labor.

It should be said first, that the issue of "rural development" was proposed as well as resisted largely from inside the agricultural establishment. Agricultural social scientists and some rural legislators supported enactment of the Rural Development Act of 1972, but little funding has been provided to implement the Act.

INTERVENTION IN THE SUBSYSTEM
OF AGRICULTURE

The dynamics of intervention by outside groups have been suggested but not well described. Emmette Redford emphasized the intervention from macro-political institutions.[28] E.S. Schattschneider suggested a scenario for "expansion of the scope of conflict."[29] Charles Jones suggested that when there is an expansion in the size of the interested public, elected officials will take initiatives to satisfy that public, and that this public-satisfying decision process overrides usual clientele group bargaining.[30]

Intervention from outside groups has occurred at various points in the agriculture policy process. In two notable cases, groups outside the agricutural subsystem not only established important agenda items but participated in making and implementing the policy. In both cases, there were several kinds of intervention:

(1) *The generation of a new environmental perspective* in the minds of both the usual decision-makers and the wider public. The information and analysis which generates public awareness typically surfaces not in scholarly articles but rather within an advocacy format. The advocate may be a specialist, as in the case of Rachel Carson, whose *Silent Spring* predicted environmental disasters resulting from the use of "persistent" pesticides.[31] In the case of food stamps, the attention of a wider audience was achieved by advocacy research, television documentaries, Congressional hearings, and a White House Conference.

Subsystem spokesmen may first attempt to discredit this new perspective by charging:

(a) that the person(s) presenting it lack(s) credentials. (The problem with this tactic is that the argument succeeds mainly with subsystem actors themselves, who thereby become the only people who fail to take the perspective seriously.)

(b) that the person has bad motives, either is settling a grudge or seeking profit through notoriety. (The outside critic may have the best of this argument, too. Indeed, the outside critic may raise it first, because the institutional rewards for subsystem defenders may be more apparent to the interested public than are the rewards from criticizing that subsystem.)

(c) that the facts do not support a "crisis" interpretation. There is a likely paradox here, in that some subsystem actors *may* have seen the problem as serious but lacked political support to engage it. They have resisted labeling it a "crisis" for fear of an overreaction (as many agricultural experts feel did happen with reforms of pesticide regulation) and, of course, because it may also imply subsystem negligence. The paradox is that a crisis is a threshold-crossing device for gaining media attention and creating public awareness. Therefore, it is a means of providing political support to engage the problem.

(2) *The demonstration of subsystem negligence.* In the case of pesticides, the book *Silent Spring,* an indictment of persistent chemical pesticides such as DDT, appeared in 1962 well *before* the period of peak

use of these chemicals. Five years or more after *Silent Spring* appeared, three outside investigations occurred—the HEW Secretary's Advisory Commission on Pesticides (The Mrak Commission),[32] a study by the General Accounting Office,[33] and a report by the House Government Operations Committee.[34] These charged gross negligence on the part of the USDA's pesticide regulatory agency.

In the food stamp controversy, proponents of food stamps charged that program inadequacies could be traced to the fact that the USDA's principal objective was not hunger prevention, but surplus removal.[35]

(3) *The activation of legislative agencies outside the subsystem.* The federal Environmental Protection Agency submitted a proposal for strengthened pesticide control.

In the Congress, the House Agriculture Committee produced a weakened version of the EPA bill acceptable to farm and agribusiness groups. But in the Senate, there were hearings on the bill not only in the Senate Agriculture Committee but also in the Senate Commerce Committee, which produced a "tougher" bill than that of EPA.

In the case of food stamps, the important breakthrough to enactment and implementation came with the creation of a Senate Select Committee on Nutrition and Human Needs. The Committee included both subsystem legislators and their critics from the Senate Labor Committee, and was under the leadership of a food stamp proponent, Senator George McGovern. The invasion of the subsystem's jurisdiction, through use of Select Committees, cross-jurisdictional committees (such as Government Operations), and investigations by other standing committees, has apparently been a major method of subsystem intervention.

(4) *Implementation and monitoring.* In the case of food stamps, the Senate Select Committee put forward specific eligibility criteria and payment rates which were written into the statute. The Committee staff then maintained close contact with those who wrote administrative rules. These criteria became the vehicle for uncontested increases in the number of recipients and in the funding level of benefits.

Pesticide regulation, in contrast, was transferred from the USDA to the EPA as a means of getting action.

(5) *Access to courts.* The regular courts are usually considered to be outside of subsystem influence, and the question of whether to allow citizen lawsuits challenging policy and administration was a key issue in the struggle over pesticides law.

In the cases of both pesticides and food stamps, the interventions in subsystem politics may seem to illustrate a process of checks and balances which was heretofore unrecognized.

This discussion of the subsystem and its outside critics precedes a review of the major agenda items.

MAJOR FOOD POLICY ISSUES

Commodity Programs

At the heart of the agricultural subsystem's political interests are the commodity programs, which are intended to guarantee producers an adequate income and to stabilize markets for major agricultural products. These major products include corn and other grains fed to animals (the price of which also has impact upon meat, dairy, and poultry products), and wheat (which is a major U.S. export), cotton, soybeans, rice, dairy products, and wool. These programs as revised in 1973 contain three mechanisms for income security: *deficiency* payments, to compensate farmers when prices go below "target prices" (target prices are based upon prices paid by farmers for production items, taxes, and other business expenses); *disaster* payments, when crops fail; and *commodity* loans, which make it possible for farmers to maintain cash flow while they store their crops in anticipation of higher prices. Stored grain, in private and government stocks, has provided some protection against upward instability of prices.

These are imperfect mechanisms to deal with the considerable instability in supply and demand for major U.S. crops. As examples of the extreme variations with which stabilization policy must cope: (1) U.S. corn production was reduced both by serious disease and drought during the same year; (2) wheat production is chronically and often extremely variable, in part because the crop throughout the world is located in "dryland" areas subject to frequent drought. World wheat supplies were dramatically increased by the "green revolution," (discussed later) which temporarily raised the prospect for a return to large surpluses. But high world stocks of wheat were temporarily drained by massive purchases by the U.S.S.R. Subsequently, in response to the Soviet run on U.S. stocks, the U.S. government instituted export controls and finally negotiated a commodity agreement which fixed the amount (within a narrow range) which must be purchased each year by the U.S.S.R.

A World Food Reserve

Humanitarians in many countries have long expressed the desire for a world reserve of food grains. In the United States, humanitarian interests are given political representation by religious and other charitable organizations which have directly participated in international food distribution programs and by emerging grass roots organizations such as Bread for the World. Commercial farmers in all countries have one reason to oppose food reserves—severe scarcity results in very high prices. Although large government stocks accrued under U.S. (and Canadian) farm programs between 1945 and 1968, and were used quite effectively as a world food reserve, these stocks resulted from the failure to control production rather than from the desire to achieve humanitarian objectives. As Ross Talbot has pointed out, the U.S.may again be "stumbling backward into a food reserve—unplanned, uncoordinated, and even unwanted.[36] One can make the case that a large national food reserve serves the interest of the U.S. economy: a dependable grain supply makes other nations more ready to rely on our producers and permits very large U.S. sales at high prices during periods of scarcity. In those results, U.S. farmers also benefit from a reserve. On that thread of mutual producer and national interests, a food reserve policy may be fashioned.

The U.S. political interest in unilaterally maintaining an adequate "world food reserve" is a subject for serious discussion. Raymond Hopkins has argued that "food is one of the few major sources of uniquely American leverage. It may be the last resource effective in coping with problems of economic development and excessive world population."[37] Robert Paarlberg has pointed out that "the U.S. can unilaterally maintain something of an open world food trading system" (by virtue of the fact that U.S. exports account for approximately half of world exports of wheat, feedgrains, and soybeans).[38] However, both of these political scientists provide persuasive arguments, from past experience and from a study of the current environment, that U.S. food exports cannot be used "as a weapon,"for example, to mandate Third World agricultural development or to assure adequate oil supplies from OPEC countries or to achieve political aims vis-à-vis the Soviet Union.

A Domestic Food Policy

The achievement of cheap food for U.S. citizens (in the sense that food is a smaller portion of the family budget than in other nations) is a significant contribution to the welfare of low-income citizens. In addition, USDA food programs provide direct assistance through school lunch programs and the food stamp program, the largest item in the U.S. Department of Agriculture budget. However, these programs, as created by agricultural interests, were efforts to dispose of surplus stocks and were used more to manipulate than to assist the poor. Food assistance programs were transformed into effective welfare programs by a determined "hunger lobby" composed of outside groups operating through a Senate Select Committee on Human Nutrition.[39] The expanded food stamp program has been much criticized by subsystem conservatives, such as former Secretary of Agriculture Butz, who strongly resent the generous use of "agricultural" funds for welfare. The program is criticized also by interests who resent "in-kind" rather than cash welfare programs; and all decry the organizational anomaly of administering major welfare programs through the Department of Agriculture. However, there are certain political facts which have led both agriculture and welfare interests to keep the program in place: The $6 billion food stamp program has been sustained in Congress through trading votes on farm programs (and vice-versa); the program does indirectly increase agricultural markets; and a national income maintenance program has yet to be enacted.

Administrative Reorganization

Organizational anomalies within the Department of Agriculture are partly a residue of its distinguished history, first as a pre-eminent research institution and then, after 1933, as a "new department" which undertook to preserve family farmers by providing services obtained in other industries through oligopolistic structures. The USDA provided farmers with capital, research, and technical assistance; it protected them from suppliers and middlemen; and it also controlled prices and undertook soil conservation. Thirty years before OEO, the USDA embraced parici-patory democracy by creating farmer committees which made local administrative decisions and also served as a recruitment pool for the Bureau's career personnel. During the Great Depression, the Department established broad services for the rural poor, experimenting with relocation of subsistence farmers, housing construction, rural electrification, community development, food stamps, and even socialized health care.[40] It is this history, despite attempts by rural conservatives to erase it, which explains the presence of large housing, food, and community development programs within the USDA today.

Because its eclectic missions overlap those of other federal departments, the USDA has long been in jeopardy from those who seek functional reorganization. Roosevelt's Committee on Adminstrative Management, however, concluded that the sprawling Department was well-administered and therefore should be left intact.[41] The first Hoover Commission also resisted the temptation to remove major USDA agencies, finding that they were given essential support by the USDA's competent research agencies.

In recent years, however, the department's reputation has suffered from its poor record on civil rights and services to the rural poor, and from charges of laxity in regulating pesticides, in forest management, in grain inspection, and in overseeing commodity exchanges. Note was taken of its faithfulness to big farmer and agribusiness interests enforced by "revolving doors" leadership and despotic rural congressmen. Although President Nixon failed in his general reorganization, which would have split the Department into four parts for inclusion in four new departments, the USDA faces an uncertain future, thanks in part to its recent inadequacies and also because it has failed to generate much support among the non-farmer clienteles which it serves.

Environmental Issues

Chemical pest control has been, at the very least, a great convenience. Indeed, in some cases, it has been a necessity in high productivity agriculture. Because of this, the USDA refused to ban toxic chemicals which persisted in the natural environment and accumulated in man's body, even when repeatedly urged to do so by the Public Health Service, the Food and Drug Administration, and other federal health agencies. Reforms in pesticide regulation, stimulated by environmental groups and implemented by the Environmental Protection Agency, have resulted in a mandatory shift to less persistent pesticides. One effective regulatory instrument against harmful agricultural pesticides is the 1958 "Delaney Clause" which provides that no tolerance can be granted to any food additive (including pesticide residues in food) which is found to be cancer-inducing.[42] New techniques for detecting small residues and for discovering carcinogenic effects now make it possible to challenge the use of mainline insecticides and herbicides for which there may be no effective substitutes. The Delaney Clause has proved a crude but non-symbolic measure requiring industry self-regulation in the use of agricultural pesticides.

Agricultural Research

Fantastic increases in per acre yields and the dramatic decline of labor in agriculture since World War II have resulted from the development of entire packages of new technology, including new tillage practices, more powerful machinery, fertilization, plant genetic changes, pesticides, and innovations in food processing. The public-supported research establishment, which largely produced this revolution, appears to have received more criticism than praise for its achievements. During the 1950's, farmers blamed research agencies for farm surpluses. In recent years, research has been blamed for the rural-to-urban migration which presumably ruined our great cities and decimated the small rural towns. Agricultural research has also been denounced for favoring capital-intensive (rather than small farm) agriculture and for aiding food processors in altering the taste and nutritive value of food. (The question is debated as to whether this was done to suit consumer tastes and convenience, or whether consumer tastes were manipulated to suit the convenience of the processors.) Agricultural research has received both credit and blame for the "green revolution" in developing countries, achieved by applying fertilizer to new strains of wheat and rice. This revolution has temporarily kept production increases commensurate with population increases, but critics charge that it dislocates the poor, and that is less dependable that traditional agriculture.

Paradoxically, these negative (or at best mixed) evaluations of agricultural research—both from muckrakers and scholars—are usually accompanied by claims that agricultural research can produce additional miracles in meeting food needs, if it is well supported and if the objective of profitability can be submerged in a strategy of increasing supplies for the world's poorest citizens. These evaluations of existing research, and assertions about its promise need continuing and more profound examination. Meanwhile, however, the U.S. research establishment, which has had good clientele support,[43] nevertheless has experienced a decline in prestige within the scientific community and among other interested elites. Current reorganization proposals threatened its integrity. There has been deterioration in the working relationship between the two systems which organize U.S. agricultural research—the USDA's Agricultural Research Service and the land-grant college experiment stations. A competing system of "organic farming" has gained attention. This system, which rejects industrial fertilizers, pesticides, and heavy tillage, has a developed ideology that yet remains to be proven practical.[44]

Congress appears to be moving to increase its support for objectives of U.S. agricultural research which deal with reducing energy needs, conserving the natural environment, and conserving the soil. However, actual appropriations for agricultural research, granted under subsystem criteria, have not kept pace with inflation. The future of agricultural research is being determined, not by a classic confrontation between the technological imperative and the human will, but rather by the drift of a dispirited agricultural subsystem.

Concluding Observations

Defenders of our agricultural subsystem say we should not destroy the goose that lays golden eggs, and its critics agree that it is indeed a goose. Leaders of the subsystem, though laden with higher learning, have seemed determinedly oblivious to the social and environmental consequences of their programs. Their single-mindedness and their excesses have been easy targets for environmentalists, consumer activists, humanitarians, nonagricultural scientists, and others. The interaction between the politically weakened subsystem and its outside critics has created major new policy issues relating to how we should produce and distribute our food and fiber in the U.S. and in the world. Much of the expanded conflict over these issues has been at arms-length with the subsystem using the old agricultural process machinery and with outside groups using other institutions. The policy that emerges does not embody the combined wisdom of all parties. Since food policy should be a serious subject today and because food issues are most complex, we may hope for a more constructive interaction of policy participants, both to deepen mutual understanding and to devise and implement good policy.

NOTES

1. *USDA and Food Policy Decisionmaking, A Report of the Agriculture Department's 1976 Young Executives Committee:* 10.

2. Ibid., 4.

3. Ibid., 4,5.

4. Address by Don Paarlberg, Director of Agricultural Economics, U.S. Department of Agriculture, at the National Public Policy Conference, Clymer, N.Y., September 11, 1975.

5. Emmette S. Redford, *Democracy and the Administrative State* (New York: Oxford University Press, 1969): 105.

6. Ibid., 106.

7. Philip Olson, "Rural American Community Studies: The Survival of Public Ideology," *Human Organization* 23 (Winter, 1964): 342-350.

8. Interview with Susan Demarco, 1975.

9. John M. Brewster, "The Relevance of the Jeffersonian Dream Today: A Current Look at Griswold's 'Farming and Democracy.' " (Presented June 11-14, 1962 at University of Nebraska Symposium.)

10. Charles Jones, "Representation in Congress: The Case of the House Agriculture Committee," *American Political Science Review,* 55 (June, 1961): 358-367.

11. For a description of USDA bureaus, see Wayne D. Rasmussen and Gladys L. Baker, *The Department of Agriculture* (New York: Praeger, 1972).

12. Grant McConnell, *The Decline of Agrarian Democracy* (Berkeley: University of California Press, 1953): 52-53.

13. Hugh A. Bone, *American Politics and the Party System, 4th addition* (New York: McGraw-Hill, 1971): 511-513.

14. Reo M. Christenson, *The Brannan Plan* (Ann Arbor: University of Michigan Press, 1959).

15. For a description of the Extension Service and Farm Bureau relations, see Gladys Baker, *The County Agent,* (University of Chicago Press, 1939): 21-22.

16. Theodore Lowi, *The End of Liberalism,* (New York: W.W.Norton, 1969): 102 ff.

17. Don F. Hadwiger and Ross B. Talbot, *Pressures and Protests* (San Francisco: Chandler, 1964).

18. John P. Heinz, "The Political Imapsse in Farm Support Legislation," *Yale Law Journal,* 71 (April 1962): 952-978.

19. Lowi, *The End of Liberalism:* 55-97.

20. Earl Heady, "New Priorities," in *Rural Development Research Priorities* (Ames: Iowa State University Press, 1973): 952-978.

21. Nick Kotz, *Let Them Eat Promises* (Englewood Cliffs, N.J.: Prentice-Hall, 1969).

22. Weldon Barton, "Coalition-Building in the United States House of Representatives: Agricultural Legislation in 1973," in James E. Anderson's *Cases in Public Policy-Making* (New York: Praeger, 1976): 145.

23. R.G.F.Spitze, "Agricultural and Food Policy Issues and the Public Decision-Making Environment," in *Agricultural and Food Price and Income Policy: Alternative Directions for the United States and Implications for Research* (Social Publication 43, Agricultural Experiment, University of Illinois at Urbana-Champaign, August, 1976): 12.

24. Jim Hightower, *Hard Tomatoes-Hard Times* (Cambridge, Mass.: Schenkman, 1973).

25. Michael S. Lewis-Beck, "Agrarian Political Behavior in the United States," (forthcoming).

26. See especially Leo V. Mayer, "Discussion of 'Agricultural and Food Policy Issues and the Public Decisionmaking Environment,' " in *Agricultrual and Food Price and Income Policy: Alternative Directions for the United States and Implications for Researach* (Special Publication 43, Agricultural Experiment Station, University of Illinois at Urbana-Champaign, August, 1976): 21.

27. Paarlberg, Address at the National Public Policy Conference, 1975.

28. Redford, *Democracy and the Administrative State,* chapter 5.

29. Elmer E. Schattschneider, *The Semi-Sovereign People* (New York: Holt, Rinehart & Winston, 1960): 16-18.

30. Charles O. Jones, "Speculative Augmentation in Federal Air Pollution Policy-Making," *Journal of Politics,* 36 (May, 1974): 438-464.

31. Rachael L. Carson, *Silent Spring* (Boston : Houghton Mifflin, 1962).

32. Department of HEW, *Report of the Secretary's Commission on Pesticides and their Relationship to Environmental Health* (December, 1969).

33. U.S. General Accounting Office, *Weaknesses and Problem Areas in the Administration of the Imported Fire Ant Program,* (Washington, D.C.:U.S.G.P.O., January, 1965).

34. U.S. House Committee on Government Operations, *Deficiencies in the Administration of the Federal Insecticide, Fungicide, and Rodenticide Act,* 91st Congress, 1st session (Washington, D.C.: U.S.G.P.O., 1969).

35. Kotz, *Let Them Eat Promises:* 48.

36. Ross B. Talbot, "Implementation of the World Food Conference Resolutions (Rome November 1974): Decisions and Non-Decisions by the U.S. Government, with Special Reference to the International Grain Reserve Issue." Presented at the Midwest Conference of Political Scientists, Chicago, Illinois, April 23, 1977.

37. Raymond F. Hopkins, "Lessons of Food Diplomacy": 18. (Paper prepared for forthcoming edited book.)

38. Robert L. Paarlberg, "The Failure of Food Power." Paper presented at the Midwest Conference of Political Scientists, Chicago, Illinois,April 23, 1977: 29.

39. Don F. Hadwiger, "The Old, the New, and Emerging United States Department of Agriculture,"*Public Administration Review* (March/April, 1976): 155-165.

40. Sidney Baldwin, *Poverty and Politics* (Chapel Hill: University of North Carolina Press, 1968).

41. Quoted in Gladys L. Baker, Wayne D. Rasmussen, Vivian Wiser, and Jane M. Porter, *Century of Service* (Centennial Committee—U.S. Dept. of Agriculture, 1963): 271.

42. 1970 U.S. Code, chapter 9, section 346.

43. Kenneth John Meier, "The Agricultural Research Service and its Clientele: The Politics of Food Research." Paper presented at the 1977 Annual Meeting of the Southwest Social Science Association, Dallas, Texas, April 2, 1977.

44. Garth Youngberg, "The Alternative Agriculture Movement: Its Ideology, Its Politics, and Its Prospects," Paper presented at the 1977 Annual Meeting of the Southwestern Social Science Association, Dallas, Texas, April 2, 1977.

5.

AMERICA'S NON-POLICY FOR ENERGY

DAVID HOWARD DAVIS

Cornell University

"The United States doesn't have an energy policy." President Carter says this. Newspaper editors write this. Business and labor leaders echo it. Indeed, this complaint is expressed so frequently that it may be the single aspect of energy with which nearly everyone agrees. But what do these wailers and teeth gnashers mean when they lament the lack of a national policy?

By policy, they mean a government-declared doctrine. The Truman Doctrine and the Marshall Plan are examples of government-declared plans from foreign affairs. Johnson's War on Poverty and Nixon's War on Cancer are domestic examples. But policy can also have a broader meaning. It can mean the aggregation of all factors determining the situation for a given issue. The Truman Doctrine and the Marshall Plan were part, but not all, of American foreign policy toward Europe in the post-war period. Other factors included NATO's creation, fixed currency exchange rates, private American business investments, and so forth. President Johnson's declaration of the war on poverty was only part of the government's policy toward the poor. The 1968 Housing Act, an expansionary money supply, and VISTA were also components. Likewise, President's Nixon's War on Cancer was only part of his administration's health policy, which included making medical research more responsive and standing firm against government health insurance. This second definition of policy means that there is always a policy in a given issue area, even if that policy is not formally declared or perhaps is even contrary to the declared policy.

Recent events in the energy area furnish a host of cases with which to probe the two meanings of policy. Since the 1973-1974 OPEC oil boycott, energy has emerged from comfortable obscurity to awkward prominence. Government and private participants have proclaimed policy, denounced policy, and, consciously or not, made policy.

POLICY-AS-DOCTRINE

The two definitions may be labeled "policy-as-doctrine" versus "policy-as-result." Energy-related examples of policy-as-doctrine are easily called to mind. The Project Independence, which President Nixon proclaimed in 1973, is the prime instance. A President can appoint an energy czar to break bottlenecks, bully Exxon, and inspire conservation. Congress can pass laws with inspiring titles like the Energy Reorganization Act of 1974, the Energy Policy and Conservation Act of 1975, or the Emergency Natural Gas Act of 1977. Washington can create new agencies like the Federal Energy Office, the Energy Research and Development Administration, or the Department of Energy.

A number of political scientists view the policy process as a sequence. Gabriel Almond and Bingham Powell write of interests being first articulated and next aggregated; then rules are made, applied, and judged.[1] In this framework, policy-as-doctrine is most useful as a means of articulating interests. The early, unadorned calls for energy independence, an energy czar, new laws, or bureaucratic reorganization are cases of interest articulation. Interest aggregation is a more troublesome phase, for it is at this point that disparate interests must be reconciled. Producers are at odds with consumers. Saving jobs clashes with protecting the environment. Oil importers contend with domestic producers. The rule-making phase is supposed to resolve the conflicting interests, but often the contradictions are merely papered over under the guise of the original doctrine. Did Project Independence really provide for energy independence? Did the 1975 law either set policy or conserve fuel? Did the 1977 law ameliorate the natural gas emergency? Or were the doctrines expounded as window dressings, which merely restated the original goal without making the hard choices?

Charles O. Jones has a similar, sequential view of policy.[2] The first stage is to get the problem to government. It must be perceived, defined, organized, and propounded. Once on the agenda, the government must (2) formulate a specific proposal, (3) legitimate it, (4) fund it, (5) implement it, and then (6) evaluate it. Policy-as-doctrine belongs in the latter part of the first stage of defining, organizing, and propounding a problem and the beginning of the second stage of formulating a proposal. Rhetorical calls—for independence from OPEC manipulation or for a coherent national policy, or for new governmental research, or for regulation—help to define and organize the government's response. Furthermore, it begins the process of formulating a proposal. The crucial question is whether it goes beyond this to aid in completing the process of formulating a specific proposal. As discussed above, it frequently does not. Policy-as-doctrine can easily be a superficial substitute for the action sought. If the law has an appealing name, many will assume that the substance of the law fulfills the promise its title implies. The same verisimilitude can occur with a Presidential declaration, a new agency, the appointment of a high official, or a Supreme Court decision.

Murray Edelman maintains that governments commonly exploit policy-as-doctrine as a substitute for the required action.[3] He goes so far as to assert that symbol manipulation is an end in itself. Politicians engage in dramaturgical roles. This role-taking is for the purpose of achieving and maintaining their positions of leadership, not for achieving the particular outcomes which their policy stances might imply. He further argues that business regulation is a sector especially subject to symbol manipulation. While outwardly appearing to regulate an industry, officials typically facilitate a high measure of evasion of the formal rules. Heartening speeches and legalistic language reassure the naive public that the government is protecting its interests, while it is actually providing a cocoon for inside bargaining.

Project Independence, the Energy Policy and Conservation Act of 1975, and President Ford's oft-declared goal of deregulating natural gas prices are three cases of policy-as-doctrine.

Project Independence was the earliest and most ambitious policy to surface after the OPEC embargo. In December, 1973, President Nixon boldly called for a plan to make the United States independent of foreign fuel by 1985. The Federal Energy Office began drafting a plan to match the President's inspired rhetoric. But by the time its report was ready the next fall, circumstances had changed. Nixon had resigned, and Ford had become president. The energy agency had a new head, John Sawhill. The rechristened Federal Energy Administration was now a permanent agency established by Congress. Perhaps most important, OPEC had ended its boycott. Oil was no longer scarce. When FEA Administrator Sawhill presented the new President with a tough energy plan stressing conservation, Ford rejected it. Measures such as a steep gasoline tax were contrary to his traditional Republican philosophy of minimal government interference in the market and threatened to cost the party votes in the fall Congressional campaign.

Secretary of State Kissinger had a different set of problems with the doctrine of Project Independence. America's allies in Europe and Japan felt that Project Independence threatened their interests. Unlike the United States, most of these industrial trading partners had no hope of ever being energy independent. America's declared intention to seek autarky threatened their position, for they realized that energy importation was a necessity. In response, Kissinger resorted to double talk, deliberately confusing the words "independence" and "interdependence."

Kissinger's deception proved superfluous, since Project Independence was dead-on-arrival. President Ford was so displeased with the scheme that he sent the preliminary report back to the FEA to be emasculated. While the report issued in November, 1974 promised not only that the United States would be self-sufficient by 1985, but would also be a net exporter of energy to Europe and Japan, the facts belied this. They showed that the oft-promised oil from Colorado shale was too costly, that coal mines could not be opened quickly enough, and that nuclear reactors were not economically competitive. Issuing even the toned-down Project Independence report cost FEA Administrator Sawhill his job. Sawhill stressed mandatory conservation measures, in particular a $.20 tax on each gallon of gasoline sold. Sawhill and his staff believed that such a tax would produce the greatest energy savings with the least economic disruption. The tax might be inconvenient, forcing commuters to take buses or form car pools and limit Sunday drives in the country, but it would not close factories or cause homes to be cold. Ford found Sawhill's proposal too harsh. Even though Sawhill tried to backtrack in response to the President's concern for not angering the motoring public, Ford was not satisfied. He demanded and got Sawhill's resignation on October 29.

Although eviscerated when issued in November, 1974, Project Independence did not die. It lived on as a venerated statement of national goals. President Ford, Secretary of State Kissinger, editors, businessmen, and even political scientists continued to pay homage to it. Sawhill's FEA successor, Frank Zarb, praised the report as a useful evaluation of the energy issue without committing himself to its recommendations.

The Energy Policy and Conservation Act: became law a few days before Christmas 1975, thus ending a year-long struggle between the President and Congress. The engagement began the previous Christmas when Ford, Zarb, and his other energy advisors began writing the relevant section of the President's State of the Union speech. By then Project Independence was moribund. Ford's new tactic, which he proposed in his State of the Union address to the joint session of Congress on January 15, was to challenge the legislative branch of government to come up with its own energy plan. Once the legislature set forth its proposal, the executive branch would respond. To put pressure on Congress to act, Ford announced that if no progress was made in 90 days, he would impose a $1 fee on each barrel of imported crude under a provision of the 1962 Trade Expansion Act. In anger, Congress repealed the relevant provisions of the 1962 law, but Ford vetoed the repeal. When Congress had not acted by June 1, the President raised the fee to $2. On August 11, the Court of Appeals for the District of Columbia ruled in response to a lawsuit brought by eight northeastern states that the 1962 law had not given President Ford the authority to impose an import fee on oil. But by then, Ford had another weapon at hand. The Emergency Petroleum Allocation Act of 1973 was due to expire on August 31. This act authorized the price control of domestic oil production. Ford said Congress would have to pass a comprehensive energy law, or he would simply let the existing controls end. In a last-minute compromise, Congress hastily extended the 1973 Allocation Act until November 15. Ford signed the extension in return for Congress's promise to pass a comprehensive law. In November, the deadline was once more extended until December 15, and Congress did not send the bill to the President for his signature until December 17.

President Ford's strategy of calling on Congress to take the initiative in drafting major legislation is contrary to the behavior of modern Presidents. Since at least the presidency of Franklin Roosevelt, the Administration has written the first version of a major law. Then Congress has reacted to that proposal. For Congress to take the initiative in drafting such a large and complex bill was unusual in itself. For the President to encourage, even force, such an initiative, was unprecedented in the post-New Deal era.

This reversal of roles between Congress and the Administration may derive from any of three reasons. First, the Administration could not develop a program of its own. It had just torn itself apart with the *Project Independence Report* (which had pleased no one, especially Ford), had forced the FEA Administrator's resignation, and had confounded the United States' allies. Having systematically explored a wide range of alternatives, the administration had found none. A second reason for this role reversal was the personality of the President. Ford had spent a quarter of a century as a Republican in the House of Representatives. For all but two of those years, his party had been in the minority. Hence, his experience was to react to the proposals of others—to criticize, improve, refine, but not to initiate. Besides, he was by nature as well as experience a reactive man who preferred to work within a structure defined by others. Becoming President—especially the nation's first unelected President—

did not change this basic passivity. The third reason was that Ford shrewdly recognized that energy was an inherently insoluble problem. It set one interest against another with a breadth, complexity, and intensity not found with other political issues. Since it was a no-win situation, it was better to dump the problem on the Democrats. The former University of Michigan football star wisely chose to punt.

Because of its geographical basis, energy split the Democrats more than the Republicans. Petroleum-producing Texas, Louisiana, and Oklahoma traditionally had provided many party leaders such as Representative Carl Albert (Speaker) and Senator Russell Long (Finance Committee Chairman). Petroleum-consuming states in the north traditionally had provided the other party leaders such as Representative Tip O'Neill (then Majority Leader, later Speaker) and Senators Jackson, Mansfield, Humphrey, and Kennedy.

The consequence of a lack of presidential leadership and a sharply divided Democratic party was a patchwork law which provided neither a coherent policy nor an incentive for conservation. The law's least logical provision was Title IV, which brought all oil production under federal price controls at a price of $7.66, more than a dollar below the going price. The effect was to encourage consumption and discourage production. Republicans said the Democrats were up to their old tricks of appearing to aid the consumer with an artificially low price while actually harming him by drying up the supply. Cheap gasoline is of little value if none is available. The low price would falsely signal to the motorist that fuel was plentiful, whereas he should be told via a high price that it was scarce and not to be wasted.

Natural Gas Decontrol was a policy propounded by business, labor, economists, and many others for years. The Federal Power Commission had been setting the interstate price of the fuel since Congress passed the Natural Gas Act in 1938. FPC regulation kept the price artificially low. Most gas sold for $.52 thousand cubit feet (Mcf). Some sold for $.29½. The FPC's rationale was two-fold. (1) Low prices benefited consumers, and (2) low prices had no effect on the quantity produced, since gas was a by-product of drilling for oil. The FPC view prevailed with little challenge until 1971. In that year, the nation began suffering its first gas shortage, a phenomenon that increased each year. Few politicians contested the FPC low price doctrine. Democrats in the New Deal tradition supported the Commission's policy of keeping a cap on prices. Others saw the clean-burning fuel as a panacea for pollution and wanted to maintain a low price to encourage its use. Still others in both parties agreed with the economists that the regulation distorted the market, but saw little reward in opposing the FPC policy. Low prices had a simplistic appeal to voters, whereas the case for high prices was hard to make persuasive to the economically unsophisticated. The argument was the standard one that prices should accurately reflect the value of a commodity. If the price were too low, not enough gas would be available, forcing gas consumers to switch to alternate fuels. In the words of one businessman: "A cheap price for *no* gas is *no* good." The adverse consequences were that by the early 1970s many distributing companies were not accepting new customers. New houses denied gas hook-ups used oil or electric heat instead. When OPEC embargoed oil in 1973, the results were disastrous. New factories that wanted to burn gas could not. One solution for those who could plan ahead was to build factories in gas-producing states, such as Texas and Louisiana. Because the gas there was *intra*state rather than *inter*state, it escaped FPC regulation. The unregulated *intra*state price was high, $1.50 or $2.00, but the fuel was available. Another alternative was for a manufacturing company to go into the gas business itself. Rather than sell the gas to the factory as it was burned, producers sold the entire field. Thus a manufacturer in, say, Ohio might own a dozen wells within Ohio in order to escape FPC regulation.

If artificially low prices do not truly benefit the consumer, what of the second point that higher prices would not increase production? This, too, is specious. The day is long past when natural gas was merely a by-product of oil. True, half a century ago the gas was chiefly a nuisance, a poisonous vapor incapable of transmission for more than a few miles. Then most gas was burned at the well head—flared off for the safety of the workers. But once arc welding permitted construction of long distance, nonleaking pipelines, the fuel became valuable. Petroleum engineers began to add the value of the gas to the value of the oil in calculating whether it was worth drilling more wells in a field. Today, many wells are drilled solely for their gas.

While most politicians had avoided the controversy, President Ford staunchly advocated natural gas deregulation. Such a doctrine was more compatible with Republican than Democratic philosophy. President Nixon had nudged the FPC in that direction, but had become distracted by the Watergate scandal. Ford made it part of his across-the-board policy of deregulation. He also urged competition in air fares, truck shipping rates, and so forth. On July 27, 1976, the FPC responded to the President's admonitions. The commissioners, a majority of whom were Republicans appointed since Nixon took office in 1969, voted to restructure gas prices radically. "Old gas" in production before January 1, 1973 would sell for $.52 per Mcf. "New gas" would have a higher price. That which came on-stream in 1973 and 1974 would sell for $1.01 per Mcf, and gas which came on-stream after January 1, 1975 would sell for $1.42. The commission set three tiers to avoid giving windfall profits to the producers. If old gas was profitable at $.52, it should still be profitable. The high price for new gas would encourage producers to drill new wells. The higher prices would encourage the most efficient use of the gas.

Despite its good intentions, the FPC stumbled into difficulty almost at once. Reanalysis by FPC staff economists showed a $500 million miscalculation. The Commission rectified it by reclassifying some "new gas" as "old gas" and lowering the price for 1973 and 1974 gas from $1.01 to $.93 per Mcf. Consumer groups contested the FPC price rise in court. Within two days of the original announcement, they had won the first round of what promised to be a long battle.

Not even its staunchest advocates suggested that deregulation would increase the supply quickly. Three years are needed to develop a new gas field on shore; seven are needed offshore. Production peaked in 1971 at 22½ trillion cubic feet and has declined since. Proven reserves have declined since 1967. Thus, the issue of deregulation had little practical consequence when the United States experienced its frigid winter of 1977. America had to make do with what gas it had, as Arctic air brought record low temperatures and record high snowfalls to virtually every city east of the Rocky Mountains. Snow fell in Miami. Military planes airlifted rescue equipment to Buffalo, New York. In the Midwest and East, thousands of schools and factories closed when the gas distributing companies shut off their supplies. In New Jersey, the governor invoked a World War II civil-defense law to declare a state of emergency. Retail stores and factories using gas were to turn their thermostats down to 50°F, and homes were to turn theirs down to 65°F. The police were to arrest flagrant violators.

President Carter met the crisis with a series of melodramatic gestures. On Inauguration Day, he walked down Pennsylvania Avenue in temperatures 10° below normal to his solar-heated reviewing stand in front of the White House. Those dignitaries who shared the experimental pavilion described it as "chilly." The next day, the new President turned the White House thermostats down to 65°F. A week later, he helicoptered to Pittsburgh to see for himself how that hard-hit city was faring beneath its mounds of snow and ice.

In response to the crisis, Carter proposed the Emergency Natural Gas Act. Congress rushed the bill through in a week, so that Carter was able to sign it shortly before delivering a fireside television broadcast on February 2, clad in a warm wool sweater.

The Emergency Natural Gas Act's speedy passage derived both from the winter crisis and its lack of substance. Snowbound cities, unemployed workers, and children out of school seemed to call for a response. The law empowered the President to allocate supplies, bring some *intra*state gas into the *inter*state market, and to subpoena the gas companies' information. In sum, the Act did very little of long-term consequence. It ducked the deregulation issue which, in turn, was supposed to solve a series of basic problems by restoring a market mechanism. Deregulation advocates maintained that it would end diversion of gas to *intra*state users, because *inter*state users would, under deregulation, be able to compete in price. It could generate capital for exploration and make new and marginal wells profitable because of the higher prices. The high price would discourage wasteful uses of gas, such as boiler fuel), where coal, oil, or nuclear energy could be used instead. It would make new sources, such as Alaskan and Canadian gas, liquified natural gas (LNG), and synthetic gas, more profitable.

During his campaign for President, Jimmy Carter had said he favored deregulation, without committing himself to any specifics. The Emergency Act evaded confronting the problem directly, although it did spark debate on the underlying issues. Members of Congress from gas-producing states sought complete deregulation, not just the three-tier system the FPC had established. Members from consuming states were more ambivalent. Their constituents liked low prices, but they were becoming aware that expensive gas is better than no gas. A frequent accusation was that the gas producers were deliberately holding back supplies to exacerbate the crisis, thus increasing pressure for deregulation. Certainly FPC regulation encouraged companies to seek alternatives to the *inter*state market. But evidence of coordinated or illegal withholding was elusive. In fact, gas producers had no need to conspire. Each company working in its own self-interest would produce the same results. In response to criticism that the Emergency Natural Gas Act avoided the big issues, Carter concurred, saying his concern was for the immediate crisis and that he would send Congress a comprehensive program in April.

President Carter's response to the 1977 winter crisis fits Edelman's criteria of symbolic action. The solar-heated reviewing stand, turning down the White House thermostats, the helicopter trip to Pittsburgh, the fireside chat, and the Emergency Act were all dramaturgical actions. As a brand-new President, Carter would be especially eager to assert his position of leadership. This role-playing conveyed an image that he was innovative (solar heat), self-sacrificing (65°F), concerned (Pittsburgh trip), accessible (fireside chat), and able to act in a crisis (the Emergency Act). Few would disagree that Carter was manipulating symbols in this activity, but a further test is whether this dramaturgy was a facade hiding a safe sphere within which the gas producers could carry on business as usual (or worse, secure some new privileges and higher profits), or whether this dramaturgy was true leadership, encouraging Americans to innovate, sacrifice, communicate, and resolve the problem.

POLICY-AS-RESULT

If policy-as-doctrine examines goals, policy-as-result looks at reality. This second approach to policy defines its subject as the totality of all forces acting in a certain issue area. Indeed, it looks beyond government influences, though all the while using government activity as its central concern. When President Nixon heralded Project Independence, the United States was importing a third of its oil. Four years later, it was importing more than half. Was American policy really independence from OPEC? The 1975 energy law promised to establish a rational national policy and to conserve energy. Did it do so? The 1977 natural gas law promised less—merely to get the country through the winter. But why was such an emergency law necessary in an industry that the FPC had been regulating since 1938?

Several theoretical models are compatible with viewing policy-as-result. The pluralist paradigm expounded by David Truman[4] sees outcomes as the result of multiple pressures pushing and shoving. The policy equilibrium is a temporary one, equivalent to price on the economist's supply-and-demand graph. A different array of pressures would produce a different outcome, but the basic mechanism would be the same. Elite models also may explain policy-as-result. This approach maintains that only a small core of influentials, blessed with money and occupying key junctures, determine the policy outcomes affecting the entire public. Robert Dahl, Robert Engler, and others meld the two approaches while maintaining that the policy process is segmented.[5] A series of issue areas or subgovernments exist according to the particular issue. Educational policy is determined independently of housing policy, which in turn is determined independently of energy policy. Some argue that even within the energy issue area, the various fuels each have their own subgovernments.[6]

Oil Imports which everyone seemed to agree should decrease, actually increased. Moreover, virtually all of that increase came from the Moslem states of the Persian Gulf. America's chief foreign source remained Venezuela, but Venezuela had no extra oil to give. The added imports had to come from the very countries that had instituted the 1973 embargo in retaliation for American support of Israel in the Yom Kippur War.

American energy doctrine was to develop domestic oil reserves and alternate sources. The Alaskan oil discovered in the late 1960s seemed a godsend. So did new fields off the East Coast. But both were costly to tap. The Alaskan oil required a long pipeline which environmentalists considered dangerous. Congress overruled their objections, and construction was begun. Once the pipeline was close to completion, a new problem arose. The costly crude, pumped from beneath the Arctic tundra and piped across the 49th state for shipment to the West Coast, was not needed on the West Coast, but rather in the Midwest. In its anxiety to bring the oil on stream quickly, the government had not fully considered where it was needed. East Coast offshore oil exploration, leasing, and development was several years behind the North Slope oil; but it promised to be even more costly. Both sources would only prove profitable if OPEC maintained its artificially high price. With current technology, shale oil was not economically feasible. The same was true for the tar sands. Nor could coal be converted into liquid or gaseous fuel at a profit.

More progress was possible in the area of fuel for stationary rather than mobile energy generation. An electric-generating plant or manufacturing plant could burn coal directly. In 1975, coal consumption grew to 640 million tons, a level topping the previous high in 1947, which was before the era of cheap oil and natural gas. Coal, however, was far from a panacea. Little slack remained in the industry. Output per man-shift dropped from 16 tons to 11 tons. Some blamed the Coal Mine Health and Safety Act of 1969 and the vigorous action by the Mining Enforcement and Safety Administration of the Department of the Interior. Others blame the "missing generation of miners." Because of the 15-year slump in production, no miners entered the field. Hence, there was a shortage of experienced manpower. There were environmental constraints, too. The Clean Air Act made high-sulfur coal unburnable or expensive to purify. On two occasions, Congress passed and President Ford vetoed an anti-strip-mining bill.

Nuclear energy's contribution to generating electricity increased markedly. From 1970 to 1975, its share went from 1 percent to 9 percent. But as the nuclear contribution grew, so did public opposition. Environmentalists moderated their affront against routine radiation and thermal pollution as the electric companies poured more concrete for shielding and installed more elaborate cooling systems. The new concern became the risks of core meltdowns. An accident at the Brown's Ferry plant showed how easily a reactor could heat up out of control. Water coolant might then cause a steam explosion, blowing apart the plant and sending a radioactive cloud out into the atmosphere. The electric companies had no plans to evacuate those in danger. In many instances, the plants are so close to cities that evacuation would be impossible. The Zion facility is only 30 miles from Chicago and only five miles from Waukegan.

The federal government's response was to belittle the danger. In 1974, the AEC (to become ERDA in 1975) published a report, named for its principle author, Dr. Norman Rasmussen. The Rasmussen Report calculated that the chances of one person being injured by one plant in a given year were one in five billion. Critics branded this as misleading. They said that the calculations were incorrect, that many plants were added each year, and that a single accident could cause hundreds, even thousands of casualties.

Retarded development of alternate energy sources is only a partial explanation of the increasing American appetite for oil imports and the problems associated with that appetite. Demand and the OPEC stance also plays a part.

Energy consumption—especially oil consumption—declined sharply during the 1973-1974 OPEC embargo. It was far from voluntary restraint. Motorists bought less gasoline because service stations had less to sell. Dealers rationed five gallons to a customer and often ran out by 11 a.m. Heating oil distributors could not supply their customers. But other restraints were planned. Highway speed limits went down to 55 m.p.h. The Los Angeles Power Department charged a 50 percent penalty to customers who failed to cut their previous winter's consumption by 10 percent. Second offenders found their power cut off for two days. As a result, the city exceeded its conservation goal, reducing demand by 14 percent. Much of the electricity conservation continued after the emergency program ended in the spring of 1974. President Nixon ordered the federal government to reduce consumption by 7 percent. Air force pilots flew fewer practice sorties, thermostats were turned down, and buildings were "delamped." The result was four times the 7 percent goal. Government usage ran at a rate 30 percent below the previous year.[7] As in the case of Los Angeles, much of the energy-saving continued after the emergency was over.

But the 1973-1974 energy savings proved to be only a dip in the long upward trend. The country returned to an annual growth rate of 4 to 5 percent. The four-fold increase in crude oil prices was not enough to change life styles, though it was enough to spur inflation. Consumers' reaction to the increased fuel costs was sluggish. In part, this was because fuel is only one of the factors in producing a product. While the raw material of gasoline—crude oil—increased 400 percent, the price at the pump increased only 25 percent because the costs of transporting, refining, distribution, and taxation at first remained constant. Later, as all sectors of the economy felt the impact, the other costs rose too, but still not as extremely. Some consumers could shift from oil to other fuels. Coal or natural gas can substitute for oil as a boiler fuel. Still, such substitution raised the prices of coal and gas. The consumers reacted slowly to higher prices in their life-styles as well. The suburbanite living in a poorly insulated, all-electric house, and driving a nine mile per gallon gas guzzler might have a completely rational understanding of his energy quandary but have few options. Not many could or would sell their houses to move back to a more energy-efficient apartment or house in the city, close to public transportation. Even installing six inches of insulation, a new furnace, or trading in a big car for a small one was not an immediate option for most.

Though OPEC's price boost could not produce a prompt response from the consumer, it could wreak havoc with the economy as a whole. The consequence was stagflation, a condition Keynesian economic theory had previously considered impossible. At the same time that inflation moved into the double digits, thousands of people were unemployed. Business was stagnant but prices climbed. While the OPEC price rise was not the sole cause, it was a major one.

Beside upsetting the domestic economics of the United States and other industrial nations, the OPEC price rise upset the international monetary system. A new word appeared—petrodollar. To pay the vastly increased costs for crude oil, the United States sent dollars to OPEC. Germany, France, Britain, and Japan likewise sent marks, francs, pounds sterling, and yen. Several of the OPEC members, most notably Saudi Arabia, could not spend the foreign exchange as quickly as it flowed in. The United States and other industrial countries looked on with trepidation as the huge reserves of petrodollars OPEC piled up. These petrodollars represented mounting claims on future goods and services. On one hand, they feared that the OPEC barons would buy them out, and, on the other hand, they feared that they would not. A sustained, diversified flow of purchases would stimulate the stagnant economies of America, Europe, and Japan. But much of the OPEC treasure simply accumulated. These large liquid reserves seemed like a potential avalanche that could unexpectedly crash down upon the already battered industrial nations. In fact, the dangers of OPEC petrodollars proved exaggerated. All of the suddenly rich cartel members launched internal development plans. They bought ships, factories, and farm machinery and hired Americans and Europeans to teach them how to use them. Of course, they also bought personal luxuries and military equipment.

Iran's development program was among the most ambitious. In fact, it was too ambitious. The Shah proposed a five-year plan to invest over

$100 billion. The king of kings foresaw that Iranian oil would eventually run out, and he wanted his country to build a modern industrial economy in the meantime. In the process, the Shah overextended himself. Oil production in 1975 actually dropped 11 percent from 1974. Petroleum reserves were $3 to $4 billion lower than expected.[8] Ironically, OPEC's second wealthiest member suffered a balance of payments deficit.

Such a problem has not yet hobbled the cartel's largest producer— Saudi Arabia. With much more oil and a much smaller population, the kingdom enjoys a huge trade surplus. The Saudis have their development plan, too. Their greatest problem is physically moving their imports into the country. Ships often wait months in the harbor, until docks are available for unloading.

Saudi Arabia and the small sheikdoms along the Persian Gulf hold the large reserves of petrodollars which worry American financiers. The funds are in highly liquid form. With a few exceptions, the Arabs have eschewed direct investment. They have not bought American refineries and service stations, the "downstream" sectors of the petroleum industry. Nor have they bought other American businesses. Indeed, the form and location of the Arab funds is mysterious. Discussion evokes whispers of gold bullion, Swiss banks, and secret purchases. Much does seem to be in gold and in bank accounts. Other reserves are invested in stocks. A little shows up directly. The Iranian royal family builds a skyscraper in New York and Arab princes buy historic country estates near London. One prudent sheik only bought an English mansion after trying it for a weekend with his harem. Early fears that the OPEC members would purchase a stranglehold on the American economy with their petrodollars proved unfounded. Perhaps fearing obvious retaliation, they have not used their wealth to buy American energy companies.

Soon after the oil embargo ended, the American government tried to rally support for a consumers' cartel to counter OPEC. The United States and 15 other industrial nations met in Paris in November, 1974 to establish the International Energy Agency (IEA). Secretary of State Kissinger, who once described himself as a lone cowboy, wanted a posse to help bring OPEC to justice. In organizing the IEA, Kissinger realized that its united bargaining front depended on a common price and that the common price would have to be higher than the old $3 a barrel. Only in the Persian Gulf could oil be pumped so cheaply. He proposed $7. This approximated the average U.S. domestic price and was high enough that coal, natural gas, and new petroleum discoveries could just compete. The IEA countries lukewarmly agreed "in principle" to have a price floor but did not commit themselves to the $7 figure. The IEA's reluctance to set a firm price for bargaining foretold its general weakness. The consumer's cartel was not able to present a common front strong enough to stand up to OPEC.

Morris Adelman, Christopher Stone, and Jack McNamara among others, believe IEA unity was not necessary to bring the OPEC price down.[9] The United States could do it alone. First, Congress would pass a law that all oil imports would be government-controlled. The government would conduct a double auction. Foreign sellers would submit secret, sealed bids, and domestic buyers would do the same. The government would simply match the bids without revealing the prices. Then each seller would deliver the oil. The government would never actually possess any oil, but would merely be a clearing house. Poor OPEC countries like Indonesia and Nigeria that needed cash would be able to sell as much cheap oil as they could, exceeding the strict OPEC quotas now limiting them. The plan simulates a free market, albeit government run.

Critics of the cartel often blame the large multinational oil companies for slavishly following OPEC dictates, even when this harms their home countries. OPEC administers its artificially high prices through Exxon, Standard of California, Shell, British Petroleum, and others. If the petroleum giants were to stand up to OPEC, the cartel would collapse. While the indictment may be true, it assumes the interests of the oil companies to be identical with those of their home country and contrary to those of OPEC. In fact, the companies have much to gain by working OPEC's will, and much to lose by defying it. In 1974, at the same time Americans waited hours in line to buy gasoline and shivered in cold houses, the oil companies admitted record profits when called before Senator Henry Jackson's committee investigating the embargo. The companies claimed that these were paper profits, resulting from reval-uation of inventories. Many observers were not persuaded. If the oil companies were to defy OPEC, its members could seize the companies' property in the OPEC countries and deny the companies access to the oil. Since many producing countries now own much or all of the fields, wells, pipelines, and ports; this is less of a sanction than it once ws. Lack of access is an equal or greater threat. A blacklisted company could not supply its refineries, and hence, its distributors and customers. Thus, multinational oil companies have neither the incentives, the unity nor the power to stand up to OPEC. Notwithstanding this, some suggest that patriotism should motivate the multinationals.

Economists are fond of declaring that cartels are inherently unstable. Eventually, the varying interests of the different members split the united front. For more years than expected, OPEC held firmly together. Then the December 1976 meeting at Qatar showed the first crack in the façade. Eleven of the 13 members voted to raise the price 10 percent. Saudi

Arabia and the United Arab Emirates broke rank, limiting their increase to 5 percent. Since the Saudis were by far the largest producers (8.5 million barrels a day in 1976) and had a small population to satisfy, their desertion was a mortal threat. Worse still, the Saudis could raise production to 11.9 million barrels per day. The 3.4 million barrel difference exceeds the total production of any other OPEC member except Iran. The bifurcation occurred because the 11 nations were no longer willing to comply with the Saudis' wishes. After the initial fourfold increase in the early 1970s, the Saudis had insisted on moderation. The price rises approximated the inflation rates of the currencies in which they were paid and with which they bought their imports. Saudi Arabia could enforce this moderation because it could hold so much excess production capacity in reserve. By December 1976, Saudi Arabia had accumulated much more money than it could spend, whereas other OPEC members such as Iran, Nigeria, and Indonesia needed more money. The United Arab Emirates' economic position was similar to that of Saudi Arabia, and the Saudis dominate them geographically and culturally. As the new plutocrats, the Saudis had become concerned about the world-wide recession to which they had contributed. The recession made their imports more expensive, and their foreign investments less profitable. Furthermore, the Saudis revived the question of Israel. Their oil minister, Sheik Yamani, announced that the United States could show its appreciation for the economic restraint by pressuring Israel to accept a peace settlement. Beside keeping the price rise down, the Saudis had paid for the Pan-Arab peace-keeping force that halted the Lebanese civil war and had moderated the Palestine Liberation Front. It was time for the United States to do something in return. When asked for a response, Jimmy Carter, then President-elect, avoided linking Israel to oil. To acknowledge that the two were linked would invite the Arab members of OPEC to once again, as they had after the Yom Kippur War, use oil to pressure the United States to pressure Israel.

OPEC's disunity at the Qatar meeting was far from the death knoll of the cartel. True, the Saudis did announce their intention to expand production by 40 percent, to 11.9 million barrels per day. This jump in production pressured the 11 other members to hold their increases below the 10 percent. Discounts and generous credit arrangements could achieve a lower price without seeming to retreat from the 10 percent figure. Still, the much vaunted split is only 5 percent, and Saudi Arabia and the United Arab Emirates cannot supply all of the world's crude oil. The disunity could disappear quickly by unofficial discounts or by the 11 foregoing further increases while the Saudis catch up.

The Qatar bifurcation is more notable as a symptom of Saudi Arabia's emergence as a foreign policy actor. Prior to 1973, the desert kingdom had been an international relations hermit. Its conservative, theocratic rulers shunned foreign involvement. At the end of the Yom Kippur War, it reluctantly took the lead in the embargo when its brother Arab states of Egypt and Syria failed to reconquer territory lost in the 1967 war. Meeting with success in this venture, it intervened through diplomacy and subsidies to end internecine fighting and quarrelling in Lebanon, within the PLO, and between Egypt and Syria. Saudi foreign policy toward the United States has been favorable. It seeks American friendship, technology, imports, and oil sales. Its technocrats are largely American-trained. It is staunchly anti-Communist. The United States is not so eager to reciprocate as positively, because of American support for Israel. Arabs (though not Saudi Arabs) have fought four wars with the Jewish state since 1948 and have steadfastly refused to make peace or even recognize Israel's existence. In suggesting that Saudi Arabia's moderation in price deserved American reciprocation (U.S. pressure on Israel), the Saudis took a leading role in the Arab cause. While the United States government reflexively rejected linking oil and Israel, former ambassador Richard Nolte, for one, argued in favor of encouraging the Saudi role.[10] He maintained that Saudi Arabia was the most moderate Arab state and that its goal of stability in the Middle East was compatible with American goals. The Saudis could lead and cajole the more volatile Arabs to accept a settlement palatable to Israel. Furthermore, the United States needed Saudi Arabia for its own security and prosperity. By the end of the decade, a quarter of American crude oil imports would come from the desert kingdom. America's European allies and Japan would be even more vulnerable to an oil embargo.

While American petroleum experts fretted about OPEC and especially its lynchpin, Saudi Arabia, during the mid-1970s, portentious discoveries occurred much closer to home. Mexico located new oil fields. The largest finds were in the southeastern provinces of Tabasco, Chiapas, and offshore of Campeche in the Gulf of Mexico. Mexican reserves were over 60 billion barrels, 10 times the Alaskan reserves and 40 percent as great as those of Saudi Arabia, the petroleum giant. Mexico would thus be as large a producer as Venezuela. In spite of its proximity to the United States, the Mexican bonanza was not automatically the solution to the American shortage. Mexico was wary of the United States. In 1938, American exploitation led Mexico to expropriate foreign production and to organize a government corporation—Pemex. Pemex played down news of its huge discoveries until it was apparent that the fields were so large that it would have to hire foreign companies to exploit them. Even then, Pemex did not plan to grant concessions based on a percentage of the oil produced, but to hire foreign developers on a fee-for-service basis. Mexico was not an OPEC member, though it did charge the OPEC price for its exports. The discovery of the new reserves caused Mexico to consider joining the cartel. If it were to become one of the world's biggest exporters, should it join OPEC? If Mexico were awash with 60 billion barrels of oil, could it expect the United States really to try to achieve energy independence?

Domestic Oil policy was as complex as import policy. Completion of the trans-Alaska pipeline in 1977 called attention to a host of problems. Although Congress had self-consciously dealt with the North Slope oil on numerous occasions, the situation as the oil began to flow through the pipeline illustrated policy-as-result much more than policy-as-doctrine. The chief problem was that the pipeline would deliver the crude to the wrong place. From the terminus at Valdez, ships were to take it to the West Coast. But the West Coast did not need the oil. It could use no more than half of the 1.2 million barrels per day projected. The oil was needed in the Midwest, but transporting the oil there was an obstacle. The oil companies wanted to unload it at Los Angeles and pipe it eastward. Los Angeles objected to the pollution this would cause. Crude could be shipped through the Panama Canal only in small tankers. The Jones Act required that these tankers be of American registry. American ships and crews were more expensive than foreign ones, and not enough were thought to be available, anyway. One option would be to ship the Alaskan crude to Japan in exchange for Middle Eastern oil, but Congress outlawed this when the pipeline was authorized.

The West Coast oil surplus and Midwest oil shortage caused belated reevaluation of the original selection of the route. At the time the Alaska pipeline was under consideration, many had advocated a trans-Canadian pipeline that would deliver the oil to the Midwest. Objections were that it would take at least a year longer to build and that it would run through a foreign country. Furthermore, the oil companies forecast that West Coast demand would be high enough to absorb the full capacity. The recession, fuel conservation, and environmental concern reduced the West Coast's demand for oil. As it was, construction lagged several years behind the original schedule, so one additional year did not seem that critical. The fears of running the pipeline through Canada seemed exaggerated. In fact, such a joint venture would foster a desirable degree of interdependence. While the victory of the Parti Quebeçois in 1976 did threaten the delicate fabric of Canadian unity, this same potential instability made the Canadian federal government less likely to engage in petty quarrels with the United States. And anyway, the pipeline would go nowhere near Quebec.

The oil discovery and production revolutionized the 49th state economically and politically. In order to get the wells drilled and the pipeline built, Congress had to resolve Eskimo, Indian, and Aleut claims to land, resolutions that had been postponed in the Alaska Statehood Act of 1958. The resolution was the Alaska Native Claims Act of 1971, which established a series of 200 corporations owned and managed by the natives. With the oil boom of the 1970s, these corporations became wealthy enterprises owning land, banks, and buildings. The state government received 12½ percent of the revenues from oil and launched an ambitious development plan much as the OPEC countries had.[11]

Since the state's royalty revenue depends on the price of the oil at the wellhead, it intervened in the proceedings of the Interstate Commerce Commission to determine the tariff the pipeline will charge. Because the price is set at the south coast port of Valdez, the higher the charge for piping the oil 400 miles across the tundra, the lower the price at the wellhead and the lower the royalty. The ICC is to set a tariff that will give the pipeline company a 7 percent return on its capital investment. The state argued that the company had high capital costs because it mismanaged the construction, and that the ICC should not allow it to charge a higher rate, because it did a poor job of building the pipeline in the first place.

Whatever price the ICC settled on, the Alaskan oil was bound to be high. The North Slope was the world's most hostile oil field. Arctic cold, high winds, frozen tundra, and months of darkness made drilling expensive. The trans-Alaskan pipeline had to be built across steep mountains, icy rivers, and permafrost. A truck driver earned $11 an hour. Skilled laborers earned more. As a result, Alaskan oil cannot compete unless OPEC keeps its price at the artificially high level.

The mid-1970s also saw expensive domestic oil being developed at the opposite side of the United States. In August, 1976, the Department of Interior leased 93 tracts off the New Jersey shore in the undersea Baltimore Canyon. Preliminary drilling showed the area likely to be rich in oil and gas deposits. It might contain as much as 2.6 billion barrels of crude oil and 10 trillion cubic feet of natural gas. Like the Alaskan oil, this oil would be costly to produce. Drillers would have to erect platforms 50 to 100 miles offshore in deep water. Once oil was discovered, the company would have to ship the oil by undersea pipeline or by tanker. The pipelines would be expensive and environmentally offensive during construction. If pipelines proved impractical, the crude would go by tanker. The tankers present a greater environmental risk, since they may leak during loading and unloading and are subject to accident.

The federal government's desire to speed development of oil and gas clashed with the federal government's desire to protect the environment.

On February 18, 1977, only weeks before drilling off New Jersey was to begin, a federal judge in New York ruled that the Interior Department's leases of drilling rights in the Baltimore Canyon violated the National Environmental Policy Act of 1969 (NEPA). The judge's scathing opinion listed five ways in which Interior had ridden roughshod over NEPA and cited evidence that the Secretary of the Interior acted in bad faith in his rush to lease the tracts. The offshore development schedule was set back but not terminated. Too many government officials, oil companies, and East Coast consumers wanted the petroleum.

The dangers of tanker accidents, which the judge gave as one of his five violations of NEPA, applied to tankers from abroad as well as from offshore platforms. Coastal states like New York, Delaware, California, and Washington had passed laws regulating such ships. For example, Washington forbade "supertankers" of more than 125,000 tons from sailing in Puget Sound. The shippers feared piecemeal regulation. If they could not have leniency, at least they could have standardization. Anticipating voluminous shipments of its Alaskan oil, the Atlantic Richfield Company challenged Washington State's right to pass such legislation. It argued to the Supreme Court that the federal government preempted the field in 1972, when Congress passed the Ports and Waterways Safety Act. Washington responded that the 1972 law did not preempt the field and that federal regulation was haphazard and ineffective.

Most of the tankers are beyond the immediate authority of either state or federal government. Because American safety and labor regulations are strict, most tankers, even those that are American-owned, sail under flags of convenience. Liberia and Panama are the leaders of the international competition for leniency. The Jones Act precludes such vessels from domestic routes such as Valdez to Puget Sound. American law could reach foreign tankers by setting certain standards for ships entering American ports. Environmentalists blame the Coast Guard for too much deference to the shippers it is supposed to regulate. During the interagency squabbling, EPA Administrator Russell Train asserted that the problem was "the wall of conservatism at the Coast Guard."

Conflict between two House of Representatives committees working on the Carter administration's proposed energy law illustrated the extent to which seemingly minor changes in the legislation could have a major impact. Carter's chief means of saving precious oil and gas was the mandatory conversion to coal of large industries and public utilities. Conversion would account for half of the total petroleum saved. The administration bill did this with tax penalties. But the Ways and Means Committee was overly generous, providing so many exemptions that the savings vanished. The Carter package originally was to save the equivalent of 3.3 million barrels of oil a day. Ways and Means exemptions reduced the savings to one million barrels a day. After the Ways and Means Committee had emasculated the program, Speaker Thomas O'Neill sent the bill to the Ad Hoc Energy Committee, a committee he had created specially to insure that Carter's program got through intact. The Ad Hoc Committee undid most of the Ways and Means damage. A decade earlier, perhaps even one Congress earlier, such harsh treatment of petroleum and of the Ways and Means Committee would have been unthinkable. Ways and Means was long the silent weapon of petroleum interests. Previous Speakers like Sam Rayburn and Carl Albert from oil-producing states had always been careful to select Ways and Means members sympathetic to oil and gas. For half a century, the industry benefited from the infamous depletion allowance. It still has generous tax write-offs for intangible drilling expenses.

Thus domestic oil policy proved just as fragmented as import policy when viewed in terms of the results. Indeed, it shared many of the features of importation. New onshore discoveries were declining sharply within the "Lower 48" (as the Alaskans call it). The emerging domestic sources were from Alaska or offshore, both of which presented problems much like importation. Furthermore, the environment frequently related to imported oil and foreign ships foundering and colliding in American waters.

Natural Gas displays less of a bifurcation between policy-as-doctrine and policy-as-result than imported or domestic oil, because the fuel is much more extensively regulated. Presidents Nixon and Ford both advocated deregulation, but while the effect was pricing closer to the market, it was still a regulated price.

The previous section discussed how the FPC's doctrine of a low price had the result of low supply as producers forewent opportunities to drill for gas that would then be profitable at $.52 per Mcf, or committed such supplies to the unregulated *intra*state market. Yet the FPC price ceiling was not the sole cause of declining supplies. Wildcatters were drilling fewer oil wells, since the most easily tapped supplies already were exploited. Until 1973, Middle Eastern oil was far cheaper than new domestic supplies. Shipping the oil from the Persian Gulf was easy, often easier than from Texas. Persian Gulf crude can be lifted and loaded for as little as $.20 a barrel. The tanker can then sail directly to the refinery. Gas from Middle Eastern wells cannot be transmitted so easily. As in Texas and Oklahoma before pipelines were feasible, the gas is flared off. Bright flames in the desert night testify to this waste. A small amount is liquified at --259°F and shipped in special cryogenic tankers. Such liquified natural gas (LNG) costs $5 per Mcf delivered to New York or Boston, compared to a little more than $1 (including transmission) for American gas.

The natural gas subterraneously trapped with the large oil reserves on the Alaska North Slope is not so remote from users as is the Middle Eastern gas. Competing pipeline companies offered three alternative routes. The Arctic Gas Company proposed the most direct one. Unlike the trans-Alaskan oil pipeline, it would run directly east from the North Slope fields to the Mackensie River in Canada, where it would pick up additional supplies from the newly discovered gas fields in that region. Then, it would continue south to Calgary, Alberta, from there would connect with existing pipelines to California and the Midwest. Two objections to the Arctic Gas Company route were that it makes transmission subject to Canadian interference and that it will run through the Arctic National Wildlife Range. The former seems exaggerated. The two countries have a treaty forbidding this. If Canada were to interrupt supplies, the United States could retaliate by cutting off the oil routes to eastern Canada that run through the United States. The Arctic Gas Company proposed to meet the latter objection by laying the pipeline during the winter, when the wildlife would have migrated south. Unlike the oil pipeline which has hot oil, the gas pipeline can be cold and will not damage the tundra. The rival Alcan Company proposed a similar pipeline that would follow a trans-Canadian route further south. The El Paso Company proposed a route parallel to that of the oil pipeline to Valdez, where the gas would be liquified. Cryogenic tankers would deliver the gas to the West Coast.

Normally, the FPC would license the preferred route under provisions of existing legislation. In this case, Congress feared that the decision was so important (i.e., lucrative) that any FPC decision would inevitably face a court challenge from the losing bidders. So Congress passed the Alaskan Natural Gas Transportation Act that provided for the President and Congress to ratify the FPC determination. This firm legislative authority would preclude the lengthy litigation so common with the Commission's decisions. After considering costs and environmental impact, the United States and Canada agreed to the route following the Alcan highway.

Neither Alaskan gas nor LNG offer much hope to consumers seeking a cheap fuel, nor to environmentalists seeking a clean one. LNG has sold for up to five times the price of Texas and Louisiana gas. Transmission costs alone for Alaskan gas will run between $1.50 and $2.50 in the northeast. This compares with $.65 to pipe gas from Texas.

Conservation is one solution proposed for the gas shortage. This would involve retro-fitting. Gas is an ideal fuel for home heating because it is clean, easily distributed, and efficient. But most houses built during the 1950s and 1960s were insufficiently insulated, and few homeowners are willing and able to lay out the money to insulate their houses. One solution is for the federal government to subsidize such capital investment with an income tax deduction. Another is for the local gas company to pay for the insulation, then collect payment with a higher gas bill over the next 10 to 30 years. Because state utility commissions typically base a company's rates on its capital investment or its sales, insulating customers' homes to reduce consumption would be contrary to the gas companies' self-interest, unless the value of the insulation could be included in the companies' investment base.

Proposals to conserve gas are often confused with proposals to allocate it more efficiently. The American Gas Association found that electric generation consumed 10 percent of the nation's gas. This would be enough to heat four million homes. Coal, oil, or uranium could substitute for this purpose. To burn gas as a boiler fuel is wasteful. Gas is also wasted when it is used to heat many large factories and office buildings, and for many industrial processes. Sometimes gas may be needed to prevent air pollution, and a few industries such as glass-making need a clean fuel, but a major proportion of the gas is not burned where it is most needed. State utility commissions bear the onus. Because they calculate profits as a percentage of investment, the companies have an incentive to increase volume. Before the early 1970s, when supplies were both cheap and easily available, gas companies gave discounts to large buyers even though there were no significant economics of scale. The gas companies justified the discounts by making service interruptible. The buyer could be cut off temporarily if supplies were scarce, but until the mid-1970s such interruptions were rare. The utilities did not want to alienate their biggest customers. Consequently, the interruptible customers did not bother to install alternate fuel systems to tide them over during an interruption. When the shortage did develop, these factories and offices were unprepared and had to shut down.

The FEA offered one answer when it ordered several thousand plants using natural gas as a boiler fuel to switch to coal. The EPA objected at once, saying that in many cases, this would cause pollution in excess of air quality standards. The businesses objected that the process was too costly. The result was that virtually none of the plants complied. For example, of all the electricity generating plants ordered to convert, only one did so. The most persuasive argument was that retro-fitting was too costly. The FEA backed down and concentrated on influencing new construction.

In the long term, deregulation would allocate gas efficiently. If gas were expensive, it would only be used where most needed: for home heating, to meet pollution standards, and for industrial processes requiring a clean fuel. President Carter surprised many New Deal-minded Democrats in his outspoken support for deregulation. Only Republicans were expected to advocate free market solutions so boldly. Three weeks after signing the Emergency Natural Gas Act authorizing him to allocate gas by fiat, the President said, "If I were running an oil company, I would reserve the right to release or reserve some supplies of natural gas. [12] Carter advocated deregulating natural gas prices experimentally for a period of five years. While philosophically supporting deregulation, the American Gas Association economic forecasts showed that five years of deregulation would not be long enough to return production even to the 1973 level. President Carter's FEA Administrator, John O'Leary, estimated that $5 per Mcf. would be the appropriate price to encourage enough drilling. Such a price would make LNG from the Middle East competitive. Were this to happen, the United States would find itself dependent on the same foreign countries for natural gas as for oil. America would be moving farther away from the occasionally remembered goal of Project Independence.

It would also be moving away from the nonmarket, administrative solutions that the federal government has favored since the New Deal. Though the Republicans are supposed to be the champions of the free enterprise system, the Eisenhower, Nixon, and Ford administrations have all used nonmarket mechanisms. Eisenhower established the oil import quota, Nixon organized the FEA, and Ford imposed import fees, to cite just a single energy example for each. For a Democratic President to deregulate natural gas when Republican Presidents have failed to do so would be ironic.

CONCLUSION

Comparing energy policy-as-doctrine to policy-as-result in three areas—oil imports, domestic oil, and natural gas—reveals the two sorts of policies to be very different. Indeed, doctrine and results often are opposite. The very name Project Independence implies America should be independent of imported oil. Rather than reducing dependence on unreliable OPEC sources, the United States has become more dependent. And virtually all of the increase in imported oil has come from the Persian Gulf states that proved willing to embargo the United States in retaliation for its support for Israel in 1973.

Domestic oil policy embodies similar contradictions. The Energy Policy and Conservation Act of 1975 promised two things: a unified policy and conservation. Merely reading the law shows that there is no unified policy set forth. The act enshrines the status quo. Its chief impetus and accomplishment was the extension of price controls on crude oil. The controls dated back to President Nixon's 1971 wage-price freeze and had gone through several incarnations. The 1975 law reshuffled the details but maintained regulation. The law's formula to set the price of crude kept it approximately at the same level while cynically giving a temporary reduction the consumer would enjoy until after the 1976 election. The law provided little more conservation than it did unified policy. In accepting roughly the current price of crude, the act also did nothing to discourage use or encourage new drilling. Title I did provide for a national reserve of crude, but a year and a half later, no oil had been pumped into the salt domes chosen as natural storage tanks. Title III did provide for automotive fuel economy standards.

The Emergency Natural Gas Act of 1977 had virtually no long-term impact. Its main success was in mollifying the cold public. The presidential allocation of supplies actually had been easily worked out by the gas transmission companies themselves. The law merely protected them from violating existing FPC regulation and clearly stated that their supplying additional gas would not be considered a precedent that would force them to do the same permanently. If emergency administrative allocation under the 1977 act was a sham, permanent FPC administrative allocation under the 1938 Natural Gas Act and pursuant to the 1954 *Phillips* case was a failure. The Commission's doctrine of keeping prices low resulted in limited supplies and maldistribution of those supplies. At the height of the 1977 cold spell, energy sages spoke gravely of the futility of having enough fuel for "a hundred-year winter," but meteorologists (acknowledging they had measured record-breaking cold temperatures) had data showing that it was not a hundred-year winter, but more like a ten- or twenty-year winter. If winters were to be that cold five or ten times a century, natural gas supplies were inadequate.

What are the reasons that policy-as-doctrine is so different from policy-as-result? The dichotomy seems to be more than the symbolism of which Murray Edelman writes. Or if it is symbol manipulation, it does not appear to be conscious. Congressional debate on the 1975 act indicated that the members sincerely felt that they were solving the nation's energy problems. If those who voted for passage were ill-informed and misguided, it was in spite of their colleagues on the floor who clearly pointed out the weaknesses and contradictions in the bill. When serious criticism failed to persuade, opponents ridiculed the bill labeling it "the Cold Homes and Dark Factories Act," "The Energy Dependence Act," and "The OPEC Relief Act."

Neither symbolism nor sincerity explains why policy-as-doctrine diverges from policy-as-result. Can it be ignorance? Are Presidents and Congressmen unable to see the implications of their handiwork? Why do the "unintended consequences" of government policies loom so large in hindsight? Political leaders are notorious for their present-mindedness. They focus on the immediate crisis and the next election. When viewed from the perspective of a President or Congressman, this present-mindedness proves quite rational. Project Independence lasted longer than the Arab oil embargo. (It even lasted longer than the Nixon Presidency.) The Energy Policy and Conservation Act provided both President Ford and the Democratic Congress something to brag about in the 1976 election, and it is conveniently due for renewal just prior to the 1980 election. The Emergency Natural Gas Act allocation authority expired on April 30. Coincidentally, it was then spring.

Clearly, policy-as-doctrine diverges from policy-as-result in the three cases considered here. Is this divergence characteristic of other cases within the energy area? Is it true outside the energy area?

There is little reason to believe other energy case studies would show less divergence between doctrine and results. Coal is a highly competitive industry, close to the economists' ideal free market with many buyers and sellers and easy entry and exit. The federal government role is slight. It has authority to regulate health and safety under the 1969 law. State regulation, however, is more extensive. The federal government's role in coal is greatest with respect to western reserves just beginning to be mined. The western coal is low in sulfur and easily strip mined. The government holds title to many of the coal fields because the land is entirely in the public domain, or because mineral rights were retained when the land was homesteaded. Environmentalists and some local residents oppose development. Congress twice passed and President Ford twice vetoed a surface mining bill that would have strictly regulated the extraction. Thus, with respect to coal, government has little policy-as-doctrine.

In contrast, the government has much doctrine with respect to nuclear energy. The Energy Reorganization Act of 1974 abolished the venerable Atomic Energy Commission (AEC). A stated goal was to avoid the overemphasis on nuclear power. Yet the AEC's successor, the Energy Research and Administration (ERDA) bears a suspicious resemblance to the old AEC. Eighty-five percent of its funds and personnel came from its predecessor agency.

The divergence between doctrine and result might not hold true for policy areas other than energy. Energy is essentially a problem of resource allocation. It is a zero-sum situation. Fuel burned by one cannot be burned by another. Oklahoma oil producers are inherently in conflict with New England consumers. Importers are in conflict with domestic producers. If homeowners install six-inch insulation and replace pilot lights with electric spark starters, gas company sales will decline. In spite of a high degree of government involvement, energy is basically an economic problem. This contrasts with issues such as defense, foreign policy, and air pollution where there is a shared public interest. These are not zero-sum situations. Providing anti-missile defense, negotiating treaties, and cleaning up the air provide benefits that must be shared. Energy cannot.

The divergence of policy-as-doctrine and policy-as-result is pathological. If the contradiction derives from ignorance, energy policy will be inferior to what it could be. While few Congressmen and Presidents are trained as economists, the resource allocation decisions that law-making demands of them are elementary. Staff analysis is readily available from their own committees and the bureaucracies. Indeed, Congressmen hear enough testimony and read enough analyses. It just does not influence them. Of course, more than information is involved. The Congressman's function of representation leads logically to a beggar-thy-neighbor policy. The dynamics of pleasing constituents places a premium on parochial goals. Just as with tariff politics prior to the 1930s, the aggregation of constituent demands yields a suboptimal result.

If the contradiction between policy-as-doctrine and as-result derives from deception, this too is pathological. Exponents of the American democratic system may dismiss this deception as incidental, even innocent—an inevitable by-product of political leadership. Politicians must over-promise and exaggerate in order to overcome the inertia of the bureaucrat, the businessman, the consumer, or the voter. The system fosters competition in deception. Thus, Congressmen pin hortatory titles on legislation and President Carter proposes to consolidate the FEA, ERDA, the FPC and 10 other bureaus into a new Department of Energy.

The pathology may yield to two remedies. One is the standard prescription of better information and planning. If the results are not those sought, it may be because the consequences were not adequately analyzed. Air pollution is just as much a product of an electric generating plant as kilowatts. Offshore drilling produces oil spills and injured workmen as well as crude oil. Analysis is becoming increasingly sophisticated. The FPC included the "negative salvage costs" of eventually removing the trans-Alaska pipeline when it calculated the tariff. The federal judge who halted drilling in the Baltimore Canyon did so because of failure to assess the environmental impact.

The other remedy for the divergence between doctrine and result is to proclaim less doctrine. If the United States does not have an energy policy, so what? It also does not have a national music policy or a clothing policy or a population policy. Indeed, the First Amendment expressly forbids it to have a religious policy. To the extent to which energy is a problem of internal resource allocation, the market offers the best resolution. This does not necessarily have to be a private market. Conceivably, it could be a shadow market run on a government computer, providing it is not a distorted market but one in which the price reflects the true costs including pollution, workmen's compensation, and so forth. Government does have some legitimate roles to play where there are common interests or where bargaining would be unequal. As common carriers, pipelines and electricity transmission lines should be supervised for access and when exercising eminent domain. Natural monopolies such as local gas and electricity distribution systems require supervision. Worker health, safety, and protection from coercion are legitimate governmental concerns. National security requires a government role. The military would be useless without gasoline and jet fuel; more generally the entire economy needs a cushion against an oil embargo. If the United States cannot find dependable foreign supplies (perhaps from Mexico's 60 billion barrels), the government should stockpile enough to deter or ameliorate a future embargo. With these peripheral conditions subject to government supervision and a market mechanism functioning, Americans could relax, boasting that "the United States doesn't have an energy policy."

NOTES

1. Gabriel A. Almond and G. Bingham Powell, *Comparative Politics* (Boston: Little, Brown, 1966): 73-127.

2. Charles O. Jones, *An Introduction to the Study of Public Policy,* 2nd ed. (Belmont, Cal.: Duxbury, 1977).

3. Murray Edelman, *The Symbolic Uses of Politics* (Urbana, Ill.: 1964): 152-171.

4. David B. Truman, *The Governmental Process* (New York: Knopf, 1951).

5. Robert A. Dahl, *Who Governs* (New Haven, Conn.: Yale, 1961); Robert Engler, *The Politics of Oil* (New York: Macmillan, 1961).

6. David Howard Davis, *Energy Politics* (New York: St. Martin's Press, 1974); Don Kash et al., *Our Energy Future* (Norman: University of Oklahoma Press, 1976): 39-47.

7. National Academy of Sciences, Committee on Nuclear and Alternative Energy Sources, Decision Making Resource Group, *Energy Conservation,* [Roger W. Sant] (October, 1976): 36, 37.

8. Cynthia H. Enloe, "Iran," chapter 9 in Donald Kelley (ed.) *The Energy Crisis and the Environment* (New York: Praeger, 1977).

9. M.A. Adelman, "The Hinge of Energy Policy" in Gary Eppen (ed.), *Energy: The Policy Issues* (Chicago: Chicago, 1975); Christopher D. Stone and Jack McNamara, "How to Take on OPEC," *New York Times Magazine* (December 12, 1976): 38. Richard Nolte, "The Saudi Connection and the Arab Boycott," *New York Times* (February 18, 1977).

11. Mary Clay Berry, *The Alaskan Pipeline* (Bloomington: Indiana, 1975).

12. *New York Times* (February 24, 1977).

Part II

THE QUALITY OF LIFE

DO NATIONAL POLICIES ACCOMPLISH MORE THAN PIOUS HOPES AND FALSE EXPECTATIONS?

6.

ENVIRONMENTAL POLICY: FROM INNOVATION TO IMPLEMENTATION

HELEN M. INGRAM

Resources for the Future, Washington, D.C.

DEAN E. MANN

University of California, Santa Barbara

Environmental policy has moved from an era of commitment to environmental quality goals to a period of searching for efficient, economical, and politically feasible techniques and mechanisms for protecting the environment. In the early 1970s, far-reaching pollution control legislation swept through Congress on the wave of public recognition of environmental degradation and public belief that the government had not done nearly enough to halt pollution. As the decade has progressed, the economic and social costs, the trade-offs for a clean environment, and the immense governmental task of administering ambitious legislation have become increasingly salient. Neither the public nor governmental officials appear willing to renege on the commitment to clean air, less noise, clean and safe water, more livable cities, and so forth. However, energy shortages, economic dislocation, and administrative conflicts have led to questions about whether too much is being attempted too fast and in ineffective ways.[1]

As Anthony Downs pointed out, the period of euphoria over cleaning up pollution has been replaced by a growing awareness of costs.[2] Kneese and Schultze estimate that air and water programs together may cost some $375 billion in the 1972-1985 period, and possibly half again as much if nonpoint sources of water pollution and storm water discharges are included.[3] Whether or not these costs exceed the value of the benefits is difficult to evaluate, since many benefits are unquantifiable. Even so, such colossal amounts are sobering and reasonably raise questions of efficient expenditure. What is a small incremental improvement of air and water quality really worth? The tough rhetoric of the early pollution policy was "clean up or shut down." Closing the American automobile industry, for instance, is economically, socially, and politically unacceptable, considering that one job in seven in the United States is dependent, directly or indirectly, on the manufacture, sale, and service of automobiles. Experience has shown that when the costs of shutting down polluters are very great, threats are empty; and government must ultimately back away from "either-or" encounters. The distribution of the costs of pollution control has also become controversial. Public acceptance of and compliance with regulations depends partly on public perceptions of the fairness of those regulations.

The administrative burden imposed by pollution legislation has been extremely heavy. The Environmental Protection Agency (EPA) has been the focus of both the high expectations fostered by ambitious and explicit environmental laws and the bitter opposition of the interests brought under regulation by these laws. As the product of reorganization, EPA is a composite of the organizational units publicly judged inadequate in the late 1960s. While EPA's public works projects received greatly augmented funds in the early 1970s, the new regulatory programs of EPA are not given sufficient resources to allow the agency to transcend its bureaucratic heritage.[4] Pollution legislation has also placed a large obligation upon state and local governments which they have often had neither the resources nor the commitment to fulfill. EPA has had a rocky relationship with its counterparts at other levels of government.

The intent of this essay is to describe and analyze public policy in three specific environmental programs: air pollution, water quality, and land use planning. The first two programs were bold Congressional initiatives and were mainly the progeny of Senator Edmund Muskie's Senate Public Works Subcommittee on Air and Water Pollution. Land use planning was fathered by Senator Henry Jackson in the Senate Committee on Interior and Insular Affairs, but such planning never managed to pass the House. While not embodied in a comprehensive national law, land use planning is a current federal government concern, and many state and local governments have passed legislation promoting such policy. A review of all three programs will serve to illustrate the emphasis upon adequate means of implementation in current environmental policy.

AIR POLLUTION POLICY

The Clean Air Act Amendments of 1970 promised air clean enough to protect the public health by July, 1975 and still cleaner air by July, 1977. But both deadlines have passed, and the millennium in air quality has not yet arrived. The 1976 annual report of the Council on Environmental Quality (CEQ) indicates that modest progress in cleaning up the air has been achieved in some areas of the country. At the same time, the CEQ speaks in terms of the early 1980s before most regions will meet the primary health standard for some major pollutants and admits that there are both troublesome types of pollutants and areas with difficult problems which cannot be controlled even in that time span.[5] Furthermore, the current rate of improvements, while limited, has entailed extraordinary organizational, legal, and political problems. The present focus of activity in air pollution policy is upon the torturous process of implementing the Clean Air Act (CAA) and amending federal law where implementation has raised particularly thorny problems.

Policy Escalation and the Clean Air Act Amendments of 1970

The clean air program has been plagued by exceedingly problematic implementation for a variety of reasons including, importantly, very large changes from practices common in the past at which the 1970 legislation was aimed. The ambitious goals of the act, which exceeded what was known to be technically achievable; the stringent regulations which set stiff penalties and specific deadlines; and the extent of federal dominance over states and localities in setting standards went far beyond anything which might have been projected from the evolution of past policy. Table 6.1 displays the major provisions, techniques, and organizational arrangements embodied in federal air pollution legislation from 1955 to the present. The table indicates a gradual shift of responsibility from local and state to the federal level and a trend away from simple subsidies to more coercive regulatory techniques.

However, until 1967, the federal pollution program had mainly offered subsidy "carrots" rather than regulation "sticks" to coax polluters to clean up. Authority and responsibility over such clean-up efforts were left on the state and local level. Ironically, in terms of subsequent problems of implementation, it was frustration with the pace of the actual clean-up progress, along with growing public awareness of the environmental problem, which prompted the policy change in the Clean Air Act.[6] Federal legislation in 1967 required states to set standards and to formulate implementation plans. States acted slowly and ineffectively. Between 1967 and December, 1970, only 21 state implementation plans had been submitted; and none had been approved by 1970.[7] Congres-

Table 6.1. Escalation of Air Pollution Policy, 1955–1970.
Modification of Air Pollution Policy, 1970 –

Legislation	Major Provisions	Main Techniques	Distribution of Administrative Authority
Air Pollution Control Act of 1955	Research funding for 5 years, $5 million per year.	Research grants (Subsidy).	Federal research leading to exercise of state and local authority.
1959 of the Air Pollution Act	Research grants continued for 4 years, $5 million per year.	Research grants (Subsidy).	Federal research state and local authority.
Motor Vehicle Exhaust Study Act of 1960	Additional federal research, concentrated on vehicle emissions.	Continuation of research. Standards setting considered and rejected.	Federal research state and local authority.
Clean Air Act of 1963	Grants to state and local control programs. Extension of research to publication of "criteria" documents. Conference procedure for abatement.	Research grants. Institution building grants (Subsidy). Remote possibility of regulation.	Gentle federal prodding towards state and local action.
Motor Vehicle Air Pollution Control Act of 1965	Accelerated federal research and demonstration. Secretary of HEW given authority to set standards.	Research grants (Subsidy). Regulation of auto emissions.	First federal regulatory program—restricted to auto emissions HEW secretary given flexibility States retain most authority.
National Emissions Standards Act of 1967	Large increase in research funds ($185 million for 1969). HEW secretary required to set air quality control regions, issue criteria, and recommend techniques. States required to set standards.	Research grants (Subsidy). Standards required (Regulation).	Federal government requires states to establish state, local, and regional air pollution program.

Table 6.1. Escalation of Air Pollution Policy, 1955–1970. Modification of Air Pollution Policy, 1970 –

Legislation	Major Provisions	Main Techniques	Distribution of Administrative Authority
1969 Amendments	Extension of research provisions.	No new provisions.	No new arrangements. Frustration expressed at pace of progress.
1970 Clean Air Act Amendments	Continued federal research, but "technology-forcing" provisions. Grants to states. National emissions standards. Specific timetables and deadlines.	Research and institutional grants (Subsidy). Mandatory national standards (Regulation).	Federal government makes most decisions. States and localities have a role in implementation.
1974 Energy Supply and Coordination Act	Allowed EPA to waive. Auto emission limits. Extends auto deadlines. Exempted Air Act from NEPA	Delays regulation	No new arrangements
1976-77 Amendments Proposed to CAA	Proposes extensions of auto emissions deadlines. Raises NOX standard. Classifies deterioration allowed in clean air areas. Charges and penalties for delayed compliance	Provides for more flexibility. Delays regulation.	Larger role for states in determining standards for Clean Air Areas. More flexibility in EPA enforcement.

Sources: John E. Bonine, "The Evolution of 'Technology-Forcing' in the Clean Air Act," *Environment Reporter* 6 (July 25, 1975): 1-29. Charles O. Jones, "Speculative Augmentation in Federal Air Pollution Policy-Making," Journal of Politics 36 (1974): 438-464. J. Clarence Davies III and Barbara Davies, *Politics of Pollution* (2nd ed., 1976): 46.

sional policy makers felt further thwarted by what they believed to be recalcitrance and bad faith on the part of the automobile industry in ignoring and suppressing development of pollution technology unless forced to do so.[8]

The 1970 Clean Air Amendments, embodying complex and comprehensive provisions, were a sharp departure from past policy, both in terms of goals and in the mechanisms chosen for implementation. With the passage of the 1970 legislation, the pragmatic, functional definition of air quality, restricted to what was economically and technologically feasible, was abandoned, and clean air was legislated as a national value.[9] The Senate Committee Report on the legislation determined "the health of the people is more important than the question of whether the early achievement of ambient air quality standards protective of health is technically feasible". . . .[10] The means for accomplishing this goal have been characterized by legal authorities as "draconian."[11] The act required the EPA to set specific standards for various types of pollutants. These standards were to be achieved through techniques specified in implementation plans formulated by states and approved by the EPA. Tight deadlines were set for the achievement of primary and secondary standards of ambient air quality. The act also directed the EPA to set "new source performance standards" which limit the emission of pollutants from new industrial plants to an amount no greater than that attainable by "the best adequately demonstrated control technology." Specific emission standards were established for hydrocarbons and carbon monoxide for new model cars in 1975, and an additional standard for oxides of nitrogen was to be met in 1976. The act, in effect, called for a 97 percent reduction compared with uncontrolled conditions. An enormous $10,000 fine per vehicle was established for violations.[12]

Vagaries of Implementation

Among the numerous problems encountered in administering the Clean Air Act Amendments was the energy crisis—its impact could hardly have been anticipated by its Congressional authors. The first legislative modification of the act, The Energy Supply and Environmental Coordination Act, was passed on June 22, 1974 to encourage the burning of domestic coal rather than imported oil in stationary pollution sources such as power plants. While the energy supply legislation restated the commitment to clean air, the use of coal greatly complicates pollution control. EPA has insisted upon stack scrubbing devices to remove coal ash, sulphur oxide, and other emissions. The costs of such environmental controls contribute to increasing energy costs. Further, electrical utilities have argued that scrubbers are unreliable technology. The energy crisis has also brought new problems to the control of auto emissions. Auto manufacturers maintain that pollution controls introduce fuel penalties which the nation cannot afford in a time of petroleum shortage; hence, they argue, emission targets should be deferred. The failure of technology has also hampered the implementation of the Clean Air Act. Particularly in automobiles, pollution control presents an enormous technical puzzle. Since there are more than 130 million cars, trucks, buses, and motorcycles on American roads, with about 100 million separate owners, as contrasted with only a few thousand serious stationary sources of pollution, the authors of the Clean Air Act chose to place a heavy burden for achieving primary standards by 1977 upon the automobile.[13] The initial thrust of the act was on reducing by 90 percent the emissions from 1970 cars, which was clearly beyond the technical capability of the automobile industry at the time. The legislation was specifically intended to quicken the pace of the industry's emissions research. Should the standards set for 1975 prove to be technologically infeasable to achieve, the act allowed the administrator of the EPA to grant one year delay. Administrator Ruckleshaus resorted to a one year extension of the target date, after his initial denial of extension was overruled by the court because the issue of technical feasibility had not been sufficiently considered. In June 1974, Congress legislated an additional one year delay to save energy as a part of the Energy Supply and Environmental Coordination Act. The belief was that pollution control technology imposed fuel penalties in the performance of new cars. Technology became an issue again in 1975 when the Administrator of EPA granted yet another extension because of fears that the catalytic converter devices that were being used to meet the interim standards might be generating serious sulphur oxide emissions. Some commentators argue that, rather than forcing technology, the CAA has actually caused automobile companies to concentrate on the "quick-fix" of catalytic converters (which, among other problems, are difficult to maintain) rather than on more advanced automotive designs and alternatives to the internal combustion engine.[14]

The failure of the CAA to clean up new car emissions by 1977 has shifted the burden for meeting ambient air quality standards to the existing automotive fleet and stationary sources. There is some question as to whether the average motorist puts sufficient maintenance into even new cars to keep pollution devices working. Older cars get less frequent tune-ups and are dirtier than they need to be. Emissions testing for older cars could accomplish much to clean up the air in areas with heavy traffic. However, car inspections inconvenience many motorists, and states have moved slowly to make them a requirement.[15]

The technical difficulties encountered in administering the act with regard to stationary sources are nearly as nettlesome as those with automobiles. Under the act, the EPA was to set new-source performance standards. The substantive standards chosen, as well as the decision-making procedures used by the EPA, have been subject to controversy. In the case of electric power plants, one issue is what constitutes adequately demonstrated control technology. While the EPA has favored scrubbers, the industry contends that the equipment is unreliable and expensive. Utilities prefer tall stacks, which dilute pollutants before they reach the ground, and intermittent and supplementary controls such as production cut backs or switching to cleaner fuels, according to prevailing weather and pollution conditions.

An enormous amount of litigation concerning the implementation of the 1970 act has occurred, but whether or not court rulings have been a help or a hindrance is a source of disagreement among legal scholars.[16] Congress left implementors and the courts with a tremendous interpretive burden. The act is peppered with vague phrases, the meaning of which must be inferred from inconclusive legislative histories. While the act set a three-year deadline for achieving ambient air quality, it has taken more than five years simply to resolve in the courts the EPA's responsibility to weigh the economic, technological, and social feasibility of the measures polluters must take to meet standards. Among the plethora of litigation, one case particularly highlights the importance of the courts' role in implementation. In Sierra Club v. Ruckelshaus, (1972) the D.C. District Court ruled that the Administrator had violated the Clean Air Act by requiring states to do no more than to prevent ambient pollution levels from exceeding secondary standards, and thus, in effect, permitting the degradation of air quality in areas where the air is more pristine than required by secondary standards.[17] The court relied on statements in the 1967 and 1970 acts, which stated that Congress's purpose was to protect and enhance the quality of the nation's air resources.[18] Further, the court traced adminstrative history, which indicated previous agency interpretation of "significant deterioration" as contrary to the act.[19] The courts opinion had far-reaching implications for future industrial, commercial, and residential development throughout the United States. Mineral and coal development in the West was likely to be particulary affected.

The decision initiated a review and policy modification process by the EPA. The EPA administrator first proposed four alternative plans for protecting the air in clean air areas and invited a wide range of public comments. Thirteen months later, the agency proposed a specific detailed plan which became the final plan in five additional months. In August, 1976, the District of Columbia Circuit Court upheld these regulations in Sierra Club v. EPA.[20] The policy controversy is not yet at an end, however, and significant deterioration became an important issue in the proposed 1976 amendments. Ultimately, this resulted in deadlocking the Senate.

Complexities of intergovernmental relations have also bedeviled the implementation of federal air pollution statutes. Until 1970, states and localities had the primary responsibility for setting standards. The 1970 legislation gave the EPA much of the standard setting responsibility and left states with the often onerous task of implementing rules for which there were neither adequate administrative resources nor political support. State formulation and EPA review of state implementation plans (SIP) has been fraught with problems. Even after EPA and an individual state came to an agreement about the contents of the SIP there remained problems of enforcement. Effective sanctions against polluters require court actions and the cooperation of the state attorney general, who is often an elected state official responsible to a state constituency. Consequently, enforcement under the Clean Air Act has varied from state to state, according to the balance of political power and public opinion.[21]

The most controversial problem of intergovernmental relations in controlling air pollution has been in the area of urban transportation. In 36 cities where primary standards could not be met by controlling stationary and automotive emissions, the EPA insisted that the SIP incorporate a variety of incentives to reduce traffic, including parking restrictions, systematized car pooling, increased bridge and tunnel tolls, bus lanes, and so on. The history of transportation control plans has been one of foot-dragging, protests, litigation, and general nonaccomplishment, all culminating in lawsuits challenging the EPA's authority to dictate to the states. Finally, in 1977, the agency said it was largely abandoning mandatory measures because of local resistance and would seek voluntary cooperation instead.[22]

Amending the Clean Air Act

While no such action has occurred by this writing, amendments to the Clean Air Act are certain to happen during the 94th Congress. Congress adjourned without final action on the 1976 amendments because of the objections of some western Senators to nondegradation provisions. Further delay is unlikely. The auto industry has proceeded with plans to produce 1978 autos to comply with 1977 standards, and it is unlikely that Congress will allow the EPA and the courts to deal with the problem of massive noncompliance, without itself participating in the reformulation of policy. Besides extending the deadlines and relaxing the standards for auto emissions, Congress must resolve the issue of nondegradation. The amendments proposed in 1976 were very similar to the classification system proposed by the EPA and upheld in EPA v. Sierra Club. Further, the Congress will consider provisions for allowing the construction of new pollution sources in areas which have not yet met primary standards, provided it can be shown that such areas have made substantial progress in improving air quality. Many other issues which have evolved during the implementation process are also before the Congress for policy adjustments.

The legislative setting of air pollution policy has changed substantially since 1970. The Senate Subcommittee on Air and Water Pollution, headed by Senator Edmund Muskie, eclipsed the House in influencing landmark legislation in that year. In recent years Representative Paul G. Rogers of Florida, Chairman of the Environmental Health Subcommittee of the House Interstate and Foreign Commerce Committee, has grown into a leadership role parallel to that of Senator Muskie. Without the same pride of authorship which Senator Muskie and his staff continue to have in the 1970 legislation, Congressman Rogers has been more open to considering modifications of air policy.[23] The Carter Administration, committed to environmental policy and energy conservation, increasingly is likely to challenge the Congressional hegemony which has thus far existed in fashioning air policy.

Many economists and physical scientists believe that the difficulties encountered in implementing the Clean Air Act justify a completely different approach to air pollution control. For instance, Kneese and Schultze suggest a system of effluent charges which will result in reduced pollution but leave the basic decisions of how and when to abate to the polluter.[24] However, there has been such an enormous political and organizational investment in the regulatory approach that legislators are likely to be more open to suggestions for improving the existing machinery rather than for totally revamping it. In particular, Congress might welcome an alternative to the "all or nothing" impact of such standards, under which polluters must comply or shut down. One such suggestion has emerged from the Connecticut pollution agency where EPA Administrator Douglas Costle once served. Under the Connecticut plan, polluters who fail to reach emission standards by deadlines are subject to civil assessments exactly equal to the amount of money the firm is saving by not being in compliance. These polluters have a financial incentive to comply, and policy makers need not be responsible for loss of jobs by plant closures.[25] Whether or not the Connecticut scheme is adopted, it seems likely that more finely tuned administrative controls which promise more efficient and less conflict-ridden implementation will find favor in Congress.

THE NATION'S WATER QUALITY PROGRAM

In 1972, the nation charted a new course for its program to clean up its polluted waterways. A "politically potent but intrinsically uneasy marriage between environmental idealsim and pork barrel practicality," supported both by environmentalists and public officials representing the cities and states facing the high costs of sewage abatement, overcame the resistance of the Nixon Administration by passing the Federal Water Pollution Control Act Amendments[26] over a Presidential veto.[27] Its passage reflected rather general dissatisfaction with the water quality enhancement programs of the previous two decades. That experience had demonstrated a number of important lessons: the complexity of the problem and its resistance to simple solutions, the difficulty of setting standards and gaining compliance, and the problems of achieving goals by spending money without other necessary incentives. That experience however, was not necessarily reflected in the new program on which the nation embarked. Table 6.2 displays the major provisions, techniques, and organizational arrangements embodied in federal water pollution legislation from 1948 to the present.

Philosophy of the Act

The new departure in the federal water quality program lay in the adoption of the principle of effluent limitations and the requirement for permits for all those who discharge waste into streams. The ultimate goal, as stated in the legislation, was essentially "no discharge" by the year 1985, but an interim goal for 1983 was "water quality which provides for the protection and propagation of fish, shellfish, and wildlife and provides for recreation in and on the water. . . ." The law called for the achievement by July 1, 1977, of effluent limitations on nonpublic point sources of pollution (chiefly industrial sources) requiring the application of the best practicable control technology (BPT) and effluent limitations of publicly owned waste treatment works based on secondary treatment. By July, 1983, it would be expected that effluent limitations on nonpublic point sources would be based on requirements for application of the "best available technology" (BAT) that was both economically reasonable and contributory to progress toward the no-discharge goal. Similarly, public waste treatment plants would be based on evaluation of alternative means of achieving the "best practicable waste treatment technology over the life of the works. . . ."[28]

The new law adopted effluent limitations as the basic technique of water quality improvement. While it retained water quality as a guide on writing effluent limitations, the law rejected water as the principal guide in pollution control. Those who defended the receiving-water approach argued that water had varying qualities for assimilating waste and that this approach allowed pollution control to be achieved in relationship to the highest use to which the waters would be put. If society could not use water for its chosen purposes, the water was polluted and should be cleaned up. Otherwise, it was not polluted. As expressed by the National Water Commission:[29]

Table 6.2. Major Federal Water Pollution Control Legislation 1948–1972

Legislation	Major Provisions	Main Techniques	Distribution of Administrative Authority
Water Pollution Control Act of 1948	Research and Development	Loans for treatment plants. (Research and subsidy)	Temporary authority to Public Health Service (PHS). Major responsibility in states.
Water Pollution Control Act Amendments of 1956	Grants for treatment plant construction, $50,000,000 annual authorization.	Conference—hearing court action process for interstate waters. Grants (publicity and subsidy)	Permanent authority to PHS Major responsibility in states.
Federal Water Pollution Control Act of 1961	Grants authorization of $80,000,000 in 1962. $90,000,000 in 1963. $100,000,000 annually 1964-1967.	Grants, field labs authorized (research and subsidy).	Federal jurisdiction extended to navigable waters.
Water Quality Act of 1965	Authorization of $150,000,000 in 1966 and 1967.	Federal-state standard setting. Streamlined enforcement. (possibility of regulation)	Authorization for states to set ambient water quality.
Clean Waters Restoration Act of 1966	Authorization of $450,000,000 in 1968. $700,000,000 in 1969. $1,000,000,000 in 1970. $1,250,000,000 in 1971.	Larger federal grants and larger federal share. Quality standards for waters receiving sewage treatment plant discharges. (regulation and subsidy)	Responsibility for Oil Pollution Act transferred to Secretary of Interior. Federal government to initiate court cases after 180 days notice.
Water Quality Improvement Act of 1970	Polluters to take absolute liability for oil spills	Regulation of oil spills. (regulation)	Responsibility transferred to the Environmental Protection Agency (EPA).

Table 6.2. Major Federal Water Pollution Control Legislation 1948–1972

Legislation	Major Provisions	Main Techniques	Distribution of Administrative Authority
Water Pollution Control Act Amendments of 1972.	National goal of eliminating water pollution. Federal effluent standards. Federal-State permit system. Additional grants for waste treatment up to $7,000,000,000 in 1975.	Federal standards. Deadlines for "best practicable" and "best available" technology. (regulation)	Federal government sets standards and enforces them. States may recover implementation responsibility.

Sources: J. Clarence Davies III and Barbara Davies, *Politics of Pollution,* 2nd edition, p. 30, (1976): 40. Lettie McSpadden Wenner, *One Environment Under Law* (Pacific Palisades, Calif.: Goodyear Publishing, 1976): 74.

a reduction in waste disposal beyond that necessary to protect existing or anticipated future uses of receiving water would create costs unrelated to any social benefit and would result in needless expenditures and waste of other resources such as air,land,minerals, and energy. Absolutely pure water simply is not necessary for many uses, and these include uses such as recreation and fish propagation. Adoption of a no discharge policy thus amounts to the imputation of an extravagant social value to an abstract concept of water purity; a value the Commission is convinced the American people would not endorse if the associated costs and effect on other resources were fully appreciated and the policy alternatives clearly understood.

The new law, however, was an expression of impatience with the rate at which the waters were, in fact, being cleaned up and doubt about the possibility of enforcing a law that was based on the proposition that one could relate the quality of water in a given segment of a stream to a precise effluent source. Under previous legislation, the "enforcement conference" was the basic instrument of enforcement.Such conferences involved lengthy and prolonged hearings, negotiations, recommendations, preferred plans, sometimes more but usually less compliance, and, ultimately, the possibility of an injuction. Most watercourses were not subjected to proceedings; few conferences ever closed; few formal hearings were held; and only one enforcement aciton was initiated. The federal agencies were, moreover, utterly dependent on information provided by the polluter. Various observers had concluded that the allegation that a given polluter had caused a given deterioration in stream water quality was legally unenforceable. As a result, polluters were less than likely to succumb to the demands of the enforcement agency. Only with the brief revival of the 1899 Refuse Act, which requires permits for dumping into navigable streams, and a procedure that allowed the EPA to short-cut the conference approach did enforcement activity increase just prior to the adoption of the 1972 act.

Effluent Guidelines and the Permit System

Rather than rely on the relationship between stream quality and the effluents of given polluters, the new Act required the EPA to establish effluent guidelines which, in turn, provided the basis for specific permits for industries discharging waste into streams. These guidelines established nationally applicable effluent water treatment programs for achieving BPT and BAT, the 1977 and 1983 goals.[30] The EPA divided industrial groups into various categories and promulgated guidelines for each category and subcategory as deemed appropriate. As of 1976, 76 major industrial categories with 492 subcategories had been established. For each industry, the guidelines spelled out the specific factors to be taken into account in determining the control measures and practices to be applicable to point sources in that category or class. The categories and subcategories may reflect age and plant size, manufacturing process, raw material used, or other factors that may require discrete effluent limitations.

These guidelines constituted the basis for permits required for every municipal and industrial polluter under the National Pollutant Discharges Elimination System (NPDES). These permits established effluent limitations for each polluter, or, in the event that the polluter was unable to comply, established a compliance schedule for installation of the necessary pollution control plant and equipment for achieving both BPT and BAT. The job was staggering. As of January 1, 1976, 45,865 permits had been issued by all jurisdictions out of a total of over 62,000 identified dischargers.[31] And lying ahead, the EPA estimates, are an additional 50,000 to 100,000 dischargers such as feedlot and stormwater sewers and largely nonpoint sources such as irrigation return flows that ultimately must receive permits also. (The Government Accounting Office placed the figures at 1.8 million feedlot owners, 100,000 agricultural and silvicultural activities.)

The effluent guideline and permit writing process is itself extremely complex and subject to challenge. As the staff of the National Commission on Water Quality expressed it:

As effluent limitations do not, and can not, cover every possible situation, permits frequently reflect a composite— produced from the best information available to a particular permit writer including (in addition to interim guidance documents and interim and final effluent limitations) "best professional judgment" based on past training and experience and knowledge of research and technical studies.

The application of a single number criterion to complex and variegated industrial processes appears unrealistic and requires flexibility in the design of the permits. It is clear that the application of the same standards to all plants in a single category could wreak economic havoc on a given area. Thus, EPA allowed substantially lower abatement requirements for the steel plants in Mahoning River Basin in Ohio than for steel plants elsewhere because of the potential economic and employment disruptions.[33]

As the job of composing effluent guidelines and issuing permits is completed, the burden of the program must rest more decidedly on the areas of monitoring, compliance, and enforcement. The record thus far is inadequate to make a judgment. Permits have been in existence for only a brief period of time, and there is little evidence regarding the extent to which compliance schedules are being met. Both federal and state officials appear to agree that there will be much bargaining, negotiation, and compromise.

Legal Challenges

It is certain, however, that this legislation has been and will be litigated extensively. A considerable part of the delay in the pollution abatement program has been the number of administrative and legal challenges to the guidelines and permits. By the time of the issuance of the 1975 Council on Environmental Quality (CEQ) annual report, there had been 150 lawsuits filed, mostly by industry, challenging the guidelines for industrial categorizing specifically called for in the act.[34] Requests for administrative hearings were pending for more than one-tenth of the major industrial permits issued by the EPA as of March 31, 1976.

Environmentalists attacked the EPA failure to issue guidelines in timely fashion in accordance with the law. In response, the court established its own timetable for EPA compliance.[35] The EPA had endeavored to reduce its impossible burden of issuing permits for every point source by exempting certain small point dischargers, but this tactic failed under legal challenge from the NRDC.[36]

Industrial challenges have concentrated on the industrial effluent guidelines. The principal argument has been that the EPA did not have the authority to issue such guidelines except as part of the permitting process. Industry has also argued (1) that the EPA must further justify its categorization of industrial processes, (2) that guidelines should provide ranges of effluent reductions, not single numbers, (3) that variances should be permitted more broadly, (4) that the EPA's use of exemplary plants as guides for effluent reduction for 1977 and 1983 was unreasonable, (5) that the EPA has not adequately considered economic, energy, and environmental costs, and (6) that the law potentially creates a massive new criminal code. Most of these issues are still being litigated, but the EPA won a major vicory in early 1977 in E.I. DuPont de Nemours and Company, et al., v. Train.[37] DuPont, representing eight chemical companies, challenged the authority of EPA to issue or to approve of 42,000 permits well before the 1977 deadline, a position the Court felt Congress would not have taken.[38]

The Rules of the States

P.L. 92-500 mandated an important role for the states in implementation of the pollution abatement program. The EPA administrator is empowered to certify states to carry out the provisions of the Act—issuance of permits, monitoring, and enforcing compliance—if the states develop adequate program authority and support. As of November 1, 1975, permit-granting authority had been granted to 26 states, and it was considered possible that as many as 39 states might seek certification. The picture is less clear, however, because many state pollution control agencies perform much of the permit-drafting inspection and planning work without having formal authority to issue and to enforce permits.

The Construction Grant Program

The pork-barrel side of the 1972 act was the authorization of $18 billion for three years for the construction of municipal sewage treatment plants. The federal government would pay 75 percent of the total cost of each plant. The distribution formula was designed to ensure that money would be distributed to each and every Congressional district.

Unfortunately, the sewage treatment plant construction program failed to move ahead at the pace necessary to meet the 1977 goal of secondary treatment. The reasons for the tardiness were manifold: the difficulty of devising guidelines, the consequent delay in their issuance, and the multiple revisions. The three-step process involving facility planning, plans and specifications, and construction stretched out the process so that the entire sequence required from 2½ to 8½ years.[39] President Nixon impounded $9 billion of the $18 billion until this action was struck down by the Supreme Court as beyond his Presidential reach.[40] Given the uncertainties involved,municipalities were slow to gear up for the new procedures, and those that had formulated plans on the basis of the previous law had to revise their plans to conform to the new requirements. Some municipalities had difficulty in financing their share of the costs. Finally, the sheer number of grant applications and the inadequate staff to handle them meant that for nearly 19 months virtually nothing happened at all. Inflation also took its toll. It was estimated that the impoundment of $9 billion during the 1973-1975 period resulted in a decline of the buying value of those funds by $1.7 billion, thus substantially reducing the number of plants that could be built with those funds.[41]

The result was that by 1977 only $7.3 billion had actually been spent, $12 billion were committed to EPA-approved projects, but nearly all of it was obligated. It was predicted, because of this record, that by 1977, more than one-half of all municipal dischargers would fail to meet the deadline for having secondary treatment which was designed to mitigate 85 percent of the existing pollution. Ironically, without further authorizations, many states that had proceeded rapidly with their construction programs would be completely out of money by July, 1977.

The amount of money required to complete the sewage treatment program is highly debatable subject. One thing is certain: a great deal more money will be required. The National Water Commission estimated that the achievement of "Best Known Technology" in 1983 would require the expenditure of $352 billion in 1972 dollars.[42] Utilizing a "needs" survey conducted in1974, the EPA estimated a total cost of $342 billion.[43] The validity of such estimates is somewhat questionable, and the estimates very much depend on what kinds of treatment facilities are constructed. By far the largest component of these figures is for treatment and/or control of stormwaters, for which there is little agreement as to acceptable solutions. But estimates of these magnitudes do raise questions regarding priorities and the relative size of federal shares. Which categories of treatment and construction should receive priority? Should the federal share remain the same for every category? And should funding in some categories be provided for all states before funding is made available to some states in other categories? Given "needs" of these magnitudes, the Staff Report of the National Commission on Water Quality asked appropriately: "To what extent did the 92nd Congress commit the Nation to a long-term continuing municipal grant-in-aid program?"[44]

Planning

The act includes several planning provisions, one of which has potential impact on land-use planning thoughout the United States. Section 106 requires an annual state water quality program plan with specific objectives and a statement of resources to be applied toward their achievement; section 201 constitutes step one in the construction program for waste-treatment facilities; and section 303 requires continuous state planning, usually on a basin-wide basis, and incorporates water quality standards and priorities for their achievement in each basin. Ideally, these plans set priorities for construction grants and guide the issuance of permits on the basis of the classification of stream segments. In practice, with about one-third completed by 1976, they have "ranged from poor (purely descriptive, nonprogram oriented) to very good, program-directed studies."[45]

Section 208 is the act's most powerful planning tool, but its significance has yet to be tested. Its potential impact lies in its possibilities as an instrument of land-use planning. The planning is area-wide and is designed to provide the following outputs:

(1)   treatment works necessary to meet anticipated needs for 20 years;
(2)   construction priorities and schedules for such treatment works;
(3)   a regulatory program to control point and nonpoint sources, *to control the location, modification, and construction of any facilities within the area;* assure pretreatment requirements for industrial waste dischargers; [emphasis added]
(4)   measures to execute the plan: financing, time required, costs, and economic and environmental impacts;
(5)   a process to identify agriculturally, silviculturally, mine-, and construction-related nonpoint sources of pollution and means (including land-use requirements) to control such sources.

In other words, a 208 plan should provide for implementation of a water-quality improvement program for a given region.

The planning implications are clear. Development in an area must be consistent with the capacity of receiving waters to assimilate waste without disturbing community and environmental values. Such limitations might alter local zoning and subdivisions regulations. Because of this potential impact, the possibilities of political strife are apparent.

Planning under Section 208 is important for another very important reason: it is the principal means by which the pollution control program can get at nonpoint sources of pollution: agricultural, construction, silvicultural, and stormwater run-off. Such run-off is the source of a considerable proportion of the rivers' pollution, but relatively little is known about how much there is or how to control it. Discharge permits are not presently required nor do they appear feasible. Thus, the emphasis is on "best management practices," which are relatively undefined and must reflect the nature of the discharge and the feasible practices to control it.

The EPA was slow in issuing 208 planning guidelines, as well as effluent limitations and guidelines, for a number of reasons: (1) limited resources;(2) time required to obtain state comments on proposed guidelines; (3) costs of the program; and perhaps most of all, (4) the reluctance of the Nixon Administration to get involved in land-use regulation.[46] One result was a serious delay in the completion of such plans from a July 1, 1976, deadline to November, 1978. Even the latter deadline may be impossible to meet for some areas.[47]

The more important result was that wastewater treatment construction applications were processed, grants made, and discharge permits issued essentially without reference to area-wide planning. Thus, for five to six years of the act's existence, the instrument for rationalizing the water quality planning effort was lacking. Present planning will have to reflect the existence of treatment plant construction and discharge permits, rather than control them. The EPA is now endeavoring to convince the states that it is serious about 208 planning, and that new and revised permits and construction grants must reflect those plans.

Planning under 208 is supposed to be a principal responsibility of the states and local governments. The governors are required to designate local planning agencies for areas having substantial water quality problems, and states are required to plan for nondesignated areas. Councils of Governments (COG) have been typical recipients of this planning authority and of the federal money that has gone with it. A crucial point is that these planning agencies must have the authority to implement their plans. Given the fact that COGs are voluntary associations of governments, that local governments jealously guard their authority to make land-use decisions, and that the states now have mandated roles in coordinating these programs, the possibilities of political conflict are clear. Although the EPA considers 208 planning a state and regional-local responsibility, it has impressive powers to achieve compliance with its conception of an effective planning effort. Among these powers are withdrawal of construction grant funds, denial of permits and civil suits, and injunctive relief for discharging without them.

Through mid-1975, 149 designated agencies had been created and $163 million obligated to them. But only $53 million was appropriated and spent. The EPA estimates that an annual expenditure of $125-150 million will be requried to maintain the vitality of the planning, but the Ford Administration requested only$15 million for fiscal year 1977. Total cost of the initial planning effort has been estimated to be $40 million.[48]

Numerous uncertainties remain: Whether the regions, states, and the EPA can staff the planning effort adequately; whether the various levels of government can develop a cooperative relationship; whether economic conditons will lead to increasing demands for development with little reference to water quality; whether federal funds will be forthcoming; and what the relationship of this planning effort to that of 20 other federal agencies engaged in area planning, (such as the HUD-701 program, air quality planning, coastal zone management planning, and numerous others) will be.[49]

The Status of the Water Quality Effort

The bottom line of a discussion of the water pollution abatement must be an evaluation of the progress in cleaning up the nation's waters. There is unanimous agreement that the goals envisioned in 1972 for universal secondary treatment for municipal waste treatment plants and for the adoption of the best practicable technology by industry is not achievable, although the latter goal will come close to being met. This fact further implies that the 1983 deadline will not be met either. But the National Commission on Water Quality found bases for concluding that substantial progress was being made in achieving water quality benefits under the 1977 goal:[50]

> Based on the analysis of the Commission's 41 environmental sites, application of the 1977 requirements will *restore* a large portion of the Nation's presently polluted waters to a level of physical and chemical quality sufficient to provide for achievement of the interim goal. The chief exceptions are caused by toxics, pulse leads discharged from point and nonpoint sources during and following storms, and delays in actual achievement of the 1977 requirements. *Maintaining* that level of quality with continued growth will depend upon timely and effective compliance with outstanding permits and the effective application of more stringent limitations that may become necessary following adoption of water quality standards where the volume of pollutant discharges begins to produce lower quality water.

Because of natural conditions or as the result of previous efforts, much of the nation's waters already meet the interim goals, and application of the law's provisions will maintain these levels. Some streams are so polluted that it is doubtful that the interim goals will ever be achieved. Waste treatment plants will reduce the coliform levels, and the levels of dissolved oxygen should improve to the point where half of the waters now not meeting minimum standards will do so.

On the other hand, run-off from nonpoint sources remains a problem that has hardly been touched. Toxic substances remain a serious problem not adequately addressed by the EPA. And with growth of population, location of industry, and possible low flows of rivers, one may expect significant deterioration of some waters unless water quality standards are raised, and abatement measure implemented. And as the permit issuance and construction grant programs reach their peak and are completed, attention must shift to enforcement: monitoring, inspection, and assurance that qualified personnel are available to make the program work.[51]

Proposals for Change

The water pollution control legislation passed in 1972 was considered sufficiently revolutionary to require a review to assess the progress under this new approach. Such a review was produced by the National Commission on Water Quality in 1976. In general terms, the commission believed that the nation was on the right track in dealing with water pollution and recommended a continuation of most of the current effort. It urged, however, a mid-course correction with respect to the achievement of the 1983 BAT goals. The commission clearly rejected the elimination of discharge goal and raised serious questions concerning the need for going beyond the 1977 goals. It urged a case-by-case waiver of the 1977 deadlines for those public and private polluters which for good cause could not meet the deadlines. It also recommended a delay in the application of the 1983 standards for from five to 10 years in order to assess the identifiable marginal benefits from such technological improvements. The commission argued that other measures be taken, including revision of effluent limitations to reflect advances in control technology; enforcement of higher levels of treatment where necessary to meet approved standards; implementation of toxic pollutant standards; further decentralization of program administration; and funding of the construction grant program at a level of $5-10 billion for a period from 5 to 10 years.[52]

That these recommendations, plus others, for revision of 92-500 were controversial became immediately obvious as Congressional committees endeavored during 1976 and 1977 to come to grips with the numerous thorny issues. Senator Muskie, the principal author of 92-500, fought against what he considered weakening amendments, particularly anything that suggested a relaxation of the technology-based approach and a return to the receiving water standard.[53] Critical issues appeared to include the extent of state authority to certify compliance with EPA requirements to qualify for construction grants; restriction of the authority of the Corps of Engineers to issue permits for discharges to navigable waters and not into wetlands; postponement of compliance deadlines; the allocation formula for construction grants; and the level of federal funding. Not surprisingly, a bill of this significance dealing with a public works program of this size became immediately embroiled in controversies. In early 1977, it was involved in conflicts over President Jimmy Carter's program to provide jobs and stimulate economic activity and his efforts to eliminate certain water development projects throughout the country.[54]

It shoud be noted that little or no attention was given to recommendations made by many economists that an effluent charge on polluters would be a far more effective and efficient method of dealing with water pollution. Commitment to the effluent standard—discharge permit—construction grant program seems strong and likely to remain the basis of the water pollution program into the foreseeable future.[55]

Safe Drinking Water Act

A second facet of the federal water pollution control program concerns protection of the nation's drinking water supplies. Legislation that had languished in Congress for four years suddenly regained remarkable vitality with revelations of serious deficiencies in the water supplies of many cities. In 1974, the EPA published a study of the New Orleans water supply, revealing that it contained no less than 66 organic chemicals, some of which were suspected carcinogens. A study by the Environmental Defense Fund in the same year found that the water supplies of cities in 11 states had similar characteristics.[56] Despite Administration opposition, the Safe Drinking Water Act was passed within two weeks after these revelations.[57]

The act[58] required the Environmental Protection Agency to adopt primary drinking water regulations for protection of public health. These regulations must specify maximum contaminant levels and means of reducing them. Under the act, the EPA must also adopt secondary regulations pertaining to conditions of drinking water such as the odor and appearance of the water. These conditions do not necessarily affect the public health, however. The EPA was also required to publish regulations for state underground injection control programs because of their obvious implications for urban water supplies.

In contrast with the relatively tough enforcement stance adopted with respect to water pollution in general, the EPA was cautious with regard to drinking water regulation. As required by the act, EPA set interim standards for contaminants during 1975 but backed off on many of them, particularly organic pollutants, because it claimed to lack sufficient information to justify them. Critics argued that recent studies had revealed to be present in many water supplies known and suspected carcinogens and other toxic substances, such as chloroform, asbestos, and heavy metals. They alleged that existing monitoring and testing programs were inadequate to determine the degree and the presence of these substances and pointed to National Cancer Institute studies, which indicated that 60 to 90 percent of all cancer was environmentally induced. According to these critics, action to clean up these pollutants was imperative.

Aside from uncertainty about how health and contaminants are linked, the EPA has apparently been reluctant to act more vigorously because of the act's requirement that primary responsibility for enforcement of the statute be given to the states. The EPA has back-up authority in the event the states are unwilling or incapable of taking on this responsiblility. By mid-1976, 48 states had indicated their intention of taking responsibility for enforcement. Undoubtedly, this was a relief to the EPA, as it would otherwise be faced with monitoring, testing, and enforcing standards for 240,000 water systems throughout the country. State representatives appear satisfied with EPA performance, seeing in it a welcome contrast to the water pollution program experience.

Also influencing the EPA's approach to setting drinking water standards has been the National Drinking Water Adisory Council, mandated by the act. Consisting of equal numbers of members from state and local agencies concerned with water hygiene and public water supply, five members from other private organizations with similar interests, the Council has played a major role in setting policy and directing EPA researach.

Environmental groups expressed dissatisfaction with interim standards. A suit, alleging inadequacy of the standards, was settled, however, by an agreement under which the EPA is required to issue regulations to control the discharge of 65 toxic chemicals before 1980.[59] By early 1977, however, the controversy heated up again, with the Environmental Defense Fund going to court again to force EPA to set federal standards that place a ceiling on the maximum permissible levels of organic chemicals in drinking water.[60]

Sludge Management

The no discharge concept adopted in the 1972 Act suggested that the water pollution control program was designed to be a closed system with all costs and physical interactions contained or internalized. But it appears that one externality was not given sufficiently careful attention—sludge. Although an increasingly large quantity of sludge would be produced by municipal waste treatment plants, no provision was made for its disposal. Obviously, it couldn't be dumped in the rivers and lakes, it was too expensive to burn, and even if burned, such an action would create air quality problems. For sea coast cities, ocean dumping had been the traditional answer, but the EPA had ordered New York City, Philadelphia, and 100 nearby communities to stop ocean dumping by 1982.

The Comptroller General, however, in 1977 urged the EPA to reconsider its enforcement dates and its prohibition against ocean dumping in order to allow time to assess the effects of alternative sludge management approaches.[61] Chicago and other cities disposed of their sludge on land, with Chicago transporting it to Southern Illinois. But land disposal threatened the ground water with pollution, and the effects of toxic substances and heavy metals in the sludge were uncertain. Clearly, the answer for one community would be unsatisfactory for another.[62]

Federal policy for sludge disposal or treatment was virtually non-existent. Some work had been done by the Agricultural Research Service and by contractors under grants from the National Science Foundation, but less than $3 million was being spent on management research.

In 1976, Congressman Robert Drinan (Dem., Mass.) with 30 co-sponsors, introduced the Sludge Management Act of 1976.[63] The bill would authorize a major research and development effort and would establish a regulatory regime for sludge management. The regulatory system would include permits and requirements that no wastewater construction grants could be made without a plan for sludge management. The bill did not gain approval, but was reintroduced in 1977. One thing is certain—the problem will not go away.[67] A survey by Public Technology Corporation reported that local officials consider sludge management one of the top 10 energy and environmental problems. One Chicago official warned that something had to be done "or else some day people of Chicago are going to flush their toilets and nothing is going to happen."[65]

FEDERAL LAND-USE PLANNING LEGISLATION

As indicated above, the federal government has a substantial role in land-use planning, under a host of statutes dealing with specific federal policies. These have to do with housing, transportation, water and air pollution, and coastal zone management. In addition, the federal government makes an enormous impact on state and local land use, if not on planning, through its own decisions on programs and installations. The Federal Housing Authority (FHA) program has been cited as having a decided influence on the tendency of affluent whites to leave central cities. The location of a large federal installation in a given place can heavily influence industrial, commercial,and residential location patterns. Federal land management decisions and practices, particularly in the West, can clearly have an effect on land use. For example, under the Land and Water Conservation Fund Act of 1965, federal funds are available to the states for the acquisition of recreational lands.

But there is no *general* land-use planning legislation at the federal level. Efforts to obtain passage of such legislation have foundered on an ideology that finds a federal role in this area clearly unacceptable. Prodigious efforts were made to pass such legislation during the early 1970s. Bills sponsored by Senator Henry Jackson passed the Senate in both 1972 and 1973. However, similar legislation sponsored by Congressman Morris Udall died in the House of Representatives in 1971, 1974, and 1975. Reflecting on his experience, Udall stated that the attacks on his bill were "probably the leading example of legislative slander in modern times."[66]

Depending on one's perspective, federal land-use legislation was either a necessary first step toward the protection of critical land-use areas through state and local planning efforts with federal support, or the first federal wedge in the door leading to federal decisions on "every piece of land in America to the detriment of individual property rights."[67]

Using the 1974 Jackson bill as a representative model, the proposals essentially provided money in the amount of $100 million per year to the states to undertake their own land-use planning.[68] It declared no well-defined federal standards to guide state planning but emphasized that the planning had to be comprehensive, the state agency had to have implementation authority, and the public had to be allowed to participate fully. The principal sanction would be the withdrawal of funds for lack of a good faith effort. The state would be expected to assume decision-making authority only for "critical areas and uses." leaving existing local entities with authority to make most decisions. The state planning agency would have to devise a strategy to deal with existing land-use problems and to anticipate those of the future. Critical land uses and areas of more than local concern would involve (1) controlling growth-inducing forces, (2) regulating large-scale subdivisions, (3) preventing arbitrary exclusion of development by local governments, and (4) protecting lands of peculiar social and environmental significance. The planning agency would have to control land-use for "key facilities" such as major airports, highways, recreational facilities, and major housing developments, especially proliferating second-home developments in many rural areas.

The rhetoric against the land-use legislation emphasized states' rights, but the array of organizations in opposition suggests concern for the impact of the legislation on development. They included the Chamber of Commerce, associations of organizations in the construction industry, and mining, cattlemen's associations, and the American Farm Bureau Federation.[69] Labor nominally favored the legislation, but much local union opposition groups argued that the procedural requirements had substantive implications that would lead to the exercise of federal sanctions if states did not conform to expectations regarding the adequacy of state programs. Earlier efforts to have the Secretary of the Interior define areas of critical environmental concern and to include "cross-over sanctions "(i.e., authority to withhold the state's share of three major federal funding programs for failure to comply), were eliminated, but the opponents justifiably found much to suspect about the backers' motives.[70]

The future of general land-use legislation is unclear. Udall is clearly unwilling to lead without clear-cut Administration support for such a bill. Without that leadership from elsewhere on the issue, he said, "I don't really think it's worth the time and energy to take on all these old turkeys again. . . ."[71]

Coastal-Zone Planning

Ironically, general land-use planning legislation for the coastal zone is already on the statute books: the Coastal Zone Management Act of 1972.[72] Described by one critic as "poorly drafted, deficient in substantive standards, vague on policy, and uncertain regarding agency responsibility,"[73] it is, nevertheless, an important piece of legislation to control the devastation taking place in the scarce shoreline areas of the United States.

Originally, the legislation provided several kinds of grants to the states for planning: program development grants, administration grants, and estuarine sanctuary grants. Funding was low: $16.2 million in program development grants during fiscal years 1974 and 1975.[74] Under the impact of proposed leasing programs for the offshore oil and gas, Congress reacted in 1976 by passing amendments which established a Coastal Energy Impact Fund with $1.2 billion for purposes loans ($800 million) and grants ($400 million) to help coastal states and communities to construct necessary facilities to accommodate increased populations brought about by the leasing program.

Under the terms of the 1972 act, each state was encouraged to prepare—with the federal government paying ⅔ of the cost (increased to 80 percent by the 1976 Act)—a coastal management program which contains the following elements: (1) definitions of the coastal-zone boundaries; (2) permissible land and water uses within the boundaries; (3) the means of regulating activity within the zone; (4) guidelines for priorities of use; (5) designation of areas of particular concern; (6) demonstration that the plan does not unreasonably restrict uses of regional benefit; (7) public participation; (8) an organizational structure with adequate authority; and (9) evidence of coordination with other public entities. Once prepared and approved, the federal government (represented by the National Oceanic and Atmospheric Administration) is required to certify the program. By Mid-1976, 32 of the 34 eligible states were participating. However, only one program, that of the State of Washington, had been approved.

The slowness with which states proceeded with program development reflected a number of factors: inexperience, the complexity of their settings, and the nature of the federal presence. Moreover, the Comptroller General found wide variations in progress owing to the difficulty of obtaining adequate legal authority for the coastal zone agencies; resistance to coastal-zone management, particularly from local governments; and lack of political and financial support.[75]

A major problem thus far encountered has been in obtaining federal participation. By the terms of the act, once a state program has been approved, all federal agencies must conduct their activities and develop their projects in a manner consistent with the state management program. According to the Comptroller General, neither the federal agencies nor the states have done enough to ensure adequate communication and coordination. And, as offshore oil and gas deposits are exploited, this requirement of federal consistency looms large in the future as a possible point of conflict between the federal government and the states. Can the states, under their management plans, forbid or place such severe constraints on the location of on-shore refining or power plant facilities so as to severely restrict the obtaining of additional oil and gas supplies so important to the national interest? Consultation with federal agencies (required by the act) would presumably preclude approval of a plan that included such restrictions, and the procedures adopted by the federal agencies in pursuing oil and gas development can assist the states in preparing their management plans to deal with future oil and gas development.[76]

CONCLUSION

The travails of current environmental policy are a vivid reminder that it is at least as complex and difficult a matter to implement a policy as it is to formulate and legislate one. Both air and water pollution programs have been plagued by time-consuming litigation over differing interpretations of language. Both programs have placed burdens on administration which, at present, the administration can't handle, because of lack of financial resources, manpower, technical knowledge, or political sup port. The difficulties of inadequate resources were particularly exacerbated in the water program, where funding for waste treatment plant construction was impounded by the Nixon administration.

Pressman and Wildavsky have suggested that implementation is such a conditional and uncertain matter that reviewers of policy should be pleasantly surprised at whatever indications of positive policy impact can be discovered.[77] Signs of the progress in environmental quality are mixed. While both the air and the water seem to be somewhat cleaner because of far-reaching regulatory legislation of 1970 and 1972, improvement has been slow and uneven. Neither the interim goals in water nor the primary standard in air was achieved in the timetable set down in legislation. The deadlines for reduction of auto emissions have been set back three times; still yet another postponement seems certain. While there is wide agreement that land-use planning is necessary, policy makers are still grappling with the question of who should do it. In those states with land-use and coastal-zone planning law, experience has been so varied as to provide few clear directives for the future.

It is hard to determine whether the shortcomings in implementation of environmental law are greater than those in, say, economic, health, or other policy. Insofar as the 1970 air and the 1972 water amendments legislated especially ambitious goals and envisioned particularly complex standard setting and enforcement processes, following the law is more difficult than it would be in simpler policies. The choice of numerical standards to be achieved by certain dates has highlighted policy failures. An obvious question for policy analysts is whether more is accomplished by setting policy aims higher than can reasonably be reached to prod painfully slow governmental bureaucracies, or whether blatant policy failure simply fosters cynicism about government.

A very important component of the policy-making process is the education of public tastes and values. The bold environmental legislation of the early 1970s served in part to mobilize a consensus about environmental quality as a national value. With that matter more or less settled, the current concern has been with finding economical, efficient, and politically feasible mechanisms for getting the job done. The lesson of the last half-decade of national environmental regulation is that the issues are terribly complex, and solutions are seldom easy, even in the scientific and technical sense. The challenge to environmental policy makers is to design more flexible means of preventing environmental degradation.

Such means must be more sensitive to specific conditions and problems. To ease the burden of implementation, decision-making may be less concentrated at the federal level in the future. Economic incentives and disincentives which motivate clean up, but leave the choice of appropriate means to the polluter, are likely to appear increasingly attractive. Policy analysts whose ideas and findings promise to add rationality to environmental policy have never been more welcome.

NOTES

1. The Council on Environmental Quality (CEQ) *Environmental Quality: The Seventh Annual Report of the Council of Environmental Quality* (Washington, D.C.: U.S.G.P.O., 1976): 1-4.

2. Anthony Downs, "Up and Down with Ecology: The issue Attention Cycle," *Public Interest,* (Summer, 1972): 38-50.

3. Allen V. Kneese and Charles L. Schultze, *Pollution, Prices and Public Policy* (Washington, D.C.: The Brookings Institution, 1975): 70.

4. National Academy of Sciences-National Research Council, *Decision Making in the Environmental Protection Agency,* a report to the U.S. Environmental Protection Agency from the Committee on Environmental Decision Making, Analytical Studies for the U.S. Environmental Protection Agency, Volume II (Washington, D.C.: National Academy of Sciences, 1977): 1.

5. CEQ, *Environmental Quality; The Seventh Annual Report* (1976): 213.

6. John E. Bonine, "The Evolution of Technology-Forcing in the Clean Air Act," *Environmental Reporter* 6 (July 25, 1975): 8.

7. J.Clarence Davies III and Barbara S. Davies, *The Politics of Pollution,* 2nd ed. (Indianapolis: Bobbs-Merrill, 1975): 54.

8.Henry D.Jacoby and John D. Steinbruner, "The Context of Current Policy Discussions," in *Cleaning the Air,* Henry D. Jacoby et al., [eds.] (Cambridge, Mass.: Ballinger Publishing, 1973: 10-11.

9. Helen Ingram, "The Political Rationality of Innovation: Federal Air Pollution Control Legislation," in *Approaches to Controlling Air Pollution,* Ann Friedlaender [ed.] (Cambridge, Mass.: MIT Press, 1978, pp 12-56.

10. "U.S., Congress, Senate, Committee on Public Works, National Air Quality Standards Act of 1970: Report with Individual Views to Accompany S. 4358," 91st Cong., 2nd sess., 1970, S.Rept 1196: 2-3.

11. Richard B. Stewart, "Judging the Imponderables in Environmental Policy: Judicial Review Under the clean Air Act," in *Approaches to Controlling Air Pollution,* pp 68-138.

12. Kneese and Schultze, *Pollution, Prices, and Public Policy:* 51-53.

13. Edwin S. Mills and Lawrence J. White, "Government Policies Toward Automotive Emissions Control," in *Approaches to Controlling Air Pollution.* pp 348-410.

14. Jacoby *et al., Cleaning the Air.*

15. Mills and White, "Government Policies Toward Automotive Emissions Control."

16. Bruce M. Kramer, "Economics, Technology, and Clean Air." *Ecology Law Quarterly* 6, 1 (1976): 161-231.

17. Sierra Club v. Ruckelshaus, 344 F. Supp. 253, 4 ERC 1205 (D.D.C. 1972), affirmed, 4 ERC 1815 (D.C. Cir. 1972), cert. granted, 41 U.S.L.W. 3392 (U.S. Jan. 15, 1973), affirmed by tie vote, 41 S.L.W. 4825 (U.S. June 11, 1973).

18. Public Law No. 90-148, Sec. 101 (b) 81 Stat. 485 (1967; Clean Air Act Sec. 101 (b), 42 U.S.S.C. S/857 (b) (1970).

19. Kramer, "Economics, Technology, and Clean Air": 223.

20. Sierra Club v. EPA, F. 2d-, 9ERC 1129 (D.C. Cir. 1976).

21. Marc Roberts with assistance of Susan Farrell, "The Political Economy of Implementation: The Clean Air Act and Stationary Sources," in *Approaches to Controlling Air Pollution,* pp. 152-182.

22. Gladwin Hill, "A Murky Future for Smog Control," *New York Times,* (January 30, 1977) sec. 13: 1.

23. Arthur J. Magida,"Clean Air Act Deliberations—The Changing of the Guard," *National Journal,* 8 (13 March 1976): 340-342.

24. Kneese and Schultze, *Pollution, Prices and Public Policy:* 2.

25. Ann Friedlaender, "Introduction," in *Approaches to Controlling Air Pollution,* p 7.

26. P.L. 92)500, 86th Stat. 816.

27. J. Dicken Kirschten, "Plunging the Problems from the Sewage Treatment Grant System," *National Journal,* (February 5, 1977): 196; also Dean E. Mann, "Political Incentives in U.S.Water Policy: Relationships Between Distributive and Regulatory Politics," in *What Government Does,* Matthew Holden, Jr. and Dennis L. Dresang (eds.). *Sage Yearbook in Politics and Public Policy* (Beverly Hills, Cal.: Sage Publications 1975): 94-123.

28. Section 201 (g) (2) (A).

29. National Water Commission, *A Water Policy for the American People,* (Washington, D.C., 1973): 70.

30. CEQ, *Environmental Quality: The Seventh Annual Report,* pp. 12-13.

31. Ibid., 15.

32. National Commission on Water Quality (NCWQ), *Staff Report, to the National Commission Water Quality* (1976): V-19.

33. CEQ, *Environmental Quality: The Seventh Annual Report:* 12-13.

34. Council on Environmental Quality, *Environmental Quality: The Sixth Annual Report,* (Washington, D.C.: U.S. G.P.O., December 1975): 61.

35. Natural Resources Defense Council v. Train 510 F. 2d 692, 166 U.S. App. D.C. 312 (1975).

36. Natural Resources Defense Council v. Train 396 F. Supp. 1393 (1975).

37. *The United States Law Week,* 45 LW 4212 (February 22, 1977): 19.

38. Ibid., 4217.

39. NCWQ, *Staff Report:* V-41.

40. Train v. Campaign Clean Water 420U.S. 136, 43 L.Ed. 2d 82 95 S.Et. 847 (1975).

41. NCWQ, *Staff Report:* V-88.

42. National Water Commission, *A Water Policy for the American People:* 75.

43. NCWQ, *Staff Report:* V-78.

44. Ibid., V-78.

45. Ibid., V-108.

46. Mark Pisano, "208: A Process for Water Quality Management" and Rob MacDougall, "The State's Role in Section 28," *Environmental Comment* (January, 1976,): lff, 16-19.

47. Victoria Greenfield, "The States and Section 208 Water Quality Management Planning." Paper presented at the Western Political Science Association, Phoenix, Arizona, April 12, 1977: 26.

48. U.S. Senate, Committee on Public Works, *Fiscal Year Budget Review,* Hearings, 94th Cong., 2nd Sess., Serial No. 94-H33 (1976): 285.

49. See, for example, Daniel R. Mandelker and Susan B. Rothschild, "The Role of Land-Use Controls in Combating Air Pollution Under the Clean Air Act of 1970," *Ecology Law Quarterly,* 3, 2 (Spring, 1973): 235-276.

50. NCWQ, *Staff Report:* I-20.

51. See U.S.,House of Representatives, Committee on Public Works and Transportation, *Implementation of the Federal Water Pollution Control Act, Hearings* before the Subcommittee on Investigations and Review, 94th Cong., 2nd Sess. (1976).

52. NCWQ, *Report to the Congress by the National Commission on Water Quality* (March 18, 1976).

53. See Senator Muskie's response to the National Commission on Water Quality's report, ibid.: 43-44.

54. James R. Wagner, "Water Pollution Stalls Jobs Bill," *Congressional Quarterly Weekly Report,* 35, 15 (April 9, 1977): 635-638.

55. Allen V. Kneese and Charles L. Schultze, *Pollution, Prices, and Public Policy,* (Washington, D.C.; The Brookings Institution, 1975); chapter 7 and Epilogue.

56. Arthur J. Magida "Implementing the Drinking Water Act—A New Approach for EPA," *National Journal* 8 (June 12, 1976): 822-824.

57. "House Backs Standard for Drinking Water," *Congressional Quarterly Weekly Report,* 32 (November 23,1974): 3183-3184.

58. P.L. 93-523, 88 Stat. 1660.

59. Resources for the Future, *Resources* (January March 1977): 14-15

60. Los Angeles *Times* (March, 1977): 2.

61. General Accounting Office, *Problems and Progress in Regulating Ocean Dumping Sewage Sludge and Industrial Waste,* Report to the Congress by the Comptroller General of the United States, 1977.

62. P. J. Kendrick, "Cities Struggle with Sludge Problem," *Journal of the Water Pollution Control Federation,* 48 (December, 1976): 2646-2648.

63. H.R. 14638, 94th Congress.

64. H.R. 851, 95th Congress.

65. *National Journal,* 8 (September 11, 1976): 1286.

66. *Congressional Quarterly Weekly Report,* 35 (April 2, 1977): 605.

67. Quoted in *Congressional Quarterly Weekly Report,* 33 (March 1, 1975): 431.

68. For a thorough discussion of this bill, see Martin R. Healy, "National Land Use Proposal: Land Use Legislation of Landmark Environmental Significance," *Environmental Affairs,* 3, 2 (1974): 355-396.

69. *Congressional Quarterly Weekly Report,* 33 (March 1, 1975): 430.

70. See John McClaughry, "The Land Use Planning Act—An Idea We Can Do Without," *Environmental Affairs,* 3, 4 (1974): 595-626.

71. *Congressional Quarterly Weekly Report,* 35 (April 2, 1977): 605.

72. 86 Stat. 1280, 16 U.S.C. par. 1451-1464 (1974).

73. Zigurds L. Zile, "A Legislative-Political History of the Coastal Zone Management Act of 1972,"*Coastal Zone Management Journal,* 1, 3 (1974): 236.

74. General Accounting Office, *The Coastal Zone Management Program: An Uncertain Future,* Report to the Congress by the Comptroller General of the United States (December 10, 1976): 2.

75. Ibid., 21.

76. Kenneth A. Rubin, "The Role of the Coastal Zone Management Act of 1972 in the Development of Oil and Gas from the Outer Continental Shelf,"*Natural Resources* Lawyer, 8, 3 (1975): 399-436; also Helen Alexander Cassidy and Sultana Kaldis, "The Environmental Protection Agency and Coastal Zone Management; Striking a Federal-

State Balance of Power in Land Use Management," *Houston Law Review,* 11 (July, 1974): 11521193.

77. Jeffrey L. Pressman and Aaron Wildavsky, *Implementation: How Great Expectations in Washington Are Dashed in Oakland; Or, Why It's Amazing that Federal Programs Work at All, This Being a Sage of the Economic Development Administration as Told by Two Sympathetic Observers Who Seek to Build Morals on a Foundation of Ruined Hopes* (Berkeley: University of California Press, 1973).

AUTHOR'S NOTE: This article was drafted in May 1977. Since that time, Congress passed substantial amendments to both the Air and Water Pollution Acts that had the effect of postponing deadlines, and, hopefully, improving implementation.

7

THE SEARCH FOR NATIONAL URBAN POLICY: FROM KENNEDY TO CARTER

DENNIS R. JUDD
FRANCIS N. KOPEL

Washington University

THE CHANGING FEDERAL ROLE

Three important periods of national involvement in the cities can be traced from the Kennedy to the Carter Administration. In the first, which characterized the Kennedy-Johnson years, a plethora of social programs was enacted to achieve great "national purposes." The 89th Congress (1965-1967) clearly was the most activist and ground-breaking in enacting social legislation.

The second period witnessed a "backlash" against the Great Society. It began with the Congressional elections of November, 1966, and continued through the 1968 Wallace campaign and the Presidential victory by Richard M. Nixon. It subsequently escalated into a generalized reaction involving many liberals, who attacked the federal bureaucracy with as much enthusiasm as the conservatives had mustered. This period lasted until the Watergate events had run their course.

From sometime in the early Ford Presidency to the present, there has been a consolidation of support for federal urban and social programs. It would now take strong Presidential leadership to attack or cut social programs in any serious fashion. This third period is characterized by such strong consolidation of political support that the political reaction of 1968 through 1974 would be difficult for even conservatives to sustain; their criticisms now focus upon program details, not their right to exist.

THE SOCIAL WELFARE EXPLOSION

When President John F. Kennedy was sworn in on January 20, 1961, his Administration was already committed to a larger federal role for the cities. Even before his campaign, Kennedy had concluded that the problem of the cities "is the great unspoken issue in the 1960 election."[1] Not only did Kennedy feel that the election would be decided by the votes of key cities in a few industrial states, but he also felt that the problems of urban dwellers were, on their own merits, worth special attention. During the 1960 campaign, the Democrats played the city issue with scarcely a contributing or disturbing role from the opposition. The Republicans, in fact, actively tried to avoid such issues. "If you ever let them campaign only on domestic issues," confided presidential nominee Richard M. Nixon to his aides, "they'll beat us . . ."[2] As President, Kennedy

emerged as an eloquent spokesman for a new political generation. In Presidential message after message Kennedy spelled out in more detail than the Congress or the country could easily digest the most complete programs of domestic reforms in a quarter century.[3]

In August, 1965, the Watts riot dramatically demonstrated the conditions of life in the black ghettoes of American cities. Under President Lyndon Johnson, the "War on Poverty" and other major pieces of social legislation had been steered through Congress. The federal commitment began to pick up steam, and the trouble in the cities made it seem more imperative than ever.

The growth of grants economy tying the cities to the federal system is dramatically illustrated by the number and size of federal grants committed to cities and states during the 1960s. In 1960, 44 separate grant-in-aid programs were available to state and local governments.[4] Four years later, a Senate subcommittee report compiled by the Library of Congress identified 115 grant programs and a total of 216 separate authorizations under these programs.[5] The next two years brought another large increase. An analysis done by the Legislative Reference Service in 1966 counted a total of 399 authorizations.[6] By 1969, the count was approaching 500, and it reached about 530 a year later before leveling off (see Figure 7.1).[7]

The amount of money spent through federal grants also increased dramatically. Federal grants-in-aid totaled more than $70 billion by 1977, as shown in Table 7.1. In 1950, only $2.2 billion had been spent in this fashion. By 1960, this had increased to $7 billion. In the first year of the Nixon Administration, 1969, the national government was spending $20.3 billion for grants-in-aid. When Nixon left office in 1974, the amount had more than doubled, to $49.7 billion.

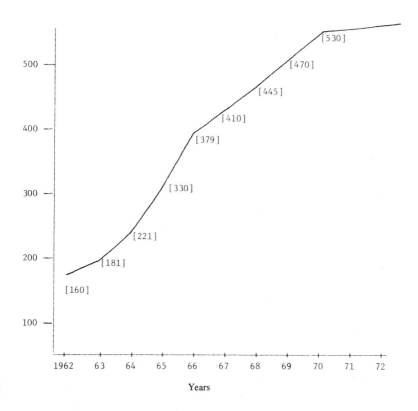

Figure 7.1. Growth of Grants-in-aid Authorizations, 1962–1972

Sources: Adapted from U.S. Congress, Senate Committee on Governmental Operations, *Intergovernmental Revenue Act of 1971 and Related Legislation, Hearings* before the Subcommittee on Intergovernmental Relations, Senate, 92nd Congress, 1st session (1971), p. 379; and Michael D. Reagan, *The New Federalism* (New York: Oxford University Press, 1972), p. 55.

Over this same period, state and local governments became increasingly dependent upon federal dollars. In 1950, about one dollar in 10 spent by the state and local governments originated in Washington. Ten years later, this figure had increased fo 14.7 percent and to 19.4 percent in 1970. In 1977, every fourth dollar spent by state and local governments came originally from the federal treasury.

Table 7.1. Federal-Aid Outlays in Relation to State-Local Expenditures

Fiscal Year	Amount (millions)	Percentage of State & Local Expenditures**
1950	2,253	10.4%
1955	3,207	10.1
1960	7,020	14.7
1965	10,904	13.5
1969	20,255	17.4
1970	24,018	19.4
1972	34,372	22.0
1973	41,832	24.3
1974	43,308	22.7
1975	49,723	23.2
1976	59,037	24.7
1977 (est.)	70,424	26.7
1978 (est.)	71,581	25.0

**As defined in national income accounts.

Source: Adapted from U.S. Office of Management and Budget,*Special Analyses, Budgetof the United States Government: Fiscal Year 1978* (Washington: U.S. Government Printing Office, 1977), p.273; data for 1969 from U.S. Office of Management and Budget, *Special Analyses, Budget of the United States Government: Fiscal Year 1975* (Washington: U.S. Government Printing Office, 1974), p. 210.

Between 1962 and 1970, a total of 370 new programs had been made available to the states and localities by the federal government. In the 10-year period between 1960 and 1970, the Congress had quintupled the number of programs that had been accumulated over the preceding 175 years.[8]

All of this represented a radical departure from the past. Although the federal role had expanded during the New Deal years, the amount of money going to state and local governments had remained very small. In 1960, only 6.4 percent of the federal domestic budget went to grant-in-aid programs—programs which, through specific grants, aided states and localities in giving relief, building sewers, water mains, and highways.[9] By 1973, more than one-fourth of the federal domestic budget—268 percent—went for grants-in-aid. This declined to 22.3 percent in 1976.[10]

The explosion in federal spending for programs designed to go into localities was accompanied by an attempt at the national level to achieve *national purposes.* Not since the closing of the frontier in the 1870s had the national government attempted to so clearly define a national domestic purpose. In that earlier period, by giving away land to states and railroads, in establishing a post office and financing internal improvements, in following a militant policy toward the Indians, the national government had declared its intention to open up the West and secure its territory.[11] Now, in the 1960s, the President and Congress again tried to formulate an overall national policy and assert the right of the national government to extend its authority. This assertation of purpose is clearest in the case of the Civil Rights Act of 1964, in which the government served notice that its new civil rights statutes would override state and local racial practices. In the case of grant programs, the preambles to legislation of the New Frontier and Great Society articulated many new purposes. For example, from the Manpower Development and Training Act of 1962:[2]

> *It is in the national interest that* current and prospective manpower shortages be identified and that persons who can be qualified for these positions through education and training be sought out and trained, *in order that the nation may meet the staffing requirements of the struggle for freedom.*

Or the Economic Opportunity Act of 1964:[13]

> *The United States can achieve its full economic and social potential as a nation* only if every individual has the opportunity to contribute to the full extent of his capabilities and to participate in the workings of our society. *It is, therefore, the policy of the United States* to eliminate the paradox of poverty in the midst of plenty in this nation.

Or the Demonstration Cities and Metropolitan Development Act of 1966:[14]

> The Congress hereby finds and declares *that improving the quality of urban life is the most critical domestic problem facing the United States.*

Imagine these kinds of statements-of-intention introducing hundreds of different pieces of legislation, ranging from rent supplements and teacher training to federal school aid to crime control, and the complexity of the new system of grants becomes readily apparent. Hardly an economic or social problem escaped attention. And each program carried with it complicated methods of implementation. Recipient institutions were subjected to close scrutiny and control. After all, it makes no sense to announce a "national purpose" unless the money is going to be used carefully, according to prescribed guidelines and standards.[15]

This era of activist policy-making by the federal government was facilitated by a new conception of the legitimate role of the national government with respect to the individual and society. The Congress, at the prodding of two Democratic administrations, enacted several programs which aimed primarily at broadening the scope of individual opportunity and development. The cumulative effect of these programs [was] to place the principal emphasis of federal aid . . . on health, labor, and welfare activities—as well as to give added impetus to education and housing and community development efforts.[16]

This shift to a social welfare orientation happened primarily between 1963 and 1967, when Congress enacted 136 new grant authorizations. Among the many programs added were the major social reforms of the 1960s—including food stamps, regional and community health facilities, the war on poverty, Medicaid, Appalachian regional development, aid for elementary and secondary education, and "model cities."[17]

Most of the new programs fit within the general rubric of "human resources." Fiscal year 1965 marked the beginning of a dramatic upswing in outlays for social programs, particularly in the areas of health, education, and manpower. Grants-in-aid to state and local governments within these fields rose from 14 percent of federal domestic aid in 1960 to a third in 1970. Similarly, the proportion of assistance outlays for housing and community development nearly quadrupled during the decade, rising from 3 to 11 percent of the domestic budget.[18] Obviously, urban issues were becoming more important. In fact, the 1960s were unique, for never before had the cities received so much direct attention.

A NEW PLACE FOR THE CITIES IN THE FEDERAL SYSTEM

Before the Kennedy Administration, the only major federal aid programs to be targeted especially to cities were urban renewal and public housing. The partisan change in Washington in 1961 marked the beginning of a new era. A concern for urban problems in the 1950s by the national Democratic party developed into a full-fledged commitment to and preference toward metropolitan areas. Reflecting these Democratic policy concerns and political interests, direct aid was increasingly made available to local governments. Federal assistance in urban areas increased from $3.9 billion in 1961, the last Republican fiscal year, to $14 billion in President Johnson's last budget eight years later. Over the decade, the money went to people and problems in the cities—a far cry from the pre-New Deal days when federal highway assistance funds to cities were forbidden by law.

The extent of the new urban commitment is shown in Table 7.2. While aid to urban areas increased 590 percent from 1961 to 1972, total federal aid spending increased by 450 percent. Aid to nonurban areas increased

Table 7.2. Federal Aid Outlays to Urban Areas, by Functional Area, for Selected Years

Functional Area	Fiscal Year (millions) 1961	1964	1969	(est.) 1972	Percentage Increase 1961–1972
Agriculture and Rural Development	155	271	417	375	142
Natural Resources and Environment	54	18	180	943	1,646
Commerce and Transportation	1,434	2,142	2,539	3,205	124
other than highways	37	199	314	559	1,411
Community Development and Housing	214	338	1,612	3,328	1,501
Other than public housing and urban renewal	3	43	569	1,783	5,933
Education and Manpower	561	722	2,963	4,362	677
Health	99	300	2,296	3,262	2,194
Income Security	1,341	1,695	3,899	8,181	510
General Government and Defense	35	77	159	803	2,194
General Revenue Sharing	—	—	—	2,813*	—
TOTAL for urban areas	3,893	5,588	14,045	26,848	590
TOTAL federal aid outlays	7,112	10,141	20,255	35,940	405
Percentage of total federal aid outlays to urban areas	54.7	55.3	69.1	75.0	—

*Tentative estimated impact

Sources: Adapted and calculated from U.S. Office of Management and Budget, *Special Analyses, Budget of the United States Government: Fiscal Year 1972* (Washington: U.S. Government Printing Office, 1971), p. 241.

by only 182 percent. By far the largest increment in spending was in the new programs associated with community development and housing, which were distinctly urban in orientation.

The importance of the stepped-up federal effort in the cities is illustrated in the case of the City of New York. In 1952, prior to any significant federal urban programs, New York relied on the federal government for only 3.8 percent of its expenditure budget. Even in 1963, after the implementation of the massive National Defense and Interstate Highway System, federal assistance amounted to only $142 million, or 5.5 percent. However, with the advent of the massive federal explosion of social welfare programs in the mid-1960s, the federal share of the city's budget rose rapidly. In 1965, the federal proportion of the budget reached 11 percent, and by 1969 it accounted for 15.9 percent. And finally, in the four years following, the total rose from $508 million to just over $2 billion—and 19.4 percent of the city's budget.[19]

THE GROWING DISSATISFACTION WITH FEDERAL ACTIVISM

It is important to note that a significant portion of the new federal money did not go directly to city governments themselves, but to nongovernmental, nonprofit organizations. Application procedures and funding arrangements varied considerably. Grants-in-aid went directly to local governments, to state agencies performing urban functions, and to private groups. Many programs encouraged or even mandated the creation of "special districts" or new agencies to receive funds, bypassing general purpose municipal governments. The extremely rapid growth of programs, their complexity and varying purposes, and complex application procedures quickly led to serious problems of coordination, impediments to Congressional oversight, and conflicts among agencies and groups at the local level.

Governors, mayors, and other state and local officials expressed frequent consternation about the lack of coordination among programs, the complexities of application and administration, and the lack of available information on programs. The chief culprit was institutional fragmentation.

There were numerous sources of information on grant programs. For example, the Advisory Committee on Intergovernmental Relations issued a bibliography in January, 1967, entitled "Catalog and Other Information Sources on Federal and State Aid Programs," that was nine pages long.[20] It listed publications by federal agencies, organizations of public officials, and local governments. A study contracted by the Department of Housing and Urban Development reported in September 1967 that federal agencies had no standardized procedures for conveying information on their grant programs, and that there were few common practices concerning the frequency of updating information.[21] During 1966, four major agencies issued four different catalogues with information on programs of both their own agencies and those of others.[22]

This fragmentation was reflected at the local level. In July 1967, administrators reported that they turned to an average of 8.2 different sources to obtain information about grant programs.[23] The most frequently used sources were federal agency publications and federal agency personnel at local and regional offices. Newspapers were the next most widely used source.

Such concerns over the problems of the grants-in-aid system were not new. Red tape, inflexibility, and poor coordination were the objects of much discussion during the postwar decades. It was the explosive expansion of the system during the 1960s which heightened these concerns and brought on concerted efforts to redress the problems.[24]

In attempting to simplify the system, officials in the Johnson Administration sometimes made matters worse. HUD official Robert Wood testified before the Senate Subcommittee on Intergovernmental Relations in 1966 that HUD was participating in 31 interagency committees, task forces, and other coordinating groups.[25] At the same hearings, officials from the Office of Economic Opportunity testified that they cooperated in 29 "committees and similar groups" with other federal agencies, and in 20 agreements with six other departments.[26] Labor Secretary Willard Wirtz listed five interagency agreements in which the Department of Labor was participating.[27] But the Secretary of Health, Education, and Welfare enumerated the greatest number of efforts. He served as the chairman of six committees, as a member of 23 others, and designated a person to represent him on six more. The Office of Education participated in 17 "formal" committees, 11 informal ones, and five interagency agreements.[28]

Several formal mechanisms were developed to replace these voluntary attempts at administrative cooperation. The Economic Opportunity Council was established by the Economic Opportunity Act to help coordinate the federal government's antipoverty efforts. In August, 1966, an executive order authorized the Secretary of HUD to convene agency representatives for exchange of information.[29] The President also urged simplified grant procedures and authorized the Bureau of the Budget to study and report on intergovernmental relations problems.[30] The Bureau subsequently reported some success in eliminating redundant data requirements among programs, reducing technical reviews, and increasing preapplication consultation among local, state, and federal officials.[31]

Federal agencies also pushed local grant applicants to demonstrate strong efforts at comprehensive planning—in fact, in Model Cities and other programs, planning and coordination were the passwords for satisfactory applications. Between 1964 and 1966, 47 separate aid programs requiring some measure of planning were enacted. "Many of these were intended to improve areawide planning for metropolitan regions."[32] As with attempts at coordination, however, planning requirements often exacerbated rather than improved the grant process. In testimony before the House Subcommittee on Intergovernmental Relations in 1967, Secretary of the Treasury Schultze noted that:[33]

> Certain planning requirements necessarily demanded as a condition of grants may be overlapping. This duplication can defeat the very purpose for which planning is sought. Such requirements may themselves become a significant generator of confusion, and have an adverse effect on program policy and execution.

Too many programs had been passed too fast for anyone to keep up. From the point of view of local public officials, the worst of it was not that there were so many programs, but that so many of these programs went to agencies and groups outside city hall. The governmental institutions of the cities were being by-passed in favor of new institutions—particularly those associated with the Economic Opportunity Act and Model Cities. In Oakland, California, for example, elected officials were disturbed that "substantial federal funding was going to a local organization which was openly hostile to the city government." The mayor's local nemesis, the local community action agency (The Oakland Economic Development Council, Inc.) received more than five times the $1 million in federal aid received by the city government in 1968.[34] Political officials and the local administrative agencies responsible for the delivery of municipal services felt that the federal government was fomenting "revolution" through its social programs.

Before long, a full-scale counterattack was being launched against "national purpose" legislation. Many of the same people who had been strong advocates of the social programs began to argue against federal power to dictate national goals. One of the chief proponents of federal activism in the 1960s had been Senator, then Vice-President, Hubert Humphrey. By 1972, he was testifying before a Senate committee that:[35]

I have listened to and talked to many thousands of people and hundreds of elected officials and if there is one unmistakable message, it is this—never before in the history of this nation has the diversity of our people, our cities, our countries, our communities, and our states placed such an importance on how government programs are constructed, how policies are implemented, and how revenue transfers are made.

We can no longer pass legislation that through bureaucratic red tape and underfunding stifles the ability of local officials to deal with indigenous problems.

We can no longer assume that solutions developed in Washington will automatically work in Louisiana, Montana, Utah, Connecticut, Iowa, and California.

We can no longer make minute, detailed choices as to how funds will be spent in every city and community of this nation.

We simply must recognize that cities, states, and local governments are different because people are different.

These differences call for new departures—if the needs of the people are ever to be met.

Revenue sharing is a new departure.

Decrying the proliferation of federally sponsored programs and the long delays and uncertainties inherent in the federal bureaucracy, liberals began to shift their ground.

The confidence and optimism which launched the Great Society social programs had waned rapidly. The Congressional election of 1966 and the Presidential election of 1968 revealed very clearly a political backlash against social legislation. In 1966, the Republicans gained four seats in the Senate, and in the House it raised its proportion of the membership from below one-third to 43 percent.

THE NIXON REORIENTATION: REVENUE SHARING AND THE NEW FEDERALISM

As a result of the 1968 election, the Republicans held 62 percent of the governorships and installed an anti-urban President pledged to clean up the federal assistance mess and to return "power to the people" through the decentralization of domestic policy and a "New Federalism."[36]

"The Sixties are ending," observed the Advisory Commission on Intergovernmental Relations,[37]

with substantial support of a "New Federalism" championed by the Nixon Administration by which increased reliance is placed upon State and local governments to make the multitude of public decisions required in the pursuit of domestic goals.

Immediately following his 1968 election victory, President Nixon emphasized his desire to decentralize governmental domestic programs, and he became more outspoken on the subject during 1971 and 1972. In his 1969 revenue sharing message, he spoke of the grant programs as producing a "gathering of the reins of power in Washington," which he saw as "a radical departure from the vision of federal-state relations the nation's founders had in mind." He referred to his proposal as "a turning point in federal-state relations, the beginning of decentralized relations of governmental power, the restoration of a rightful balance between the state capital and the national capital."[38] This was a rather modest statement of a theme he was to turn back to many times, perhaps most expressedly in his October 21, 1972, radio address on "The Philosophy of Government":[39]

Do we want to turn more power over to bureaucrats in Washington in the hope that they will do what is best for all the people? Or do we want to return more power to the people and to their state and local governments so that people can decide what is best for themselves? It is time that good, decent people stopped letting themselves be bulldozed by anybody who presumes to be the self-righteous moral judge of our society. In the next four years, as in the past four, I will continue to direct the flow of power away from Washington and back to the people.

The President devised a two-fold strategy. First, he ordered reviews of the major programs left over from the Johnson Administration. Throughout his first term, he repeatedly attempted to reduce spending on social programs.

In a more positive vein, the President proposed a new revenue-sharing program through which the federal government would give money to state and localities with few restrictions on how it could be spent. This would, he said,[40]

reverse the flow of power resources from the States and communities to Washington, and start power and resources flowing back from Washington to the States and communities, and more important, to the people all across America.

The time has come for a new partnership between the Federal government and the States and localities.

His revenue-sharing proposal, submitted to Congress in 1971, promised to give state and local officials substantial freedom to spend federal money according to their own priorities. This was fundamentally different from the objectives which had been stated in the national purpose bills. The preamble to the revenue-sharing legislation promised:[41]

to restore balance in the Federal system of government in the United States; to provide both the flexibility and resources for State and local government officials to exercise leadership in solving their own problems; to achieve a better allocation of total public resources and to provide for the sharing with State and local governments a portion of the tax revenues received by the United States.

The revenue-sharing plan was to be the centerpiece of domestic policy for the Nixon Administration. Full implementation of the plan would, it was contended, go a long way toward addressing the complaints that local officials had expressed about the complexity of the grant-in-aid system. Of the $16.1 billion proposed for distribution under revenue sharing for the first year, $5 billion was to be in the form of general revenue sharing and $11.1 billion was to be allocated to state and local governments through "special" or categorical revenue-sharing in six functional areas.[42]

The Presidential proposal, though not unexpected, stole the initiative from Democratic leadership. The idea of revenue-sharing had been around for years. It initially was developed by Walter W. Heller, a former University of Minnesota professor and Chairman of the Council of Economic Advisors in the Democratic adminsitrations of the early 1960s. He, like so many others, had noticed that "prosperity gives the national government the affluence and the local governments the effluents."[43] The paradox of the federal income tax structure was such that tax revenues from this source grew at a rate one and one-half times that of the economy—for every 10 percent increase in economic growth, the government registered a 15 percent increase in tax revenues. The result, by 1963, was the prospect of excess revenues in the federal treasury.[44]

Concerned that the projected budgetary surpluses might constrain economic growth and expansion, Heller proposed that the national government share its surplus with the nation's cities and towns. Especially for the big cities, which were caught in a constant revenue crunch, federal revenue sharing would be a boon.

Revenue-sharing was never seriously considered by the Democratic Presidents. Instead, the wide array of national purpose programs captured their attention. Additionally, much publicized tax cuts were enacted in 1962 and 1964. Spending on social and economic programs and reductions in the tax rates had high political visibility. The Democratic party leadership surmised that the public would take notice of such actions long before they appreciated intergovernmental transfers of revenue for general purposes.[45]

The adoption of revenue sharing as a national domestic policy was secured through the cooperation of two rather different political groups. One was composed of state and local public officials, including mayors, governors, city managers, county executives, and others. Their main incentive for pursuing the matter through the halls of Congress was to gain access to additional (i.e., federal) resources in order to ameliorate their fiscal problems.

The second major group was drawn together by ideological and political concerns over the expansion of the federal government's role in domestic policy. Conservatives were appalled by the centralization of domestic policy which had occurred during the Great Society years.

Political conservaties, now led by President Richard Nixon, fully understood the dynamics of the political system with which they were tinkering. At the national level, the power of political interest groups was balanced differently than in local politics. "The plain fact is that large population groups are better represented in the constituencies of the President and the Congress than they are in the constituencies of the governors and legislatures."[46] On the national level, the general values of equity, equality, and social justice receive a fuller hearing than they do at other levels of government. At lower levels in the American system, in state legislatures and city halls, before utility commissions and airport authorities, the often narrow, usually specific, and always compelling individual economic and social interests work against the more widely diffused social values.[47.]

At the national level, for example, a civil rights law is somewhat abstract. In local politics, it translates into access to jobs, housing, or schools. Liberal values are more easily championed in the abstract, rather than in specific situations.

In the early 1960s, this fact led to broad support for federal activism. Liberals had succeeded in placing conflict over policy at the national level because of the electoral advantage of the Democratic party in the cities and because of the frustrations of the city officials who lacked resources to deal with social disorder. City officials wanted to move policy issues out of the state legislatures and to the national level because they knew national political leaders would be more sympathetic to their fiscal plight. "City leaders sought to promote direct federal aid as a defensive weapon against state intransigence."[48]

But a consequence of moving social policy to the national level was that local political leaders lost some of their autonomy. Their control over politics slipped; anti-poverty workers protested city hall decisions; nonprofit housing organizations proposed federally funded housing projects in white areas; and so forth. The cost of compromising with federal bureaucrats was high, and naturally local officials sought escape.

The revenue-sharing issue did not concern *what would be done* with policy; it concerned *who would decide*. Social welfare values were not directly attacked, but it was apparent that if the national purpose legislation were abandoned in favor of revenue sharing, social programs would suffer.

The forces in support of revenue sharing were dominated by a group of public interest groups known as the "Big Seven." The institutional members of this powerful coalition included the National League of Cities (NLC), United States Conference of Mayors (USMC), the National Governors' Conference, the National Legislative Conference, the Council of State Governments, the National Association of Counties, and the International City Management Association (ICMA). It was a wide array of groups which covered the spectrum of all important state and local policy-making institutions. The last mentioned group was a "new comer" to the intergovernmental lobbying structure. Representing "professionals" who long viewed political activities as beyond their purview, they had broken with a 50-year tradition of "neutrality" vis-à-vis legislative issues to support revenue sharing vigorously.[49]

With these groups solidly behind the concept of shared revenues, the ensuing political battle largely pitted the fiscal interests of local elected officials with the ideological and philosophical concerns of social welfare liberals.

Many of the liberal and social reform groups which had been an important part of the liberal-urban coalition that supported the expansion of the federal role now opposed the retrenchment implicit in the New Federalism's revenue sharing. Organized labor, excepting for the American Federation of State, County, and Municipal Employees (AFSCME) which correctly perceived that its members would be prime beneficiaries of the plan, decried the concept. The AFL-CIO, long a friend of urban interests and an important component of the Democratic electoral coalition, championed the liberal interests of federal primacy in domestic policy and opposed the lack of national purpose or federal oversight in the proposed "give-away" sharing plan.[50] The union group's executive council articulated their position in February, 1971:[51]

> The AFL-CIO urges complete rejection of this revenue sharing proposal. We are firmly convinced that such no-strings money will not add one Federal penny to the money available to the states and localities. It will merely be a substitute for the full fundings of existing programs . . . critical needs could be by-passed in the expenditure of these federal monies. There is no reason to believe that each of the fifty states and 81,000 cities, boroughs, townships and school districts is in a better position to weigh and balance national priority needs, and use Federal funds to meet them more effectively and efficiently. Moreover, without specified and enforceable federal performance standards, there is no assurance that federal civil rights guarantees and fair labor practices will be applied to projects supported by no-strings federal grants.

Civil-rights groups also opposed revenue sharing, fearing that social programs favorable to minorities would be abandoned.

Many liberals opposed revenue sharing because they thought it placed too much trust in the competence and intent of local governments. Local governments, they argued, lacked the vision to attempt good social programs and could not be depended upon to respond to social needs:

> Fiscal poverty and poverty of ideas often go together in state government, especially when the programs are designated to help the least affluent and influential of citizens . . . states are loath to spend additional dollars unless compelled to.[52]

. . . revenue sharing is a cop-out as regards the almost universally admitted inadequacies of state and local governmental structure and financial systems.[53]

Conservatives and liberals were not uniform in their positions regarding revenue sharing. Some conservative organizations, for example, did not see revenue sharing as an alternative to social programs. They didn't want either. One of the more active groups of this type was the United States Chamber of Commerce (USCC). Its opposition stemmed largely from its general ideological position of opposition to any expansion of the public sector—at any level. It is significant to note, however, that the USCC Committee on Urban Problems, its only linkage to the crises of urban America, advocated suport of the revenue-sharing proposal within the organization. The compelling philosophy of private enterprise and the unfettered market won out in the end, however, and the USCC became a very active opponent of the "Big Seven"—going to the extreme of issuing an "Action Call" to all its affiliated local chambers to pressure their respective Congressmen to vote against the revenue sharing proposal.[54]

Another always conservative, anti-urban group, the American Farm Bureau Federation, referred to the proposal as "deficit-sharing" during its testimony in opposition to the plan.[55]

The Democratic party and the liberal-urban coalition were deeply split by the President's initiative on revenue sharing. The mayors, a key element in both the policy and electoral coalitions, were strongly in support of the proposal by this time. Their fiscal crisis had deepened with no end in sight, and even the liberal mayors were forced to support practically any new source of revenues.

In a report commissioned by the National League of Cities in 1967, the cities of the nation were estimated to be facing a gap between revenues and expenditures totaling $262 billion over the decade ending in 1975. Less than half of this staggering figure could be expected to be made up by the federal grant programs. Even assuming increased municipal revenue rates and stepped-up state funding, total city debts could be expected to rise by $63 billion to meet the gap (see Table 3).[56] The National Urban Coalition predicted in 1971 that the gap between the revenues and expenditures of the nation's cities would reach $94 billion annually by 1976—even assuming passage of the revenue-sharing act. The needs of the nation's cities were indeed critical.[57]

The seriousness of the fiscal gap was evidenced by major cutbacks in municipal services. The 1971 National Municipal Survey reported, for example, that:[58]

Pittsburgh recently closed 14 fire stations;

Philadelphia would soon have to reduce various police support units;

Cincinnati was cutting back on school libraries, kindergartens, and teaching staffs;

Hamtramck was so very near bankruptcy that its mayor requested that HEW stop the flow of federal funds—the city could no longer supply the necessary matching funds;

Detroit was forced to lay off 600 municipal employees and keep 2200 authorized positions vacant due to the lack of sufficient funds, and given the plight of the city's treasury, would need an additional 26 million new dollars to keep from backsliding any further—just to stay even;

New York had 1 million persons on its welfare rolls—requiring annual welfare outlays of 600 million dollars in that category alone.

Table 7.3. Estimated Annual Revenue Gaps and Recommended Funding Sources for the 1966–1975 Period

(billions of dollars)

Year	Estimated gap	Funding sources			
		Federal Government	States	Increases in city charges	Increases in net city debt
1966	$ 4.5	$ 1.0	. . .	$ 0.5	$ 3.0
1967	8.0	3.0	$ 1.0	1.0	3.0
1968	12.0	6.0	2.0	1.0	3.0
1969	16.5	8.0	3.0	1.5	4.0
1970	22.0	10.0	4.0	2.0	6.0
1971	28.5	13.0	5.0	2.5	8.0
1972	34.5	16.0	6.0	3.5	9.0
1973	40.0	19.0	8.0	4.0	9.0
1974	45.5	23.0	9.0	4.5	9.0
1975	50.5	26.0	11.0	4.5	9.0
TOTAL . . .	262.0	125.0	49.0	25.0	63.0

Source: National League of Cities, U.S. Conference of Mayors, and International City Management Association, *The Fiscal Plight of American Cities,* Table X, as presented in Richard E. Thompson,*Revenue Sharing: A New Era in Federalism* (Washington: Revenue Sharing Advisory Service, 1973), p. 146.

In St. Louis, the budgetary crisis was becoming so severe that then Mayor A. J. Cervantes appeared before the Board of Aldermen with this speech:[59]

Having delivered several budget speeches over the years, I know that you will say that every year is another crisis. Today, however, the situation is even more desperate than in the past, and we must face up to the fact that we are scraping the bottom of the revenue barrel.

This is the last year the City can make a budget which will come anywhere near adequately meeting the needs of our citizens. Working under the limitations of state constitution and state law, there are no other viable means of local revenue, in my opinion.

As a result, the Metropolitan Youth Commission, the Regional Development Corporation, the Challenge of the 70s Committee, and the Meramec Hills Home for Delinquent Girls were eliminated from the budget. And, in order to try to make ends meet, the Board of Estimate and Apportionment also curtailed the following: Child Guidance Program, Street Department, Human Development Corporation, Fire Department, Traffic Division, Forestry Division, Recreation Department, City Hospital, and maintenance for municipal buildings.[60]

The Congressional leaders of the Democratic party, although sympathetic to the plight of the cities, resisted giving in to the pressure to approve revenue sharing. With a national election just a year away, the Democratic legislative leadership and Presidential aspirants were loath to give the Republican incumbent any type of domestic victory. Such Democratic mayors as Pittsburgh's Peter Flaherty and Cleveland's Carl Stokes considered this attitude an "ill-advised . . . partisan reflex"[61] to what they considered a nonpartisan issue.

The tension between the partisan needs of the Democratic leadership and the fiscal needs of the big city mayors came to a peak in a March, 1971, private meeting between the House leadership and the U.S. Conference of Mayors' Legislative Action Committee.

As one of those in attendance recalls it, New York's Mayor John V. Lindsey had just gotten up to speak, when Majority Leader Hale Boggs (D-La.) suddenly slammed his fist on the desk and shouted: "You don't need to make any points. Revenue sharing is dead. I'll see that it never passes. So let's get on to something else." Flabbergasted, Lindsey slid back into his seat. There was a moment of embarrassed silence—and then a rolling southern drawl rang out from the back of the room. "Hale," said New Orleans Mayor Moon Landrieu, "that's the rudest treatment I have ever witnessed, and I think you better talk about revenue sharing and you better listen. Because, Hale, if you don't start thinking about helping the cities, I want you to know that you'll never be welcome in the city of New Orleans again." Now it was Boggs' turn to be flabbergasted.[62]

After the heated exchange, the national leadership began to reassess the soundness of its position. Party Chairman Lawrence O'Brien worked to mend the deteriorating urban pillar of the party's electoral coalition, straining to bind the party together. Finally, representative Wilbur Mills, the powerful chairman of the Ways and Means Committee, dropped his opposition to the concept of revenue sharing. A back burner Presidential aspirant, he proposed a plan of his own—a $3.5 billion emergency aid plan for the cities—and opened the way for Democratic approval of the revenue-sharing concept. The internal wounds of the party began to heal.[63]

Even within the "Big Seven" lobby, there was dissension over the policy implications of the revenue-sharing proposals. The principal points of contention among the several groups centered around the appropriate formulae for dividing up the federal monies. Mayors and governors both, naturally enough, desired to maximize their own "equitable" share of the revenue pie. Ideas ranged from all the money going to the states, with pass-through provisions to be worked out at that level, to all funding being allocated to the cities and the states being left out completely (the Mills plan). After several months of haggling, a compromise was reached. Two-thirds of the amount given to the state would be directly allocated to the cities (and other local governments) and one-third to the state's government.

Having emerged moderately victorious in that battle, urban interests turned toward the apportionment formula. In this vital matter, there was a direct conflict between the urbanized and nonurbanized states. Reflecting the composition of the Ways and Means Committee membership which drafted the legislation, the House adopted a five-factor formula which closely approximated a "fair" per capita share—balancing allocation between urban and rural interests. The Senate, on the other hand, did not concur with the House allocation procedure. Again reflecting the make-up of the appropriate substantive committee (the Finance Committee, chaired by Russell Long of Louisiana) and the overall small-state bias of representation in the Senate as a body, the Senate adopted a three-factor allocation formula which reduced the proportion that would go to urban areas. By substituting a factor for poverty and total tax effort, the Senate version allocated a higher proportion of the total funds to the smaller, poorer, rural states of the South and Southwest.[64]

Urban interests watched intently as the two bills were sent to the House and Senate Conference Committees. Adoption of the House formula, as opposed to the Senate version, would benefit the big cities. A classic compromise was worked out. Both formulas were to be used, with the choice up to the individual states.[65]

The passage of the State and Local Fiscal Assistance Act of 1972[66] marked the culmination of four years of intense efforts by big city mayors and other governmental officials to access the federal treasury in a largely unrestricted manner. It reached that final point as a result of four basic political facts: (1) all the groups concerned—primarily the "Big Seven"—agreed upon it as a high priority measure; (2) a shaky but essential consensus was hammered out with respect to the division of money between the states and their local governments; (3) it received the highest priority from the President; and (4) the Democratic Congressional leadership reluctantly had to agree to allow the President a domestic policy victory on this issue.[67]

The signing of the revenue-sharing bill might have been taken as a bad omen by social welfare liberals who thought it presaged neglect of the nation's social problems. Officials from every level of the American system were present in Philadelphia for the outdoor ceremony. But after the signing, the new law was left behind as officials scurried off. The State and Local Fiscal Assistance Act of 1972 nearly suffered the windy fate of a candy wrapper as the document was left unattended.

> after the great ceremony of signing under the shadow of Independence Hall, nobody picked up the bill. And after everybody else had left, it was still sitting there. One of the policemen picked it up and asked: "Does anybody want this?"[68]

THE IMPACT OF "NEW FEDERALISM"

Under the revenue-sharing legislation, local officials gained more autonomy in spending federal money. Unlike the grants-in-aid programs, few "strings" and little "red tape" were attached to the funds. Such guidelines as had to be followed were very minimal and virtually meaningless in the face of the reality of governmental accounting procedures. Because of the lack of detailed federal oversight, revenue-sharing dollars are indistinguishable from other money in the over 39,000 state, county, township, and municipal treasuries across the nation. As such, they cannot be traced beyond the actual use reports filed by local officials with the Department of the Treasury. They are, as they were intended to be by the "Big Seven" and the Nixon administration, a very loosely restricted supplement to the general revenues of state and local governments.

The actual amount of revenue sharing money has constituted only a small component of the budgets of local governments. In 1974, the 4.5 billion dollars apportioned among 35,077 local governments accounted for only 3.1 percent of their revenues for that year. The relatively small size of the general revenue-sharing contribution in relation to the total resources of the cities prevents it from having a very significant impact on the municipal balance sheet.[69]

Local governments, and cities in particular, reported that they channelled the largest proportion of their revenue-sharing funds into govern-

Table 7.4. Reported Use of General Revenue Sharing Funds January 1972–June 1973 (amounts in millions of dollars)

Function	States (51 states) Amount	%	All Cities (15,785 cities) Amount	%	Cities of 250,000 and over (55 cities) Amount	%
Public Safety	20.0	2	434.0	44	208.9	59
Environment/Conservation	7.4	1	126.0	13	40.0	12
Transportation	55.6	5	148.7	15	35.2	10
Health	30.7	3	50.3	5	10.5	3
Recreation/Culture	3.7	*	76.6	8	27.8	8
Libraries**	—	—	10.4	1	3.8	1
Social Services	61.2	6	11.7	1	7.8	2
Financial Administration	18.5	2	16.0	2	3.8	1
Education	664.3	65	4.7	*	0.2	*
General Government	5.9	1	68.7	7	9.3	3
Housing/Community Development	1.1	*	14.4	2	1.2	*
Economic Development	2.2	*	14.4	2	1.2	*
Economic Development	2.2	*	7.3	1	3.3	1
Other***	151.9	15	11.7	1	0.4	*
Operations and Maintenance	959.1	94	546.3	56	277.9	79
Capital expenditures	63.4	6	431.2	44	75.2	21

*Less than 0.5 percent

**State expenditures for "libraries" are included under "other"—"libraries" not being a separate reporting category for states.

***Includes "social development"

Source: Adapted from U.S. Department of the Treasury, Office of Revenue Sharing, *Revenue Sharing: The First Actual Use Reports,* by David A. Caputo and Richard L. Cole (Washington: U.S. Government Printing Office, 1974), pp. 4, 10-11, 29.

mental functions outside the general rubric of social services. Most cities during fiscal year 1973 put money into transportation, environment and conservation, and public safety (refer to Table 4).

A substantial portion of these funds were allocated to the latter category—public safety—which largely meant police and fire protection services. Townships and counties reported that they spent 33 percent of their revenue-sharing funds on this in 1973. Cities spent even more, 44 percent of their revenue-sharing funds, on public safety. Large cities, which were in the worst financial shape, put even more into fire and police. The nation's 55 largest cities spent 59 percent of their revenue-sharing funds this way.[70]

These figures are in striking contrast to the reported expenditure patterns of the states. Because of the substantially different political culture and the tradition that police and fire services are primarily a local matter, the states spent very little—2 percent of the total in 1973—on public safety. The largest expenditure by the states, completely reversing the priorities of the cities, was education.

One of the significant aspects of the reported actual use of revenue sharing is the distinction between capital expenditures for such things as highways, parks, and new equipment, and operating and maintenance expenses. Only 33 percent of the revenue-sharing funds spent in 1973 went for capital improvements. Financially strapped big cities spent most of their funds just to "keep things going." While cities in general spent 56 percent on operations and maintenance, cities with populations over 250,000 reported spending 79 percent in this category. The five largest cities—New York, Chicago, Los Angeles Philadelphia, and Detroit—reflecting their intractable day-to-day fiscal problems— reported spending 497 percent of their revenue-sharing funds for operations and maintenance.[71]

It appears that the enactment of general revenue sharing resulted in a drop of 10 percentage points for the human resources portion of the federal assistance program to states and localities. Human resources accounted for 69 percent of all grants-in-aid outlays in 1972, the last pre-revenue-sharing fiscal year. Primarily as a result of spending 11 percent of domestic outlays on the revenue-sharing program, human resources suffered a net loss of 14 percentage points in its share of the budget.[72] The states and localities reported spending 35 percent revenue-sharing monies—approximately 4 percent of the total federal outlays for grants-in-aid—on human resources. By adding this to the fiscal 1973 budget, we find that 59 percent of all federal assistance to state and local governments in 1973 went into human resources, a drop of 10 percentage points in a single year.[73] The largest "winner," understandably, was general government, which registered a gain in its proportion of the federal grants-in-aid budget—from 2 to 8 percent.[74]

Most mayors were satisfied with the general revenue-sharing program. The program had given the city halls greater autonomy. The only substantial criticisms of the program came from liberal and civil rights groups who objected to the political implications of policy decentralization. The Reverend Jesse Jackson, a Chicago civil rights activist and director of Operation PUSH typified this sentiment when he decried the anti-poor bias of general revenue-sharing:[75]

> Most statehouses, county courthouses, and city halls are dominated by the more advantaged sectors of the body politic.
> Revenue sharing funds, in contrast to certain categorical aids targeted on the poor as a group do not flow in sufficient quantities to help those local governments, particularly the major central cities, with extraordinary concentrations of poor people.

The Democratic leadership in the Congress continues to be uneasy with general revenue sharing. Political self-interest alone would lead them to be unhappy with the decentralization of decision-making accompanying wide distribution of the federal largesse. The liberal orientation of the Congressional party leads them to support federal primacy in the formation and implementation of national goals. Many Congressional liberals feel that the social needs which had been the object of so many policy initiatives during the 1960s are being slighted under the revenue-sharing program.[76]

Only months after the first checks were sent out by the Revenue Sharing Office, Congressional Democrats began to complain about the illiberal manner in which the money was being spent. Representative Shirley Chisholm of New York voiced concern "that the program failed to aid the disadvantaged and minority groups."[77] Other Congressmen were concerned that revenue-sharing funds were not going to those who needed it the most, but were, instead, being used to aid the "haves."[78]

Liberal acquiescence to the program had been bought with the promise that general revenue sharing would be in addition to, not instead of, the multitude of federal assistance programs. The liberal outcry was immediate and loud when it became clear in the Nixon Administration's fiscal 1974 budget that "the birth of general revenue sharing is being used to justify the homicide of selected social programs."[79]

Despite the offended ideological and political interests of Congressional liberals and the Democratic leadership, general revenue sharing was extended in 1976. Again, it was the unrelenting political pressure by representatives of the "Big Seven," especially the big city mayors, which prodded the Democratic Congress to act. The U.S. Conference of Mayors, a major components of this pressure coalition, adopted a resolution "suporting reenactment of the general revenue sharing program and promising to make renewal a key local issue in the Congressional campaigns."[80]

The extension of general revenue sharing reflects only a partial success for the interests of the Big Seven and the political conservatives. As adopted, the extension does not provide for annual increments in the level of funding. Under the impact of inflation, the level of funding, measured in 1972 dollars, will have dropped 17 percent between 1972 and 1979.[81] Also, instead of extending the program for five and three-quarters years, as proposed by the Ford Administration, revenue sharing was extended for only three and three-quarters years. Both of these decisions reflect the basic wariness of the Congressional Democrats toward revenue sharing. The ideological conflict over revenue sharing is far from settled.

OTHER REPUBLICAN INITIATIVES

While revenue sharing was surely the cornerstone of President Nixon's New Federalism, he pursued other policy initiatives which affected the interests of urban America. His domestic policy "centered around the New Federalism objectives of simplifying government operations and transferring planning and management functions to State and local governments."[82]

Early in Nixon's first term, the Office of Management and Budget issued a series of Executive Orders which were intended to rationalize the grant-in-aid programs. Metropolitan and regional planning and coordination was encouraged through the most famous of these circulars—A-95. Other such memoranda strengthened the powers of elected officials to control federal programs within their jurisdictions and provided for uniform federal practices with regard to grant relationships.[83]

Another early strategy of the Nixon Administration included the "planned variations" component within the Model Cities program. Twenty cities were invited to participate. The first variation allowed cities to expand the Model Cities projects beyond the target neighborhoods into the entire city—with additional funds being provided for that purpose. A second variation greatly simplified the regulations of the Model Cities program, thus cutting some of the red tape and delay surrounding its implication. The third, and most popular, variation provided for the evaluation and recommendations of the city's chief executive of all federal grant applications arising from his city.[84]

But the primary thrust of federal urban policy in the Nixon Administration was an attempt to consolidate grant programs, to collapse the plethora of national purpose programs into a manageable handful of broad block grants. The primary object of such consolidations was, as in the case of general revenue sharing, to minimize the relative power of the national government with regard to domestic affairs and to maximize the authority of state and local government officials. The major administration initiatives along these lines were the special revenue-sharing proposals of 1971. Under these programs, $11.1 billion—twice the amount proposed for the subsequently enacted general revenue plan—was to be apportioned among the eligible jurisdictions. The monies were to be applied by state and local governments to programs within six broad areas: urban community development ($2 billion), rural community development ($1 billion), education ($3 billion), manpower training ($2 billion), law enforcement ($0.5 billion), and transportation ($2.6 billion).[85]

These proposals were not well received by the Democratically controlled Congress and were not enacted all together as proposed by the

Nixon Administration. Portions of the plan, however, did find their way into the statute books.

Under the Comprehensive Education and Manpower Act of 1973, 10,000 federal manpower contracts arising out of the national purpose legislation of the 1960s were replaced with 50 state and 350 big city block grants. In keeping with the underlying philosophy of New Federalism, the powers of the big city mayors were greatly enhanced under the provisions of the act. Federal grant money for manpower programs in cities of 100,000 or larger were sent directly to the offices of the mayors. Implementation of the provisions of the statute proceeded at the direction of the local chief executive.

The Housing and Community Development Act of 1974 was the most important attempt since the Model Cities program to formulate a comprehensive national policy for the cities. Like the Model Cities legislation, it recognized that urban communities have severe problems that required "systematic and sustained federal aid," and also like Model Cities, which hoped to involve private and public resources and to promote coordination and planning, Community Development promised "increased private investment and streamlining of all levels of government programming."[86]

President Nixon had first proposed a consolidation of housing and urban programs in 1970. His proposal had invited an onslaught of counter-proposals from Democrats in Congress. But finally, in August, 1974, the Community Development Act was signed into law. It took effect on January 1, 1975. The act evolved as an amalgam of New Federalist efforts to decentralize domestic policy-making and Democratic efforts to increase funding levels for urban programs. The act "secured a continuation of the traditional public housing and subsidized housing programs" as well as new, consolidated "community development and housing assistance programs that rely, heavily, on local goverment and private market activies."[87]

THE COMMUNITY DEVELOPMENT ACT

The Community Development Act of 1974 replaced seven major categorical grant programs with a single block grant authorization. Among these superceded programs were several which were of special importance to the nation's cities—grants for water and sewerage systems, neighborhood facilities and land acquisition programs, code enforcement and neighborhood development, urban renewal, and Model Cities. Of the $8.4 billion authorized by Congress for the first three years, Standard Metropolitan Statistical Areas must, by law, receive 80 percent of the funds. Most, but not all, of the money is distributed according to a formula based on population, the extent of poverty, and housing overcrowding.

This program was of great significance to the urban areas of the nation, for it facilitated some redistribution of grant funds administered by the Department of Housing and Urban Development away from the smaller cities and towns toward the larger cities (see Table 5). The average city of over 100,000 registered a 1 to 4 percent net increase in federal funding. The annual amounts of grants-in-aid under HUD-administered programs to cities of smaller size decreased, with cities of less than 10,000 persons suffering an average 38 percent loss in funding. Ironically, the implementation of the Nixon Administration's philosophy of decentralization actually penalized the Republican party's natural base of support in "middle America"—the smaller cities and towns where conservative, pro-Republican sentiments predominate.

Table 7.5. Comparison of Community Development Block Grants and H.U.D. — Categorical Grants: Average Annual Monetary Grants, by City Size*

City size (1970 census)	Number of cities	Average annual grants (thousands of dollars)		Percentage change
		Categorical grants (FY 1968-1972)	Community development block grants** (FY 1974)	
500,000+	26	23,459	23,776	+ 1
250,000−499,999	30	9,841	9,981	+ 4
100,000−249,999	97	3,381	3,722	+ 4
50,000− 99,999	232	1,191	1,149	− 4
25,000− 49,999	455	954	922	− 3
10,000− 24,999	1,127	600	554	− 8
− 9,999	16,699	332	207	−38

*Data exclude Puerto Rico, the Virgin Islands, and Guam, as well as places not considered incorporated by the Bureau of the Census.

**SMSA discretionary funds not included.

Source: Adapted from U.S. Department of Housing and Urban Development, Office of Community Planning and Development, Office of Evaluation, *Housing and Community Development Act of 1974, Community Development Block Grant Program: First Annual Report* (Washington: U.S. Government Printing Office, 1975), p. 142.

Unlike general revenue sharing, governments must apply for Community Development block grant funds, with a portion of the monies awarded on a competitive basis and in accordance with specific detailed performance standards and review procedures.[88] In fact, Congress specified unusually detailed administrative procedures, no doubt reflecting a lack of confidence in HUD's ability to formulate adequate standards. The legislation calls for yearly application and evaluation and requires a three-year development plan from the applying community. The plan must, among other things, project "long-range community objectives," include a housing assistance plan for the poor and elderly, respect equal opportunity and environmental protection guidelines, and give "maximum feasible priority" to low and moderate-income areas.[89] The last item is probably the most clearly-stated "national purpose" in the legislation.

The first few months of implementation were characterized by delays and confusion. HUD was in the midst of a bureauratic shake-up which made policy-making extremely difficult. Carla Hills took over as HUD Secretary in March, 1975. But the real confusion was to be found in the middle ranks, where bureaucrats had to devise new regulations and procedures. For the first several months, the HUD bureaucracy repeatedly changed its mind on nearly everything: eligibility, review requirements, forms, deadlines, and so forth.[90]

Through it all, HUD claimed great advances over past practices. By the end of the first year, Carla Hills said that HUD had reduced the average review period from two years for the programs which Community Development replaced to 49 days, and that applications averaged 50 pages, compared to 1,400 for the old urban renewal applications.[91]

The most important features were not to be found in process, however, but in results. How was the money spent? In its first annual report, HUD reported that 71 percent of all community development funds went to priority areas.[92] A year later, in its second annual report, HUD had revised its calculation to represent the actual proportion of lower-income residents in such areas, rather than courting the areas themselves. In the cities, the percentage of funds being spent for low- and moderate-income groups averaged 44 percent.[93]

Some evidence seems to indicate that affluent areas are receiving much more than these figures indicate. According to the Southern Regional Council, "the very mixed achievements of southern cities have shown that local diversions from national purpose are not just occasional abuses, but rather form a pattern inherent in the implementation of the Act."[94] The national purpose the Council had in mind was that funds should be spent in low- and moderate-income areas.

That community development funds would be spent in affluent areas is hardly a surprising turn of events. With local discretion largely governing expenditures, local political elites have a controlling voice in the allocation process. Poorer areas, naturally, lack influence. In Little Rock, Arkansas, for example, 150 thousand dollars from that city's Community Development Block Grant was spent to construct a tennis court in an affluent section of town. When questioned about this use of funds, the director of the local Department of Human Resources noted that: "Ninety-nine percent of this money is going to low and moderate income areas." But he revealingly continued that: "You cannot divorce politics from that much money. We remember the needs of the people who vote because they hold us accountable. Poor people don't vote."[95]

One strategy that local communities can employ in inflating the figures for priority areas is simply to draw their funding districts in such a way as to include affluent and less affluent areas in the same territory, as in gerrymandering Congressional seats. In Gulfport, Mississippi, for example, the city council declared the entire city to be an urban renewal area in order to facilitate use of Community Development Block grant funds on city-wide projects—notably a new central fire station. "When you expand fire protection, everybody in every census tract benefits from lower insurance rates," including, ostensibly, the primary target population of the Act, the low- and moderate-income residents.[96] Whether census tracts or planning districts are utilized, the result is often the same.

Another indication that this is happening derives from HUD's policies. HUD's prime consultant on the Community Development program was Anthony Downs, then president of the Real Estate Research Corporation in Chicago. Downs was concerned that community development funds be used as seed money which would encourage private reinvestment in transitional neighborhoods; he did not want it poured into areas which could not be brought back. Thus, he recommended that areas within cities be divided up into three basic categories: healthy, transitional, and deteriorated. Transitional neighborhoods, he thought, should receive highly visible projects to stimulate private investment.[97] Under the terms of the Community Development Act, these transitional areas would normally qualify as "priority" areas. Thus, poor neighborhoods might receive nothing, even though the terms of the Act would be met.

Under the Carter Administration, HUD's policy has been turned even more in the direction of stimulating investment. According to Patricia R. Harris, the new HUD Secretary, "The specific intent of action programs will be to stimulate new and increased private investment while establishing private sector confidence that will protect current investment."[98] Such an orientation, and the evidence that money is being used for affluent areas, has stimulated many critics to suggest basic revisions in the Housing and Community Development Act. For example, Senator William Proxmire has suggested a bill, "The Neighborhood Preservation Act of 1977," which would require further concentration of community development funds in low-income areas.

The Carter Administration has also begun to crack down upon communities which ignore the Congressional intent that funds be targeted toward low-income areas. "HUD Secretary Patricia R. Harris and Assistant Secretary Robert C. Embry have told mayors bluntly that they will also have to concentrate their CD [Community Development] programs in poorer areas, instead of scattering projects all over town."[99]

Unlike the Ford Administration, the Carter Administration is now carefully examining the applications of grant recipients. The impact of the new commitment has already made itself felt:

An application by Hempstead, New York, was turned down recently because of the community's poor record on low-income housing. Recently the city council of Boca Raton, Florida, hurriedly approved a subsidized housing project in order to save a $400,000 grant.[100]

There is concern, particularly in the urbanized areas of the northeast, that the major urban centers will receive a smaller share of the Community Development funds as time passes. From a level of nearly 83 percent of the monies in fiscal 1975, the Illinois Bureau of the Budget projects that only 60 percent will go to older cities of the north in 1980.[101] Under the 1974 formula, cities in critical need of federal community development funds would suffer dramatic declines in assistance levels. By 1980, Newark would lose over 52 percent of its block grant allocation, Philadelphia nearly 45 percent, Detroit 22 percent, and Rochester, New York, almost 70 percent. The "lost" money would be largely allocated to the growing cities of the sunbelt. Because of the biases of the formula, Dallas would receive a 549 percent increase in its CD block grant by 1980, Fort Lauderdale a 436 percent increase, and Phoenix would gain by nearly 727 percent.[102]

Precisely because of this phenomenon, several groups initiated efforts to substitute a new formula. In response to the needs of the governors of 14 northern industrial states who expressed concern over this at the Conference on Federal Economic Policies in October, 1976, the Illinois agency devloped an alternative formula which would benefit the older urbanized areas.[103] Similarly, The Brookings Institution and HUD's Office of Policy Development and Research have actively pursued improvements in the allocation formula which will aid the declining "frost belt" cities.[104]

As evidence mounts that the Congressional intent regarding spending in priority areas is not being implemented, pressures for amendment of the Housing and Community Development Act and its formulae have increased. Responding to the pressing needs of the cities of the northeast, the Carter Administration proposed a new formula which includes factors attempting to measure the processes of urban deterioration. Legislation before the House in May, 1977 would dramatically increase the Community Development entitlement funds available to the urban centers of the northeast. Fiscally troubled New York City, for example, would receive a 50 percent increase in its entitlement in 1978, and in 1980 would receive 256 million dollars—over $100 million more than it can expect to receive under the present formulae. Other older cities—Chicago, Detroit, St. Louis, Buffalo, Cleveland—would more than double their entitlements under the proposed legislation. In order to make these relative increases politically acceptable, the increased entitlements would come out of a $1 billion per year increase in appropriations for the program, so that the previously advantaged newer cities of the sunbelt will not be absolute losers.[105]

The Senate version, which contains a factor measuring the age of a city's housing stock, passed that body in June, 1977, by a close 45 to 43 margin, in a vote which underlined the interregional conflict involved.[106] The Senate bill, which proposes several alternative formulae in the style of revenue sharing allocations, reflects the composition of that body. It is opposed by the Carter Administration and House conferees. The revision of the CD block grant allocation, provided by the Administration and suported by a wide array of urban interests, "still has a long way to go" in the fall of 1977.[107]

THE SOCIAL WELFARE ESTABLISHMENT

Under the Nixon and Ford Administrations, there was a concerted effort to consolidate categorical grant programs which funded social welfare and urban activities. There was also a large dose of rhetoric about balancing the federal budget by paring the number and size of such programs. But despite all this, federal social welfare spending continued to rise. As can be discerned from Table 6, outlays for grants-in-aid for state and local governments—including revenue sharing—increased from $34.4 billion in Fiscal 1972 to $71.6 billion in Fiscal 1978. The proportion disbursed through block grants increased from just 2.8 percent to 34.5 percent. It is important to note that the block grant approach represented a tinkering with the manner in which money was disbursed—certainly not a reduction in the amount of spending.

Despite the great emphasis on shifting the locus of decision-making to lower level governmental institutions, there has been only a slight shift away from the emphasis on social programs in the federal grants-in-aid budget. Only in the case of general revenue sharing has there been a

Table 7.6. Outlays for Grants-in-Aid to State and Local Governments: By Type (dollar amounts in millions)

	Fiscal Year			
	1972	**1974**	**1976**	**1978***
General-purpose grants				
General revenue sharing . . (1972)	—	$ 6,106	$ 6,243	$ 6,814
Other general-purpose assistance and shared revenues . . .	$ 516	655	807	1,324
Sub-total, general purpose grants	516	6,761	7,050	8,138
Block grants				
Community development block grants . . . . (1974)	—	—	983	3,112
Comprehensive health grants . . . . (1966)	90	89	128	94
Employment and training (1973)	—	—	2,603	2,598
Social services . . . . (1974)	—	—	2,251	2,533
Criminal justice assistance (1969)	281	518	519	522
School aid to federally affected areas	602	529	558	433
Local public works. . . . (1974)	—	—	—	802
Financial assistance for health care . . . (proposed for FY 1978)	—	—	—	12,302
Child nutrition . . . (proposed for FY 1978)	—	—	—	2,000
Financial assistance for elementary and secondary education . . . (proposed for FY 1978)	—	—	—	336
Sub-total, block amounts	973	1,136	7,042	24,732
Categorical grants.	32,883	35,411	44,945	38,711
Total grants	34,372	43,308	59,037	71,581
(as a percentage of total grants-in-aid)				
General-purpose grants. . . .	1.5	15.6	11.9	11.4
Block grants	2.8	2.6	11.9	34.5
Categorical grants.	95.7	81.8	76.2	54.1
Total grants-in-aid. . . .	100.0	100.0	100.0	100.0

*Tentative figures as proposed in the Ford Administration FY 1978 budget

Source: Adapted from U.S. Office of Management and Budget, *Special Analyses, Budget of the United States Government: Fiscal Year 1978* (Washington: U.S. Government Printing Office, 1977), p. 276.

marked decrease in the general area of human resources. General revenue sharing aside, the movement toward consolidation of national purpose type he nation—and in particular the urban majority of the nation—in priorities. The percentage of federal assistance outlays allocated to human resources has remained steady and has even increased slightly—from 55 percent of total grants-in-aid outlays in 1973 to 58 percent in 1978.[108]

By the Ford Administration, social and urban programs had become an entrenched part of the federal governmental apparatus. Whereas firm Presidential leadership was required to create the programs of the 1960s, and they had come under attack under the Nixon Administration, by 1975 they were beyond the kind of attack launched in 1968. Even concerted Presidential leadership could not dislodge them. Under President Carter, there will probably be a further expansion.

A dramatic growth of national interest in the domestic problems of the nation —and in particular the urban majority of the nation— occurred during the Democratic administrations of the 1960s. The tangible electoral needs of the party leadership and the idealistic reform visions of its liberal elements converged upon the fiscal, social, and physical ills of the big cities to create an intricate array of solutions. However, the increasingly pro-urban domestic policies of the federal government under the leadership of the Democratic party were accompanied by a broad expansion of national authority into areas which had theretofore been primarily or exclusively of local concern. It also brought on centralized administration of programs in these functional areas.

The centralization which resulted offended both the ideological sensitivities of conservative elements as well as the political sensitivities of the big city mayors. For differing reasons, both sought to increase the control of local executives over the vast quantities of federal funds which were being targeted in cities across the nation. The result was a tenuous union of common interests between the big city mayors and the conservative Republican leadership.

Now those interests have been united with the Carter Administration, and the union will no doubt result in new initiatives in federal policies for the cities. "We have every reason to believe," remarked Newark's Mayor Kenneth A. Gibson, "that this is the beginning of a new relationship between the White House and the nation's mayors."[109]

Mayors have long expressed support for an increased federal responsibility in welfare. They will presumedly support the Carter Administration's 1977 proposals for a guaranteed annual income, public service jobs, and a larger federal role in funding welfare programs.[110] "I am cautiously optimistic that this proposal is a significant step in the right direction," remarked Syracuse Mayor Lee Alexander, president of the United States Conference of Mayors.[111]

The Carter Administration is also considering the idea of an urban development bank to help cities in financial trouble.[112] The concept has received the support of various groups including the Coalition of Northeastern Governors, the United States Conference of Mayors, and the National Association of Housing and Redevelopment Officials. Such a program would tie city officials into an even tighter alliance with the federal government.

The Carter Administration will continue to consolidate social welfare programs and to streamline the federal bureaucracy. In this respect, it will follow policies set in motion by the Republican Presidents. Block grant programs and revenue sharing will continue to emphasize local initiative. Any change from this policy would invite concerted criticism from Democratic mayors as well as liberals and conservatives who thrive on the bureaucracy issue. Sometime in the late 1970s, an income policy coupled with federalization of welfare will probably be implemented. All of these policies, incidentally, were set in motion by Republican Presidents in search of a palatable alternative to social welfare categorical grants-in-aid. What they achieved, instead, was the legitimation of federal involvement in social policy and in the cities.

NOTES

1. Reported in the *New York Times* (December 1, 1959): 27, and quoted in Mark I. Gelfand, *A Nation of Cities: The Federal Government and Urban America,* Urban Life in America Series (New York: Oxford University Press, 1975): 295; see also John F. Kennedy, "The Great Unspoken Issue," *Proceedings, American Municipal Congress 1959* (Washington: American Municipal League, n.d.): 23-28; and John F. Kennedy, "The Shame of the States," *New York Times Magazine* (May 18, 1958).

2. Quoted in Theodore H. White, *The Making of the President, 1960* (New York: Athenum Publishers, 1962): 206; Nixon's strategy, which White contends was no strategy at all, was a "national" one, in which he committed himself to visit all 50 states; Kennedy, on the other hand, utilized an "urban" strategy centered around the great industrial states (see pp. 267, 352).

3. John C. Donovan, *The Politics of Poverty* (2nd ed.; New York: Pegasus, A Division of the Bobbs-Merrill, 1973): 19.

4. U.S. Advisory Commission on Intergovernmental Relations, *Eleventh Annual Report* (Washington, D.C.: U.S. Government Printing Office, 1970): 2.

5. U.S. Congress, Senate, Committee on Government Operations, *Catalogue of Federal Aids to State and Local Governments,* Senate, 88th Cong., 2nd sess. (April 15, 1964).

6. U.S. Congress, Library of Congress, Legislative Reference Service, *Number of Authorizations for Federal Assistance to State and Local Governments,* by I. M. Labovitz (Washington, D.C.: Legislative Reference Service, July 5, 1966).

7. Michael Reagan, *The New Federalism* (New York: Oxford University Press, 1972): 55. In 1971 and 1972 there was virtually no growth in the number of grant programs, largely because of Presidential vetoes; Nixon vetoed 16 bills in 1972 (U.S. Advisory Commission on Intergovernmental Relations, *Fourteenth Annual Report: Striking A Better Balance* [Washington, D.C.: U.S. Government Printing Office, 1973]: 12).

8. Reagan, *The New Federalism:* 55.

9. U.S. Office of Management and Budget, *Special Analyses, Budget of the United States Government: Fiscal Year 1975* (Washington, D.C.: U.S. Government Printing Office, 1974): 210.

10 Ibid.; and U.S. Office of Management and Budget, *Special Analyses, Budget of the United States Government: Fiscal Year 1976* (Washington, D.C.: U.S. Government Printing Office, 1975): 148.

11. Refer to Daniel J. Elazar, *The American Partnership: Intergovernmental Cooperation in the Nineteenth Century United States* (Chicago: University of Chicago Press, 1962).

12. Manpower Development and Training Act of 1962, Public Law 87-415, 87th Congress (1962); emphasis added.

13. Economic Opportunity Act of 1964, Public Law 88-452, 88th Congress (1964); emphasis added.

14. Demonstration Cities and Metropolitan Development Act of 1966, Public Law 89-754, 89th Congress (1966); emphasis added.

15. See James L. Sundquist and David W. Davis, *Making Federalism Work: A Study of Program Coordination at the Community Level* (Washington, D.C.: The Brookings Institution, 1969): 3-5.

16. U.S. Bureau of the Budget, *Special Analyses of the United States Budget: Fiscal Year 1969* (Washington, D.C.: U.S. Government Printing Office, 1968): 158.

17. Refer to U.S. Advisory Commission on Intergovernmental Relations, *Eleventh Annual Report:* 2; and U.S. Advisory Commission on Intergovernmental Relations, *Fiscal Balance in the American Federal System,* Vol. I (Washington, D.C.: U.S. Government Printing Office, 1967): 151.

18. U.S. Office of Management and Budget, *Special Analyses: Fiscal Year 1975:* 207.

19. "Citizens Budget Commission Summaries, 1952-1973," and *Mayor's Annual Report and Expense Budget Message* (May 1973), as cited in Donald H. Haider, *When Governments Come to Washington: Governors, Mayors, and Intergovernmental Lobbying* (New York: Free Press, 1974): 94.

19. "Citizens Budget Commission Summaries, 1952-1973," and *Mayor's Annual Report and Expense Budget Message* (May 1973), as cited in Donald H. Haider, *When Governments Come to Washington: Governors, Mayors, and Intergovernmental Lobbying* (New York: Free Press, 1974): 94.

20. See U.S. Congress, Senate Committee on Government Operations, *Creative Federalism, Hearings* before the Subcommittee on Intergovernmental Relations, Part 2a, *The State-Local-Regional Level,* Senate, 90th Cong., 1st sess. (January 31; February 1, 2, 6, 1967): 576-585.

21. Midwest Research Institute, "Federal Aid Program Information—A Survey of Local Government Needs" (September 1967): 15.

22. U.S. Bureau of the Budget "Summary of Recent Activities to Promote Improved Intergovernmental Relations" (memorandum), March 14, 1967.

23. Midwest Research Institute, "Federal Aid Program Information": 64.

24. See U.S. Advisory Commission on Intergovernmental Relations, *Improving Federal Grants Management, The Intergovernmental Grant System: An Assessment and Proposed Policies* (Washington, D.C.: U.S. Government Printing Office, 1977): 1-23.

25. U.S. Congress, Senate, Committee on Government Operations, *Creative Federalism,* Part 1: 138-139. HUD also was participating in 41 different "interagency agreements, understandings, Executive Orders, and Directives."

26. Ibid., 232-233.

27. Ibid., 264.

28. Ibid., 287-289. He also listed interagency committees and agreements with the Vocational Rehabilitation Administration and committees in which the Welfare Administration was participating.

29. U.S. Executive Office of the President, Executive Order 11297, August 11, 1966.

30. See U.S. Executive Office of the President, *Weekly Compilation of Presidential Documents,* (vol. 3): 482-494.

31. U.S. Bureau of the Budget, "Summary of Recent Activities to Promote Improved Intergovernmental Relations" (memorandum), June 21, 1968.

32. U.S. Advisory Commission on Intergovernmental Relations, *Fiscal Balance* (vol. 1): 175-181; see also H. Ralph Taylor, "Greatest Opportunity—Making Model Cities Work," *Public Management,* L (February, 1968): 46; and Bernard J. Frieden and Marshall Kaplan, *The Politics of Neglect: Urban Aid from Model Cities to Revenue Sharing* (Cambridge, Mass.: M.I.T. Press, 1975), for a discussion of the "efficiency and economy" values underlying the push for planning.

33. U.S. Congress, Senate, Committee on Government Operations, *Creative Federalism* (part 1): 391.

34. Jeffrey L. Pressman, *Federal Programs and City Politics: The Dynamics of the Aid Process in Oakland,* The Oakland Project (Berkeley: University of California Press, 1975): 60-61.

35. U.S. Congress, Senate, Committee on Governmental Operations, *Intergovernmental Revenue Act of 1971 and Related Legislation, Hearings* before the Subcommittee on Intergovernmental Relations, Senate, 92nd Cong., 1st sess. (1971): 102-103.

36. Haider, *When Governments Come to Washington:* 109.

37. U.S. Advisory Commission on Intergovernmental Relations, *Eleventh Annual Report:* 1.

38. Quoted in Reagan, *The New Federalism:* 97.

39. Quoted in Timothy B. Clark, John K. Iglehart and William Lilley III, "New Federalism 1: Return of Power to States and Cities Looms as Theme of Nixon's Second-Term Domestic Policy," *National Journal: The Weekly on Politics and Government* (December 16, 1972): 1911.

40. U.S. Congress, House, Committee of the Whole on the State of the Union, *The State of the Union, Address* of the President of the United States, House, 92nd Cong., 1st sess. (January 1971): 4-5.

41. H. Res 4185, 92nd Cong., 1st sess. (1971).

42. U.S. Office of Management and Budget, *Special Analyses, Budget of the United States Government: Fiscal Year 1972* (Washington, D.C.: U.S. Government Printing Office, 1973): 237.

43. W. W. Heller, *New Dimensions in Political Economy,* (Cambridge, Mass.: Harvard University Press, 1967): 129.

44. Richard E. Thompson, *Revenue Sharing: A New Era in Federalism* (Washington, D.C.: Revenue Sharing Advisory Service, 1973): 20.

45. Thompson, *Revenue Sharing:* 20, 55-57.

46. Duane Lockard, *American Federalism,* (New York: McGraw-Hill, 1969): 95.

47. Refer to E.E. Schattschneider, *The Semi-Sovereign People: A Realist's View of Democracy in America,* reissued with an introduction by David Adamany (Hinsdale, Ill.: The Dryden Press, 1975), for insights on the significance of the level at which political conflict takes place.

48. Haider, *When Governments Come to Washington:* 50.

49. See Thompson, *Revenue Sharing:* 4, 45; refer also to Paul R. Dommel, *The Politics of Revenue Sharing* (Bloomington and London: Indiana University Press, 1974); and Richard P. Nathan, Allen D. Manvel, Susannah E. Caulkins, and Associates, *Monitoring Revenue Sharing* (Washington, D.C.: The Brookings Institution, 1975), for discussions of the politics of passage.

50. U.S. Congress, Joint Committee on Internal Revenue and Taxation, *Summary of Testimony on General Revenue Sharing at Public Hearings, June 2 to June 28, 1971, Held by the Committee on Ways and Means on the Subject of General Revenue Sharing* (committee print), Joint Committee on Internal Revenue and Taxation, 92nd Cong., 1st sess. (1971): 2, 14; and Thompson, *Revenue Sharing:* 55-56.

51. Statement of the AFL-CIO Executive Council on Revenue Sharing, Bal Harbour, Florida, February 15, 1971: 2-3; as cited in Thompson, *Revenue Sharing:* 67; Dommel cites this vehemous opposition by organized labor as a major contributing factor in Lyndon Johnson's lack of enthusiasm for the revenue sharing concept (The Politics of Revenue Sharing: 51).

52. Reagan, *The New Federalism:* 117.

53. Ibid., 130-131.

54. U.S. Congress, Joint Committee on Internal Revenue and Taxation, *Summary of Testimony:* 8; and Thompson, *Revenue Sharing:* 103.

55. U.S. Congress, Joint Committee on Internal Revenue and Taxation, *Summary of Testimony:* 11.

56. National League of Cities, U.S. Conference of Mayors, and International City Management Association, *The Fiscal Plight of American Cities* (excerpts), as reprinted in Appendix A of Thompson, *Revenue Sharing:* 145.

57. Robert S. Benson and Harold Wolman (eds.), *The National Urban Coalition Counterbudget: A Blueprint for Changing National Priorities 1971-1976,* foreword by Sol M. Liniwitz, (New York: Praeger Publishers, 1971): 129.

58. National League of Cities, United States Conference of Mayors, and the International City Management Association, *The Fiscal Plight of American Cities,* as reprinted in Thompson, *Revenue Sharing:* 130-132.

59. Quoted in Ibid., 130.

60. Ibid.

61. Refer to *Washington Post,* March 22, 1971, as cited by Thompson, *Revenue Sharing:* 69.

62. *Newsweek* (May 24, 1971): 94.

63. Thompson, *Revenue Sharing:* 72.

64. Ibid., 114-116.

65. Ibid., 118.

66. Public Law 92-15, 92nd Cong. (1972).

67. Haider, *When Governments Come to Washington:* 64.

68. Related by Senator Howard Baker (R-TN), and quoted in Thompson, *Revenue Sharing:* 120.

69. U.S. Department of the Treasury, Office of Revenue Sharing, *Reported Uses of General Revenue Sharing Funds 1974-1975: A Tabulation and Analysis of Data from Actual Use Report 5* (Washington, D.C.: U.S. Government Printing Office, 1976): 5.

70. U.S. Department of the Treasury, Office of Revenue Sharing, *Revenue Sharing: The First Actual Use Reports,* by David A. Caputo and Richard L. Cole (Washington, D.C.: U.S. Government Printing Office, 1974): 10, 12, 29.

71. Ibid., 25.

72. Calculated from data in U.S. Office of Management and Budget, *Special Analyses, Budget of the United States Government: Fiscal Year 1973,* (Washington, D.C.: U.S. Government Printing Office, 1973): 240; the volume in the same series for *Fiscal Year 1978:* 271; and U.S. Department of the Treasury, Office of Revenue Sharing, *Revenue Sharing:* 4-5.

73. Ibid.

74. Ibid.

75. U.S. Department of the Treasury, *Renewal of Revenue Sharing* (Washington, D.C.: U.S. Government Printing Office, 1975): 11.

76. For a discussion of this topic see Richard P. Nathan, Charles F. Adams, Jr., and Associates, with the assistance of André Juneau and James W. Fossett, *Revenue Sharing: The Second Round* (Washington, D.C.: The Brookings Institution, 1977): 1-23.

77. Ibid., 2, citing *Congressional Record,* February 20, 1973: 746.

78. See, for example, *Congressional Record,* February 22, 1973: 987; and *Congressional Record,* March 1, 1973: 1160.

79. *Revenue Sharing Bulletin* (June, 1973): 2.

80. *Revenue Sharing Bulletin* (July, 1974): 2.

81. U.S. Office of Management and Budget, *Special Analyses: Fiscal Year 1972:* 204.

83. See Robert Jacob Kerstein, "The Political Consequences of Federal Intervention: The Economic Opportunity Act and Model Cities in the City of St. Louis" (Unpublished Ph.D. dissertation, Washington University, St. Louis, 1975): 23-28; refer also to U.S. Advisory Commission on Intergovernmental Relations, *Grants Management:* 6-7, 17-20.

84. Kerstein, "The Political Consequences of Federal Intervention": 30-31.

85. U.S. Office of Management and Budget, *Special Analyses: Fiscal Year 1972:* 237.

86. Kerstein, "The Political Consequences of Federal Intervention": 30-31.

85. U.S. Office of Management and Budget, *Special Analyses: Fiscal Year 1972:* 237.

86. Housing and Community Development Act of 1974, sec. 101.

87. Ernest Erber, *The Emergence of the "Housing Density Bonus"* (Washington, D.C.: National Committee Against Housing Discrimination, 1974): 14.

88. Most of the funds are allocated to entitlement cities with populations of 50,000 or more, SMSA central cities, and certain urban counties. Jurisdictions which participated in the previous categorical programs included in the Housing and Community Development Act also received "hold-harmless" grants under which the level of funding could not decline. About 20 percent of the monies are distributed without regard to the formulas. These latter three funds represent the competitive portion of the program.

89. Housing and Community Development Act of 1974, sec. 104(a).

90. See the "Community Development Monitor" series, *Housing and Development Reporter* (1976).

91. "New Directions Cited in First Annual Block Grant Reports," *Housing and Development Reporter* (January 12, 1976): 761.

92. U.S. Department of Housing and Urban Development, Office of Community Planning and Development, Office of Evaluation, *Housing and Community Development Act of 1974, Community Development Block Grant Program: First Annual Report* (Washington, D.C.: U.S. Government Printing Office, 1975): 38.

93. Reported in *Housing and Development Reporter* (January 10, 1977): 684.

94. Quoted from the Report of the Southern Regional Council in *Housing and Development Reporter* (April 5, 1976): 1051.

95. Citing an interview by SGMP investigator Sharon Cribbs with Nathaniel Hill, Director, Department of Human Resources, Little Rock, Arkansas (Summer, 1975), Southern Governmental Monitoring Project, *A Time for Accounting: The Housing and Community Development Act in the South,* A Monitoring Report by Raymond Brown with Ann Coil and Carol Rose (Atlanta: Southern Regional Council, 1976): 53.

96. Ibid., 51.

97. See Leanne M. Lachman, "Planning for Community Development: A Proposed Approach," *Journal of Housing* (February, 1975): 58.

98. Quoted by Robert L. Joller, "HUD Secretary Quiets Critics," *St. Louis Post-Dispatch* (April 18, 1977): 38.

99. "Grants With Strings Attached," *St. Louis Post-Dispatch* (August 6, 1977): 4A (reprinted from *The Washington Post*).

100. Ibid.

101. State of Illinois, Bureau of the Budget, Federal Relations Unit,*Equity in Federal Funding: A First Step* (Springfield: State of Illinois, Bureau of the Budget, December 9, 1976):2.

102. Rochelle L. Stansfield, "Federalism Report: Government Seeks the Right Formula for Community Development Funds," *National Journal: The Weekly on Politics and Government* (February 12, 1977): 242.

103. See State of Illinois, Bureau of the Budget, Federal Relations Unit, *Equity in Federal Funding:* 32.

104. Refer to Stansfield, "Government Seeks the Right Formula."

105. Robert Reinhold, "More Aid on Way for Older Cities," *St. Louis Post-Dispatch* (May 9, 1977): 3C (c 1977, New York Times News Service).

106. "Shot in the Arm for Older Cities: Senate Passes Housing Bill," *St. Louis Post-Dispatch* (June 8, 1977): 1A.

107. Ibid.

108. U.S. Office of Management and Budget, *Special Analyses: Fiscal Year 1976:* 238; and U.S. Office of Management and Budget, *Special Analyses, Budget of the United States Government: Fiscal Year 1978* (Washington, D.C.: U.S. Government Printing Office, 1977): 271.

109. "Washington Update: Administration Officials, Mayors Have Love-Fest," *National Journal: The Weekly on Politics and Government* (January 29, 1977): 189.

110. "Carter Proposes All New Welfare System," *St. Louis Post-Dispatch* (August 6, 1977): 1A.

111. "Carter's Sweetening of His Welfare Plan Blunts Some Criticism," *St. Louis Post-Dispatch* (August 7, 1977): 5A (c 1977, New York Times News Service).

112. "Administration Studying Proposal for Development Bank to Aid Cities," *St. Louis Post-Dispatch* (March 20, 1977): 26A.

8.

NATURAL RESOURCES POLICY: PROCEDURAL CHANGE AND SUBSTANTIVE ENVIRONMENTALISM

PAUL J. CULHANE

University of Houston

For many Americans, natural resources policy—the management of the public lands and water resources development—seems an arcane field, laden with technical and legal issues, which affects them little. The substance of natural resources policy is, of course, critically important to certain sectors of society: those in the industries dependent on natural resources agencies, environmentalists, and the people in the western United States generally. Water resources programs are the second largest (after highways) of the regular federal public works programs, at $3.66 billion in 1975.[1] The major public lands agencies of the federal government manage a total of 31.4 percent of the United States.[2] There was a time when the politics of natural resources rightly received high billing on the national stage, but until recently that time had passed.

For public policy analysts, however, the primary importance of natural resources administration has been that these policy subsystems were seen as archetypes of federal policy processes generally. The politics of natural resources have been thought to be clear examples of the phenomenon of irresponsible interest group domination of policy making, to the exclusion of the general "public interest." As Grant McConnell put it:

> The complexities of the twentieth century have enveloped the issues of land and agricultural politics, so that it is not often easy to state what is essential in them. In the nineteenth century the issue was most frequently the simple

taking possession of public land; in the twentieth it has more often been the taking possession of public policy. This has not been peculiar . . . to the sphere of land and agriculture. But the process has perhaps been somewhat clearer in matters relating to land and agriculture than elsewhere.

Water resources projects, moreover, have been considered the prime example of budgetary irresponsibility—pork barrel politics in an uncontrolled policy subsystem.[4]

The philosophical debates in the natural resources field have historically run parallel to these academic critiques. In the early part of the twentieth century, natural resources politics had already become the battleground of the "special interests" and the champions of the "public interest." The doctrine of the early conservationists was an amalgam of scientifically based prudence and the political grievance of the Progressive Movement. The public lands should not be exploited solely to benefit the timber and cattle barons, nor should public hydropower resources be monopolized by the private utilities. Resources should be managed wisely by professionals and used—as Gifford Pinchot, Theodore Roosevelt's natural resources advisor, put it—"for the greatest good of the greatest number in the long run."[5] The same political grievance is at the heart of the ideology of the modern environmental movement, the philosophical successors of the turn-of-the-century preservationists and progressive conservationists. Just as the General Land Office was viewed in Teddy Roosevelt's day as the accomplice of the exploiters, federal natural resources agencies are regarded by today's environmentalists as the captives of exploitative special interests, with "public interest" the loser. They see sins against Nature—not to mention the public purse—wrought by an unholy alliance of agency developmentalist professional norms and missions, narrow economic greed of clienteles, grants of excessive discretionary authority to the agencies, and subsystem politics generally.[6]

But for the environmentalist and the academic observer of natural resources policy, it must seem that the federal government of 1977 has been born again!

The past decade has witnessed a gradual process in which the political environment of natural resources agencies has changed radically, causing progressively clearer movement of policy towards a more balanced, if not pro-environmental, position. Two events in 1970 marked the beginning of this change.[7] First, the environmental movement, and general public sentiment favoring the environment, broke into full flower, with Earth Day, 1970, being both symbolic of the new environmentalism and a media event which spurred the growth of the movement. Public concern for the environment rose from 2 percent in 1968 to 24 percent in 1970, second only to the Vietnam War (at 54 percent).[8] Of greater importance for the political impact of environmentalism was a considerable increase in the number and size of environmental interest groups in the late 1960s and early 1970s. The number of environmental groups doubled after 1969, and the membership, activism, and budget of existing groups all increased after Earth Day. The Sierra Club's membership, for example, has grown from about 85 thousand in 1969 to 164 thousand in 1976.[9] Second, the National Environmental Policy Act (NEPA) was signed into law in January, 1970, establishing a broad policy of environmental consciousness for federal agencies to be enforced by the mechanism of Environmental Impact Statements(EISs). While applicable to all federal agencies, the natural resources agencies were the major targets of NEPA, and they have been the most affected by it.

The rise of environmentalism and NEPA have been the driving forces behind change in natural resources policy. Initially, agency responses were incremental, and often of a procedural, as opposed to a substantive, nature. Increasingly, however, the receptiveness of natural resources agencies to NEPA and environmentalists—reinforced by the courts—led to discernible and sometimes astounding substantive policy developments. The process has been capped, moreover, by the election of President Carter, who gives every sign of being the most conservation-oriented chief executive since Theodore Roosevelt during the heyday of the progressive conservation movement.

THE NATIONAL ENVIRONMENTAL POLICY ACT

The statutory vehicle of change in natural resources policy is the National Environmental Policy Act.[10] For a law with such consequences, NEPA's explicit provisions and legislative history are fairly innocuous. NEPA contains three major provision. First, section 101 advances a broad, hortatory policy, stating the federal goverment should:

> Maintain conditions under which man and nature can exist in productive harmony; [and]
> Fulfill the responsibilities of each generation as trustee of the environment for succeeding generations.

The policy implied that uncoordinated federal programs, carried out with a disregard for environmental consequences, were the major public policy concern. NEPA's section 105, as well as its legislative history, clearly indicated the NEPA policy was "supplementary to" those same uncoordinated, incremental missions, but section 103 of the Act instructed agencies to report back to Congress on existing statutory mandates which might conflict with NEPA's environmental goals.

Second, NEPA's section 102 established a mechanism to insure agency compliance with the section 101 policy. The "action forcing" mechanism of section 102(2)(c) was that for "major federal actions significantly affecting the quality of the human environment, a detailed statement" had to be prepared as a primary decision document. The statement was to be a form of rational decision making, including a discussion of the environmental impacts of a proposed action, long-term effects of the action, and alternatives to the proposal. In addition, the EISs were viewed as a mechanism for coordination of proposals with other governmental agencies and the President and were to "be made available. . . . to the public" (a provision which turned out to be the root of NEPA's effectiveness).

Third, Title II of NEPA (sections 201-207)[11] established the Council on Environmental Quality (CEQ) in the Executive Office of the President. CEQ had been viewed by some of its proponents as an environmental ombudsman, but its statutory "powers" are very limited. Its duties are to advise the President on environmental issues generally and to write the President's annual environmental report. While its annual reports have been excellent reference documents, CEQ was not one of the more important staff units in the Ford and Nixon Executive Offices.

If the provisions of NEPA seem innocuous, the reader has made the same appraisal as most observers of the legislation in 1969. NEPA was a noncontroversial bill, passing Senate, for example, on a voice vote. Not subjected to significant lobbying, the major legislative fights over NEPA were intercommittee jurisdictional disputes (principally between Senators Muskie and Jackson in the Senate, and Representatives Dingell and Aspinall in the House).[12] Congress—and most other observers—thought a nice piece of symbolic legislation had been passed.

Development of NEPA Case Law

Legal scholars are fond of debating whether judges "make law." One thing is certain; judges made NEPA. During its first year, federal agencies approached NEPA's requirements very tentatively. Only a small proportion of the agencies adopted their own NEPA procedures; and agencies seemed not to realize the impact NEPA might have on their programs, since only one reported, in its so-called section 103 statement, on the Act's implications for their programs.[13] Moreover, the section 102(2)(C) EISs produced in 1970 were few and short, vague documents which did not approximate what is now considered an adequate EIS. Agency hesitancy was somewhat understandable. NEPA was a very vague statute which failed to define key phrases: how "major" and "significant" did an action have to be to trigger the EIS requirement? How "detailed" did an EIS have to be? CEQ, in its 1970 guidelines, failed to resolve these issues. But the courts would attempt to.

The courts were a potentially useful tool for environmentalists attempting to force agency compliance with NEPA, but environmentalists faced a major potential roadblock in using the courts to further NEPA's ends—the threshold legal doctrine of "standing to sue."[14] Traditionally, only "aggrieved parties" with a "legal interest" are allowed to obtain relief from the federal courts; and the legal interest generally had to involve individualized economic loss at the hands of the respondent agency. This rule of standing would make access for public interest, environmental plaintiffs very difficult; individualized interests were not the ones to be litigated, but rather, broad "public" interests were. In environmental cases, also, the interests were almost wholly noneconomic.

Fortunatley for environmentalist litigants—and in large part because of environmental litigation—the law on standing was significantly liberalized from 1965 to 1973. The liberalization began with the Scenic Hudson case, involving Federal Power Commission (FPC) licensing of the Storm King pumped storage project.[15] In Scenic Hudson, the court held that the environmentalist plaintiffs with a personal, if noneconomic, interest had standing under the Federal Power Act. In two 1970 decisons, Data Processing[16] and Barlow,[17] the Supreme Court set forth a two-part test of standing based on the Scenic Hudson decision: (1) plaintiff had to show direct "injury in fact" to either economic or noneconomic interest, including "aesthetic, conservational, or recreational interests"; and (2) the injury had to be "arguably within the zone of interests to be protected by the statute." These tests did not completely allow public interest litigation under NEPA: even though environmental interests were within NEPA's "zone of interests to be protected," plaintiffs were granted standing only to protect personal interests. The Sierra Club attempted to expand the rule in the Mineral King case, arguing that its general interest in conservation conferred it standing. The Supreme Court, in its 1972 decision on Mineral King,[18] did not accept this position, reiterating essentially the Data Processing and Barlow test. But it did suggest that an environmental organization could obtain standing through injury to its members' personal interests (the Court suggested hiking use by members would meet the personal interest test) and could then litigate general public interest issues. Finally, in the SCRAP case,[19] the Supreme Court adopted a very broad meaning of "injury in fact." A group of law students sought standing to challenge an Interstate Commerce Commission (ICC) freight rate increase alleged to discriminate against recycled materials on the grounds that the freight rate structure caused overexploitation of natural resources, including forests, streams, and mountains. Some of these were in the Washington, D.C., area and were used by the students for "hiking, fishing . . . . and other recreational, aesthetic purposes." After the Court granted SCRAP standing, it would be fair to say that environmentalist individuals or organizations who are part of a "public" with even a broad and diffuse public interest can obtain standing and act essentially as "private attorneys general."

While, as noted above, the agencies had moved slowly on NEPA in 1970, the courts proved very receptive to NEPA, especially during 1971-1972. A Supreme Court decision under the highway laws paved the way for the development of NEPA law. The Overton Park[20] case was a challenge to the routing of a highway through a park in Memphis, Tennessee. The Court was concerned about the absence of a well developed reviewable record of agency decision-making. In the absence of such a record the Court held that the decision could be reviewed to determine whether it was "arbitrary and capricious" and thus not in accord with the provisions of the relevant law. In addition, the Courts could thoroughly investigate agency decision processes in connection with the "arbitrary and capricious" standard, but, critically, could not overrule the agency decision on matters of judgment.[21] Thus the Court set the stage for the two-part pattern of decisions on NEPA compliance: (1) a fair, complete and formal decision process, but (2) ultimate reliance on agency judgment about substantive policy choices once fair decision processes had transpired.

The first, and still most important, of the NEPA cases was Calvert Cliffs,[22] decided by the District of Columbia Circuit in July, 1971. The case involved a challenge to the licensing of a nuclear power plant on Chesapeake Bay and deficiencies in Atomic Energy Commission (AEC) procedures implementing NEPA. The Court first established that NEPA would be subject to judicial interpretation and that the courts would require strict compliance with the act. The court also held that NEPA required environmental consideration to "the fullest extent possible" at each significant agency decision stage.[23] Two other decisions of the period indicated that the primary way the courts would evaluate full consideration would be by evaluation of the thoroughness of the EIS. The Gillham Dam case[24] involved a Corps of Engineers project on the Cossatot River in Arkansas. The district court opinions, in particular, in Gillham stress that NEPA compliance requires the development of a rigorous and good faith analysis and "full disclosure" of alternatives and environmental impacts. The Hanly I case, involving the construction of a federal detention facility in New York City, stressed the role of the EIS as a reviewable record of agency decision-making.[25]

The Calvert Cliffs and Gillham decisions clearly indicated the courts would not accept the superficial, 1970-style agency efforts as meeting NEPA's call for "detailed" statements. However, the Gillham and Tennessee-Tombigbee[26] opinions noted that the agencies need not engage in unlimited analysis. As District Judge Eisele said in Gillham, "It is doubtful that any agency, however objective, however sincere, however well staffed, and however well financed, could come up with a perfect environmental impact statement in connection with any major project."[27] In other words, NEPA requires more than superficiality, but less than perfection—not a very precise standard. However, it is possible to discern some patterns in court decisions on the scope of NEPA analysis.

Both the Calvert Cliffs and Gillham opinions indicated that the courts, in reviewing the adequacy of EIS's, would place heavy emphasis on full evaluation of alternatives to a proposed action. The leading case on the consideration of alternatives is NRDC v. Morton,[28] which involved a challenge to the Bureau of Land Management's (BLM) Outer Continental Shelf (OCS) leasing program. The D.C. Circuit argued in NRDC v. Morton that all reasonable alternatives should be considered. That the court meant "reasonable" to be construed broadly was indicated by its holding that the BLM had to even consider alternatives which were not within its authority to implement (so as to inform reviewing decision makers of those options).

The courts, again led by the Calvert Cliffs decision, also indicated that analysis "to the fullest extent possible" was required, in discussing environmental impacts, but, as with alternatives, limited by a "rule of reason." The guiding rule was best discussed by Judge Eisele in Gillham: The EIS should contain a "full disclosure" of all environmental impacts of the action known to, or which could be anticipated by, the agency. Closely related to the "full disclosure" criteria, the courts have examined the agency's treatment of comments on the draft EIS; failure to consider evidence advanced by outside commentators would be an indication of less than full disclosure. This point was stressed in Hanly II,[29] as well as Gillham. The Amchitka decision, involving a challenge to a detonation of a nuclear device on an Alaska island also held that good faith consideration of comments was required, but used the narrower language of "responsible" comments.[30]

Of course, the gross volume of EISs, and alternatives and impacts discussed therein, is less important that the relationship between EIS's analysis and the decision on a proposed action. A nagging question has been whether NEPA requires "substantive" or only "procedural" compliance. Does NEPA mandate, as Judge Skelly Wright put it in his Calvert Cliffs opinion, "no more than the physical act of passing certain folders and papers, unopened, to reviewing officials along with other folders and papers?"[31] At an explicit level, the courts have held that NEPA does require substantive compliance. Again the leading cases were Calvert Cliffs and Gillham Dam. In Gillham, the Eighth Circuit argued that NEPA was not just a "full disclosure" law, but a statute which created substantive environmental rights and duties. Specifically, according to Calvert Cliffs, agencies had to "balance" environmental costs against economic and technical benefits. But the court's rulings about substantive balancing are subject to a "catch-22": beginning with Overton Park, the courts held they could not substitute their own judgment on the merits of cases for the agencies'. So the courts assigned themselves a less direct test to enforce NEPA's substantive requirements by requiring the very strict procedural test of full, good faith analysis leading to a proposal which was not "arbitrary and capricious" when compared with reviewable EIS record. The "arbitrary and capricious" standard forbade agency decisions which weighed factors outside agency authority, and, most importantly, which gave undue weight to any factors; this, in theory, would achieve "balance." Moreover, the absence of agency consideration of the points of view of responsible commentators, as the Hanly II, Gillham, and Amchitka decisions indicated, would be a clue that the agency decision was "capricious."

The precedential decisions in the early phase of NEPA implementation were all at the circuit court level. These circuit court decisions were either not appealed to the Supreme Court, or certiorari was denied. Other than the Mineral King and SCRAP I cases, which involved standing, the Supreme Court, did not decide a NEPA case until 1975. The three Supreme Court decisions on NEPA in 1975-1976 did not alter the basic case law on NEPA but did adopt a fairly narrow reading of what an agency action was for the purpose of an EIS. In SCRAP II,[32] the Court upheld the ICC's EIS as adequate, finding that the across-the-board rate increase—not the underlying rate structure—was the relevant agency action. In the Kleppe case,[33] involving coal-related energy developments in the Northern Great Plains, the Court held no programmation EIS was required on the series of actions in the region, such as leasing tracts of land for coal strip mining, because no regional plan existed to constitue a "federal action."Finally, in the Flint Ridge case,[34] the Court held that the Department of Housing and Urban Development need not prepare and EIS on a subdivision property report because acceptance of such a report within 30 days of receipt is a nondiscretionary requirement unless the report is incomplete. While not ruling explicitly on the issue, the Court's decision overturned a Tenth Circuit ruling that NEPA constituted grounds for examination of the environmental consequences of the development, even though only the accuracy of the report was covered in the act requiring the report.[35] While fairly narrow, these decisions did not alter the basic structure of NEPA requirements developed in Overton Park and the 1971-1972 circuit court decisions. In any case, by 1975, the horse was out of the barn.

Administrative Implementation of NEPA

Observers of NEPA generally agree that during 1970, almost all federal agencies, including the Council on Environmental Quality (CEQ), were quite uncertain about what NEPA required of them.[36] As a result, most agencies waited to see whether they would be compelled to comply with the Act. The strict interpretation of NEPA in the 1971-1972 Court decisions was the cue that NEPA would have to be implemented.

One of the first areas in which the Court decisions were reflected was CEQ's NEPA guidelines. During 1971 and 1972, CEQ revised its guidelines twice and issued a number of supplementary memoranda; the guidelines and memoranda all required considerable improvements from the agencies. It was quite clear that CEQ's stance was being significantly influenced, if not lead, by Court decisions, especially Calvert Cliffs. The CEQ guidelines and memos stressed a number of themes in the Court decisions: the role of EISs at all decision stages, full disclosure, balancing, etc. CEQ also suggested that the avoidance of "legal difficulties" would be the major incentive for agencies to comply rigorously with NEPA.[37] The area in which CEQ had perhaps its greatest impact, however, was in the openness of the EIS process to the public. Court rulings, especially Gillham and Hanly II, had placed a premium on agency response to comments. But these rulings merely solidified CEQ's initiatives. From the outset, CEQ's guidelines and memos had opened the door to public comments on EISs. In many ways, perhaps the single most important CEQ rule in its 1970 "interim" guidelines was the requirement that draft EISs be prepared, circulated to other agencies *and "the public,"* and then a final EIS written, revised in light of comments. Subsequent revised guidelines and memos always stressed the importance of agency responsiveness to public comments. Thus, while NEPA's Congressional sponsors seemed in 1969 to have a fairly passive role in mind for the public (in the style of Freedom of Information Act openness), CEQ was largely responsible for fostering active public participation in the EIS process, which led to the opening of agency decision processes generally.

Under pressure from the early court decisions and CEQ's guidelines, federal agencies began to implement NEPA. During this "formal compliance" phase,[38] agencies gradually developed NEPA procedures, began to take a more liberal view of their responsibilities under the Act, wrote improved (and certainly longer) EISs, and usually develped special NEPA staff sections. There was quite a bit of variation among agencies in terms of both the timing and the rigorousness of their formal compliance with NEPA. The Corps of Engineers, for example, could be considered to have entered the phase in 1970, even before CEQ's first set of guidlelines were issued, while the Soil Conservation Service (SCS) did not enter the phase until 1972;[39] and by 1974 the Forest Service had written approximately 24 times the number of EIS's of the Bureau of Land Management, an agency with a comparable workload.[40] But all major agencies began to formally comply, at least to some extent, with NEPA.

For a number of agencies, formal public participation programs were an important part of NEPA compliance. Public participation programs were viewed as a logical extension of the requirement for agency consideration of public comments on EISs (though some agencies' programs were developed independently of NEPA). The programs, though often identified with public hearings, also consisted of much less formal consultations between agency administrators and interest groups. The major importance of public participation, of course, was that the "public," which was added to the agencies' constituencies, consisted primarily of environmentalists. There was more variation in public participation programs than in formal NEPA procedures. Several agencies have well developed participation programs, among them the Corps and the Forest Service, who are also leaders in the development of participation methods. Other agencies have less commitment to participation, with some—notably the FPC and the Nuclear Regulatory Commission (NRC, formerly the AEC)—using formal, quasi-legal intervention procedures which have the effect of limiting broad and easy participation in administrative proceedings.[41]

NEPA's Significance

From the beginning, NEPA implementation has presented a fundamentally ambiguous evaluative problem. NEPA itself, its legislative history, CEQ and agency regulations implementing the Act, and case law interpretations have clearly stressed the importance of changes in decision *procedures*. Detailed, good faith EISs were to be prepared, and were to be incorporated into decision routines. Environmental staffs were to be developed. And, in many agencies, public participation was to be a part of the NEPA process. These changes have, with some variation, definitely occurred. In 1972, some elements in Congress, particularly the Joint Committee on Atomic Energy and the public works committees, attempted to significantly modify NEPA. When those efforts failed,[42] resistance to NEPA per se collapsed. By 1973-1974, NEPA was an established facet of federal natural resources policy processes.

However, both academic observers of and participants in the process were uncertain for several years about the effects of NEPA on substantive policy.[43] Even agencies with excellent NEPA procedures still pursued missions which seemed environmentally destructive (i.e., dams, channelization, nuclear power, clearcutting timber sales,and so on). And projects which conservationists thought of as "environmental disasters" still made it through the NEPA process: Calvert Cliffs is now operational; the Amchitka device was detonated; the Alaska pipeline is now operational; and so forth. According to the pessimists, Judge Skelly Wright's fears of agencies producing unread documents, while missions and projects supported by pre-NEPA clienteles proceeded unhindered, have materialized.

Such pessimism rather misconstrues both the goals of NEPA and its significance. First, the ambiguity between procedural and substantive compliance is built into NEPA. The courts were not overly restrained in requiring strong procedural compliance, but ultimately relied on agency judgments on final decisions. NEPA's language and its legislative history clearly show Congress to be similarly ambiguous. The glowing environmental policy of section 101, which the section 102(2)(C) EISs were to enforce, was balanced with section 105. NEPA was not meant to repeal by implication the "existing authorities"—that is, traditional missions, as well as already authorized projects. Agencies were to develop procedures to incorporate environmental criteria into their decision-making, and that is exactly what they have done.

Second, NEPA's procedural reforms address a major criticism of administrative policy-making. The major cause of adverse environmental consequences of federal programs, NEPA implies, is that agencies produce proposals in an incremental, arrational policy process, hidden from public scrutiny and responsive solely to narrow clienteles.[44] This charge is, of course, a very general critique of administrative behavior. Lowi, critiquing this pattern of policy-making (under the label "interest group liberalism"), suggests that one solution to the problem of incremental, clientele-bargaining styles of policy-making is to return to a rule of administrative formalism.[45] In the natural resources field, the formalist solution to the incremental-clientelist problem is most clearly associated with Charles Reich's *Bureaucracy and the Forests*.[46] Like Lowi, Reich criticizes Congress' excessive grants of discretionary authority to natural resources agencies. In the absence of comprehensive Congressional policy-making, Reich advocated three administrative reforms to protect the public interest: (1) preparation of an open, written, formal report on the reasons for particular decisions to provide public scrutiny of decisions; (2) diversification of agency staff to counteract problems of domination of agencies by single professions with professionally biased norms and traditions; and (3) greater public access to administrative decision-making, facilitated by liberalization of the standing doctrine. NEPA may mandate primarily procedural reforms, but those reforms involve a point-by-point enactment of Reich's recommendations. EISs are an open, formal report on decisions which force agencies to think about the consequences of their programs. NEPA itself [section 102(2) (A)] and the administrative requirements of the EIS process have led to the development of special agency environment staffs which represent environmental values in internal agency processes.[47] And the liberalization of the standing rule, CEQ guidelines on the public review of EISs and agency participation programs address Reich's third point.

Finally, NEPA has been intertwined with the rising effectiveness of the environmental movement. NEPA whould not have had any effect had it not been for environmentalists. The courts' broad construction of NEPA in 1971-1972, leading to the act's rigorous procedural implementation required environmentalist plaintiffs. The Sierra Club, the Natural Resources Defense Council (NRDC), the Environmental Defense Fund (EDF), SCRAP, and a host of other environmental groups were more than willing to litigate under NEPA. Similarly, without NEPA, environmental groups would not have had a vehicle to use the courts, and consequently the broad access to agency decision-making, which success in the courts spawned, might well not have developed.

The creation of legitimate access to agency decision-making is the single most important consequence of NEPA. Environmentalists are significantly opposed to the kinds of programs favored by the traditional clienteles of most natural resources agencies. Thus, the inclusion of environmentalists in agency policy systems is a significant balancing of agency constituencies. The old capture thesis no longer holds water with respect to natural resources policy. That thesis is predicated on the existence of a political environment in which an agency's only attentive public is a narrow subset of all affected interests.[48] Since agency constituencies now include environmentalists along with traditional clients, such a situation no longer exists in natural resources subsystems.

As a result, natural resources policy is probably the most balanced of all American policy systems. As a reform, constituency balance is quite different from administrative formalism. Constituency balance is the fulfillment of the pluralist dream Lowi so condemned (and correctly, since although it is a key assumption of pluralism, "countervailing power" rarely existed in policy subsystems). But whether pluralist balance is philosophically good, bad, or irrelevant, the fact is the natural resources system *is* balanced and that balance is the driving force behind substantive policy change.

It is understandable that NEPA would initially produce only procedural changes. The EIS process was NEPA's major specific requirement and was conceived of as a means to the end of increased environmental consciousness in decision-making. Thus consolidation of NEPA's procedural changes could be viewed as a precondition to integrating environmental values into decision-making.[49] This seems to be occurring, leading to changes in substantive policy of two kinds. First, the traditional programs and projects of agencies have been constrained to some extent. Some projects have been substantially delayed, and in a few cases cancelled, because of NEPA. But more often, the NEPA process results in incremental changes which mitigate the adverse environmental consequences of projects. Second, positive policies favored by environmentalist critics which were given little or no emphasis pre-NEPA are on the agencies' agendas and are being acted on favorably. The water resources development and public lands management policy areas provide good examples of these kinds of changes, and it is to these areas that we now turn.

WATER RESOURCES DEVELOPMENT POLICY

The four main federal water resources development agencies are the U.S. Army Corps of Engineers, the Department of the Interior's Bureau of Reclamation (BuRec), the Department of Agriculture's Soil Conservation Service (SCS), and the Tennessee Valley Authority (TVA), an independent agency. With the partial exception of the SCS, all are multipurpose agencies whose projects, depending on the project and the agency, can have some or all of the following economic benefits: flood control, navigation, water supply/irrigation, or hydroelectric power production. Within classes of projects, there is little intrinsic difference between agencies. Corps and SCS channelization projects have about the same environmental effects; a BuRec and a TVA dam have about the same environmental impacts. Differences in economic impacts (the projects' benefits) among the agencies' projects are more a function of financial arrangements built into the agencies' statutory authorities than of the projects' engineering functions. The U.S. Army Corps is the oldest (established in 1802) and largest ($1.9 billion in FY75) of the four agencies, and the one with the most nationwide program (as opposed to the regional focus of BuRec, TVA, and to a lesser extent, SCS programs.).

Water Resources Development Issues

Water resources projects have not been controversial solely on environmental grounds (nor, of course, are most projects environmentally controversial). The still-classic indictment of the Corps, Arthur Maass' *Muddy Waters*, critiqued the Corps primarily for engaging in irresponsible subsystems politics. The Corps has traditionally had a close working relationship with the public works committees of Congress because of Congressional perceptions of the Corps' projects as the choicest pork in the barrel. This relationship's worst feature, according to Maass, is that it effectively eliminates Presidential coordination of executive programs. And, indeed, the Corps' successful running battle with BuRec is a classic example of bureaucratic imperialism in American politics.

Economic arguments have been the best tactical weapons of environmentalists and other critics of water projects. By their very nature, water projects primarily benefit local areas at public expense. The benefits of such projects are often quite narrow, even in the local area. BuRec's $87.9 million Fruitland Mesa project, for example is designed to irrigate at a cost of $1.2 million each only 69 large ranches.[50] Another common complaint is that Corps inland waterway projects are a thorough subsidy of the barge industry, the only transportation industry whose right-of-way is wholly capitalized and maintained from public funds without compensation. Critics also point out that the goals of water projects often conflict with other government programs. In the past, for example, the Department of Agriculture's land bank and surplus food purchase programs attempted to keep food commodities off the market, while the SCS and BuRec's irrigation and reclamation programs sought to bring arid or flood-prone land into agricultural production.

Water projects are justified by an explicit cost-benefit (B/C) calculation, which critics routinely perceive to be mere quantitative prestidigitation. The Corps routinely includes in its estimated flood control benefits the value of protection of developments to be built in a flood plain after the area is protected. BuRec's Palmetto Bend project in Texas, as another example, was justified as providing water for future industrial sites in a rural area in which abundant underground pumped water is one-third the cost of the reservoir's water.[51] Very few projects' B/C ratios would exceed 1:1 without recreational benefits. These recreational benefits almost always seem exaggerated to critics, and all the more aggravatingly so to environmentalists, whose recreational preferences do not lean toward slackwater powerboating. For example, one impoundment in the Tennessee-Tombigbee project, which is in an area in which every other river has an impounded lake, will supposedly accommodate some 29,000 visitors per day on a 9,000-acre lake at a density of 1.4 fishermen or boaters per acre, the recreational equivalent of an urban expressway during rush hour.[52] A key assumption in B/C analysis is the "discount rate." Analagous to including interest in figuring the fully financed costs of a capital purchase, the discount rate decreases future costs and benefits by a certain percentage. (Since most water projects' costs occur at construction, the discount rate primarily affects benefits, which accrue over the life of the project.) The current discount rate if 6.4 percent, but most projects were authorized many years ago, under rates in the 2 to 4 percent range. Raising the discount rate from the average of 3.2 percent on current projects to 6.4 percent can halve a B/C ratio, which would drop many projects below 1:1. Finally, water recources B/C estimates are subject to considerable cost overruns, further confounding the calculations. These problems, particularly the cost-overrun problem, led Senator William Proxmire to bestow on the Corps his 1976 "Golden Fleece of the Year" award.

As major engineering undertakings, many water projects also provide good examples of the problem of simple technological solutions to complex problems, solutions which produce adverse unintended consequences. BuRec's Teton Dam, which failed in 1976, causing 11 deaths and a billion dollars in damages, might be considered a horrible example of such unintended consequences. However, Teton is the only federal dam failure to date, and BuRec's engineers had made extensive efforts to overcome the problem which eventually caused the failure. Several projects have been subjected to increased scrutiny since Teton: Auburn-Folsom Dam in California is being reevaluated because it is in an earthquake zone, and one of the controversies surrounding Meramec Dam in Missouri is that it is in an area of caves far larger than the fissures which caused the Teton failure. But dam safety had generally not been a major, systematic problem. The recurring problem is with unforseen consequences which require technological solutions which then have more unforseen effects: problems whose "solutions" become problems requiring more "solutions."

The corps' flood-control program provides a good example of these kinds of problems. The Corps traditional flood-control efforts consisted of "structural" solutions to flooding problems. To protect areas from flooding, the Corps typically either channelized the "offending" river and/or protected the floodplain with devices such as levees. These structural approaches have environmental impacts in the narrow sense: channelization, for example, alters natural streamflow and drains marsh-lands which are critical fish and wildlife habitat. But more importantly, recent evidence suggests that these structures may also exacerbate the flood conditions they were intended to solve. Flood waters must go somewhere. When, as is the case now on the Mississippi River system, a substantial proportion of the river is protected, unprotected areas must absorb all the flood waters, increasing flood damage downstream of the protected areas. Thus, as more of the Mississippi has been protected from floods, flood damage has increased.

Increasing conflict over these issues—pork barrel politics, question-able economics, and unintended technological consequences—has put unprecedented pressure on the four water project agencies, with environ-mentalists being their leading critics. The Corps is, by far, the target of more political conflict than the other agencies. The Corps, for example, is the target of a large volume of critical literature,[53] while there is only one (to the author's knowledge) general, critical piece on any of the other three[54]. The Corps has led the other agencies on other indicators of conflict as well: it has consistently had more projects under litigation and on "hit lists" (CEQ's, OMB's, as well as groups like EDF's) than the other three combined. While most projects are not subject to conflict over these issues, such pressure, of course, is at the root of the NEPA-related changes in water resources policy.

Changes in Traditional Water Resources Programs, 1970-1977

There were considerable differences in the water resources agencies' procedural reforms under NEPA. BuRec's and TVA's implementation records on NEPA were fairly typical of most federal agencies'. Like most agencies, they waited to see how much would be required of them. The SCS was one of the more recalcitrant agencies on NEPA. Like the Environmental Protection Agency and the National Park Service, the SCS took the position that, because it had traditionally had a (soil) conservation mission, it was not significantly affected by NEPA. While there was some sympathy for EPA's and the Park Service's positions, the SCS's small watershed program was precisely the sort of mission at which NEPA was aimed. It was not until 1974 that the SCS's procedures were, long after the other agencies, brought into full compliance with NEPA.[55]

The Corps was quite another matter. The Corps was the first federal agency to establish NEPA procedures in 1970, and its procedures are still considered among the best of all federal agencies. Moreover, the Corps was a leader in the development of public participation in natural resources decision-making, stressing early and continuous involvement of groups (especially, of course, environmentalists) in the planning process.[56] The Corps even began a public relations campaign to communicate its new environmental awareness: one writer reported that, during an interview with the Chief of Engineers, he had a "The Corps Cares" button foisted on him.[57] Perhaps an even more apt slogan, however, for the Corps' turnabout is its traditional motto, *Essayons*—"let us try." NEPA instructed the Corps to write EISs and to consider environmental values. The Corps did this with the same efficiency, skill, and esprit de corps with which it had carried out its water project planning and Congressional relationships before NEPA. Since the Corps was also bearing the brunt of environmental criticism of water resources development, compliance with NEPA might even help to alleviate some pressure.[58]

While procedural changes in project planning were considerable, especially in the case of the Corps, NEPA evaluations generally did not generate an immediate substantive change in ongoing projects. NEPA evaluations frequently led to relatively minor, incremental changes in project design. For example, a problem with Corps dredging projects is that dredge spoils from urban harbors are usually fairly polluted and leakage of the spoils from dredging disposal areas can pose a pollution problem. Thus, improving the capability of a dredging site's dike is a relatively minor design change which minimizes the adverse impact while allowing the project to go forward. Fish and wildlife mitigation policy is another example of such design changes. The Fish and Wildlife Service, state game agencies, and the wildlife interest groups are all interested in the fish and wildlife habitat, which is invariably affected by major water projects. The Fish and Wildlife Coordination Act[59] requires water resources agencies to consult with the Fish and Wildlife Service and provides for the acquisition of land to be set aside for wildlife purposes to mitigate the loss of habitat caused by a project. The wildlife agencies, supported by the wildlife federations, have placed considerable pressure on the water resources agencies and have been insistent that mitigation lands be included in project designs.

Despite these design and mitigation changes, most water projects which were in the pipeline when NEPA was passed are still progressing today. A national mail survey in late 1971 and a regional interview- and document-based study in late 1976 show that less than a quarter of all Corps projects for which an EIS was prepared are affected in a substantive way by NEPA, and the overwhelming majority of the effects

(60 percent of projects affected in the 1971 survey and 79 percent in the 1976 study) were delays, not cancellations or major modifications.[60]

Court interpretations, as noted above, were critical to NEPA's implementation, and many people assume that litigation is the major cause of delay and/or cancellation of water projects. A number of major water projects have been affected by NEPA litigation, including the Cross-Florida canal, the Tennessee-Tombigbee waterway, Tellico Dam, and the Trinity River project. But litigation affects only a small fraction of all water projects. From 1970 through June, 1975, the Corps released EISs on 1339 projects (93.6 percent of the total of 1430 EISs on water projects). During the same period, the Corps was subjected to relatively heavy litigation, with 63 cases completed or pending (9.6 percent of all NEPA cases); and the Corps' projects were relatively hard hit by injunctions, with 24 temporary and four permanent injunctions (25 percent of all NEPA injunctions against all agencies, and 67 percent of all permanent injunctions).[61] But these cases, while generally affecting the more important projects, are a small proportion of all projects: total cases are 4.7 percent of EIS projects, and injunctions only 2.1 percent. Moreover, the Corps (through June 1975) officially cancelled a dozen projects because of NEPA but unrelated to litigation, compared with only two permanent injunctions in completed cases.[62]

Two cases which are similar in many ways provide a good insight into the kinds of effects NEPA and environmental pressure have had on some major, ongoing water projects. In the first case, the Corps' Tennessee-Tombigbee waterway, NEPA caused a delay on a project which is now back under construction. The second project, TVA's Tellico Dam, was recently permanently enjoined in a precedent-setting decision. The reader should bear in mind, however, that these cases are examples of only that minority of controversial projects in which there is some nonminor change attributable to environmental considerations.

Tennessee-Tombigbee Waterway: "Tenn-Tom" as it is generally known, is a 253-mile, nine-foot-deep channel connecting the Tennessee River with the Gulf of Mexico at Mobile. At a current estimated cost of $1.4 billion, Tenn-Tom will shorten the trip from Tennessee to the sea by 800 miles. The project is massive: more earth will be moved on one 27-mile segment of Tenn-Tom than was moved to build the Panama Canal; earth displaced by the project will fill and level off 43 valleys in the area.

Tenn-Tom's issues are fairly typical of controversial projects, except that its impacts are an order of magnitude greater than usual. The Tombigbee is a nice little river. Local opposition to the project is led by a group called Committee for Leaving the Environment of America Natural, headed by a Mississippi State University ichthyologist (fish zoologist), Glenn Clemmer. According to Clemmer, Tenn-Tom would: destroy a river that, "in terms of fish life, [has] the second richest fauna of any river in the United States, [making it] a great biological laboratory," and inundate 600 archeological sites and 40,000 acres of hardwood forest and wildlife habitat.[63] Tenn-Tom has also been denounced on social grounds.[64] As usual, economic aspects of the project are in dispute. The barge industry, of course, will pay nothing to use Tenn-Tom, leading to charges of subsidy to special interests. Tenn-Tom has a relatively low B/C ratio of 1.1:1. The B/C ratio is computed with a 3.25% discount rate (since the project was authorized in 1946), so at the current statutory discount rate, Tenn-Tom's B/C ratio would be only .87:1.0. Moreover, Tenn-Tom's design raises some practical questions. The waterway is designed to accommodate a normal eight-barge tow, but the existing downstream locks can handle only six. Cynics suggest the Corps plans further work for itself downriver once the current project is complete.[65]

Tenn-Tom was among the first projects litigated under NEPA. In 1971, a D.C. District Court temporarily enjoined the project until an adequate EIS was prepared.[66] The Corps then prepared a massive EIS, which, in some respects, is a good example of the generally extensive efforts of the Corps to comply with NEPA's procedural requirements. The EIS and project plan also provided for a number of design changes to minimize environmental impacts. After a change of venue, the Corps filed the EIS with the District Court for the Northern District of Mississippi, and the injunction was dissolved.[67] The court held that the EIS, while not perfect, was a good faith attempt to consider all relevant alternatives and impacts and hence satisfied NEPA's procedural requirements. The circuit court affirmed, noting that, in the Tenn-Tom case, the procedural requirement of the EIS was the major concern; the court rejected environmentalists' attempts to have the substantive decision examined on its merits, especially the allegedly deficient B/C analysis, because Congress had effectively reviewed the decision and B/C analysis and B/C calculation by appropriating funds for the project. With the lifting of the injunction, the construction of Tenn-Tom resumed. Although the project has come under renewed attack in recent months, its construction still continues today.

Tellico Dam: Located a couple of hundred miles east-northeast of the Tenn-Tom area, the Tellico Dam gained widespread notoriety in January 1977. In what many who are unfamiliar with the project considered to be simple-minded, bird-lover style preservationism, Tellico's completion was permanently enjoined because the dam threatened an endangered— and little-known—species, the snail darter, a three-inch long member of the perch family.[68] Before the January, 1977, decision, Tellico had been fairly typical of NEPA controversies. A $100 million project, Tellico would dam the Little Tennessee River in eastern Tennessee, creating a 16,000-acre reservoir to foster industrial development, provide hydro-electric power, slackwater recreation, and flood control benefits. Local opposition was led by owners of the land to be flooded by the reservoir and biologists at the University of Tennessee, but national groups, principally EDF, have also been involved. Opponents' principle concerns are to preserve one of the last free-flowing river segments in the Tennessee basin and maintain about 25,500 acres of agricultural land in farm use. As usual, the project's economics were the subject of debate, with critics arguing that: demand for new industrial sites in the region had decreased drastically, and industrial benefits would thus not offset the approximately $27 million of annual foregone agricultural production; hydroelectric benefits are overstated, since Tellico would have no generators, but would only pump water to increase the powerhead at nearby Ft. Loudon Dam, and at several times the average cost in the TVA system; and free-flow river canoeing and trout fishing are more valuable recreationally in an area with 22 reservoirs within a 50-mile radius.[69]

The recent decision is the third round of litigation over Tellico. Tellico was authorized in 1966, and construction began in 1967. Opposition arose almost immediately, but was unsuccessful until NEPA was passed. EDF and others sued TVA in 1971, and a temporary injunction was granted in 1972 on the grounds that TVA had not prepared an adequate EIS.[70] Project construction was delayed for a year and a half while TVA prepared a revised EIS. In 1973, the courts held the revised EIS to be adequate and dissolved the injunction.[71] TVA then recommenced construction of the dam. Up to this point, Tellico was typical of NEPA litigation: compliance with the procedural EIS requirement, but no decision on the merits of the case.

In late 1973, just as EDF was losing the second round of Tellico litigation, several new developments occurred. In August, David Etnier, a University of Tennessee ichthyologist, discovered the snail darter. Then in December, 1973, the Endangered Species Act[72] was passed, providing that the Fish and Wildlife Service maintain official lists of endangered species and prohibiting federal agencies from taking actions which jeopardize endangered species' critical habitats. In 1975, the Fish and Wildlife Service placed the snail darter on the endangered species list (on petition from environmentalists opposed to Tellico) and defined the Little Tennessee River as its critical habitat. Environmentalists then sued TVA again to halt completion of Tellico, this time under the Endangered Species Act. They lost at the district court level, the court holding that the dam was 80% complete and that an injunction would be inequitable.

(Opponents argue, by the way, that $80 million of present project costs were for land acquisition and needed roads and other improvements which would not be "lost" if the project was abandoned, and which have since, in fact, increased in value to more than total project costs.[73]) However, just as the dam was to be closed in January, 1977, the Sixth Circuit ruled that the letter of the Endangered Species Act did not exempt Tellico and permanently enjoined completion of the dam. In its opinion the court suggested that if Congress did not want the Endangered Species Act to halt the dam, Congress could do something about it. TVA appealed the decision to the Supreme Court, and, collaterally, supported Congressional amendments to explicitly exempt the Tellico project from the Act. Although the Supreme Court upheld the Sixth Circuit's injunction in June, 1978, the Congress has been actively considering amendments to the act; the amendment which seems most likely to pass (sponsored by Senators Culver of Iowa and Baker of Tennessee) would create an interagency review board (composed of the Secretaries of Interior, Army, Agriculture, the heads of the Smithsonian Institution, CEQ, and the Environmental Protection Agency, and the affected state's governor) which could exempt projects from the Act.[74] Even if the Culver-Baker amendent passed, however, Tellico would not be out fo the woods since from three to five of the federal board members might be expected to vote against the Tellico exemption.

Thus, the snail darter was used to obtain a tactical victory which 10 years of interest group activity and four NEPA suits had failed to accomplish. On the surface, this fish story might seem to reflect badly on NEPA: if NEPA has wrought such great changes, why is it that the best example of a stopped project occurred not because of the agency's NEPA-induced evaluations or even NEPA litigation, but because of a three-inch-long fish? In large part, of course, ongoing projects are not a good test of NEPA's effectiveness. A project like Tellico which is underway when an EIS is written has considerable momentum because of the time, effort, money, and prestige committed to the project. NEPA may cause minor, if often useful, alterations in projects, but it is extremely rare for NEPA alone to cause the abandonment of a program into which an agency has sunk significant organizational costs. It is in other areas that the best examples of NEPA's impact can be found.

New Policy Developments

NEPA—and the NEPA-related rise in environmental influence— seems to have led to three types of significant, discernible, substantive policy changes in federal water resources policy. First, NEPA conflict tended to make the agencies more cautious about new projects under their traditional missions. This reticence about new starts affected all four agencies to some extent but is most pronounced for the Corps. Second, the Corps attempted to develop a major new program area which, while involving its traditional professional skills, was much more environmentally acceptable. Third, a traditional regulatory responsibility of the Corps, which is only peripherally related to the agency's primary mission and skills, took an astoundingly pro-environmental turn, especially with one 1976 decision.

While the water agencies generally attempted to complete projects which were in the mill when NEPA was passed, the NEPA learning process, conflicts reflected in public hearings and EIS comments, and litigation all made their point for the agencies—business was not going to ever be "as usual" again. Officials in the water project agencies (and most federal agencies, for that matter) report that potentially controversial projects are scrutinized very carefully and delayed or avoided as much as possible.[75] The most systematic policy level area in which this change is important is in flood control projects. The Corps' new policy is that "structural" flood control measures will now be adopted only as a last resort.[76] To back up this new policy, the Corps obtained Congressional sanction for a program of "nonstructural" flood control measures (basically, the prevention of development in flood plains by turning flood plains into open space, parks, and the like) in the Water Resources Development Act of 1973.[77] The act authorized three pilot nonstructural projects on the Upper Charles River, Boston; South Platte River, Littleton, Colorado; and Prairie du Chien, Wisconsin. The new Corps policy favoring nonstructural flood control is a *major* reversl in its approach to flood management and a reversal which almost wholly adopts the environmentalist position on the issue.

A second, policy-level Corps departure was the so-called urban studies program. In 1971, the Corps requested authorization to conduct studies of regional wastewater management plans in five urban areas. The sewage treatment program would use the Corps' civil engineering skills and would give it a program strongly supported by environmentalist opponents of its other programs. The problem with the urban studies program has been that the field has been essentially preempted by the Environmental Protection Agency (EPA), which controls the $18 billion construction grants authorization and "section 208" regional water pollution planning programs under the Federal Water Pollution Control Act. Thus the Corps has played only a minor role in the overall wastewater program to date. However, the studies begun in 1973-1975 represented a third of all Corps pre-authorization studies, a substantial commitment of opportunity costs to the program.[78]

The third area of policy change again involves the Corps. Since 1899, the Corps has had the responsibility for regulating dredge and fill activities on the navigable waters of the United States.[79] Dredge and fill projets have come under increasing attack in recent years because they destroy wetlands, which are increasingly recognized as an important resource. Coastal wetlands are the prime breeding ground for fish and shellfish populations and are estimated to generate two-thirds of the world's commercial fish harvest. Also, because of their nutrient demand and other biological processes, wetlands are a major pollution removal system. Thus wetlands have considerable economic value; a study of one Georgia marsh estimated its economic productivity at $3,100 per acre annually.[80] However, these economic values of wetlands can rarely be recaptured by the holders of title to the land. Thus the pattern of "development" of wetlands has been to fill them in with material dredged from the bottom of nearby waterways, creating dry land real estate, while destroying the economic productivity of the site.

Corps approval of dredge and fill permits had been fairly routine before the 1970s. However, in 1970, the Corps denied a permit for a small, 11-acre dredge and fill on Boca Ciega Bay, Florida. The Corps action was upheld in Zabel v. Tabb,[81] the court holding that NEPA granted the Corps the authority to consider environmental factors in addition to its traditional navigation-related criteria under the 1899 Act. While Zabel set a precedent for denial of permits on environmental grounds, it did not immediately alter the Corps' overall wetlands and dredge and fill policies.

The Federal Water Pollution Control Act Amendments of 1972[82] (FWPCA) incorporated the Corps' water pollution authorities under the 1899 Refuse Act,[83] including the dredge and fill authority, into a revised and expanded pollution program, with Section 404 of the FWPCA containing the wetlands program. The Corps retained authority over the Section 404 program, but EPA was given an effective veto over the permits, and, as usual, the Corps had to consult with the Fish and Wildlife Service (under the Fish and Wildlife Coordination Act). Initially, the Corps did not move aggressively to implement the 404 program and adopted the view that Section 404 applied only to its traditional responsibility for navigable waters. Environmentalists, however, challenged the Corps, and prevailed in a 1975 suit. When the court held that Section 404 applied to the "waters of the United States" (not the much narrower "navigable waters"), the Corps was pushed into the business of wetlands regulation.[84] The Corps attempted to generate a backlash to this decision, issuing a press release which claimed that its revised regulations would require permits for ranch stock ponds, farmers plowing wet fields, and so on. But pressure from EPA, Department of the Army superiors, and environmentalists forced the Corps to retract this misleading statement and issue the required regulations. The revised regulations required, in a three-phase staging, permits for dredge and fill operations in the navigable waters, interstate waters, waters used in interstate commerce, as well as the tributaries and wetlands associated with all three categories of bodies of water.[85]

Marco Island:[86] Soon after the Corps' revised 404 regulations were issued in late 1975, the regulations were tested in the Marco Island case, involving one of the country's largest coastal developments. The Corps was faced with a decision on three permit applications related to development of Marco Island, Florida, by the Deltona Corporation. Deltona had been developing Marco for some years as a resort and retirement community of 35,000 inhabitants, dredging a mangrove wetlands into homesites and canals. Part of the development was completed before 1975, with several dredge and fill permits issued under the Corps' pre-404 program. However, the most recent, in 1969, was considerably delayed at the time of the Zabel controversy. The three 1975 permit applications were for the Barfield Bay (943 acres), Big Key (1,096 acres), and Collier Bay (1,100 acres) sections of the Marco development. The development was quite controversial, opposed by a coalition of local and national environmental groups, the Fish and Wildlife Service, and EPA, but strongly supported by Deltona (of course), local building trades unions, and other development interests. To try to mollify critics, Deltona had arranged a side payment to the State of Florida, donating the 4,000-acre Caxambas Sanctuary in exchange for state dredge and fill permits.

After the state permits were issued, it was the Corps' turn. After filing an EIS (accompanied by a bitter public hearing), the District Engineer, Col. Donald Wisdom (a name environmentalists regard as apt), recommended denial of the Barfield Bay and Big Key permits on environmental grounds, citing protection of the mangrove wetlands. Since considerable development had already occurred in the Collier Bay section (which had only 113 acres of mangroves), Wisdom recommended issuance of that permit. Wisdom's recommendation was sustained in an April, 1976 decision of the Chief of Engineers, leading to absolute dismay on the part of Deltona (which is litigating the decision) and amazed delight on the part of environmentalists. The decision may cost Deltona dearly. About 90 percent of the two wetlands tracts which may not now be developed have already been sold. As the 4,000-odd sales contracts come due, Deltona will either have to refund more than $60 million or provide other lots. Moreover, the State of Florida will apparently keep a choice piece of beachfront, developable property, which it received in Caxambas Sanctuary in the side payment deal for the now-useless state permits. As Deltona's president, Frank Mackle, fumed: "It was absolutely astounding, the biggest miscarriage of justice in my lifetime. The Corps—they've been like us. They're engineers, our kind of people. If this kind of thing prevails, what kind of businessman is going to risk his money?"[87]

While the Marco ruling is a major substantive decision in its own right, its major significance is that it sets a precedent for strict Corps enforcement of its Section 404 policy. The decision led to a serious effort in Congress to amend Section 404. The so-called Breaux Amendment[88] would have stripped the Corps of its wetlands authority by returning 404 jurisdiction to the pre-1972 "navigable waters" definition, thereby excluding 85 percent of the nation's wetlands. The Breaux Amendment led to a situation most observers would not have thought possible a few years ago—environmentalists lobbying full force on the Hill to defend a Corps of Engineers program. The Breaux Amendment died in the last days of the 94th Congress, when the Houses could not agree on a conference report. (Senator Edmund Muskie, the chairman of the Senate Public Works Committee controlling the FWPCA, strongly opposed the Breaux Amendment.) Thus a major Corps preservation policy still stands. The Breaux Amendment revision of Section 404 was the main focus of debate over amendment of the FWPCA in the first session of the 95th Congress. The House-passed amendment included a version of the Breaux Amendment, but the Senate-passed version retained the full Section 404 program. Thus, pending resolution of the differences by the conference committee, a major Corps preservation policy still stands. The Corps is not always the developer's "kind of people" any more.

THE MANAGEMENT OF THE PUBLIC LANDS

The four principal federal land management agencies—the Forest Service in the Department of Agriculture, and Interior's Bureau of Land Management (BLM), National Park Service, and the Fish and Wildlife Service (F&WS)—manage a total of 713,813,890 acres of federally owned land, 31.4 percent of the United States. The two largest agencies, the Forest Service and the BLM, which manage 187 million and 474 million acres respectively, are the "multiple use" agencies. The "multiple use" acts[89] direct the Forest Service and the BLM to manage their lands to provide an optimum and high level mix of timber, livestock, wildlife, watershed, recreational, mineral, and aesthetic benefits, while trying to maintain the long-term productivity of the land and minimizing conflicts among uses. The Park Service and the F&WS manage 24.7

million and 28.7 million acres, respectively, for natural area preservation and recreational purposes. Commercial commodity uses are generally prohibited in National Parks, Monuments, and Wildlife Refuges, and, where permitted, they are not primary management objectives.

While public land management and water resources development differ both administratively and in terms of the scale of physiographic impacts, the politics of the two policy areas have been rather similar. Public lands agencies have been the subjects of substantive charges that some of their policies and programs are environmentally harmful, and they have been subjected to the same kind of political process critiques as the water project agencies. However, while the water agencies' programs all had similar effects and the same political line-up (development interests pro and environmentalists con), there are major differences between the programs and political environments of the public land agencies. Most of the uses on the multiple use list benefit definable industries, and the agency and professional norms of the Forest Service and BLM encourage such uses. Thus the Forest Service and the BLM policy arenas, like the water resources arenas, are marked by issues of environmental trade-offs for economic benefits and related rhetoric about political capture of the agencies by development interests. Since natural area preservation is a primary mission of the Park Service and the F&WS, they have not been subjected to nearly as much conflict as the multiple use agencies. The Park Service's other primary mission, recreation, sometimes conflicts with its preservationist mission, bringing it into conflict with environmentalists. Proposed scenic highways through a park, or concessions for rustic hotels in parks, are common examples of such conflicts. Even the F&WS has been involved in programs which were criticized on environmental grounds, such as the predator control program of a few years ago.[90] But, by and large, environmentalists are the supportive clientele and allies in interagency disputes of the Park Service and F&WS. The role of the F&WS in the Tellico Dam case, discussed earlier, is a good example of this relationship.

The Forest Service has been the target of more intense conflict than the other public lands agencies. The largest of the four agencies, with a FY75 budget of $963.4 million,[91] it manages almost as much acreage in the lower 48 states as the BLM (166.5 million versus the BLM's 174.6 million,) and its land is considerably more productive and in demand than the Bureau's semi-desert land. The two primary, and usually interrelated, issues of recent National Forest management are timber production and wilderness.

The Forest Service is the largest single manager of commercial timberland in the country, with 91.9 million (18.4 percent) of the 499.7

million acres nationally. Because private timberlands, particularly the forest products industry's lands, are more productive—and because public agencies did not want to compete with private timber, thus lowering prices on private timber—commercial harvest of Forest Service timber was relatively low for many years and logging on industry lands relatively high. Hence, the Forest Service's relative proportion of timber inventory has increased over the years because of depletion of private stands. In 1970, the Service had 42 percent of the nation's standing sawtimber. As its own inventories of sawtimber decreased, the forest products industry turned increasingly to National Forest timber.[92] This increase in demand had some advantages from the Forest Service's point of view. The main management tool of foresters is logging, and they feel they cannot achieve many of their silvicultural objectives without a reasonable demand for timber sales. But the increasing demand, and the generally positive Forest Service response to that demand, brought the agency increasingly into conflict with environmentalists. Timber sales themselves are controversial. Logging operations cause a certain amount of damage, and some practices such as clearcutting are viewed as especially destructive; timber roads often provide the infrastructure for other controversial developments; and there are significant questions about whether present cutting levels can be sustained over the long run in conformance with sustained yield principles. But most importantly, environmentalists were concerned that the National Forests were being given over to a dominant commercial use.

A major goal of the more ideological environment groups is to preserve substantial tracts of public lands free from development as Wilderness, an even more rigid form of protection, in some ways, than even National Park status. The concept of officially designated wilderness developed in the 1930s as a result of the work of several individuals in the Forest Service and culminated in the passage of the Wilderness Act in 1964. The Wilderness Act defines an eligible wilderness as an undeveloped tract of federal land of at least 5,000 acres "affected primarily by the forces of nature," and with "outstanding opportunities for solitude or a primitive and unconfined type of recreation."[93] All Forest Service areas which had been administratively classified as "wilderness" became statutory wilderness areas with the passage of the act, and the Forest Service and Interior were instructed to review "primitive" and roadless areas and recommend possible future additions to the National Wilderness Preservation System. This issue will be discussed more fully later in the text, but environmentalists have felt that the Forest Service, because of its professional norms and forest products industry pressure, has recommended insufficient additions to the Wilderness System.

The BLM has been the target of environmental criticism in two areas. First, the Bureau's mainline public lands program is the management of the 175 million acres of "national resource lands" in the 11 states (except Alaska) west of the 100th Meridian. The large bulk of this land has been managed as a part of grazing districts established under the Taylor Grazing Act of 1934.[94] Although the Taylor Grazing Act was intended, in part, to rectify problems of range deterioration caused by overgrazing, some 83 percent of BLM lands remain in unsatisfactory condition.[95] Arid conditions, poor stock handling practices, and wildlife use affect range conditions, but environmentalists lay the blame on the level of domestic livestock grazing.

The second major BLM management function is to process claims and leases of public lands' mineral or oil and gas resources under the mining laws.[96] The Bureau's responsibilities extend to public lands (primarily, of course, their own and those of the Forest Service), land in private ownership on which the government has retained mineral rights, and the Outer Continental Shelf (OCS, the area seaward from the old three-mile, or three-league in Texas' case, limit to the point at which the sea floor drops sharply). The federal lands have traditionally been exploited for a variety of minerals from gold to sand. Of primary importance today, most new energy-related exploration and development—including oil, gas, coal, and uranium—takes place on the public lands, making public lands a major pawn in debates over new domestic energy supplies. Environmentalists, in addition to their involvement in energy issues generally, have been critical of some of the environmental impacts of federal minerals policy, including concern over oil spills in the OCS, strip mining, and mining in the National Parks and Wilderness systems.

The public lands agencies have also been subjected to the same kinds of political or administrative responsibility critiques as other natural resources agencies. The BLM has been used in the past as a textbook example of a captured agency. Phillip Foss' *Politics and Grass* described the ways the western livestock industry dominated the Bureau, from Washington-level subsystems politics down to (and especially) the role of stockmen's "advisory boards" in controlling local BLM managers.[97] The Forest Service has also been accused of being captured by its major user group, the forest products industry,[98] but it has also been viewed (especially by academic observers) as one of the most professional agencies in the federal bureaucracy and therefore relatively immune to capture.[99] The Park Service and the F&WS have not been generally critiqued as captured agencies; but of course the agencies' relationships with groups like the National Parks and Conservation Association, National Wildlife Federation, Sierra Club, and the like, are perfect examples of clientelism.

NEPA Implementation and Public Land Management

The pattern of procedural implementation of NEPA among the public lands agencies was almost identical to the pattern among water resource agencies. The Forest Service was among the first agencies to develop its own NEPA procedures, and it has been consistently recognized as the agency which has implemented NEPA best of all federal agencies. From the start, the Service produced EISs on a large proportion of its decisions (the Service ranks third in number of EISs filed, after the Federal Highway Administration and the Corps), and its EISs are usually of high quality. CEQ singled the Service out for special praise in its 1974 Annual Report for integrating the NEPA process into agency decision-making. Indeed, the Forest Service has come to use EISs and environmental analyses (a form of prelimnary EIS) as the primary decision documents for all agency decisions.[100]

The Service has also been a leader in developing public participation as an adjunct to the NEPA process. Early in 1971, the Service converted its old public relations program into a public participation program and made public participation a primary responsibility of its line officers down to the district ranger level. Forest Service researchers have been, along with the Corps', leaders in the development of participation methodologies.[101] Thus, as the Corps, the major environmentalist target among the water resources agencies, implemented NEPA best in its area, so the Forest Service, the most criticized of the land management agencies, also performed best among its peers.

The other three public lands agencies have not matched the Forest Service's NEPA record. At first glance the BLM's record appears to be one of the worst among all federal agencies. That bureau did not begin to use EISs systematically for its public lands program until 1974-1975 (the majority of pre-1974 statements were on OCS leases). While the Forest Service was writing EISs on all major actions at the Forest level, the BLMs EISs were few and on seemingly random actions in the early years and concerned only broad national programs later. However, while the BLM did not comply extensively with the EIS requirement, it did well on other NEPA procedures. Environmental analyses are used extensively at the local level, and the bureau's local public participation program is as good as the service's. Moreover, BLM sluggishness on NEPA is slightly excusable. The bureau had made major changes in the 1960s, breaking the strangelhold of local advisory boards, making the transition to a multiple-use mandate in 1964, and becoming an increasingly profession-alized agency. In any case, at least at the local level, it is hard to systematically distinguish between the Forest Service and the BLM in terms of the spirit of implementation of NEPA's substantive goals.[102]

The Park Service's NEPA record was, initially, mixed. Though it complied with procedures early, it took the position (as did the SCS) that it was exempt (under, supposedly, NEPA section 104) from NEPA as an environmentally protective agency. However, some Park Service projects (such as a scenic highway through a park) have typical environmentally adverse effects. The Park Service was brought to recognize this, and its NEPA program is now typical of the average federal agency. In terms of NEPA procedures for its own programs, the F&WS implementation of NEPA is also average. Although its NEPA procedures are adequate, they are rather redundant—since F&WS programs are probably the least controversial (on environmental grounds) of all federal agencies. However, the F&WS implementation of NEPA has been outstanding in one area: it has put substantial, high quality effort into commenting on other agencies' EISs, with higher expenditures for reviewing EISs than any other federal agency (including EPA, which has the responsibility, under the Clean Air Act, to comment on all EISs).[103]

Thus, the public lands policy area showed a similar pattern of NEPA procedural implementation as occurred in water resources policy. The most controversial agency, the Forest Service, made the most comprehensive effort to alter decision procedures to conform to NEPA of the public lands agencies (indeed, of all federal agencies). The BLM (like BuRec) took a relatively long time to improve its procedural compliance with NEPA. And the Park Service (like the SCS) alleged initially that its pro-environmental mission excused it from compliance with NEPA. The pattern of substantive policy change in land management is also very similar to the changes in water resources policy. The NEPA process generated, usually, significant incremental or mitigating changes in projects, but did not clearly seem to alter agencies' commitments to certain kinds of controversial programs. However, programs favored by environmentalists became very significant agenda items for the agencies.

Developments in the Multiple Use Agencies' Policies

As was the case with water resources policy, it is convenient to differentiate relatively minor adjustments in programs and proposals from general changes in the programs or proposals themselves. The Forest Service and the BLM are more committed to incremental mitigation and design adjustments than any other federal agency.[104] From major projects like the Alaska Pipeline down to routine actions like timber sale layouts, land managers routinely attempt to minimize the effects of projects on aesthetic, soil and watershed, wildlife, and other values.

The agencies have become much stricter about insuring that proposed uses are designed to minimize environmental damage (often at considerable cost to project beneficiaries, particularly in terms of time). However, unlike the water project agencies, for whom mitigation strategies are an interference with straightforward designs to accomplish primary purposes, restrictions which minimize conflict among resource values are the practical applications of the multiple-use philosophy, which is the cornerstone of the Forest Service's and BLM's statutory obligations as well as their administrators' professional norms and skills.[105] NEPA has improved the ability of the BLM and Forest Service to carry out these mitigation strategies: since environmental analyses are required for almost all actions, administrators are constantly reminded of their multiple-use responsibilities, and the general pressure of environmentalists helps administrators justify stringent controls imposed on developers. The restrictions, though, are not a new policy, but increased adherence to an old routine.

Though much stricter with users, the multiple-use agencies have not abandoned their development-oriented programs or missions, even very controversial ones. Most administrators report that some new, potentially controversial projects are held in abeyance or not proposed because of administrators' judgments that the projects are politically unacceptable. Such anticipatory "decisions" are, of course, very difficult to measure.[106] As with water resources projects, most projects and programs underway at NEPA's passage have proceeded. A regional sample of Forest Service EISs from 1970 to 1976, for example, found that two-thirds of all proposals were implemented on schedule and essentially as proposed and that implementation difficulties involved delays or modifications, not cancellations.[107] Four cases, ranging from programs showing only procedural compliance with NEPA to ones with some substantive change, illustrate the effects of NEPA-related changes in the minority of complicated, controversial cases.

The BLM Grazing Program: As noted above, the BLM's livestock program has been fairly controversial. The livestock industry, of course, supports the program, as necessary for meat production. The program is the basis of its way of life and occupation. Critics argue that grazing lease levels are too high, leading to deteriorated range conditions. The program, since grazing fees are less than market value, is a subsidy to an inefficient form of agriculture; and wildlife and recreational uses of the public lands are more valuable economically than livestock grazing. One of the bureau's first systematic attempts to comply with NEPA was an EIS, released in 1974, on the bureau-wide grazing program. Although the statement was generally well done, considering its objectives, it was still attacked as unrelated to actual agency decision-making. Since the key decisions on lease-level policy are made at the district level, environmentalists argued, a national programmatic EIS avoided the main issue. An environmentalist suit on the matter was successful, with the court directing the BLM to prepare separate EIS's on the grazing program for each of its 52 grazing districts.[108] While all 52 EISs have not been prepared as yet, the early EISs ratify, rather than alter, exsiting BLM grazing policies.

Mineral King: One of the major types of developed recreation permitted by the Forest Service is alpine skiing, and one of the major Forest Service controversies in recent years has involved a proposal by Disney enterprises to build a major ski area in the Mineral King Valley in California. Although initial planning for the ski area began as early as 1945, the controversy came to a head in 1969 when the Sierra Club filed suit against the development and obtained a preliminary injunction. The complaint alleged that the development would endanger the Sequoia National Game Range in the valley, that the road to the ski area would illegally cross a national park for purposes other than park managment, and (in an amendment after NEPA was passed) that no EIS had been prepared on the project. Lower court decisions in the case denied the Sierra Club standing and were appealed to the Supreme Court, leading to the landmark decision on standing discussed earlier in this chapter.[109] Following the decision, the Sierra Club amended its complaint in June, 1972, alleging injury to its members who used Mineral King for hiking. Since the Forest Service had not prepared an EIS (and knowing it would surely lose the suit without an adequate EIS), it prepared a draft EIS, released in late 1974. The final EIS, released in February, 1976, proposed a development approximately half the size comtemplated in the draft EIS and in 1969. While the scaled-down development had some tactical advantages in terms of the ongoing litigation, it was much smaller than Disney preferred, and Disney, tired of nearly 10 years of delay, began to investigate other sites for its development. Meanwhile, beginning in May, 1975, bills were introduced in Congress to add the Sequoia Game Range (Mineral King Valley) to Sequoia National Park, thereby foreclosing development. These bills are under consideration in the 95th Congress. Then, in March, 1977, the Sierra Club's suit, which was supposed to go to trial 90 days after release of the final EIS, was dismissed for lack of prosecution. Then, in January, 1978, the Administration supported addition of Mineral King to the Sequoia National Park; as of June, 1978, the Mineral King addition to the Park had been reported favorably by the House Interior Committee and was awaiting floor action.[110]

Public Lands Energy Policy: The Department of the Interior and the BLM are in the middle of current controversies over new domestic fuel supplies, since most new energy development is on federal lands. Mining and oil and gas policy is among the most complicated issue areas in natural resources management, with fundamental questions of resource exploitation versus environmental protection, complex economics, highly technical issues, and an extensive body of statutory law. Under the Nixon and Ford administrations, Interior generally attempted to pursue a policy of fostering development of domestic fossil fuel sources. That policy often brought it into conflict with environmentalists. Coal stripmining and OSC leasing policies offer good examples of these conflicts.

Coal strip-mining policy is less simple than most natural-resources issues. The basic arguments have the familiar simplicity: exploitation of a needed economic resource versus extreme environmental damage to soil stability, water quality, and aesthetic values. But environmentalists are cross-pressured on the issue because coal is a viable alternative to nuclear power (which environmentalists fear) and strippable western, low-sulfur coal (as a replacement for eastern coal) is one alternative way of helping to meet air quaility standards in urban areas. Nor is the "other side's" position simple: a major ally of environmentalists on the strip-mining issue has been the western livestock industry (which opposes environmentalists on most other issues), because the lands to be stripped are their ranches or public rangelands which they depend on in their operations. In practice, however, all the complexity of the issue has usually reached down to the question of how much reclamation (returning the land to its original contour and vegetative conditions, with performance bonds to insure compliance) should be required of coal operators.

Reclamation of strip-mined lands became a federal problem as the locus of coal exploitation shifted to the northern Great Plains (Wyoming, Montana, and the Dakotas), because most of the coal seams there are strippable and most are on federal (BLM or Forest Service) or Indian (managed by the Bureau of Indian Affairs) lands or private lands on which the federal government or Indian tribes retained mineral rights. Led by Representative Morris Udall, the Congress passed a stringent reclamation and strip-mining control bill in 1975. This bill was, however, vetoed by President Ford. In 1976, two similar strip-mine bills were reported from committee, but failed to gain a rule from the Rules Committee, in part because of certain Presidential vetoes.[111]

Meanwhile, Interior initiated a comprehensive revision of its coal-leasing policy. From September, 1975, through January, 1977, Secretary Thomas Kleppe shepherded the BLM's so-called Energy Minerals

Activity Recommendation System (EMARS) through the EIS and rule-making processes.[112] EMARS is the cornerstone of a thorough over-hauling of federal coal leasing, including: (1) a fully competitive leasing system which eliminates preference right leases related to prospecting permits; (2) diligent development standards to eliminate holding coal leases for speculative purposes; (3) integration of the BLM's land use planning and NEPA analysis processes with a new tract valuation procedure to determine, before leasing, the value of lease tracts (to obtain fair market lease process) and prevent leasing of marginal tracts with high potential for environmental damage; (4) more stringent mining operation and reclamation standards and regulations; and (5) regional EISs on groups of leases.

Promulgated after negotiations with, and with the approval of, OMB, CEQ, and EPA, the EMARS leasing policy addressed a number of issues, from the concern, dating back to 1971, with speculative monopolization of federal coal leases, to the problem of disagreement between the Ford Administration and Representative Udall over strip-mine regulations. While the EMARS reforms were not as strict as the Udall bills preferred by environmentalists, the administrative rule-making seems to have partially undercut Congressional strip-mining initiatives. After EMARS was published as final rules in May of 1976, Congress, in August, passed the Federal Coal Leasing Act Amendments,[113] which effectively ratified Interior's EMARS program. After passage of the act, Interior hurried to revise the EMARS regulations slightly to conform to the act and negotiated agreements with four of the main western coal states (Wyoming, Utah, New Mexico, and South Dakota) to merge the state reclamation programs with the federal program. Kleppe's and Interior's haste had the effect of setting EMARS in place, presenting the new Secretary, Cecil Andrus (who, as Governor of Idaho, had taken strong environmental positions on mining issues), with a fait accompli.

When the 95th Congress convened, the new Administration supported the strong strip-mine regulations advocated by Representative Udall. No longer able to rely on a Presidential veto, the mining industry switched its attention to the Congress and was able to achieve some compromises in the bills. The resulting strip-mine bill[114] passed in July, 1977, is stronger than the EMARS surface-mining regulations, but somewhat weaker than the Administration-Udall position. The bill is weaker than environmentalists preferred in terms of returning strip-mined land to original contour, protecting nonfederal lands, and postponing compliance for smaller operators, but the bill includes some strong provisions for protecting prime agricultural land.

Oil and gas leasing in the Outer Continental Shelf is an important federal energy program because the OCS is one of the major areas of current exploration and development. The program nets the federal government alone over $7 billion annually. The BLM's OCS leasing procedure is fairly lengthy, involving a seven-step process which can take from one and one-half to two and one-half years, with another two to five years between sale and production. Potential oil spills and the effects of development onshore have made OCS sales quite controversial, especially since the 1969 Santa Barbara spill and the Nixon administration's decision to accelerate leasing after the 1973 oil embargo. The BLM's program was the subject of one of the important early NEPA decisions.[115] Despite increased criticism, the BLM has continued the accelerated OCS leasing program, since it is one of the few ways the federal government can act directly to increase domestic oil and gas supplies.

One of the more controversial recent sales was of a tract in the northern Gulf of Alaska, with the State of Alaska, EPA, and CEQ opposed to the sale. The sale, however, was upheld in the courts.[116] Then, in February, 1977, Judge Jack Weinstein of the Eastern District of New York held that Interior's EIS on Sale 40 off the Atlantic coast of New York was inadequate (factually erroneous, thus "arbitrary and capricious") and voided the sale. This decision was one of the few cases in which a massive (and fairly typical) EIS failed to convince a judge of procedural compliance with NEPA. The district court decision was overturned on appeal—even though it was based on findings of fact, not interpretations of law—and exploration has begun in the Sale 40 area. Then, just before Sale 40 exploration began, the OCS program was hit with another injunction. U.S. District Judge Arthur Garrity enjoined a sale off the Massachusetts coast because of conflicts with Interior's duties to protect the rich Georges Bank fishery; unlike the Sale 40 case, Judge Garrity's decision was upheld on emergency appeal.[117] Because they were not strong legal precedents due to the facts of the cases, however, neither the Sale 40 nor the Georges Bank cases directly affect the legal base of the whole OCS lease program.

The Sale 40 court decision, however, gave some extra impetus to the whole question of OCS leasing, a question which had been simmering since the 1973 acceleration. The Congress is currently considering amendments to the Outer Continental Shelf Lands Act (H.R. 1614). Like the EMARS reforms of the federal coal leasing process, the OCS Act amendments are aimed, to a considerable extent, at economic aspects of OCS leasing. (Much of the controversy surrounding OCS leasing off the east coast is caused by the states' dissatisfaction with the fact that the federal government obtains all the royalty income from leases, while state and local governments bear the governmental services costs associated with OCS-related developments.)

Major features of the amendments are aimed at increasing the competitiveness of OCS auctions, which currently tend to favor the major oil firms, by authorizing a variety of bidding systems. These decrease the risk in the auction to both the government and bidders by providing for a pause between exploration and development, during which the potential of a tract could be evaluated. Another proposal would give the states a percentage of the revenues from OCS leases, the only type of federal public lands revenue which does not now provide for such payments. Certain operating regulations would be strengthened to minimize environmental damage, but the main, supposedly protective controversy centers around provisions which would allow state governors to place restrictions on OCS leases. The theory is that governors from eastern states, California and Alaska would be more restrictive than Interior, but this is a fairly speculative assumption about the future actions of state officials. While it appears that the auction reforms and operating restrictions should pass the 95th Congress, the outcome of the state participation issues is still in doubt.

Clearcutting: One of the most controversial forestry practices during the 1970s was the practice of clearcutting. Clearcutting—the harvest of all trees in a given block of land—is a form of "even-aged management," the goal of which is to produce a forest composed of trees of a single species of the same age. Even-aged stands have significant silvicultural advantages in terms of the commercial value of the stand, tree growth potential, and harvesting operations. Because some tree species, especially the more commercially valuable ones, will not regenerate if other trees block the sunlight, clearcutting is used to prepare the site for even-aged management. However, clearcutting leaves an unsightly post-harvest landscape and is alleged to accelerate erosion, watershed siltation, and soil nutrient loss, and to increase the susceptibility of the forest stands to pest and disease attacks. Environmentalists also see clearcutting as symptomatic of Forest Service commitment to commercial timber production at the expense of other multiple uses, especially recreation and preservation of natural areas.

The practice of clearcutting has been intensely controversial since 1970, both within the forestry profession and between the Forest Service and conservationists.[118] The controversy's turning point came with the "Monongahela decision." The Izaak Walton League sued the Forest Service over clearcutting on the Monongahela National Forest in West Virginia, alleging clearcutting violated the letter of the 1897 Organic Act, which authorized the sale of only "dead, matured or large growth" trees which are individually marked. When the Fourth Circuit upheld a district court decision in favor of the Izaak Walton League, the Forest Service's

sales program in much of the East and later Alaska was effectively
halted.[119] The Service did not appeal this decision, but, as the Fourth
Circuit had implied in its decision, asked Congress to extricate it from its
difficulties. The Congress combined the Forest Service's recommendations for remedial legislation with an ongoing review of long-range Forest
Service planning, and the committee deliberations turned into a heated
lobbying battle between environmentalist critics of clearcutting and the
Service (aided by the timber industry). The resulting National Forest
Management Act of 1976[120] was a compromise: the Organic Act was
amended, removing the language the Monongahela decision was based
on, but Congress issued strong mandates for multiple-use and sustained-
yield timber management, reforestation, watershed and soil protection,
and aesthetic timber sale design, and prohibited strictly commercial
silvicultural methods and logging on marginal timberlands.

The four issue areas discussed in the preceding pages show a pattern of
public policy similar to water resources development policy. Just as
major water projects were often delayed by NEPA and environmentalist
pressure, but usually moved toward construction; so traditional public
lands policies were often delayed and sometimes modified, but still
continued with basic goals and objectives intact. The BLM still carries
out its grazing and minerals programs. The Forest Service still uses
"even-aged" timber management. Some programs may be delayed—a
year in the OCS Sale #40 case—but these are a minority of all projects.
Modification of programs can, on occasion, be substantial (e.g., the
Forest Management Act's restrictions on clearcutting, or the Surface
Mining Act's restrictions on mining on prime agricultural lands), but the
basic controversial program survives. It is also interesting to note that,
while almost all water project issues involved only NEPA, many of the
most significant public lands cases involved other laws: Mineral King
litigation was based on the game range designation and general National
Park statutes and is being resolved legislatively by addition of the area to
the Sequoia National Park, the EMARS policy was closely related to
administration efforts to stave off the strong strip-mining control bills;
and the Monongahela decision was based on the 1897 Organic Act.

As with water resources policy, however, the major change in public
lands policy is not to be found so much in the traditional multiple-use
programs, but in the importance of new agenda items. These new agenda
items, as was the case with the Army Corps' new agendas, are programs
favored by environmentalist constituents of the public lands agencies.

Wilderness Preservation

The preservation of areas of public lands did not begin, by any means, in the 1970s. Yellowstone, the first National Park, was established in 1872; the first National Wildlife Refuge, Pelican Island, was established in 1903; and the concept of designated wilderness began in 1939 with the Forest Service's "U regulations" and was given statutory status by the 1964 Wilderness Act. However, the 1970s will be remembered in the future as the decade in which wilderness preservation made its greatest advances.

National Park Service and Fish and Wildlife Service preservation policies have generally not been highly controversial—with a few exceptions. The Park Service has experienced steadily increasing visitations, with visits more than tripling since 1960 to 239 million in 1975,[121] which often creates severe overcrowding problems. The Park Service, in response, has gradually come to favor park preservation emphases as more important than facilitating recreational uses and has experimented in some parks with the uses of buses to decrease transportation congestion and reservation systems for campgrounds. Of more general concern, the Park Service's budget has, in the face of rising demands on the Service, been fairly stagnant. Needed capital improvements have not been made and ranger staffs have not increased, leading to severely deteriorated conditions in some units of the system.[122] The Park Service received some extra funding in 1976, supposedly for the Bicentennial, and is currently studying management improvements. Finally, mining in National Park system units, especially Death Valley National Monument, became particularly controversial in 1976, leading Congress to begin a phase-out of mining in the six park system units remaining open under the mining laws.[123]

The most important controversy involving National Wildlife Refuge system lands in recent years was a proposal to transfer the Russell, Sheldon, Kofa, and Desert Game Ranges, which had been administered jointly by the F&WS and BLM, to sole BLM management. Amid some controversy—a 1975 Wilderness Society ad in the *Washington Post* asked, "Mr. President, have you ever thought about assigning our Wildlife Refuges to the CIA?"—Congress gave the F&WS full control of the refuges and required Congressional approval of changes in Wildlife Refuge management status.[124]

Of considerably greater importance than these issues, however, new areas have been added to the various preservation systems at an exponential rate during the 1970s. The National Park system has been expanded slightly since 1970, with 21 areas, totalling 1,733,301 acres, added to the areas which existed in 1969. The Wildlife Refuge system increased only slightly. Aside from clarification of the status of the four Wildlife Ranges, the only recent addition to the system was the 50,000-acre Great Dismal Swamp National Wildlife Refuge in Virginia and North Carolina.

The major preservation decisions in recent years have involved the wilderness system. The 1964 Wilderness Act established over nine million acres of Forest Service land as 54 statutory Wilderness Areas and mandated a review of Forest Service, Park Service, and F&WS units for possible addition designations. From 1964 through 1969, only seven areas were added to the system (five Forest Service primitive areas, totalling 879,135 acres; one 63,469-acre Park Service unit; and a 3660-acre Wildlife Refuge area). Since 1970, wilderness reviews have proceeded much faster. In 1972, the Forest Service put a massive (if highly controversial) effort into its Roadless Area Review and Evaluation (RARE) process, holding hearings on almost all National Forests, and processing a major national EIS (the hearings and EIS received over 54,000 statements). The RARE process identified 1,448 roadless areas, totalling 55.9 million acres, and recommended 274 areas, at 12.3 million acres, for further study. Then, in 1973-1974, Congressional allies of environmentalists introduced legislation to designate eastern wilderness areas (almost all Wilderness Areas had been in western states), resulting in the passage of the Eastern Wilderness Areas Act,[125] which designated 16 areas initially and mandated further study of several others. Meanwhile, the Park Service and F&WS were preparing proposals to designate substantial proportions of their systems as wilderness.

The 94th Congress, particularly late in the second session, acted on many of the RARE, Eastern Wilderness, Park Service, and F&WS proposals. Currently the Wilderness Preservation System includes 175 areas, comprising 16.6 million acres. The Forest Service manages the largest share (106 areas, at 14.7 million acres), followed by the Park Service (17 areas, 1.1 million acres). In addition, Administration-endorsed recommendations for an additional 89 areas (30.9 million acres, of which 25 areas, 9.1 million acres, are Forest Service wilderness) are pending Congressional action.[126] A 1976 statute instructs the BLM to begin a review of its lands for possible wilderness designation.[127] The Bureau's 234,000 acres of "primitive areas" will probably, at a minimum, be recommended for wilderness designation, and environmentalists argue that as much as 70 million acres of BLM land qualifies as wilderness.

Most wilderness designations are quite controversial, with the forest products industry particularly opposed to Forest Service Wilderness, and environmentalists calling for even more designations. The continuing struggle over the Boundary Waters Canoe Area (BWCA) in Minnesota is a good example of such conflicts. When it was designated in 1964, the BWCA was the subject of special riders allowing uses forbidden in other Wilderness Areas (timber operations and motorized recreation in part of the area), which led to a Forest Service management plan designating about half of the BWCA as an "interior zone" managed as wilderness and the other half as a "portal zone" in which logging would be allowed. Comments on the EIS on this management plan were universally negative, with environmentalists opposed to any logging in the portal zone, and the forest products industry opposing any wilderness restrictions. Environmentalists, after failing to persuade the agency through the EIS process, took the Forest Service to court, winning injunctions in 1973 and 1975, but eventually losing at the appellate level.[128] Environmentalists turned to Congress for protection of the BWCA. In June, 1978, a bill sponsored by Representative Donald Fraser to designate most (1,077,000 acres) of the BWCA as full-fledged Wilderness passed the House.

Wilderness-like designations of two rivers were also controversial in recent years. The cases involved utility company proposals to build hydroelectric plants on the New River in North Carolina and on the Hells Canyon section of the Middle Snake River in Idaho, Washington, and Oregon. Both cases had been forcefully advanced by the utilities and just as forcefully opposed by environmentalists. After an unsuccessful suit against the FPC licensing of the Blue Ridge Dam,[129] the New River was added to the Wild and Scenic River system[130] in 1976 under the sponsorship of the State of North Carolina and with the support of Interior. (Along with four other 1976 additions, the Wild and Scenic Rivers system now includes 19 rivers, comprising 1,652 river-miles.) Hells Canyon was designated a National Recreation Area, with 193,840 acres designated as Wilderness. Both decisions preclude construction of the proposed dams.

All federal preservation efforts to the present, however, pale in comparison with the decisions to be made soon on what are somewhat cryptically called the "d-2" lands. The 1971 Alaska Native Claims Settlement Act (ANCSA)[131] established a procedure to settle the claims to federal land, which is still 97 percent of the state, by some 78,000 Alaska Eskimos, Indians, and Aleuts. Through 12 "native corporations" established under the Act, the native peoples are to receive $962.5 million and the right to select 44 million acres of federal land. Under the provisions of ANCSA and its statehood act, the State of Alaska will select another 103.5 million acres. Finally, section 17(d)(2) of ANCSA directed the Secretary of the Interior to withdraw 80 million acres as "national interest" lands and study these lands for designation as national parks, wildlife refuges, forests, and wild and scenic rivers. In a series of 28 final EISs released in late 1974, Interior proposed: 11 new national park system units, totalling 32.26 million acres; nine new units or additions to existing units of the National Wildlife Refuge system, totalling 31.6 million acres; three new national forests, and additions to an existing forest, totalling 18.8 million acres; as well as four separate wild and scenic rivers, totalling 705 miles, plus 1,900 miles within other proposed units. In addition, the proposals anticipated that 19.2 million acres of the proposed national parks and wildlife refuges would be designated as wilderness. These proposals would more than *double* the size of the existing national park, wildlife refuge, wild and scenic rivers, and wilderness systems.

Congress must act on these proposals by December, 1978 (under the provisions of ANCSA). Rep. Morris Udall, the chairman of the House Interior Committee, introduced an Alaska National Interest Lands Act (H.R. 39) early in the 95th Congress. Supported by the major environmental groups, the bill would add even more to the preservation systems than Interior's proposals: 64.3 million acres to the park system, 46.5 million to the wildlife refuge system, 4.1 million to the wild and scenic rivers system, only 1.6 million to the national forests, and all the park, refuge, and rivers acreage to the wilderness system. As could be expected, both the Udall and Interior proposals are controversial. Development interests, particularly the minerals and oil and gas industries, supported by Alaska Republicans (including Governor Jay Hammond), are supporting a plan to reduce the designations and allow commodity extraction in parts of the new units. In September, 1977, the Carter Administration, Interior and Agriculture reached an agreement, with the revised proposals totalling 91.7 million acres. Then, in May, 1978, the House, by an overwhelming 277-31 margin, passed a modified version of Udall's H.R. 39 which would establish 101 million acres in the Park, Refuge, Rivers, and Forest systems, of which fully 66 million acres would be wilderness. The House-passed bill, however, faces a threatened filibuster by Senator Ted Stevens of Alaska in the Senate. Thus, depending on the Senate outcome, the final designations are likely to be far larger than the 80 million acres contemplated by ANCSA, representing a monumental achievement in the preservation of one of the last great areas of wilderness in the world.

Preservation of public lands is the most ambitious goal of the more philosophically extreme wing of the environmental movement, the wing whose origins go back to the 19th Century romantic preservationists such as Henry David Thoreau and the Sierra Club's founder, John Muir. The preservationists have been highly successful in the 1970s. New national parks, national wildlife refuges, and wilderness areas in the East, West and, soon, Alaska, stand as monuments to the development of public lands policy in an even more pro-environmental way, in some respects, then the nonstructural and wetlands-protection trends in water resources policy.

THE NEW ADMINISTRATION

In general, one should be skeptical of the importance of changes in the Presidency. The power of the office is usually overrated, if not mythologized, in the face of Congressional control of appropriations and statutory authorizations, the semi-autonomy of agency subsystems, and the like.[132] Moreover, the effects of the party system and public opinion tend to produce Presidents who typically do not differ radically from one another on policy matters, thus mitigating the effect even a strong President might have on policy. However, if a new President does have policy preferences which differ significantly from a predecessor, he can have a significant, if marginal, effect on policy, removing hurdles which might impede some proposals or lending some extra weight to other proposals.

The new Carter Administration is having exactly this sort of effect on natural resources policy. During the 1976 election campaign, it became clear that, amid all the rhetoric about the economy, the one area in which candidates Carter and Ford differed radically was the environment. Perhaps the League of Conservation Voters summed up their differences best with its rating of Carter as "outstanding" and of Ford as "hopeless." With Carter's election, economic interests became rather apprehensive and environmentalists began to drool.[133] On almost every occasion thus far, President Carter has lived up to the one side's fears and the other's expectations.

Appointments

The earliest signs that Carter's would be an environmentalist Administration came with his appointments, beginning with the energy and natural resources transition staff. Headed by Joseph Browder, the former director of the Environmental Policy Center, a Washington lobbying group, the staff was dominated by environmentalists, including Kathryn Schirmer, a former EPA staffer, Kathy Fletcher, from EDF, and James Rathlesberger, former director of the House of Representatives' Environmental Study Conference. The most prominent and controversial member of the transition energy staff, however, was S. David Freeman, a leading advocate of energy conservation as the director of the Ford Foundation Energy Policy Project.[134] Browder resigned from the transition staff in protest when Freeman was excluded from an energy briefing by campaign staffers, supposedly because of pressure from oil industry campaign contributors. (Carter was reportedly also "furious" when informed of the exclusion.) In any case, the rest of the staff, including Freeman, remained and seems to have had some effect on the administration's early initiatives on natural resources.

Carter's major cabinet appointments continued the trend set by the transition staff appointments. The department most relevant for natural resources is Interior. The only cabinet appointee closely linked with any side of any issue—and reportedly the only appointee who had no competition for his or her position—is the new Interior Secretary, Cecil Andrus, a pro-environment former Governor of Idaho. As Governor of a public lands state (64 percent federally owned, mostly Forest Service and BLM land), Andrus was involved in efforts to preserve federal lands from mining and timber developments, supported strong pollution control programs, and even took on the AEC on the nuclear safety issue. Carter's most important cabinet appointment for environmental issues generally was James Schlesinger, designated to be the Secretary of the new Department of Energy. As a former AEC chairman, Schlesinger's appointment drew some environmentalist criticism, notably from Ralph Nader, a leading opponent of nuclear power. But the criticism is unwarranted, since, while with the AEC, Schlesinger had a healthy skepticism of nuclear power (as does Carter), pushed the AEC into full compliance with NEPA's procedural requirements, and was generally reasonable with environmentalists and aloof from the so-called atomic energy "establishment." Schlesinger, in addition, supports the conservation approach to energy policy.

Some of Carter's sub-cabinet appointments are even more environmentally oriented. EPA Administrator Douglas Costle has a good environmental record, but EPA Deputy Administrator Barbara Blum, formerly a lobbyist for Save America's Vital Environment, and Assistant Administrator for Water and Hazardous Materials Thomas Jorling, formerly on the staff of the Senate Publics Works Committee, which authored the current air and water pollution laws, are considered exceptionally strong environmentalist appointees. The best known environmentalist appointees of the Administration were Gus Speth, formerly NRDC's top attorney, and Marion Edey, the founder of the League of Conservation Voters (which publishes the "dirty dozen," a list of Congressmen with poor environmental records who are targeted for electoral defeat). Edey was not confirmed by the Senate, but Speth is now (along with Charles Warren, an environmentally oriented former California state legislator) a member of the Council on Environmental Quality. S. David Freeman, the main energy conservationist on the Carter transition staff, was appointed Chairman of the TVA board in May, 1978. Freeman is expected to thoroughly shake up TVA, and one of his first initiatives is a reevaluation of the Tellico Dam project. The most significant of the assistant secretary level appointments in the natural resources area is M. Rupert Cutler, formerly on the staff of the Wilderness Society (among many environmentalist affiliations) and later a member of the faculty of the natural resources program at Michigan State. Cutler's dissertation on Forest Service wilderness litigation—including the Mineral King and BWCA cases—was critical of the Forest Service's exclusion of environmentalists from the decision-making process before the passage of NEPA.[135] As Assistant Secretary of Agriculture for Conservation, Research, and Education, Cutler supervises the Forest Service and the SCS. Among Cutler's efforts to date are support of the transfer of Mineral King to the National Park system and full Wilderness status for the BWCA, and personal leadership of a second round of roadless area reviews ("RARE II") which is addressing preservationist criticisms of the earlier Forest Service RARE proposals by evaluating 2,686 areas (totaling over 62 million acres) for wilderness recommendation.

Administration Policy Initiatives

Carter's pro-environment leanings are demonstrated by both the timing and the content of his major policy initiatives to date: most of the major programs which were proposed early in the Administration involve natural resources—including the water resources, energy, and environmental programs—and all take a uniformly pro-environmentalist stance. Perhaps the most important program proposed by the Administration so far is the energy program. Continuing a line of policy development stretching back to the Ford Foundation Energy Policy Report and reflected in several recent statutes, the program stresses energy conservation strategies supported by environmentalists rather than the supply-exploitation strategies preferred by the energy industries.[136] The program proposed: tax incentives for solar energy and building insulation; tax disincentives on gasoline (if conservation goals are not met), crude oil, and gas-inefficient automobiles; coal conversion to conserve oil and gas; and emphasis on coal production while assigning "last priority" status to nuclear power. In cases of potential conflict between the energy program and environmental interests, the program favors the environment. For example, increased emphasis on coal production could exacerbate the strip-mining problem on public lands. But Carter and Secretary Andrus supported the strong Udall versions of the strip-mine bill which Ford vetoed.

The Carter environmental program, like the energy program, generally stressed the environmentalist side of current policy issues.[137] In the pollution field, the program promised strong implementation of the new Toxic Substances Control Act, the 1976 Resource Conservation and Recovery Act, and occupational health standards, and supported the environmentalist position on pending legislative revisions of the air and water pollution laws. On natural resources issues, Carter's program generally did not propose specific, major new initiatives, but reaffirmed the Administration's commitment to existing policy in certain issue areas or expressed support for ongoing natural resources legislative proposals. In the water resources area, the President issued Executive Order 11988, requiring all federal agencies—principally the Corps, but also other agencies such as HUD—to allow developments in floodplains only as a last resort. This order essentially ratified the understanding that the Corps had come to over the past few years. The program also expressed support for the Corps' Section 404 wetlands program. A number of the provisions of the program were aimed at public lands minerals policies. The President expressed support for strip-mining (since passed) and OCS bills pending in Congress and promised to produce Administration proposals to drastically revise the old 1872 Mining Laws (which give the BLM and Forest Service almost no control over hard-rock mining claims and prospecting nor any royalties for minerals extracted from public lands). He also directed Interior to implement the EMARS program in a strong, environmental manner. Continuing the trend of the past few years, most of Carter's public lands proposals involved preservationist actions. The program included: nine wilderness, eight wild and scenic river, and three national scenic trail proposals; an accelerated program of Forest Service and BLM roadless area reviews, plus 20 wild and scenic river studies; support for the Alaska "d-2" lands designations; increased funding for the Park and Fish and Wildlife services, including special funding for wetlands acquisition; and accelerated implementation of the Endangered Species Act. Finally, the program included Executive Order 11991, which gave CEQ the authority to issue regulations, as opposed to mere advisory guidelines, on agency EIS procedures. E.O. 11991, under the guise of reducing "paperwork," gives CEQ additional leverage in their continuing effort to reduce "extraneous background data, in order to emphasize the need to focus on real environmental issues." The Order also establishes a referral process which may increase the Council's ability to mediate interagency disputes, for example between a water project agency and the Fish and Wildlife Service.

The "Hit List"

One of Carter's first initiatives in office was, by far, the most spectacular of his natural resources policy moves. As Governor of Georgia, Carter had numerous conflicts with the Corps. His best known action was leadership in the effort to withdraw state support for the Sprewell Bluff Dam after his personal engineering evaluation of the project convinced him that the dam's benefits were overstated. Carter also reportedly once dispatched a boatload of state fish and game rangers to forcibly halt a Corps dredging operation in a St. Simons Island wetlands.[138] During the campaign, Carter noted,[139]

> We must realize that the federal government's dam building era has come to an end. Most beneficial projects have been built. It is time the Corps enters a new phase for the overall benefit of the general public.

Carter's effort to bring the federal dam-building era to an end began in earnest in February, 1977, when the Administration indicated that all major water projects would be reviewed and recommended that 19, and later 14 more, Corps and BuRec projects be "zero-budgeted" in FY1978. Three projects were subsequently reinstated and two TVA projects added to bring the list to 32 projects, with total estimated project costs of $9.47 billion and FY78 budget requests totalling $574 million (see Table 8.1). Included on the list at one time or another were some of the most controversial projects in the country: Tenn-Tom, the Central Arizona Project and several related projects in the Upper Colorado River Basin (e.g., Fruitland Mesa), Meramec Dam, the Garrison Diversion Unit, the Lincoln-Dickey Schools project, Auburn-Folsom Dam, the Cache Basin channelization, and the Bonneville Unit of the Central Utah Project. The 35 projects which made the list at one time or another, though only about a tenth of all current projects receiving appropriations, represented 26.8 percent of the 1978 construction budget. In April, 1977, the President released the results of his final review of the "hit list" projects, recommending deletion of funding and deauthorization of 18 projects, modification of five projects, and continued funding of the remaining nine projects.[140]

Carter's interference with the ongoing pork barrel projects set off squeals of anguish on the Hill. Even such environmentally oriented legislators as Representative Udall (Central Arizona Project) and Senator Muskie (Lincoln-Dickey) complained when "their" project made the list. The water project agencies, of course, have been prime examples of subsystem politics, and a succession of Presidents have tried to control the agencies and their project budgets, almost always unsuc-

Table 8.1 The "Hit List"

Project Name, State (Agency)	Tot. Fed. Cost (Est.) [$ mill.]	Orig. FY78 Request [$ mill.]	B/C @ Current 6.375% (Not Author.) Rate	Congressional Action
Projects Recommended for Deletion (Final List):				
Grove Lake, KA (COE)	$ 86.0	$ 1.0	.59	Deleted $
LaFarge Lake, WI (COE)	55.4	2.0	.98	Deleted $
Lukfata Lake, OK (COE)	31.5	0.2	1.02	Deleted $
Meramec Park Lake, MO (COE)	124.0	10.0	1.5	Deleted $
Yatesville Lake, KY (COE)	53.6	7.2	.99	Deleted $
Fruitland Mesa Project, CO (BR)	87.9	7.7	.3	Deleted $
Narrows Unit, CO (BR)	145.7	9.7	.9	Deleted $
Oahe Unit, SD (BR)	504.6	17.0	1.0	Deleted $
Savery-Pot Hook Project, CO (BR)	75.8	6.0	.4	Deleted $
Bayou Bodcau channelization, LA (COE)	14.5	2.4	1.12	Partial $ – Modif'n
Applegate Lake, OR (COE)	81.5	7.4	.64	Funded
Atchafalaya Rv. & Bayous Boeuf, Black & Chene navigation channel, LA (COE)	20.3	5.1	1.4	Funded
Cache Basin channelization, AR (COE)	93.2	2.0	2.08	Funded
Hillsdale Lake, KA (COE)	55.7	14.0	1.08	Funded
Russell Dam, GA-SC (COE)	276.0	21.0	1.3	Funded
Tallahala Creek Dam, MS (COE)	55.7	5.0	.9	Funded
Columbia Dam, TN (TVA)	142.0	20.0	.8	Funded
Auburn-Folsom Dam, CA (BR)	1131.0	39.7	1.0	Funded-pending study
Subtotal, Recommended Deletions	3034.4	177.4		
Projects Recommended for Modification (Final List):				
Mississippi Rv, Gulf Outlet navig'n, LA (COE)	286.3	0.7	1.4	Agreed-No $ Change
Tensas Basin chann'n/flood cont., AR-LA (COE)	271.4	10.0	1.03	Agreed-No $ Change
Central Arizona Project, AZ (BR)	1679.1	104.2	1.4	Agreed-3 dams drop'd
Bonneville Unit, Cent. Utah Project, UT (BR)	862.7	32.0	1.0	No Modif'n
Garrison Diversion Proj., ND (BR)	609.7	18.7	1.36	No Modif'n-pend. study
Subtotal, Recommended Modifications	3709.2	165.6		
Projects Recommended for Continued Funding (Final List):				
Dayton flood control, KY (COE)	7.6	2.9	.81	Funded
Fulton flood control, IL (COE)	12.9	4.2	.71	Funded
Red River Waterway, LA (COE)	908.5	26.0	.7	Funded
Tennessee-Tombigbee Waterway, AL-MS (COE)	1418.0	157.0	.87	Funded

Table 8.1   The "Hit List"   *(Continued)*

Project Name, State (Agency)	Tot. Fed. Cost (Est.) [$ mill.]	Orig. FY78 Request [$ mill.]	B/C @ Current 6.375% (Not Author.) Rate	Congressional Action
Tyrone flood control, PA (COE)	33.9	1.5	.69	Funded
Bear Creek Project Dams, AL-MS (TVA)	75.0	18.6	1.06	Funded
Dallas Creek Project, CO (BR)	53.7	12.2	.9	Funded
Dolores Project, CO (BR)	187.3	5.7	.6	Funded
Lyman Project, WT (BR)	29.2	4.1	.5	Funded
Subtotals, recommended Funding (Final)	2726.1	232.2		
Projects Recommended for Continued Funding (First List):				
Lincoln-Dickey Schools Lake, ME (COE)	533.0	1.0	n.a.	Funded $0.7 mill.
Freeport Project, IL (COE)	9.4	0.1	n.a.	Funded
Paintsville Lake, KY (COE)	41.6	7.3	n.a.	Funded
Subtotals, Recommended Funding (First)	584.0	8.4		
Totals, All 35 Projects	$10,053.7	$583.6		

cessfully as the Congress protected "its" projects, particularly those of the Corps.[141] So most observers felt that the Carter recommendations were sure to be overruled by Congress. Since water projects appropriations are lumped together in omnibus bills, they are generally considered fairly veto-proof. The Senate was the first to act, attaching a largely symbolic rider in March to the public works jobs bill which instructed the President to spend all funds appropriated for "hit list" projects.

In May, the House Appropriations Committee reported out bills funding 17 of the projects recommended for deletion on the final (April) list. Some of the projects seemed to be in trouble because of Carter's action: Grove Lake was deleted in the House bill, Missouri Senators Eagleton and Danforth had the Meramec project explicitly omitted from the "protection" of the Senate jobs bill rider, and Representative Udall, a prime sponsor of the Central Arizona Project, agreed to the deletion of Orme, Hooker, and Charleston Dams from the project. Though both sides (especially environmentalists) were gearing up for a major fight on the water projects, most observers predicted that few, if any, projects would be deleted. The turning point came on a House floor vote on the Derrick-Conte amendment to delete the remaining "hit list" projects from the Public Works Appropriations bill. When the Derrick-Conte amendment lost by only 194-218, it became clear that the President had enough votes to sustain his threatened veto. To avert the threatened veto, the Congressional leadership worked out a deal with the Administration deleting nine of the 18 "hit list" projects as well as the Clinch River breeder reactor. When the Senate and a House-Senate conference committee agreed to this compromise, the President and other water project opponents had won an extremely surprising victory.[142]

Initially, the "hit list" seemed to be important for primarily symbolic reasons. Certainly it was a quick reward for environmentalists who supported Carter's candidacy and presaged the Administration's conservationist positions on the energy and environmental programs. Later developments gave the "hit list" much more concrete significance: not only were nine projects deleted for fiscal 1978, and four more modified, but it seems clear that all the "hit list" projects will be threatened by continuing reevaluation in future budget cycles. The victory on the water projects also gives added impetus to a general review of water resources which was announced in the Carter Environmental program. The U.S. Water Resources Council, OMB, and CEQ conducted a year-long review of national water policy culminating in a set of major presidential proposals for water policy reform.[143] The Carter proposals recommend a major revision of the principles and standards under which water projects' cost-benefit analyses are performed, emphasis on environmental concerns and trade-offs, and increased cost-sharing by project beneficiaries via state government contribution of up to 10% of the cost of newly authorized projects. (In a separate process, Congress has almost passed a weak bill imposing fees, in the form of a fuel tax, on the barge industry which has heretofore used Corps' waterways free.) The hallmark of the Carter water project reform proposals—as was the case with the Carter energy program—is water conservation as an alternative to expensive new structural water projects. Thus the "hit list" and the water policy review are the latest in a series of developments in the 1970s which bode ill for authorization of major new structural water projects.

Reorganization

A substantial proportion of candidate Carter's campaign rhetoric involved promises to reorganize the federal bureaucracy. Apparently Carter's notion of reorganization involves reducing the number of federal administrative entities from a putative number of about 1500 (which is three and a half times the number of independent agencies plus the bureaus and other offices in the cabinet departments) down to some smaller number.

Major federal reorganization attempts have traditionally focused on two of the natural resources agencies as top priority targets. The Corps, in the Department of Defense, so the argument goes, belongs in Interior along with the Bureau of Reclamation, the second largest water project agency. (The argument never seems to target the SCS or the TVA, whose locations in the federal organization chart are just as anomolous as the Corps'.) The other target is Agriculture's Forest Service, which would be transferred to Interior to join the other public lands agencies. These proposals are rather old: the first full-scale effort was made by Franklin Roosevelt's Interior Secretary, Harold Ickes, and the most recent by President Nixon in 1970. All have, obviously, failed. The Congressional committees overseeing the Corps and the Forest Service have zealously guarded their charges. In fact, the fear of reorganization of the Corps has been the primary motivation behind procedures of the various reorganization statutes passed since 1939 (which provide for Congressional veto of Presidential reorganization plans). For their parts, both the Forest Service and the Corps appreciate their present locations. Because their missions are rather different from the rest of their departments' work, they enjoy a fair amount of autonomy.

While Interior would be expected to gain from major reorganizations in the traditional vein (receiving the Corps and the Forest Service), it actually could have lost significantly in the first round of reorganizations proposed by Carter. A key part of the Carter energy program was the creation of a new cabinet Department of Energy. A new Department of Energy could conceivably have taken over some or all of the programs of nine of the Interior Department's 18 bureaus, particularly the BLM (OCS and other leasing duties), the Geological Survey (post-lease monitoring of BLM leases), Bureau of Indian Affairs (fossil fuel leasing on Indian lands), BuRec (hydroelectric power generation functions), and the four regional power marketing administrations. However, the new Department of Energy, as recently passed by Congress, will remove only the four power marketing administrations and a few other minor programs from Interior. Although Interior and the Department of Energy will have a formal consulting relationship on the levels of energy minerals leasing, Interior will retain the programs currently administered by the BLM, BIA, and the Geological Survey (as well as almost all of BuRec's functions).

The second round of reorganization held a real surprise for people interested in natural resources issues. The first of the Reorganization Plans per se dealt with the Executive Office of the President, and early proposals included several options which would have effectively abolished CEQ. These proposals caused some bewilderment among environmentalist defenders of the NEPA process, especially since they emanated from the same "environmental administration" which had only a few months earlier increased CEQ's formal authority over the NEPA process in Executive Order 11991. Environmentalist opposition, however, led the Administration to leave CEQ intact in its July, 1977, plan for reorganization of the Executive Office.[144]

The major reorganization proposals affecting the departments and independent agencies are still in the offing as of this writing. The reorganization planners at OMB are reportedly actively considering various options involving both the Corps and the Forest Service, and the infighting (e.g., by the Forest Service) has already begun. Since organization chart-shuffling reorganizations do not, of themselves, fundamentally alter the statutory authorities, agency and professional norms, resource commitments, and political environments of bureaus, most modern students of public administration are skeptical about the ability of reorganization efforts to significantly affect public policy or the behavior of agencies. Major reorganizations (i.e., those affecting the Forest Service and the Corps), however, could affect the Carter Administration and its policy initiatives adversely by tying up personnel time and political capital which might be better spent on substantive policy matters.

Implications of the New Administration

In summary, all indications are that the Carter Administration will reinforce the trends of the past few years in environmental policy generally. Carter is personally much more sympathetic toward environmentalists than was his predecessor, and his early actions on appointments and substantive policy programs indicate he will attempt to carry through on those personal beliefs. The marginal effects of this radically different President (on environmental issues) should be most evident in pollution control and energy matters. EPA, which had to spend a certain amount of time and caution in fighting with the previous Republican Executive Offices, will now be able to act with a somewhat freer hand. Unlike the Republican administrations, which emphasized energy supply strategies, the Carter Administration has committed itself early to the conservation strategy.

In the natural resources field, the Carter Administration seems likely to support a continuation of the 1970-1976 trends: deemphasis of structural water projects, but support for the Corps' Section 404 program, nonstructural flood control experiments, perhaps even the urban studies wastewater management program, and continuation of the efforts to preserve public lands in the wilderness system. The shift of Presidential priorities from energy-supply to energy-conservation strategies should also act to moderate pressures on the public lands for full-scale exploitation of coal, oil, gas, and uranium fuel sources.

SUMMARY AND CONCLUSIONS

To date, the 1970s have been a time of considerable change in natural resources policy. Under the influence of NEPA, natural resource (and all other federal) agencies have been forced to develop procedures which have institutionalized the consideration of environmental factors in agency policy-making. These procedural changes, moreover, have reinforced the growing strength of the environmental movement by affording environmentalist access to decision processes they had difficulty participating in pre-NEPA.

Substantively, one finds the same pattern of change in both water resources and public lands policy. The old, traditional missions, which engendered so much controversy, have come through the 1970s, but significantly scathed. A project or program here and there may fail, and many projects are delayed to some extent. Many proposals are undoubtedly turned down early or not even made, because they are seen as not worth the conflict they would generate. And a majority of projects and programs are modified, sometimes significantly, to decrease their environmental impacts. But dams, waterways, timber sales, mineral leases, and so on, are still made. The most significant changes in the 1970s, however, have been the "new" agenda items. Wilderness preservation, nonstructural flood control methods, and the protection of wetlands all reflect the gradual movement toward what Barry Commoner called the third law of ecology—"nature knows best."[145]

Several interrelated factors seem to have influenced this shift in policy. First, natural resources policy has been perhaps the most litigious policy arena in the 1970s, on a par with civil rights policy. The courts helped to make NEPA's promise a reality. In their circuitous way, judges required strict implementation of NEPA's procedural mandates, but refused, following the logic of the Administratrive Procedure Act and the Overton Park decision, to explicitly overturn agency decisions alleged to violate NEPA's substantive goals. Almost every major natural resource issue (and quite a few minor ones) has been subjected to protracted litigation, as the various case studies discussed above demonstrate. But the courts resolved the substantive issues in very few of these cases. Typically, the courts either explicitly or implicitly "remanded" the case to Congress for final resolution (e.g., the Tellico, BWCA, and clearcutting cases). But the courts' enforcement of NEPA's procedural requirements facilitated continued environmentalist pressure on the agencies' traditional missions and forced the agencies to adapt to NEPA's environmental consciousness goal.

Second, the growth of the environmental movement—institutionalized by NEPA's procedural reforms and the public participation programs

NEPA spawned—changed the political environment of natural resources agencies radically. Well organized, more numerous, and increasingly sophisticated environmentalists are a powerful counterbalance to the interests the agencies had dealt with almost exclusively before the 1970s. In such a political environment, the potential for agency capture by narrow economic interests is almost nil. This sort of political balance is rare in policy systems, especially among the so-called clientelist agency systems. And the events of the past few years demonstrate that such political balance can significantly affect public policy.

Third, several agencies proved quite adaptable in the face of NEPA and environmental pressure. The conventional wisdom is that powerful agencies are fairly rigid and entrenched, protected from the need to change by powerful clients, supporters in Congressional committees, and the like. Such has not been the case in natural resources subsystems in the 1970s. The Corps of Engineers and the Forest Service are generally recognized to be two of the most powerful agencies in the federal bureaucracy. But they are precisely the agencies which proved most adaptive in the 1970s. They implemented NEPA's procedural reforms best of all agencies. Substantively, the Corps efforts, for example, in programs like Section 404 wetlands protection have astounded critics who viewed the agency as one of the most diligent of destroyers. The Corps' and Forest Service's adaptability, of course, was also facilitated by their status as the two major targets of environmentalist pressure. But it also seems possible that the professionalism and esprit de corps of the two agencies, which were major factors in the agencies' pre-NEPA power, facilitated their adaptability in the face of the new pressures of the 1970s.[146]

There is no foreseeable reason for these environmental trends to change significantly in the near future. The solidly Democratic Congress has been unresponsive to efforts to water down key statutes like NEPA, and many key Congressional leaders, such as Senator Muskie and Representative Udall, are strongly pro-environment. The courts also show no signs of retreating from their enforcement of environmental statutes. The agencies' NEPA procedures are, by now, fairly institutionalized. And the Presidency, at least for the next four years, is pro-environment. The Congress seems to be becoming slightly less environmentally oriented to balance the effect of the Carter "environmental administration" on the Executive Branch, but the net shift is still in the environmental direction. Development interests may gain some apparent victories in the future. In the next few years, preservation decisions should decrease, but that decrease will be apparent only in contrast with the high level of preservation, such as the 80 to 100 million acres of "d-2"

254 *Nationalizing Government*

lands to be designated, in the 94th and 95th Congresses. And the Congress has passed a strip-mine control bill this year that is weaker than those vetoed by Ford, but the EMARS process and the new strip-mine law should provide an adequate vehicle for strong strip-mine control in the hands of an Interior Department committed to environmental protection. But environmentalists should continue to win as many or more than they lose.

Perhaps the key to the continuation of the trends of the past few years is the continued strength of the environmental movement and general public opinion favoring the environment. Public support has not diminished, even in the face of (perhaps because of?) industry efforts to blame all manner of ills on "environmentalists." More important, environmental group membership and activism have not diminished. Perhaps Carter put it best in a campaign speech:[147]

> The title of my speech, as I noted when I got here this morning, comes from the Bible—for if the trumpet be given an uncertain sound, then who shall prepare themselves for the battle?

> I tell you that this is no time for those of us who love God's earth and the beauty of it, the purity of the air and water, to compromise or to retreat or to yield in any possible measure to the devastation or deterioration of the quality of our lives or our environment.

> If the members of the environmental and conservation groups of this nation are willing to compromise ahead of time on tough decisions relating to the quality of the lives of the American people, then who in God's world is going to maintain a staunch position from which we can make proper decisions?

The trumpet remains as strident as always.

NOTES

1. *Budget of the United States Government, Fiscal Year 1976.* (Washington, D.C.: U.S. Government Printing Office, February 1975): 218-313. Figures are for FY75 estimated outlays for Corps of Engineers, Bureau of Reclamation, Soil Conservation Service, Tennessee Valley Authority, and the four power administrations in Interior. Federal Highway Administration outlays were $4.85 billion. The third ranking category was Environmental Protection Agency sewage treatment grants, at $2.3 billion.

2. Bureau of Land Management, *Public Land Statistics, 1974* (Washington, D.C.: U.S. Government Printing Office, 1975): 10-13.

3. Grant McConnell, *Private Power and American Democracy* (New York: Alfred Knopf, 1966): 200. Also see chapter 4 in Theodore Lowi, *The End of Liberalism* (New York: W.W. Norton, 1969).

4. Lowi, *The End of Liberalism:* 306-309; Arthur Maass, *Muddy Waters* (Cambridge, Mass.: Harvard University Press, 1951), and John Ferejohn, *Pork Barrel Politics:*

Rivers and Harbors Legislation, 1947-1968 (Stanford, Calif.: Stanford University Press, 1974).

5. Grant McConnell, "The Conservation Movement—Past and Present," *Western Political Quarterly,* 7 (September, 1954): 463-478; Samuel Hays, *Conservation and the Gospel of Efficiency* (Cambridge, Mass.: Harvard University Press, 1959); Frank Smith, *The Politics of Conservation* (New York: Random House, 1966).

6. For two representative examples, see the "Nader Raider" studies on the Forest Service and the Bureau of Reclamation: Daniel Barney, *The Land Stand* (New York: Grossman, 1974); and Richard Berkman and W. Kip Viscusi, *Damming the West* (New York: Grossman, 1971).

7. Paul Culhane, "Federal Agency Organizational Change in Response to Environmentalism," *Humboldt Journal of Social Relations,* 2 (Fall/Winter, 1974): 32-35.

8. James McEvoy, "The American Concern with Environment," in William Burch, Neil Cheek, and Lee Taylor (eds.), *Social Behavior, Natural Resources and the Environment* (New York: Harper & Row, 1972): 223-224. The percentages are from an open-ended questionnaire item.

9. Council on Environmental Quality, *Environmental Quality—1973* (Washington, D.C.: U.S. Government Printing Office, September 1973): 396-402; McEvoy, 220-221; "Sierra Club Financial Report," *Sierra Club Bulletin,* 62 (February, 1977): 26.

10. The best sources on NEPA are: Frederick Anderson, *NEPA In The Courts* (Baltimore, Md.: Johns Hopkins University Press, 1973); Richard Liroff, *A National Policy for the Environment: NEPA and Its Aftermath* (Bloomington: Indiana University Press, 1976); Richard Andrews, *Environmental Policy and Administrative Change* (Lexington, Mass.: D.C. Heath, 1976); the NEPA Symposium in *Natural Resources Journal,* 16 (April, 1976); and Thomas Sullivan, "The National Environmental Policy Act," in J. Gordon Arbuckle, et al., *Environmental Law Handbook,* 4th ed. (Washington, D.C.: Government Institutes, 1976): 59-93.

11. 42 U.S.C. Section 4332(2)(c).

12. Liroff, chapter 2.

13. Ibid., 89-92, 118-119.

14. A good, available, fairly up-to-date treatment of "standing" can be found in Karen Orren, "Standing to Sue: Interest Group Conflict in the Federal Courts," *American Political Science Review,* 70 (September, 1976): 723-741.

15. Scenic Hudson Preservation Conference v. Federal Power Commission, 354 F.2d 608 (2d Cir., December, 1965), cert. denied.

16. Association of Data Processing Service Organizations v. Camp., 397 U.S. 150 (March, 1970).

17. Barlow v. Collins, 397 U.S. 157 (March, 1970).

18. Sierra Club v. Morton, 405 U.S. 345 (April, 1972), appealed sub. nom. from Sierra Club v. Hickel, 433 F.2d 24 (9th Cir., September, 1970).

19. U.S. v. Students Challenging Regulatory Agency Procedures, 412 U.S. 669 (June, 1973); the case is generally called SCRAP I.

20. Citizens to Preserve Overton Park v. Volpe, 401 U.S. 402 (March, 1971).

21. Liroff, 164-165. The "arbitrary and capricious" standard is based on the Administrative Procedure Act, 5 U.S.C. 500.

22. Calvert Cliffs Coordinating Committee v. Atomic Energy Commission, 449 F.2d 1109 (D.C. Cir., July, 1971).

23. NEPA states that the EIS "shall accompany the proposal through the existing agency review process," so the general rule has been that the EIS should be prepared early in the decision process, and before the "final decision." In SCRAP II, infra, note 30, the

Supreme Court held that the final EIS is not legally due until a report is issued on the action, which was fairly late in the process in the case at hand.

24. Environmental Defense Fund v. Corps of Engineers (Gillhan Dam), 470 F.2d 289 (8th Cir., November, 1972); 342 F.Supp. 1211, (E.D.Ark., May, 1972); 325 F.Supp. 728 (E.D.Ark., February, 1971). While the circuit court decision carries precedential weight, it affirms and relies almost entirely on Judge Eisele's District Court rulings.

25. Hanly v. Mitchell, 460 F.2d 640 (2d Cir., May, 1972).

26. Environmental Defense Fund v. Corps. of Engineers (Tennessee-Tombigbee) 348 F.Supp 916 (N.D.Miss., August, 1972); aff'd 492 F.2d 1123 (5th Cir., April, 1974).

27. 342 F.Supp @ 1217.

28. Natural Resources Defense Council v. Morton, 458 F.2d 827 (D.C. Cir., January, 1972).

29. Hanly v. Kleindienst, 471 F.2d 823 (2d Cir., December, 1972); Hanly II involves the same New York prison as Hanly I, supra, note 25.

30. Committee for Nuclear Responsibility v. Seaborg, 463 F.2d 783 (D.C. Cir., November, 1971).

31. Supra, note 22, 1 ELR at 20356.

32. Aberdeen S Rockfish RR. Co. v. SCRAP, 422 U.S. 289 (June, 1975); a continuation of SCRAP I, supra, note 19.

33. Kleppe v. Sierra Club, 427 U.S. 390 (June, 1976).

34. Flint Ridge Development Co. v. Scenic Rivers Assn. of Oklahoma, 426 U.S. 776 (June, 1976).

35. The Interstate Land Sales Full Disclosure Act, 15 U.S.C. 1701.

36. On administrative implementation generally, see: Liroff, chapter 4; Allen Wickelman, "Administrative Agency Implementation of the National Environmental Policy Act of 1969: A Conceptual Framework for Explaining Differential Response," *Natural Resources Journal,* 16 (April, 1976): 263-300; and Andrews.

37. Liroff, 38-43.

38. Wickelman, 273-290.

39. Richard Andrews, "Agency Response to NEPA: A Comparison and Implications," *Natural Resources Journal,* 16 (April, 1976): 301-322.

40. Culhane, 41.

41. Ibid., 33-35. Also see John Pierce and Harvey Doerksen (eds.), *Water Politics and Public Involvement* (Ann Arbor, Mich.: Ann Arbor Science Publishers, 1976).

42. See: Liroff, chapter 6; and Sullivan, 62. Efforts to amend NEPA generally have failed, with only a few projects (notably the Trans-Alaska Pipeline) exempted from NEPA.

43. Among many examples, see Hanna Cortner, "A Case Study of Policy Implementation: The National Environmental Policy Act of 1969," *Natural Resources Journal,* 16 (April, 1976): 323-338.

44. Liroff, *passim.*

45. Lowi, 299-303. Lowi focuses on administrative rule-making rather than EIS-like processes, but the logic of the formalism of his "juridical democracy" is quite close to NEPA's objectives.

46. Charles Reich, *Bureaucracy and the Forests* (Santa Barbara, Cal.: Center for the Study of Democratic Institutions, 1962).

47. See: Culhane, 35-36; and Wickelman, 279-283.

48. See, for example, Marver Bernstein, *Regulating Business by Independent Commission* (Princeton, N.J.: Princeton University Press, 1955).

49. Agency NEPA liaisons, especially saw procedural changes as a first step towards substantive changes: Wickelman, 291-294.

50. Office of the White House Press Secretary, "Statement on Water Projects" (Washington, D.C.: The White House, April 18, 1977): 16. Also see Grace Lichtenstein, "West's Water Fight Intensifies as Carter Plans Project Cuts," *New York Times* (March 7, 1977): 20.

51. Harold Scarlett, "Boondoggle," *Houston Post* (March 13, 1977): 1.

52. Don Moser, "Dig they must, the Army Engineers, securing allies, and acquiring enemies," *Smithsonian,* 7 (December, 1976): 47-48.

53. Maass' *Muddy Waters* is the best known academic critique. Representative of the more popular critiques is Martin Heuvelmans, *The River Killers* (Harrisburg, Pa.: Stackpole, 1973). Representative articles are: Elizabeth Drew, "Dam Outrage: The Story of the Army Engineers," *Atlantic,* 225 (April, 1970): 51-62; Michael Parfit, "The Army Engineers: Flooding America In Order to Save It," *New Times* (November 12, 1976): 25-37; and Moser.

54. Berkman and Viscusi.

55. Andrews, "Agency Responses to NEPA": 305-311.

56. See, for example: Howard Sargent, "Fishbowl Planning Immerses Pacific Northwest Citizens in Corps Projects," *Civil Engineering* (September, 1972): 54-57; Thomas Borton and Katherine Warner, "Involving Citizens in Water Resources Planning," *Environmental Behavior,* 3 (September, 1971): 284-306; and Pierce andDoerksen.

57. Moser, 50.

58. See Liroff, 133-139; Andrews, "Agency Responses to NEPA"; and Daniel Mazmanian and Mordecai Lee, "Tradition Be Damned! The Army Corps of Engineers is Changing," *Public Administration Review,* 35 (March/April, 1975): 166-172. On the importance of esprit de corps, see Francis Rourke, *Bureaucratic Power in National Politics* (Boston: Little, Brown, 1972): 250-253.

59. 16 U.S.C. 661.

60. Andrews, "Agency Responses to NEPA": 313; Paul Culhane and H. Paul Friesema, "Why Environmental Assessments Fail," American Society for Public Administration meeting paper (April, 1977): 7-9.

61. CEQ, "Environmental Impact Statements: An Analysis of Six Years Experience by Seventy Federal Agencies" Washington, D.C., CEQ Report (March, 1976): 33-34; and CEQ, *Environmental Quality—1975* (Washington, D.C.: U.S. Government Printing Office: December, 1975): 639-641. Corps data are used because, in addition to being the overwhelming majority of all water project EISs, only the Corps' figures are routinely reported in a separate category.

62. CEQ, "Environmental Impact Statements," D-2.

63. Moser, 46.

64. Johnny Green, "Selling Off the Old South," *Harpers,* 254 (April, 1977): 39-58, criticizes Tenn-Tom's impact on the traditional life-style of the rural south. Moser, 48, notes that Tenn-Tom has been critiqued as a subsidy for affluent southern whites recreationally, and the project has been picketed by civil rights groups because of the failure to hire blacks for construction jobs on the project.

65. For recent critiques of Tenn-Tom, see Moser; Parfit; and Green. On the barge subsidy issue, see Lee Lane, "Waterway User Charges: Striking a Blow for Free Enterprise," *Sierra Club Bulletin,* 62 (May, 1977): 12.

66. Environmental Defense Fund v. Corps of Engineers, 331 F.Supp 925 (D.DC, September, 1971).

67. Supra, note 26.

68. Hill v. Tennessee Valley Authority, 549 F.2d 1064 (6th Cir., January, 1977).

69. Sara Cook, et al., "The Snail Darter and the Dam," *National Parks & Conservation Magazine,* 51 (May, 1977): 10-13.

70. Environmental Defense Fund v. Tennessee Valley Authority, 468 F.2d 1164 (6th Cir., December, 1972).

71. Environmental Defense Fund v. Tennessee Valley Authority, 492 F.2d 466 (6th Cir., February, 1974).

72. 16 U.S.C. 1531. Also see: "Wildlife Protection: Section 7 of the Endangered Species Act Comes of Age," *Environmental Law Reporter* [hereafter ELR_] 7 (March, 1977): 10049-10052.

73. Cook, et al., 11.

74. Tennessee Valley Authority v. Hill, 38 C.C.H.Sup.Ct.Bull. B-3109 (U.S., June 1978). As of June, 1978, the Culver-Baker amendment, S. 2899, 95th Congress, 2d Session, had been reported favorably by the Resource Protection Subcommittee of the Senate Public Works Committee; the amendment would require a five-vote majority to exempt projects from Section 7 of the Endangered Species Act.

75. See, for example, Andrews, "Agency Response to NEPA," 314.

76. See: Ibid., 314; Mazmanian and Lee, 168-169; and Moser, 50-51.

77. 42 U.S.C. 1962.

78. Mazmanian and Lee, 170-171.

79. Under Section 10 of the Rivers and Harbors Act of 1899, 33 U.S.C. 403.

80. Don Moser, "Mangrove Island is Reprieved by Army Engineers," *Smithsonian,* 7 (January, 1977): 70; Walter Westman, "How Much Are Nature's Services Worth?" *Science,* 197 (September 2, 1977): 960-964; C. H. Wharton, *The Southern River Swamp—A Multiple Use Environment* (Athens: Georgia State University, School of Business Administration, 1970); J. G. Grosselink, E. P. Odum, and R. M. Pope, *The Value of the Tidal Marsh* (Baton Rouge: Louisiana State University, Center for Wetlands Research, 1973).

81. Zabel v. Tabb, 430 F.2d 199 (5th Cir., July, 1970).

82. 33 U.S.C. 1251-1376; Section 404 is 33 U.S.C. 1341(c).

83. Supra, note 79.

84. Natural Resources Defense Council. v. Callaway, 392 F.Supp 685 (D.DC, March, 1975).

85. See "Corps Issues Interim Rules for Discharges of Dredged and Fill Materials," *ELR,* 5 (September, 1975): 10143-10144; and "Comprehensive Wetlands Protection: One Step Closer to Full Implementation of Section 404 of FWPCA," *ELR,* 5 (July, 1975): 10099-10104.

86. On the Marco case, see Moser, "Mangrove Island Is Reprieved by Army Engineers"; Luther Carter, "Wetlands: Denial of Marco permits Fails to Resolve the Dilemma," *Science,* 192 (May 14, 1976): 641-644; and "Corps Confirms Policy Against 'Unnecessary' Developments in Wetlands," *ELR,* 6 (June, 1976): 10117-10120.

87. Moser, "Mangrove Island Is Reprieved by Army Engineers": 75.

88. HR 9560, 94th Congress, 2nd session; sponsored by Representative John Breaux.

89. Multiple Use-Sustained Yield Act of 1960, 16 U.S.C. 528; Classification and Multiple Use Act of 1964, 43 U.S.C. 1411, now expired; and Federal Land Policy and Management Act of 1976, 43 U.S.C. 1701.

90. See, for example, Conservation Foundation, *National Parks for the Future* (Washington, D.C.: Conservation Foundation, 1972); and Lewis Regenstein, *The Politics of Extinction* (New York: Macmillan, 1975): especially 127-132.

91. 1975 outlays for the other agencies are: BLM, $376.8 million; Park Service, $339.9 million; Fish and Wildlife Service, $197.3 million. *Budget of the United States Government, Fiscal Year 1976:* 220-255.

92. Barney, 19-22, 143-144. For a criticism of Service sale policies as "poorly managed and unproductive," see Marion Clawson, "The National Forests," *Science,* 191 (February 20, 1976): 762-767.

93. 16 U.S.C. 1131. On the philosophy and history of wilderness management, see Michael Frome, *Battle for Wilderness* (New York: Praeger, 1974); and Roderick Nash, *Wilderness and the American Mind* (New Haven, Conn.: Yale University Press, 1967).

94. 43 U.S.C. 315.

95. BLM, *Range Condition Report Prepared for the Senate Committee on Appropriations* (Washington, D.C.: Department of the Interior, January, 1975).

96. Principally the U.S. Mining Laws, Act of May 10, 1872, 30 U.S.C. 22, and the Mineral Leasing Act of 1920, 30 U.S.C. 181.

97. Phillip Foss, *Politics and Grass* (Seattle, University of Washington Press, 1960). Also see Wesley Calef, *Private Grazing and Public Lands* (Chicago: University of Chicago Press, 1960). Foss' account of the BLM is the prototype example of capture in Grant McConnell, *Private Power and American Democracy* (New York: Random House, 1970).

98. See Barney, *The Last Stand;* Jack Shepherd, *The Forest Killers* (New York: Weybright and Talley, 1975); and Reich.

99. See Herbert Kaufman, *The Forest Ranger* (Baltimore, Md.: Johns Hopkins University Press, 1960).

100. CEQ, *Environmental Quality—1974* (Washington, D.C.: U.S. Government Printing Office, 1974): 378-381.

101. John Hendee, et al., *Public Involvement and the Forest Service,* U.S. Forest Service Administrative Study of Public Involvement Report (May, 1973); Forest Service, "Inform and Involve" (Washington, D.C.: Forest Service, February, 1972); John Hendee, et al., "Methods for Acquiring Public Input," in Pierce and Doerksen, 125-144.

102. Paul Culhane, *Politics and the Public Lands,* Ph.D. dissertation (Evanston, Ill.: Northwestern University, Department of Political Science, June, 1977).

103. CEQ, *Environmental Quality—1975:* 636-637. Fish and Wildlife Service review/comment costs were $1.8 million in FY74, versus EPA's $1.6 million; Dept. of Commerce was third, at $1.2 million.

104. Paul Culhane, *Politics and the Public Lands:* 236-239, 271-275.

105. Ibid., 299-304. Also see George Hall, "The Myth and Reality of Multiple Use Forestry," *Natural Resources Journal,* 3 (October, 1963): 276-290; and Philip Martin, "Conflict Resolution through the Multiple Use Concept in Forest Service Decision Making," *Natural Resources Journal,* 9 (April, 1969): 228-236.

106. See, however, Culhane, *Politics and the Public Lands:* 278-284, 292-299.

107. Culhane and Friesema, 7-9.

108. Natural Resources Defense Council v. Morton, 388 F.Supp 827 (D.DC, December, 1974). As noted above, the BLM went through a major round of lease cuts in the 1960s. The BLM's major goal now is to change stockhandling practices to improve range conditions; cf., Culhane, *Politics and the Public Lands:* 71, 255-264.

109. Supra, note 18.

110. Discussion of the Mineral King case based on documentary material, correspondence, periodical and news clipping in author's files. For early accounts of this ongoing controversy, see M. Rupert Cutler, *A Study of Litigation Related to Management of Forest Service Administered Lands and Its Effect on Policy Decisions,* Ph.D. dissertation (East Lansing: Michigan State University, Department of Resource Development, 1972); and Jeanne Nienaber, *Mineral King: Ideological Battleground for Land Use Disputes,* Ph.D. dissertation (Berkeley: University of California, Department of Political Science, 1973).

111. The 1975 bill vetoed was H.R. 25, 94th Congress, 1st Session. The 1976 bills were H.R. 9725 and H.R. 13950, 94th Congress, 2nd Session.

112. "Surface Management of Federal Coal Resources," 43 C.F.R. 3041; and "Coal Mining Operating Regulations," 30 C.F.R. 211; both issued May 17, 1976. Also see "Interior's Flexible Approach to Strip-Mining: Energy Self-Sufficiency Through Minimal Environmental Protection," *ELR,* 6 (September, 1976): 10198-10200; "New Federal Coal Leasing Policy" (Washington, D.C.: U.S. Department of the Interior, press release, 10 pp., January 26, 1976); and "Surface Mining Regulations Provide Protection and Production" (Washington, D.C.: U.S. Department of Interior, press release, 9 pp., May 11, 1976). As a matter of convenience, this article refers to both the leasing and operating

113. 30 U.S.C. 201. Also see "Interior's Flexible Approach to Strip Mining: Energy Self-Sufficiency Through Minimal Environmental Protection,": 10198-10199.

114. The Surface Mining Control and Reclamation Act of 1977, 30 U.S.C. 1201.

115. Supra, note 28, and accompanying text.

116. Alaska v. Kleppe, #76-0368, 6 *ELR* 20669 (D.Dc, August, 1976).

117. The Sale 40 litigation is County of Suffolk v. Secretary of the Interior, 7 ELR 20230 (E.D.NY, February, 1977); reversed 562 F.2d 1368 (2d Cir., August, 1977); cert. denied, 46 USLW 3526 (U.S., February, 1978). The Georges Bank litigation is Massachusetts v. Andrus, 8 ELR 20187 (D.Mass., January 1978); stay of injunction denied, 8 ELR 20192 (1st Cir., January 1978). The Georges Bank decision was based largely on the Fisheries Conservation and Management Act of 1977, 16 U.S.C. 1801. Interior has refused to appeal the First Circuit ruling and has put off the Georges Bank lease sale indefinitely pending revision of the OCS Lands Act. Also see "Interior's Failure to Comply with NEPA Blocks Atlantic OCS Oil Leasing," *ELR* 7 (April, 1977) 10067-10070; "Second Circuit Puts Atlantic OCS Oil Development Back in Business," *ELR* 7 (October, 1977) 10192-10193; "Federal Court Caps OCS Oil and Gas Lease Sale," *ELR* 8 (March, 1978): 10048-10051.

118. See Barney, chapter 3; Shepherd, chapter 6; Luke Popovich, "The Bitterroot—Remembrance of Things Past," *Journal of Forestry, 73 (December, 1975): 791-793; Luke Popovich, "The Bitterroot—A Fading Polemic," Journal of Forestry,* 74 (January, 1976): 39-41.

119. West Virginia Division of the Izaak Walton League v. Butz, 325 F.Supp 422 (N.D.W.Va., November, 1973); aff'd 522 F.2d 945 (4th Cir., August, 1975). The Organic Act, 16 U.S.C. 476, is the first, and still the primary, authorization to sell National Forest timber. Also, see a related case citing Monongahela as a precedent: Zieski v. Butz, 406 F. Supp. 258 (D. Alaska, December, 1975).

120. 16 U.S.C. 1600. Also see "Major New Public Land Laws Provide Detailed Guidance for Activities of Forest Service and Bureau of Land Management," *ELR,* 6 (November, 1976): 10240-10245.

121. CEQ, Environmental Quality—1976: 92.

122. National Parks & Conservation Association, *Analysis of NPS Budgetary and Personnel Deficiencies and Its Effects on Parks Resources* (Washington, D.C.: National Parks and Conservation Association, October, 1975).

123. National Parks Mining Act of 1976, 16 U.S.C. 1901.

124. National Wildlife Refuge System Administration Act, as amended, P.L. 94-223, 16 U.S.C. 668dd.

125. P.L. 93-622.

126. Forest Service, *Roadless Area Review and Evaluation, Draft Environmental Statement* (Washington, June, 1978): 5-9.

127. The Federal Land Policy and Management Act, 43 U.S.C. 1782. Also see Linda Haverfield, "Our Largest Wilderness Resource: BLM Roadless Areas," *Sierra Club Bulletin,* 61 (October, 1976): 57-59.

128. *Minnesota Public Interest Research Group v. Butz,* 401 F.Supp 1276 (D.Minn., August, 1975); injunction dissolved 541 F.2d 1292 (8th Cir., August, 1976), cert. denied. The BWCA was also the subject of a major case involving mining in Wilderness Areas: Izaak Walton League v. Sinclair, 353 F.Supp 698 (D.Minn, January, 1973) enjoined the mining, holding mining incompatible with wilderness management; but the decision was reversed, 497 F.2d 849 (8th Cir., May, 1974), because the Wilderness Act (in what the District Court referred to as a nullity) specifically allows mining. Also see Dean Rebuffoni, "Confusion at Boundary Waters Canoe Area," *National Parks & Conservation Magazine,* 51 (January, 1977) 12-14.

129. *North Carolina v. Federal Power Commission,* 533 F.2d 702 (D.C.Cir., March, 1976).

130. Wild and Scenic Rivers Act, 16 U.S.C. 1271.

131. P.L. 92-203. Material for this section from author's file of interest group and government documents, correspondence, and clippings on the ANCSA d-2 designations.

132. On the revisionist theme on the Presidency, see Thomas Cronin, *The State of the Presidency* (Boston: Little, Brown, 1975).

133. For good point-by-point reviews of the candidates' differences, see Barbara Culliton, "Gerald Ford, Jimmy Carter: Candidates 1976," *Science,* 194 (October 29, 1976): 501-505; and "The Candidates and Conservation," *Sierra Club Bulletin,* 61 (September, 1976): 18-19. For a good example of environmentalists expectations of Carter, see *Not Man Apart,* 7 (January, 1977); "In the Battle for the Environment, The Trumpet Gives a Certain Sound," *Conservation News,* 42 (January 1, 1977): 5-11.

134. Energy Policy Project of the Ford Foundation, *A Time To Choose; America's Energy Future* (New York: Ballantine, 1974). Also see Luther Carter, "Jimmy Carter's Advisors: Drawing from the Public Interest Movement," *Science,* 193 (September 3, 1976): 868-870;

135. Supra, note 110. Also see Nicholas Wade, "Rupert Cutler: Environmentalist in the Farmers' Back Yard," *Science,* 196 (April 29, 1977): 505-507.

136. For more on energy policy see the chapter 5, this volume by Davis Davis, "America's Non-Policy for Energy." The Acts are: Energy conservation and Production Act, 42 U.S.C. 6801 (1976); Energy Conservation in Existing Buildings Act of 1976, 42 U.S.C. 6851; Energy Conservation Standards for New Buildings Act of 1976, 42 U.S.C. 6831; Energy Policy and Conservation Act, 42 U.S.C. 6201 (1975); Energy Supply and Environmental Coordination Act of 1974, 15 U.S.C. 791.

137. Council on Environmental Quality, *The President's Environmental Program— 1977 (Washington, D.C.: U.S. Government Printing Office, May 1977).*

138. J. Dicken Kirschten, *"Draining the Water Projects Out of the Pork Barrel," National Journal,* 9 (April 9, 1977): 540-541.

139. Quoted in "In the Battle for the Environment, the Trumpet Gives a Certain Sound": 7.

140. Office of the White House Press Secretary, *passim;* Kirschten, *passim.*

141. Maass, *passim.*

142. "Senate Vote Tells Carter to Spend Water Plans' Funds," *Houston Post* (March 11, 1977): 16A; "Water Projects Draw Criticism," *Houston Post* (March 28, 1977): 22A; "House Panel Approves Water Project Funding," *Houston Post* (May 26, 1977): 10B. "When Defeat Is Victory," *Conservation Report* 95th Congress, 1st Session, #19 (June 19, 1977): 299; *Public Works for Water and Power Development and Energy Research*

Appropriation Bill, Fiscal Year 1978: Conference Report, Washington, House of Representatives, 95th Congress, 1st Session, Report #95-507, July 20, 1977. As proof of the old maxim that "you can't please all of the people all of the time," some environmentalists did not see the compromise as a victory; see, "The Great Administration Water Project Sell Out," *Conservation Report,* 95th Congress, 1st Session, #23 (July 22, 1977): 355.

143. Office of White House Press Secretary, "Water Policy Message: Detailed Background" (Washington, D.C., June 6, 1978).

144. Luther Carter, "Speaking Up for an Imperiled CEQ," *Science,* 197 (July 15, 1977): 240; Reorganization Plan #1 of 1977; "Reorganization: Council on Environmental Quality Emerges Stronger, Review of Federal Agencies Continues," *ELR,* 7 (September, 1977): 10168-10171.

145. Barry Commoner, *The Closing Circle* (New York: Bantam, 1971): 37-41.

146. Also see Mamanian and Lee.

147. Supra, note 139.

9.

FEDERAL POLICY AND HEALTH: RECENT TRENDS AND DIFFERING PERSPECTIVES

ANDREW B. DUNHAM

Middlebury College

THEODORE R. MARMOR

University of Chicago

In the last decade, there have been tremendous changes in the federal government's role in the health sector. Since the mid-1960s, there has been a rapid increase in the number of programs, the regulations written, the level of concern expressed, and the amount of public money spent. The dominating fact in this field is the rapid growth in federal expenditures, which will reach $56 billion by 1978, more than 10 times the amount spent in 1965. In 1965, the federal government provided about 12 percent of the nation's total health care expenditures, and by 1976 this proportion had reached 28 percent of a much larger total. This meant that health represented 6.8 percent of total federal outlays in 1967 and has grown steadily to an estimated 12.7 percent by 1978.[1]

As the federal health budget has grown, so has the importance of the health sector in the American economy. The proportion of the gross national product devoted to health care has increased by over 90 percent, from 4.5 percent in 1950 to 8.6 percent in 1976.[2] The number of hospital beds has doubled since 1950, as has the number of active registered nurses. The physician supply has grown faster than the population. More than 4.5 million people are now employed in the health sector—the third largest occupational group in the United States. The use of medical services has increased as well. The average annual number of doctor visits per person increased from 4.5 in 1964 to 4.9 in 1974, and the number of hospital days per 1,000 people grew from 1,180 to 1,255 between 1965 and 1975.[3]

Obviously, some of the increased expenditures on health care stems from increased utilization rates, a larger and older population, and more intensive services, but much of the growth is simply a product of medical inflation. In the past 25 years, the price of medical services has risen 1.5 times as fast as the Consumer Price Index, and the rate of medical inflation has increased still faster in the last few years. Current federal activity and proposals for the future must be understood in the light of rapid and seemingly uncontrolled increases in medical costs and program expenditures.

This article reviews the recent trends in federal health activities in five parts. The first discusses ways of regarding and explaining what the role of the federal government has been in the nation's health. The second analyzes the major financing programs that pay for personal medical care. Part three is an evaluation of federal subsidies for health resources: the construction of facilities, the training of manpower, and research. The fourth section discusses recent policies directed at changing the system of delivering medical care. Part five briefly characterizes the federal role in traditional public health areas, including health education, environmental, and occupational health concerns.

FEDERAL POLICY

Conceptions, Changes, and Explanations

Costs and expenditures have become the dominant concern in federal health activity. Increases in federal expenditures have led to some program cutbacks, contributed to the stalemate over national health insurance, and provided the impetus for a diverse set of new federal regulatory initiatives. The increased federal stake in total health expenditures has changed the stance of the federal government toward the health sector and affected the character of the debate about the government's proper role in health affairs. When Medicare and Medicaid were passed in 1965, the very first section confidently asserted that no government official would attempt to change the practice of medicine. Two years later the Comprehensive Health Planning Act of 1967, PL89-749, declared that its purpose was "to assure comprehensive health services of high quality for every person, but without interference with existing patterns of private professional practice of medicine."[4] Such statements seem naive today. The federal government regards the existing patterns of medicine as too costly. It is 10 years and $50 billion too late to prevent federal intervention into private medical care arrangements.

There are, of course, various approaches to explaining this great change in the federal health role. It is useful to start by saying how not to characterize federal health activity. One should not regard this expansion of federal activity as a consequence of a deliberate "federal health policy." *There is no federal health policy per se.* There are various federal policies that affect health. Such federal action consists of a multitude of programs with differing histories, politics, goals, and results.[5]

"Health" as an analytical category is not very useful for policy analysis because it assumes a single structure to government activity in this substantive arena. It implies that because programs affect health, these programs are the product of a similar political process with similar actors and fates. This is not the case. Some programs that affect health are highly controversial and politically salient; others now have low visibility. Knowing that a federal program is a "health program" does not tell us who will be concerned, what position they will take, or what outcome is likely.

The typical explanatory approach has been what might be termed managerial. The health world is regarded as an industry, and analysis is directed at the financing, supply, and regulation of the industry's outputs. These categories, while useful to the policymaker as a map, are not directed at political explanation or prediction. Analysing Medicaid, Medicare, and veterans benefits as "health financing" programs misleadingly creates expectations that the causes and consequences of these programs will be similar. That approach does not help us understand why the benefits of the Medicaid program were cut back while Medicare's remained stable, and veterans' benefits were expanded.

From a political perspective on policy analysis, the determining aspect of these programs is not that they all involve financing of health care. Any approach that deals with "health politics" or "health policy" as if a single structure exists, whether defined by the substantive arena of health, the actors involved, or the industrial activity, is bound to be misleading. There are politics in health, but no single politics of health.

Health politics are a microcosm of general American politics, not a peculiar subfield. While some of the actors and issues are, of course, distinctive to the health area, health conflicts are marked by similarities to political struggles in other fields. From a comparative perspective, the most striking feature is the relative weakness of government authority in health. Provider opposition delayed significant government financing of medical care for the poor and indeed still prevents full coverage. What is more, even when the federal government implements programs, it has seldom gone counter to provider interests. This may be now changing in some areas. But it is still true that governmental coercion of providers is minimized. The liberal tradition in America leads to a limited exercise of government authority vis-à-vis the dominant health interest groups. The liberal ideology, coupled with the weakness of party government, particularly of a party based on a working class movement, results in policies being settled on a program-by-program basis that varies with the political market of each program.

The absence of a single political market for health also means that the struggles over initiation and administration differ sharply. A national coalition can be formed to get a program enacted, but the reform coalition is seldom unified enough to monitor the implementation of the program. Thus, Medicare passed over the opposition of the providers, but many of the key administrative decisions (e.g., how to pay the providers) escaped the detailed review of the national coalition which prompted the bill's enactment. This produces cyclical program development. National legislation amidst crisis is followed by less salient implementation problems, which, in turn, create pressures for new reforms.

The purpose of this chapter, however, is not to develop a political theory about American public policy or American health policies. Rather, its purpose is to describe federal activities in the health field for political scientists and policy analysts. For that purpose, the major federal programs affecting health are adequate descriptive categories. It is to this description that we now turn.

FINANCING MEDICAL CARE

Measured by expenditure, most federal health policies consist of programs financing personal medical care services. Medicare and Medicaid alone account for 62 percent of all public spending in the health sector.[6] In spite of these large sums, the most salient federal policy in health financing in the past decade has been nonaction: the stalemate over national health insurance legislation. In this respect, the United States is alone among the industrialized nations in not having a universal national health insurance program.

The national health insurance stalemate involves the stable long-term operation of large national pressure groups, many not usually concerned with health issues. Argument over national health insurance is markedly ideological, with positions framed on what the role of the national government ought to be in a public/private and federal/state mix. There is little room for compromise over such issues. Despite all the reports, Congressional hearings, academic studies, and repeated warnings of crisis, there is little or no adjustment of positions.

Although virtually all major participants have sponsored a national health insurance bill, there is no agreement on which problems are most pressing, let alone on what the proposed responses should be. Solutions to one problem conflict with solutions to another. As the AMA has pointed out, "any system of medical care depends basically on balancing three strong and competing dynamics: the desire to make medical care available to all, the desire to control cost, and the desire for high quality care."[7] Any two of these goals work against the third.

Even the one issue that all sides view with alarm—cost—is really three problems: cost to the consumer, cost to the government, and cost to the nation. Consumers worry about high out-of-pocket costs and the possibility of catastrophic medical expenses. Government-sponsored insurance could reduce the cost to the consumer at point of use and could protect against financial catastrophe, but such programs would fuel inflationary tendencies. This would exacerbate the second cost problem, the high percentage of the nation's resources that are devoted to medical care. While a national health insurance program such as the Kennedy-Corman bill, which would federalize virtually all medical expenses, provides at least the possibility to control the total funds spent on health, it would also vastly increase federal expenditures. Responses to the three cost problems also work against each other.

The struggle over national health insurance continues with the same stalemate of national forces that has been noted in other redistributive policy debates.[8] In the meantime, United States financing programs continue to be a series of discrete programs aimed at specific clientele. Indeed, so strong is the clientele-orientation that many of the programs will continue even if a comprehensive national health insurance program is enacted. All of the major NHI plans retain veterans' medical benefits, for example. This point again illustrates the political differences of the various financing programs. Each program must be examined individually to understand its operation and impact.

Medicare

Medicare is the most expensive federal health program. It is federal health insurance for the elderly with no income restrictions. All citizens who either reached the age of 65 before 1968 or who are covered by the Social Security or railroad retirement programs are automatically eligible for hospitalization benefits (Part A of Medicare). They have the option to enroll, for a monthly premium, in the voluntary supplementary medical insurance plan (SMI, or Part B) that covers physicians' services and some other benefits. Ninety-seven percent of the eligible elderly have enrolled in SMI. The hospitalization insurance covered 24.5 million persons in 1976 and actually paid for services for 5.7 million in that year. In addition, 14 million persons received benefits under the supplementary medical insurance program. The Medicare budget grew from $3.4 billion in 1967 to $17.8 billion in 1976 and will reach an estimated $26 billion in 1978.[9]

Because of Medicare's early development as a political issue, the benefits are not comprehensive. What began in the 1930s as a "right-to-health" movement to redistribute medical services for the entire population was, through compromises over the next 30 years, turned into a program to help defray some hospital costs for some of the elderly. The long debate—focused on the aged as the problem group, social security versus general revenues as financing mechanisms, and partial versus comprehensive benefits for some or all of the elderly—structured the content of the statutory innovations. The resultant Medicare program was designed not so much to cope with all the health problems of the elderly as to reduce their most onerous financial difficulties.[10]

The program, therefore, focuses on covering the most costly medical episodes facing the elderly. This means hospital care. Not all hospital care is covered, however. The elderly pay a deductible and some coinsurance after 60 days in the hospital, and all hospital benefits cease after 90 days (plus a lifetime "reserve" of another 60 days). Nursing home expenses are covered only if they are preceded by a period of hospitalization and are limited to 100 days of care. Part B coverage has an even steeper coinsurance and deductible structure. Given these statutory provisions, it is not surprising that use of physicians' services by the elderly did not show the marked change after Medicare that hospital utilization exhibited. Hospital days per 1,000 people increased almost 50 percent for the elderly between 1965 and 1968, while hospital days for those under 65 were actually declining.[11]

Although the access of the elderly to medical care was improved by Medicare, the major result has been to ease the financial burden of care. Public funds paid for 82 percent of the costs of hospital services of the elderly in 1973, compared to less than 50 percent in 1966. Overall, the share of the elderly's medical care bill paid with public funds rose from 30 percent in 1966 to 59 percent in 1973 (not just medicare). The elderly actually pay more now than they did in 1966, although controlling for inflation the sum is about the same.[12] However, they now receive a greater amount of more intensive care than they used to, and are better protected from financially catastrophic medical bills. Medicare pays for most of the larger bills, even if public programs pay for only 59 percent of the total medical costs of the elderly.

Medicaid

Medicaid, codified as Title XIX of the Social Security Act, was enacted as an afterthought to Medicare. It was not even originally a part of the Johnson Administration's bill. Medicaid is a welfare companion to Medicare's social insurance approach. It provides federal matching funds for state-administered programs for the poor. It allows the states, within federal guidelines, to set eligibility requirements, establish benefit levels, and determine what services to cover. Medicaid was passed with the expectation that states would restrain both the benefits and the number of eligible persons. Programs for the poor were clearly expected to be poor programs, and the original estimate was that Medicaid would add only $250 million to the $1.3 billion already projected for welfare medicine programs in 1965.[13]

This expectation allowed federal policy-makers to talk of making medical care available to all the poor and of making the benefits comprehensive by 1975. The unexpected costs of the program (stemming originally from the rise in the welfare rolls, high participation and high use, and then from medical inflation) made policy makers retreat from their commitment to the poor. In 1969, the target date for comprehensive benefits was pushed back until 1977, and states were allowed to omit certain optional services. In 1972, the requirement of progress towards comprehensive care was dropped from the law altogether. States were no longer prohibited from reducing their aggregate spending from one year to the next. Deductibles and coinsurance were also introduced on some services. The program has been a victim of its own success.

Clearly, Medicaid substantially expanded the access of some of the poor to medical care. In 1964, families below the federal poverty line averaged 4.3 visits per member to a physician. By 1973, that figure had risen to 5.6, compared to 4.6 and 4.9 for middle and upper income family members, respectively.[14] The poor tend to have more health problems than the nonpoor, so such figures do not necessarily demonstrate equal access. Equality of access would reflect equal use in relation to similar needs. In this respect, "the results are quite conclusive. The nonpoor population has considerably more physician contact per one hundred disability days than does the poor population."[15] While inequalities in care based on income remain, the position of the poor "improved with respect to frequency of exams and seeing a doctor in response to symptoms of illness" from 1963 to 1970.[16]

Days of hospital care also showed substantial gains for low income persons after the enactment of Medicaid. However, Davis points out that the poor who are not covered still lag substantially behind higher income groups in utilization, after adjustment for health status. She estimates that about eight million poor people, or about one-third of those below the poverty line, were not eligible for Medicaid benefits in 1973. She adds that as many as 50 percent of the poor may be ineligible at a given time as they move in and out of the eligibility categories. In addition, there is a substantial number of the "near poor" who have no private insurance coverage but are not eligible for Medicaid coverage. It is estimated that from 25 to 35 million Americans are without any insurance coverage, public or private.[17]

This incomplete coverage is partly a reflection of the mixed federal-state nature of Medicaid, since eligibility and benefits levels vary widely from state to state. In the West, for example, the ratio of Medicaid recipients to poor persons is 1.16, suggesting that in those states, most of the poor and some of the near poor are receiving benefits. In contrast, in the South the ratio is around .33. "The South has 46 percent of the poor population, but only 24 percent of Medicaid recipients and only 19 percent of Medicaid payments."[18]

Medicaid, as a financing program, has been less successful at overcoming nonfinancial barriers to medical care. If there are no nearby available medical services, the financing of care is moot. This problem is reflected in the wide discrepancies in expenditures between rural and urban recipients. For example, expenditures for poor children in rural areas average less than $5 a year, compared to $76 in urban regions.[19] While the federal government began several programs to overcome nonfinancial barriers to care (discussed below), these have tended to stagnate. Financing programs remain the major federal initiatives.

Medicaid has not been successful in relieving the stigma attached to medical care for the poor, and that may discourage its use. Since many states have a Medicaid fee schedule that is below "usual and customary" charges, Medicaid recipients are less desirable patients for providers. Thus, many providers do not customarily treat Medicaid patients. In fact, "between 1963 and 1970 the position of the poor relative to the rest of the population worsened as far as having a regular source of care."[20]

Perhaps more important is the barrier of continued racial discrimination. In the first weeks of Medicare's operation, "the question of certifying southern hospitals took up more time of HEW's top health officials than any other feature of the program."[21] HEW officials attempted to use federal payments to end segregation, apparently with much success. Yet the evidence of discrimination persists. Davis reports that Medicaid payments per recipient were 75 percent higher for whites than for blacks. While some of that discrepancy results from regional differences in costs and benefit levels, real discrimination remains. For example, in Georgia in 1974, expenditures for white recipients were twice as high as for blacks.[22]

While Medicaid has increased the access to medical care for some of the poor, it has not been as successful in lessening the financial burden of such medical care. Persons with income below $3,500 spent virtually the same percentage of their income on medical care in 1970 as in 1963. Those below $2,000 spent almost 15 percent of their income on medical care, compared to the average of 4.4 percent of income for the population as a whole.[23]

Medicaid has not fulfilled its goal of bringing the poor into the mainstream of American medicine. Whether the poor receive lower quality care is debatable; that they receive it in different settings and from different types of physicians is not. The poor are more likely to use general practitioners than specialists, to use hospital outpatient departments or public clinics than physicians' offices, and to have no regular source of care. The poor also spend more time traveling to their source of care and in waiting than do high income persons.[24]

By greatly increasing the money spent on health care services for the poor, Medicaid has clearly increased their contact with the medical care system. In 1976, Medicaid aided 23.2 million persons. Health status indicators tend to be crude measures. Improved access to medical care would only show up if the care prevented death or serious disability; easing of pain or prevention of minor disorders is not measured by aggregate health statistics. Still, Davis reports that certain indicators sensitive to medical care have shown marked improvement after the implementation of Medicaid. For example, infant mortality among the poor dropped 33 percent from 1965 to 1974.[25] There are grounds for criticism, but Medicaid has not been useless; it has helped recipients receive more medical care and has improved their health.

While Medicaid has, according to some critics, ignored too many of the poor, the major political attack on it has been in response to its high and rapidly increasing costs. Many state programs have cut back on benefits and eligibility in an attempt to restrict cost increases. But the cost increases result from the growth of the welfare rolls and the inflation rate in the medical sector. The program grew from 11.5 million recipients in 1968 to 23.2 million in 1976. And the real benefits per recipient were approximately the same in 1976 as in the early years. Still, in current dollars, the program exploded from the expected $1.5 billion at enactment to $14 billion in 1976.[26]

The federal share of Medicaid costs ranges from 83 percent in the poorest states to 50 percent in the wealthier states. The states are exerting great pressure to "federalize" Medicaid. The 83 percent federal share does not seem to be enough to induce poorer states to enlarge benefits or eligibility, and even the wealthier states find their 50 percent share burdensome. Although there have been serious moves in Congress to reform Medicaid, it is likely that major efforts will now wait for the new administration's expected national health insurance proposals.

The different treatment of Medicare and Medicaid expenditure growth is politically instructive. While total expenditures for the two programs have grown at about the same pace, Medicaid has been subject to extensive criticism and reductions in benefits and eligibility, while Medicare has been neither seriously attacked nor cut back. Indeed, Medicare experienced a 20 percent growth in constant dollar outlays per recipient from 1968 to 1974, while Medicaid figures per recipient were stable.[27] Medicare, as a national program in the redistributive arena, faces the same political forces that have resulted in the stalemate over NHI. While the stable stalemate has prevented the initiation of a national health insurance program, it has also prevented any cutbacks of Medicare. Expenditures have risen, but the benefits and beneficiaries have not fundamentally changed since the advent of Medicare in 1965. Further, since Medicare is largely financed through Social Security taxes, it has been partly insulated from struggles over budget distribution and has discouraged major attempts to control expenditure through program retrenchment.

The contrast to Medicaid is striking. Part of the different treatment, of course, is because the elderly are a more popular clientele than the poor. But the nature of the programs' beneficiaries cannot alone explain the different reactions to Medicare and Medicaid. Medicaid, after all, also pays for care for the elderly, since many of them are poor (37 percent of Medicaid funds in 1970 were spent on the aged). In fact, a larger proportion of Medicaid expenditures actually go to the elderly than to AFDC recipients.[28]

The key difference between Medicare and Medicaid is not their clientele but the different political markets they face. Medicaid is a state-run program. The depth and breadth of coverage is therefore a state and local matter rather than a national issue. Support for the program is fragmented in smaller, statewide constituencies where it is difficult for the poor to mobilize support and press for their own interests. State program reductions affect only a relatively few poor, rather than all 23 million elderly. The effective coalition of national organizations that support Medicare and NHI is less active at the state level. While the poor have achieved political gains in a few states, McConnell's (and Madison's) argument that smaller constituencies favor powerful organized interests is substantiated. New York and California account for 37 percent of all Medicaid expenditures; but in most states, the poor are not an important political power and so suffer from Medicaid's small constituency politics.[29]

While support for Medicaid is diffused, the opposition is intense since the state portion of Medicaid is financed out of general revenues. Any increase in benefits, beneficiaries, utilization, or medical prices must be met by an increase in state expenditures. From the very beginning of the Medicaid program, it has been vulnerable to attack. The strain on state budgets generated by increased welfare rolls and medical inflation has produced continued demands for state fiscal relief. This has come at the expense of the poor, as states have met problems of high program expenditures by cutting back on benefits and eligibility.

Other Programs for the Disadvantaged

In spite of the political difficulties of the Medicaid program, it and Medicare exhibit a growth far in excess of the other Great Society programs aimed at redistributing medical care to the underserved. In budget terms, the preeminence of these two giants is stark, over-shadowing all of the other programs. This budgetary predominance by no means reflects the perspective of the Kennedy-Johnson initiators. They were proud, as President Johnson himself reported, of the widespread efforts to reach problems across all the areas of the health industry. More legislation was, to these minds, better government. Johnson stated: "During my administration, forty national health measures were presented to the Congress and passed by the Congress—more than in all the preceding 175 years of the Republic's history."[30] The programs for the poor, passed by a strongly Democratic Congress committed to redistributive efforts, did not fare as well in times of budgetary constraint and a less sympathetic Administration and Congress.

The neighborhood health centers initiated in 1965 by the Office of Economic Opportunity were to play a major role in making health care delivery a reality in poor urban neighborhoods. The centers were established in high poverty areas and tailored their services to fit local needs. Their ambitious aims were to overcome a variety of nonfinancial barriers to medical care: the lack of medical providers in low income neighborhoods, inadequate transportation to health care centers, discrimination against the poor, and lack of education. The centers provided comprehensive medical and dental care. Some initiated programs to ameliorate inadequate housing, sanitation, sewage, or nutrition. Intended as companions to Medicaid, initial estimates were that these centers would serve 25 million individuals by 1973. Yet by that time, only a twentieth of that number—1.2 million people—were actually being served at the 118 centers, and annual expenditures were declining.[31]

The Maternal and Child Health Programs of the mid-1930s were significantly expanded during the Johnson Administration. The Crippled Children's Program, for example, grew from $62.3 million in 1960 to $152.9 million in 1970. By 1970, 491,000 children were being served. Though enormously helpful for certain groups, the comprehensive children and youth projects have never reached a large proportion of poor Americans and have also experienced budget reductions in the 1970s.[32]

Some ambitious programs have never experienced significant growth. The Early and Periodic Screening, Diagnosis and Treatment Program (EPSDT) for example, enacted in 1967, was advertised as the first federal policy mandate of comprehensive preventive health services for children. Yet final regulations for the program were not issued until November 1971; and bureaucratic wrangling, strong professional opposition, and a state disinclination to bear EPSDT's potentially considerable costs have continued to block its successful implementation.

In the area of mental health, there has been drastic change and serious controversy. The Community Mental Health Centers Act of 1963 sought to replace large mental institutions with community mental health services. Subsequent provisions were made for treatment for alcohol and drug abuse. By 1974, 626 programs were serving 1.4 million people;[33] the programs were initiated with federal funds and were expected to be self-sufficient within 10 years, although special arrangements were made for centers in low income neighborhoods.

While of central importance to professionals directly affected, none of these programs dramatically altered the distribution of access to medical care services. In individual communities, a local health center might be the difference between real and financial access to care. Nurse practitioners reached some rural residents where no doctors were available. But nowhere was the commitment to provide direct health services and personnel comparable to the Medicare and Medicaid commitment.

None of the desired programs could muster even as much political support as was behind Medicaid. A program such as the Neighborhood

Health Centers ends up being a distributive benefit to a particular community. With the erosion of support at the national level for the War on Poverty and with stricter budget constraints, these programs depended for existence on the support they could generate in the communities they were to serve. A Center in the planning stages would have few established interests with a significant stake in the continuation of the program. Even operating Centers only serve their poor, unorganized, and powerless clientele and cannot easily enlist the support of major and politically more significant groups. Medicaid at least serves important economic interests, since the payments go directly to the providers. Further, there is no limit to the benefits a provider receives: the more services given, the more payment received. While it is true that some providers will not serve Medicaid clients, the fact remains that many doctors, hospitals, and nursing homes receive substantial funds from Medicaid. They have a real stake in the continuation of the program. By contrast, very few providers have any stake at all in a Neighborhood Health Center. In fact, it may actually reduce their own business.

Programs for other Clientele

In addition to Great Society initiatives aimed at expanding the medical care received by the poor and underserved, there are a number of traditional distributive programs aimed at providing benefits to specific clienteles. These programs, all of which preceded the initiation of redistributive programs, have not generated the political saliance and conflict with which Medicare started and that Medicaid grew to have. Nor have they faced the same concern about expenditures, and indeed several of the programs have actually been expanded in the last few years. The programs have not escaped controversy because they are insignificant. The Veterans Administration and the Department of Defense will have a total combined health budget of $9 billion in 1978.[34] For a while, tax expenditures for these programs were greater than Medicaid expenditures. The difference is not the size but the beneficiaries. These distributive programs can enlist the support of powerful groups or of a strong federal bureaucracy.

The Veterans Administration operates the largest program of direct provision of services (i.e., by salaried federal employees). While eligibility was recently expanded to all of the nation's 29 million vets, priority is given to those who have a service connected disability, are over 65, or are medically indigent. Veterans over 65 have the choice of using VA services or getting Medicare benefits in the private sector. The Veterans Administration is currently expanding its long-term care facilities to deal with the aging veterans population. The cost for the direct provision of services has risen from $1.3 billion in 1969 to $3.3 billion in 1976 and will be an estimated $4.0 billion for 1978.[35]

The Department of Defense provided direct service to military personnel and dependents in 211 hospitals and 400 outpatient clinics in 1973. The number of facilities has been declining rapidly as the number of persons in active duty service declined after the peak Vietnam War years and as bases closed, and the number of hospitals will be reduced to 170 by 1978. Utilization is also declining. There are approximately 9.9 million persons eligible for services from Defense Department programs; 2.5 million active personnel and 5.7 million dependents and retired military. In 1969, the cost of direct provision of services by Defense Department personnel was $1.4 billion. It grew to $2.3 billion in 1976 and will reach an estimated $2.6 billion in 1978.[36]

In addition to the direct provision of medical services, both the Veterans Administration and the Department of Defense have programs to finance care in the civilian sector. In 1956, Congress authorized CHAMPUS—Civilian Health and Medical Program of the Uniformed Services—to help pay for care for the dependents of active duty servicemen. In 1966, this was expanded to retired military, to their dependents, and to survivors of retired military. The program was also expanded to outpatient care. The CHAMPUS program only provides civilian care if military care is not available and requires some cost-sharing. With the end of the draft, however, the military has had difficulty in obtaining physicians, so paying for care from civilian personnel has grown in importance. In 1969, CHAMPUS accounted for 11 percent of Defense Department health spending, but it had grown to 20 percent by 1974. This represented $172 million in 1969, $559 million in 1976, and will reach an estimated $654 million by 1978.[37]

The Veterans Administration has a similar program, CHAMPVA, for dependents of veterans with total, permanent service disabilities or of veterans who died of service-connected disabilities. The program is still small, but it is expected to grow. The VA also pays for some care in civilian settings. The total expenditures for indirect provision of services by the Veterans Administration was $65 million in 1969, $234 million in 1976, and an estimated $367 million by 1978.[38]

The federal government also provides direct care for 500,000 Indians and native Alaskans in 51 hospitals and 83 health centers run by the Public Health Service. The cost of this program was $46 million in 1968, $372 million in 1976, and an estimated $472 million in 1978.[39] This amounts to over $800 per beneficiary, well over the national average for medical care. Even so, the health status of native Americans, although it has been improving in recent years, is still lower than that of other Americans.

Federal tax law includes subsidies for private insurance and for taxpayers who itemize and claim medical deductions. Health insurance premiums paid by the employer are benefits to the employee but are not subject to federal income tax. This is a subsidy for employer-paid private health insurance and an incentive for employees to have health insurance coverage. Further, a proportion of the insurance premiums paid by individuals and out-of-pocket medical expenses are deductible on an individual's tax return. Therefore, federal tax law provides "an average benefit [subsidy] per taxpayer that *increases* with income."[40] Mitchell and Vogel estimated that this tax expenditure amounted to almost $4.5 billion in 1970, and they point out that federal Medicaid payments were only $2.9 billion in that year. The federal government spent more in financing medical benefits through the tax system than through its major medical program for the poor. The tax benefits have continued to grow. The Congressional Budget Office estimates that in fiscal 1977 this tax expenditure will reach $7.8 billion (with 60 percent going to taxpayers with incomes over $15,000) and that it will grow to $15 billion by 1982.[41]

In addition to the questions of equity this policy raises, the generous insurance benefits probably contribute to high-utilization and medical inflation. When insurance covers much of the cost of medical services, the consumer has few incentives to use less costly alternatives, to limit use, or to worry about medical prices. Only 10 percent of hospital costs are paid directly by consumers, for example; so insured consumers face few financial constraints in using hospital services.[42] Moreover, consumers do not even face the full cost of insurance premiums. Only 17.5 percent of health insurance premiums are for individual policies; almost 80 percent are from employment-related plans. The employer, on average, pays two-thirds of the premium of these plans, and the employer pays the whole premium in 41 percent of such policies.[43] Federal tax policy encourages financing mechanisms that reduce consumer cost consciousness, even though cost constraint is a major federal objective.

As an employer, the federal government helps pay the health insurance benefits of its employees. Coverage of the 3.6 million employees and their 6.9 million dependents will cost $1.96 billion in 1978, up from $287 million in 1969.[44]

The various federal programs that finance or provide medical care seem to offer a bewildering variety of beneficiaries and programmatic fates. The various government responses cannot be understood in terms of the health or medical needs of the beneficiaries. However, some ordering of the programs can be imposed if we look at government action as a response to the political market rather than to medical needs. The imbalanced political market explains much of the imbalanced development of federal activity.

The political market approach looks at who has an interest in government action (pro or con), at how intense the interest is, and at how effectively that interest can be expressed. This requires an examination of the organization, available resources, and constituency size of the affected parties. Put simply, those programs that have the backing of powerful organizations and constituencies with significant stakes in the program and with sufficient resources to express their demands will tend to prosper. Thus, veterans medical benefits have expanded because they have an organized clientele group and a supportive bureaucracy, while Neighborhood Health Centers have stagnated because the clientele has limited resources. In general, programs for the poor fare poorly because beneficiaries are unable to press their demands effectively. One exception is the treatment of Indians and native Alaskans, but those groups have an established federal bureaucracy to support their claims and its own organizational maintenance needs. Medicaid, as an in-kind program, is also a partial exception. Governments do not choose to spend what Medicaid cost. Although the states could and did cut benefits and eligibility, they still have to pay for what eligible patients used. And providers have an interest in insuring that states pay for what poor patients receive.

The imbalanced political market cannot provide a complete explanation for the development of federal financing and delivery programs, although it does provide a fair first approximation. It certainly is more powerful than an explanation based on the health and medical needs of program recipients, and unlike an approach that looks for the "politics of health," it can account for variations between programs. What it cannot do is explain some of both the very biggest and the littlest changes.

If one takes an international perspective, the structures of the health political markets do not easily explain why the United States is different from other industrialized countries in its approach to financing medical care. Nor does it explain why the United States initiated programs for the underserved *at all,* and why such initiatives came when they did. There was a shift in political forces at the national level, particularly with the Johnson landslide, that brought many major new initiatives in health programs as well as in other areas. Thus, the politically less-influential did acquire programs that were designed to benefit them, though the political market approach suggests that such groups seldom get their way. In short, the political market approach cannot explain why there is a welfare state, nor why the United States version of the welfare state is different from that of other industrial countries. But the political market helps to explain how, once a program is in existence, it is likely to fare relative to other programs.

The political market structure also cannot account for outcomes due to idiosyncratic causes. In 1972, for example, amendments to the Social Security Act extended Medicare coverage to the disabled and to persons with chronic kidney disease, regardless of age. These additions added approximately 1.9 million beneficiaries to the program at a cost of $1.7 billion in 1975.[45] These are not insignificant additions, but there is no systematic explanation for why they occurred. The kidney amendment passed Congress almost by chance. Certainly it is hard to understand why End Stage Renal Disease was covered, but hemophilia, heart disease, or other "catastrophic" illnesses were not. The explanation almost surely requires detailed facts on the level of specific actors, such as the skills of the promoters of kidney coverage who did extensive lobbying and arranged demonstrations by dialysis patients in front of a Congressional committee. The passage is an example of the different politics of identifiable lives and statistical lives. The political response is to a specific group who can be readily identified as beneficiaries. They have an obvious and intense stake in the outcome. By contrast, a program for, say, automobile safety might save more lives at less cost, but it has only potential beneficiaries and they cannot be identified in advance.

The kidney program can be seen as a small scale experiment for catastrophic health insurance, since it provides experience on the consequences of covering very expensive services for the chronically ill. It is estimated that the End Stage Renal Disease program cost $350 million dollars in 1974 for about 20,000 beneficiaries. Although it is estimated that only 50,000 persons can benefit from treatment, the cost is expected to exceed $1 billion by 1984.[46] Before the advent of federal coverage, there were very restrictive selection criteria for receiving kidney dialysis or transplants, and patients with other medical complications were usually screened out. Now, with financial considerations removed, physicians have little reason to restrict treatment for any who might possibly benefit. An increasing proportion of beneficiaries are elderly (some in their eighties) and many more have other medical problems that reduce the probability of rehabilitation and increase the frequency and severity of complications.

The kidney program, though still relatively small, raises the fundamental question of how, and how much, public money should be used to prolong life. The costs, even for a small group, are staggering. As the population of the United States ages, and as chronic care increases in importance, the issue will gain in importance. It is estimated that in 1963, 1 percent of the population was responsible for 17 percent of the expenditures on health services, that the figure had grown to 26 percent of total medical expenditures by 1970, and is continuing to grow.[47]

MEDICAL RESOURCES

Facilities

It is now generally agreed that there is a surplus of hospital beds in many parts of the country.[48] The federal government, which for years was involved in the construction of health facilities (mostly hospitals) through the Hill-Burton program, has virtually eliminated direct funding for general construction. Indeed, federal regulatory programs are now designed to restrict facility growth. Over the last 30 years, the Hill-Burton program has provided more than $4.5 billion for the construction and modernization of facilities, with an additional $1.5 billion in direct loans and guarantees. By 1971, this program had subsidized 10,748 construction projects, involving 344,453 hospital beds.[49] Sixty percent of the hospitals in the country got some assistance.[50] Hill-Burton concentrated on hospital construction and modernization, though it also provided funds for long-term care and outpatient facilities. The program was very successful in eliminating the shortage of hospitals and hospital beds in most of the country, in equalizing the bed supply among states, and increasing the number and improving the condition of hospitals in rural areas and small towns. It is also argued that the increased supply of hospitals in rural areas induced more doctors to settle in these areas than otherwise would have.

The elimination of facility construction subsidies represents an unusual political occurrence: the end of a pork barrel program. However, the direct subsidy of construction has been replaced by an indirect federal contribution to capital expenditures through programs that finance medical services. The Social Security Administration's concern over obtaining provider participation in the Medicare program led initially to generous depreciation and interest allowances in cost-based reimbursements. As a consequence, the federal government now pays for expansion and modernization through reimbursement mechanisms, but it has less direct control over the amount and the location than when the Hill-Burton subsidies were line items in the controllable federal budget. Indeed, this indirect subsidy is much greater than Hill-Burton ever was and is expected to amount to almost $1 billion in 1978 alone.[51]

Even this more subtle subsidy to health facilities is now being challenged. The Carter Administration has proposed a national limit on total capital expenditures by hospitals. The proposel is not assured of adoption, let alone effective implementation. But the intent is clear. Along with other regulatory programs, it represents pressure by the federal government to restrict the growth of hospital facilities. The political market in this area has been partly balanced by the increase in federal expenditures. While the hospitals still have a strong, concentrated interest in maintaining federal payments and control over their investment decisions, that interest is countered by the stake the federal government now has in the nation's medical expenditures. The pressure on federal health officials to control government health expenditures in turn results in restrictions on the subsidies to health care providers and on their decision-making autonomy.

Manpower

Federal government health manpower policy is moving from a voluntary approach, emphasizing incentives, toward a more regulated system. Until very recently, federal policy was aimed at simply increasing the quantity of physicians, nurses, and other medical personnel in the country. The problems of geographic and specialty distribution, it was believed, could be solved through the market. Increased supply was also expected to help ease the problem of the rapidly rising cost of physicians' services.

In the early 1960s, the federal government began providing subsidies to medical schools for constructing facilities and established incentives for increased student enrollments. Currently, the federal government grants $1,500 per student directly to medical schools and makes loans to students. In fiscal 1978, the federal government will provide an estimated $1.9 billion dollars for health education and training ($516 million for physicians). More than 40 percent of the revenues of American medical schools come from federal grants or contracts (this figure includes research grants, but does not include federal payments for patient treatments in affiliated hospitals).[52]

The supply of health manpower has indeed increased in the last decade. The number of active physicians per 100,000 population grew from 141 in 1963 to 157 in 1973, while the number of nurses and technicians increased even more rapidly. Yet this increased supply does not seem to affect the problems of distribution appreciably. For example, South Dakota has a ratio of 71 patient-care doctors per 100,000 population, compared to 339 in the District of Columbia. And while the total number of physicians was increasing, the number of participating general practitioners was actually falling.[53]

In 1965, Congress attacked geographic maldistribution by forgiving loans to medical graduates willing to practice in underserved areas. In 1971, Congress addressed specialty maldistribution by providing incentives to medical schools to emphasize family practitioners. In 1976, medical schools were required to have a minimum proportion of residencies in family medicine. The schools are also supposed to reserve a portion of their enrollment for students willing to practice in under-served areas. Federal capitation grants are tied to compliance with provisions designed to achieve those goals. The 1976 manpower bill also restricted the entry of "foreign medical graduates" into the United States.

Research

The amount spent on health-related research has risen rapidly in recent years. Federal outlays for health research, only $70 million in 1950, grew to $1,670 million in 1970 and will reach an estimated $3,612 million in 1978. The federal government now funds more than 60 percent of all biomedical research in this country.[54] While the aggregate increase has been dramatic, most of the growth can be attributed to inflation and to an increased emphasis on cancer and heart research.[55]

The National Institute of Health (NIH) within the Department of Health, Education, and Welfare administers more than three-fifths of the federal funding through grants, contracts, and its own internal research. In the last few years, there has been a shift towards more directed research: more internal work and a shift from grants to contracts (contracts are awarded at the initiative of the Institute; grants are awarded to investigators who submit proposals on their own initiatives). However, grants which leave discretion with the researchers still make up 63 percent of the Institute's funding. In addition, training grants have been reduced.

The increasing overlay of traditional distributive programs in the medical care industry with regulatory controls is a consequence of the greatly increased federal expenditures for medical care. Soaring government expenditures for medical care threaten other government programs and thus cause a general concern for controlling health program budgets. Distributive programs are decided on "in isolation from other units . . . [and] the deprived cannot as a class be identified."[56] But the health care budget grew so rapidly and became so large that other government programs and beneficiaries began to see themselves as deprived. Soaring expenditures drew attention to medical care. Increases in medical care resources translated into increases in medical care expenditures. Most analysts now believe that a significant amount of medical demand is provider-induced.[57] If hospital beds are available, they tend to be filled; more surgeons means more surgery; research tends to produce expensive rather than cost-saving technologies. Subsidies to providers are seen as having major implications for medical expenditures. The interests of the medical industry, which had acquired the distributive benefits, were being countered by a general governmental interest in restricting medical expenditure growth. The result was either a reduction in benefits or the addition of restrictive conditions to the benefits.

RESTRUCTURING THE MEDICAL INDUSTRY

One result of all these federal programs is that the medical care industry is now financed largely through the public sector. In fiscal 1975, the public sector (federal, state, and local governments) provided over 42 percent of all health expenditures. The public sector paid for 55 percent of all hospital care and 58 percent of nursing home expenses. While the public sector only financed 26 percent of the costs of physicians' services, the federal government alone provided more than 40 percent of the revenues of American medical schools that trained the physicians.[58] While the medical industry is still largely privately controlled, it is not a model of independent private enterprise. Yet precisely because of significant public involvement, the private decisions of providers and consumers have a dramatic impact on public expenditures. The federal government, in order to control its own expenditures, must control the behavior of the private actors in the medical care industry. In recent years, the pressures to control expenditure increases has resulted in the initiation of several regulatory programs.

Rate Regulation

There have been basically three types of federal action to control the rate of payment to providers. First, restrictions have been placed on what are considered "allowable costs." Usually, this has meant that the federal government has prohibited hospitals from spreading the costs of other patients on to federal programs. The government has also refused to pay for other than "reasonable costs," meaning that certain items (e.g., a new parking lot) or outrageously high charges have not been covered. However, since virtually unlimited revenues can be absorbed in the "allowable" categories (new services, more intensive care, fancier technology), this has been neither an effective cost-control mechanism nor a major impetus to medical reform.

In 1972, Congress attempted to prevent federal payments from contributing to the unnecessary expansion of facilities. Section 1122 of the Social Security Act stated that the costs associated with construction (depreciation and interest) would not be considered allowable costs if the hospital did not get a "certificate-of-need" from a state agency. Section 1122 did not forbid construction (discussed below); it only applied financial sanctions. The sanctions existed only in states that agreed to perform the facilities review and certify need. But the federal government paid for the review and by 1975 41 states had section 1122 review programs.[59] It should be noted that the federal government could reduce payments only after the state government denied the cetificate-of-need; the federal government could not initiate action.

The second major approach to rate regulation has been to place limits on increases in prices or charges. The prime example of this is the Economic Stabilization Program, which between 1971 and 1974 placed controls first on the cost increases that could be passed on in charges, and then, in Phase IV, on the total revenue per admission. ESP had a very definite short-term impact on hospital costs and lowered the inflation rate in the medical sector. But it apparently also triggered a "catch up" attempt and resulted in very sharp price increases, as high as a 20 percent annual rate, after the program ended.[60]

The Carter Administration has proposed a ceiling on increases in hospital revenues. This approach is administratively easy, as least compared to the even more complex forms of incentive or prospective reimbursement. But ceilings had a tendency to become floors, so that the "limit" in effect becomes the norm for rate increases. And such ceilings do not provide direct incentives for changing behavior towards increased efficiency. Because the existing operation is the base on which the increase is calculated, present inefficiencies are perpetuated.

Finally, rate regulation can involve incentive or what is now being called prospective reimbursement.[61] In essence, the rate or revenue levels are removed from the exclusive determination of the provider. Predetermined levels of charges or revenues are made, and then the provider shares some risk and/or incentives in performing within those limits. There are an immense number of different approaches possible (e.g., based on costs per admission, per patient day, per service; global, departmental, or line item budget review),[62] but they all have theoretical drawbacks and are difficult to administer.

Amendments to the Social Security Act (PL92-603), in 1972, provided funding to "develop and carry out experiments and demonstration projects designed to determine the relative advantages and disadvantages of various alternative methods of making payment on a prospective basis to hospitals." Although the federal government is vitally interested in (and affected by) the projects, and although it provides much of the funding, it does not either design or administer the programs. The 1974 Amendments to the Social Security Act authorized still more experiments to find effective prospective reimbursement schemes.

Studies of the effects of prospective reimbursement are not encouraging. Hellinger, in a review of three programs, concluded that one system provided inadequate evidence, since it was small and self-selected, and the other two "were ineffective in controlling hospital costs."[63] Harvey Wolfe, in introducing the special section on prospective reimbursement in *Inquiry,* admitted that "it is difficult to conclude that prospective payments based on prior costs or budget review are advantageous in the long run."[64] The evidence from Canada supports this view.[65] However, large cost increases and the obvious impact of federal and other third party reimbursement methods on inflation insure that the federal government will continue to search for alternative payment mechanisms.

Planning and Facilities Regulation

In 1974, Congress provided authorization for over 200 local health planning agencies in the National Health Planning and Resources Development Act (PL93-641). These Health Systems Agencies (HSA) are supposed to increase the accessibility, continuity and quality of services, and to prevent unnecessary duplication. The new program has two main approaches.

First, local planning has been reinforced. The HSAs replace a network of planning agencies established by the Comprehensive Health Planning Act of 1967. The old planning agencies never had adequate funding. By 1974, one-fifth of the country still had no established planning agencies. Of the established agencies, over one-third were still in the "developmental phase."[66] Planning agencies were often dependent on medical providers for operating funds and had been accused of being subservient to them. The new HSAs were provided with more federal funding and were forbidden to use provider contributions. Although more federal funds are now available, the establishment of planning agencies continues to be a slow process. There has been a great deal of conflict over the drawing of the HSA boundaries and over the designation of the operating agency. Much of the struggle concerned federal efforts to prevent HSAs from being public agencies. Probably more than 90 percent of them will be private nonprofit organizations. At the local level, the fights concerned who would be on the board of the HSA. Law suits and political stalemates have delayed implementation, so that two years after passage some agencies have still not been designated, let along begun operation.

HSAs are supposed to identify local health resources and needs, produce a local plan establishing the goals for the area, and develop an "Implementation Plan" describing projects and priorities to meet the goals. In particular, HSAs are supposed to encourage cheaper forms of care (e.g., ambulatory rather than inpatient), increase the continuity of the medical care system, and prevent unnecessary duplication of facilities. However, one study of state and local planning agencies found local health plans were not detailed or concrete enough to be used in determining the need for new medical facilities.[67] Another study found that there were no significant differences between local areas that had operating planning agencies and areas that did not.[68] The federal government has provided funds for planning agencies, but there is no evidence that effective planning actually takes place.

The second major approach in the 1974 Act is regulatory. Health care facilities are required to obtain prior approval from the state—in the form of a certificate-of-need—before undertaking any major capital investments. The rationale for regulatory investments is that there is a surplus of hospital facilities in this country. The Institute of Medicine says the ratio of short-term beds to population should be reduced by 10 percent.[69] Since beds tend to be used whether needed or not, excess supply has a significant impact on medical costs.[70] But surplus beds are only part of the problem. Many hospitals have expensive equipment that is not needed and often not even used. For example, 30 percent of the 800 hospitals equipped for open heart surgery in the United States had no cases in the year studied.[71] Health planning is supposed to determine the need for facilities and services in an area and prevent unnecessary duplication. HSAs must review all investment proposals in their area and recommend approval or disapproval. But it is the state government that finally decides whether to issue a "certificate-of-need" and allow new projects. The federal government does not make the decisions.

This is a major problem, since the little available evidence indicates that the state governments do not effectively exercise the authority they have. A study by Carolyn Harmon indicates that over 90 percent of all hospital project proposals were approved.[72] States were not even restricting growth, let alone reducing the present surplus. Two other studies argue that states with certificate-of-need regulation had no less capital investment than states without regulation.[73] One of these studies found, however, that regulation did reduce the increase in beds. The authors hypothesized that regulators prevented hospitals from adding beds, but that hospitals merely switched their investment choices to other items. Total dollars invested remained the same.[74]

Federal guidelines are very explicit in setting up HSAs. (1) HSAs are forbidden to take money from providers; (2) they have to have a local plan; (3) they have to review the "appropriateness" of all health care facilities in their area; (4) they have to have at least 51 percent consumer participation on their boards; (5) the consumers have to be representative of the social, economic, and racial mix of the area; and (6) at least 40 percent of the board must be providers. Yet, in spite of the detail with which the federal government has specified *who* will be involved and *how* the decisions are to be made, the federal government has no control over *what* decisions are made. In effect, the federal government has delegated authority over issues with national implications to local decision-makers. There is reason to believe that national goals will not be served. HSAs, with a local constituency, will make decisions for the local interest. Even consumer representation will not particularly alter that, since consumers as well as providers are interested in increasing the supply of medical facilities and services in their locality. This is especially true when local consumers do not bear the full costs. Ninety percent of hospital expenses are paid by third-party payers: the government and private insurance. Costs therefore are spread among taxpayers and policy holders, while the benefits go to the local community. A few states and localities may actually restrict facility growth, but the federal government has no control over those that do not. The decision-making authority rests at the state level.

Utilization Regulation

A third method of reforming the medical industry involves regulation of the utilization of medical services. The original Medicare-Medicaid bill required hospital-based "Utilization Review" committees to review cases to see if they were medically necessary. However, this provision has had neither serious enforcement nor widespread implementation. In 1972, amendments to the Social Security Act (PL92-103) authorized the establishment of a network[75] of Professional Standards Review Organizations (PSRO) to review the quality and necessity of service provided to all Medicare, Medicaid, and Maternal and Child Health patients. PSROs would review services when a hospital did not have an acceptable utilization review program.

PSROs are organizations of physicians practicing in the region. However, resistance and criticism from doctors and hospitals in some areas has greatly delayed the establishment of operating PSROs. By January 1, 1976, only 120 of the 203 areas had designated agencies.[76] Even in the areas that had operating organizations, the review process was not extensive. Only 25 percent of the clients eligible for PSRO review in June of 1976 were actually being reviewed.[77] PSROs are performing very little utilization review at this time.

The attempt to control utilization of medical services is another response to the increase in federal expenditures. If unnecessary utilization can be reduced, federal expenditures can be reduced without limiting benefits or beneficiaries. But there a few commonly accepted standards to define either the "necessity" or the "quality" of medical services. Attempts to control—or even analyze—the problems are difficult because of the disagreement among professionals. There is reason to believe, however, that some changes in utilization could reduce medical costs. First, many services could be eliminated or reduced without harming patients: they are not even medically useful. A study in New

York City found that 24 percent of initially recommended elective surgery was not confirmed by a second medical opinion. The probability of tonsillectomies varies eightfold in different areas of Vermont. In general, cross-country and cross-national studies have shown that the number of surgeries varies with the number of surgeons—not just medical need. The variation in length of stays in hospitals is also greater than can be accounted for simply by medical need. Unnecessary surgery and hospitalization are the most commonly cited problems, although excessive testing and drug use may also exist.[78]

Second, many services that do indeed help patients could still be performed in cheaper settings. Some patients could be treated equally well but less expensively at home or in nursing homes rather than in hospitals. Diagnostic tests and simple surgery could be performed on an outpatient basis rather than after admission to a hospital.

Third, some services may simply not be worth the added cost, even if they are helpful and performed as cheaply as possible. This is utilization that is inappropriate from a social, if not from a personal, perspective. The use of CT scanners[79] is a good example. Although CT scanners are apparently helpful in improving diagnostic accuracy, they are extremely expensive. The added accuracy and confidence they provide must be weighed against their high acquisition and operation costs.

Finally, utilization controls could help reduce fraud. Services that were billed but not provided or that were obviously unnecessary could be detected and perhaps prevented by utilization controls. This is a politically popular form of control since it neither reduces patient benefits nor restricts legitimate provider activity and everyone is against fraud. While there have been spectacular exposes in the press, it is difficult to estimate the actual extent and cost of fraud in government medical programs.

Doctors under a fee-for-service payment method have financial and other incentives to overprovide services, since the more services they perform the more they are paid. There is a theoretical reason to expect unnecessary or inappropriate services; the empirical data merely confirm the expectation. If patients do not pay for services at the point of use, neither the provider nor the consumer have adequate incentives to restrict utilization. Some other form of control is necessary to prevent unnecessary and costly utilization.

Any direct regulation of medical utilization requires a determination of what is necessary or adequate care for a patient. This in turn requires that the decisions of the individual physician be reviewed, which of course is why so many doctors have opposed the program. Reviewing all decisions is prohibitive. Review has focused on elective surgery and on statistically abnormal patterns of utilization: usually frequent surgery by a physician, unusually long hospitalization for an episode of illness. Studies indicate that this review of "outriders" does lead to net savings over the costs of the review, but the savings are not particularly large compared to total hospital expenditures. Such regulation only prevents abuses in individual cases or by individual physicians. If the profession as a whole over-hospitalizes, than just looking at individual nonconformers will not fundamentally change medical utilization patterns.[80]

Each PSRO is supposed to develop criteria and standards for care, and these could lead to the desired reduction in utilization. However, Havighurst and Blumstein have pointed out that PSROs run by doctors are more likely to be concerned with quality assurance than with cost control. They suggest that in any tradeoff between cost and quality, PSROs are likely to choose quality and establish standards with longer bed stays and more procedures than a cost-conscious regulator would choose. This is especially likely given that attempts to establish standards that restrict customary medical practice inevitably interfere with physicians' decisions about the best treatment for their patients and so would arouse *immense* opposition in the profession.[81]

It is interesting that no other industrial nation has tried to control utilization through direct regulation and review of physician decisions. This is partly because the dominant payment method in the United States—fee-for-service with no limits on total expenditures—creates incentives for excessive utilization. Yet Canada has similar payment mechanisms but has not attempted to regulate physician decisions directly. It is ironic that the United States, where professional dominance is so striking, has legislated the most striking intervention into doctors' prerogatives. On the other hand, as it now exists, utilization regulation would affect physicians who do not conform to the established practices of the profession. It would not regulate the behavior of the majority of physicians.[82]

Health Maintenance Organizations

One attempt to indirectly control the utilization of medical services has received a great deal of political attention in recent years. There is evidence that Health Maintenance Organizations (HMO) are less costly than the traditional method of organizing the delivery of medical services. HMOs provide comprehensive medical services for a fixed payment. The organization must keep the cost of the services it provides within the fixed budget. Therefore, HMOs, unlike private physicians and hospitals, have incentives to provide care as cheaply as possible.[83]

In 1970 the Nixon administration declared that HMOs were the centerpiece of their health policy. HMOs were popular in the conservative administration since they were potentially less costly, they promoted competition and free enterprise (patients could choose whether to enroll or not, so each HMO had to sell its product to consumers), and an HMO strategy could restructure the medical industry with a minimum of government regulation and interference.

It was not until 1973, however, that Congress finally passed the Health Maintenance Act authorizing $375 million to promote the expansion of HMOs. The Act required employers to offer their employees a choice between their usual insurance and qualified HMOs. While this was supposed to assure HMOs of access to potential subscribers, the provision was opposed by the AFL-CIO as an infringement on collective bargaining. Employee enrollment was delayed until this was settled.

Physicians and insurance companies are strongly opposed to the development of HMOs. Physicians in this country have always fought any threat to the fee-for-service standard, and they continued to oppose HMO development even after the HMO idea was expanded to include fee-for-service doctors in medical foundations. Insurance companies saw HMOs as competitors for medical care dollars. But the HMO Act did not make federally aided HMOs viable competitors.

While the bill authorized subsidies to HMOs to help in their start up costs, it also placed strict conditions on eligibility. HMOs had to provide a basic package of services, have periodic open enrollment when anyone could join, and charge the same premium to people joining as individuals or in groups. These restrictions made it very difficult for HMOs to be competitive. People with costly medical problems have incentives to join HMOs and have all their care covered without coinsurance, deductibles, or benefit ceilings. Since the Act did not allow HMOs to either reject such people or charge them extra, the average subscriber premium was increased compared to commercial insurance.

Worst of all, actual federal grants and loans to HMOs remained low. From 1974 to 1977, HEW disbursed only $70 million to HMOs. Since subsidies were too small to make up for the costly eligibility requirements, a year and a half after passage only 11 of the nation's 173 HMOs had even applied for qualification for federal support.[84]

The HMO strategy continues to get vocal support. HMOs play a central role in Kennedy's national health insurance proposal, and liberals and conservatives alike see HMOs as a desirable method of delivering medical care. But the development of prepaid group practices is hindered by the high start-up costs (physicians, staff, and facilities must be available before subscribers will join). Rapid development of HMOs would require federal subsidies, and that is hindered by budget constraints and physician and insurance industry opposition. Medical foundations, which the AMA finds less objectionable, may not be a less costly delivery method. There are now fewer than seven million subscribers in HMOs, and though the number of organizations and of subscribers is growing, HMOs will not become the dominant delivery mode in the immediate future.

Conclusion

Federal attempts to regulate and restructure the medical system exhibit certain uniformities. Perhaps the most striking is the gap between legislative action on the one hand and implementation and results on the other. Federal activity up to this point has been almost exclusively legislative. Rate regulation has been authorized, but very little has occurred (with the exception of ESP). PSROs and HSAs have been mandated, but law suits and local political struggles to block or control the new programs have delayed and in some localities prevented implementation. The political struggles over the new regulatory programs have been bitter, and the regulatory agencies are not yet fully in place, let alone operating and making decisions.

The federal government only mandates that regulatory agencies exist; it does not itself perform the regulation. Rate, facility, and utilization regulation have all been delegated to state or regional organizations. The federal government has little control over how (and so far whether) the regulatory organizations actually perform.

Finally, it should be stressed that the regulatory efforts of the federal government are in a state of flux. One analyst has pointed out that planning is now in its "third generation," as two earlier stages have been replaced by planning agencies with more regulatory "teeth."[85] Providers have a concentrated interest in avoiding or capturing the regulatory programs for their own ends. So far, the restructuring efforts seem feeble. The programs are only beginning to operate and only in some regions. The authority provided seems inadequate to achieve the stated goals, and most of the established agencies are unlikely even to use what authority is provided. Yet, compared to the federal role of a decade ago, the intervention is dramatic. As expenditures continue to rise, the interest in controlling providers in order to control expenditures also rises. As the political market for regulation becomes more balanced, we can expect still greater efforts to control the medical industry.

PUBLIC HEALTH

The increased role of the federal government in the medical care delivery system has been dramatic, but the government has also expanded its traditional public health role. The federal government funds a wide variety of programs in the prevention of health problems, control of communicable diseases, environmental health, health education, nutrition, and consumer and worker safety. The federal budget lists a total of $1.5 billion spent in 1976 on "prevention and control of health problems," up from $645 million in 1969.[86] Since much of the federal activity consists of regulating the behavior of the private sector, expenditures are only a fair indicator of the federal role.

The federal government operates the Center for Disease Control in Atlanta to monitor and detect epidemic diseases and to control them through immunization and quarantine. However, the bulk of the $589 million spent on disease prevention and control is in the form of grants to the states to support public health activities.

A number of federal "health" programs do not involve medical care at all. Indeed, the relationship between medical care and health is not as strong as is usually assumed. In the first place, many health problems are not disease-related and are largely impervious to medical solutions. For example, the three leading causes of death among young white males are motor accidents, other accidents, and suicide. Among young black males, homicide is the leading cause, followed by accidents and suicide. The death rate for males 15 to 24 was 15 percent lower 20 years ago than it is now.[87] Advances in medical care, although no doubt saving many victims who previously would have died, cannot overcome other societal trends. The 55-mile per hour speed limit or gun control legislation might have more of an impact than medical programs on the health status of this age group.

Medical care is obviously not the only determinant of health. Many health problems are caused by where and how we live. Cancer and heart disease, the leading causes of death among middle aged males, seem to be linked to the environment and to life style. Indeed, "cancer appears to be, in large part, a man-made disease."[88] Even if there were a cure for cancer, medical care might not be the most effective method of controlling cancer.

There is a good deal of evidence that the *marginal* value of most medical care is low. Despite the great increases in medical care services and expenditures, the crude death rate in America remained constant in the last decade. One analyst concluded "the end of medicine is near. Medical care as provided by physicians and hospitals is having less and less impact on our health.[89] Ivan Illich goes so far as to say that medicine actually has a negative impact on health.[90] But one does not have to accept these extreme formulations to recognize that there are limits to the usefulness of medical intervention. Medical science may produce a significant breakthrough that will cure or control a dread disease. An easing of the maldistribution of current services would be beneficial to the health status of certain groups. But, in general, more medical care will not produce significantly better health. Some of the federal programs that most affect health are not directly related to medicine.

Consumer safety and information programs have the potential to affect health significantly. Each year, 30,000 people are killed in accidents at home, and another 46,000 on the highway.[91] The federal government spent $520 million on consumer safety in 1976, including programs of the Food and Drug Administration, the Consumer Product Safety Commission, the Department of Transportation, and the Department of Agriculture's food inspection programs.[92]

Every year 14,000 people are killed in work accidents, and an estimated 100,000 more die of occupational-related diseases.[93] Labor unions have been dissatisfied with state regulation of the workplace, and the Occupational Safety and Health Act of 1970 gave the federal government the dominant role in occupational safety. From the beginning, OSHA has been extremely controversial and the business community has attacked it for being insensitive to the cost-effectiveness of safety measures. Obviously, finding a balance between reducing the incidence of disease or accidents among certain workers on the one hand and the necessity for large investments in safer facilities and increased prices for millions of consumers on the other is not easy. However, labor has continued to provide strong support to OSHA, and the federal government is gradually expanding its role in occupational safety.

Environmental control has always been part of the traditional governmental public health role, but in recent years federal regulation of the environment has increased. It is beyond the scope of this paper to discuss the Environmental Protection Agency and other federal policies that affect the environment. We will merely repeat that air and water pollution have been shown to be associated with higher death rates from certain diseases. Environmental quality has an important affect on health status.

Finally, there are a number of federal programs designed to promote better health habits and more healthy lifestyles. There has been a growing recognition of the importance of lifestyle in determining health. However, the imbalance of the political market is quite striking in this area. Not only are laws restricting individual freedom understandably unpopular, but there are often groups with a sizeable stake in maintaining the existing lifestyle. An obvious example is cigarettes, where federal expenditures to discourage smoking are small compared to the continued subsidy of the tobacco industry. Expenditures for health lifestyle programs amount to only one-half of one percent of 1976 federal health expenditures.[94] What we do to ourselves, and what others do to us, may be more important in determining health than what the medical profession can do for us. But federal health programs are likely to continue to be mostly medical programs.

NOTES

1. *Special Analyses, Budget of the United States,* Fiscal Year 1978 (Washington, D.C.: Government Printing Office, 1977): 202; *Special Analyses, Budget of the United States,* Fiscal Year 1972 (Washington, D.C.: U.S. Government Printing Office, 1971: 149.

2. Robert M. Gibson and Marjorie Smith Mueller, "National Health Expenditures, Fiscal Year 1976," *Social Security Bulletin,* 40, 4 (April 1977): 4.

3. *Special Analyses, Budget,* Fiscal Year 1978: 204, 206.

4. Quoted in Joel May, "The Planning and Licensing Agencies," in Clark Havighurst (ed.), *Regulating Health Facilities Construction* (Washington, D.C.: American Enterprise Institute, 1974): 48.

5. The growth of federal programs has not been uniform, but neither has it been concentrated in areas that would have the greatest impact on health status of Americans or on groups that have the greatest health needs. In fact, overall expenditure growth was not the result of choice at all. The expansion of the federal role seems to be a classic case of unplanned consequences, as some program outlays increased beyond the wildest dreams of supporters and even beyond the nightmares of opponents.

6. Gibson and Mueller, "National Health Expenditures 1976": 8.

7. AMA Statement on National Health Insurance (by Dr. Max Parrot), *Hearings on National Health Insurance,* Ways and Means Committee (October/November, 1971): 1951.

8. See, for example, Theodore Lowi, "American Business, Public Policy, and Political Theory," *World Politics,* 16 (1964); and Theodore Marmor, *The Politics of Medicare* (London: Routledge & Kegan Paul, 1970).

9. *Special Analyses, Budget,* Fiscal Year 1978: 219-220.

10. See Marmor, *The Politics of Medicare* for a full discussion of the development of the Medicare issue.

11. Theodore Marmor and James Morone, "The Health Programs of the Kennedy-Johnson Years: An Overview," in David Warner (ed.), *Toward New Human Rights* (Austin: LBJ School of Public Affairs, University of Texas, 1977): 172-3.

12. Karen Davis, "A Decade of Policy Development in Providing Health Care for Low-Income Families," *Process* (Washington, D.C.: The Brookings Institution, July, 1975): 25-26; published also in Robert H. Haveman (ed.), *A Decade of Federal Anti-Poverty Policy: Achievements, Failures, and Lessons* (Madison: Institute for Research on Poverty, University of Wisconsin, 1977).

13. John Holahan, *Financing Health Care for the Poor* (Boston: D.C. Heath, 1975): 3.

14. Cited in Theodore Marmor, "Welfare Medicine: How Success Can Be a Failure," *The Yale Law Journal* 85, 8 (July, 1976): 1153.

15. Ronald Andersen, Joanna Lion, and Odin Anderson (eds.), *Two Decades of Health Services* (Cambridge: Ballinger Publishing Co., 1976): 13.

16. Ibid., 15.

17. Karen Davis, "Achievements and Problems of Medicaid," *Public Health Reports* 91, 4 (July/August, 1976): 313; and Anne R. Somers and Herman M. Somers, "A Proposed Framework for Health and Health Care Policies," *Inquiry* 14, 2 (June, 1977): 137.

18. Davis, "A Decade of Policy Development": 12.

19. Ibid., 13.

20. Anderson, et al., *Two Decades:* 15.

21. Marmor, *The Policies of Medicare:* 92.

22. Davis, "Achievements of Medicaid": 314-15.

23. Davis, "A Decade of Policy Developments": 20-21.

24. Ibid., 18.

25. Davis, "Achievements of Medicaid": 311-12.

26. Ibid., 311.

27. Louise Russell, Blair Bourque, Daniel Bourque, and Carol Burke, *Federal Health Spending, 1969-74* (Washington, D.C.: National Planning Association, 1974).

28. Holahan, *Financing Health Care:* 9.

29. Computed from table 19 in Committee on Interstate and Foreign Commerce, Subcommittee on Health and the Environment, U.S. House of Representatives, "Data on the Medicaid Program: Eligibility, Services, Expenditures Fiscal Years 1966-76," (Washington, D.C.: U.S. Government Printing Office, 1976): 29-30.

30. Lyndon Baines Johnson, *The Vantage Point* (New York: Holt, Rinehart & Winston, 1971): 220.

31. Russell, *Federal Health Spending:* 57.

32. Marmor and Marone, "Health Programs of Kennedy-Johnson Years": 178-79.

33. Ibid., 179.

34. *Special Analyses, Budget 1978:* 228.

35. Russell, *Federal Health Spending:* 73; and *Special Analyses, Budget 1978:* 226-28.

36. Russell, *Federal Health Spending:* 72, 79; and *Special Analyses, Budget 1978:* 221, 226-28.

37. Russell, *Federal Health Spending:* 54; and *Special Analyses, Budget 1978:* 226-28.

38. Russell, *Federal Health Spending:* 60; and *Special Analyses, Budget 1978:* 226-28.

39. Russell, *Federal Health Spending:* 75; and *Special Analyses, Budget 1978:* 222.

40. Bridger Mitchell and Ronald Vogel, "Health and Taxes: An Assessment of the Medical Deduction," *Southern Economic Journal* 41, 4 (April, 1975): 670.

41. Congressional Budget Office, *Budget Options for Fiscal Year 1978* (Washington, D.C.: U.S. Government Printing Office, February, 1977): 143, 147.

42. Gibson and Mueller, "National Health Expenditures 1976": 8.

43. Council on Wage and Price Stability, "The Complex Puzzle of Rising Health Care Costs: Can the Private Sector Fit It Together?" (Washington, D.C.: Council on Wage and Price Stability, December 1976): 84.

44. *Special Analyses, Budget 1978:* 222.

45. Marjorie Smith Mueller and Robert M. Gibson, "National Health Expenditures, Fiscal Year 1975," *Social Security Bulletin,* 39, 2, (February, 1976): 6-8.

46. Richard A. Rettig and Thomas C. Webster, "Implementation of the End-Stage

Renal Disease Program," paper presented at the 1975 American Political Science Association meeting in San Francisco, September 2-5, 1975: 3.

47. Judith A. Kasper, Ronald Andersen, and Charles Brown, "The Financial Impact of Catastrophic Illness as Measured in the CHAS-NORC National Survey," processed. Prepared for the National Center for Health Services Research, February 4, 1975.

48. See, for example, Institute of Medicine, "Controlling the Supply of Hospital Beds," Washington, D.C., National Academy of Sciences, October 1976.

49. Judith R. Lave and Lester B. Lave, *The Hospital Construction Act* (Washington, D.C.: American Enterprise Institute, 1974): 14.

50. *Special Analyses, Budget 1978:* 215.

51. Ibid., 215.

52. Ibid., 213-14.

53. Robert A. Diseker and James C. Leist, "From Incentives toward Regulation," *Medical Group Management,* 22, 5 (July/August, 1975): 8.

54. *Special Analyses, Budget 1978:* 212.

55. Russell, *Federal Health Spending:* 22.

56. Lowi, "American Business": 690.

57. See, for example, M. Roemer and M. Shain, *Hospital Utilization under Insurance,* Monograph Series No. 6 (Chicago: American Hospital Association); and Martin S. Feldstein, "Hospital Cost Inflation: A Study of Non-Profit Price Dynamics," *American Economic Review,* 61 (December, 1971): 853-872.

58. Gibson and Mueller, "National Health Expenditures 1976," computed from table 2 (p. 5) and *Special Analyses, Budget 1978:* 213.

59. Jack Wood (ed.), *Topics in Health Care Financing,* 2, 2, (Winter, 1975): 93, appendix C, "State 1122 Agreements"

60. Council on Wage and Price Stability, "The Complex Puzzle of Rising Health Care Costs": 79.

61. Technically, they are not the same. An incentive reimbursement system requires that the provider be at risk and therefore have incentives to be cost-restrictive. A prospective system simply means costs are estimated and established in advance. If adjustments to this established budget are easily made, there may be no incentives involved.

62. See, Lewin & Associates, "Nationwide Survey of State Health Regulations," Contract No. HEW-OS-73-212 (Washington, D.C.: Lewin and Associates, September 16, 1974): chapter 2.

63. Fred J. Hellinger, "Prospective Reimbursement through Budget Review," *Inquiry,* 13, 3 (September, 1976): 319.

64. Harvey Wolfe, "Introduction," *Inquiry,* 13, 3 (September, 1976): 276.

65. See discussion in Theodore R. Marmor, "Can the U.S. Learn from Canada?" in Spyros Andreopoulos (ed.), *National Health Insurance: Can We Learn from Canada?* (New York: John Wiley & Sons, 1975): 234-35.

66. United States Senate, Labor and Public Welfare Committee, Senate Report No. 93-1285, "National Health Planning and Resources Development Act of 1974," in *Legislative History:* 7850.

67. Comptroller General of the United States, "Comprehensive Health Planning as Carried Out by States and Areawide Agencies in Three States" (Washington, D.C.: U.S. Government Printing Office, 1974): 18.

68. Joel May, "The Planning and Licensing Agencies."

69. Institute of Medicine, "Controlling the Supply of Hospital Beds."

70. The implication of the "availability effect" is that "excess" beds are costly both

because idle capacity is wasteful and because excess beds leads to unnecessary utilization. See sources in footnote 56.

71. Howard H. Hiatt, "Protecting the Medical 'Commons'—Who Has the Responsibility," in *The National Leadership Conference on America's Health Policy* sponsored by the *National Journal,* Representative Paul Rogers and Representative Dan Rostenkowski, Hyatt Regency, Washington, DC (April 29-30, 1976): 20.

72. Carolyn Harmon, "The Efficiency and Effectiveness of Health Care Capital Expenditures and Service Controls: An Interim Assessment," in Herbert H. Hyman (ed.), *Health Regulation* (Germantown, Md.: Aspen System Corporation, 1977): 27-52.

73. David Salkever and Thomas Bice, "The Impact of Certificate-of-Need Controls on Hospital Investment," paper presented to CHAS workshop, October 8, 1975, University of Chicago; and Fred J. Hellinger, "The Effect of Certificate-of-Need Legislation on Hospital Investment," *Inquiry,* 13, 2 (June, 1976): 187-197.

74. Salkever and Bice, "Impact of Certificate-of-Need."

75. The PSRO and HSA boundaries are usually not the same.

76. Health Policy Program, "Cooperation between Health Systems Agencies and Professional Standards Review Organizations," HEW contract No. HRA 230-75-000-71 (San Francisco: University of California, School of Medicine, January 23, 1976): 13.

77. Data collected from interviews by Rich Krieg.

78. Cited by Bruce Stuart, "Utilization Controls," in John Holahan and Bruce Stuart, *Controlling Medicaid Utilization Patterns* (Washington, D.C.: Urban Institute, 1977): 35-37.

79. Computed tomographic scanners are full body x-ray machines.

80. See, for example, Alan R. Nelson, "Relation between Quality Assessment and Utilization Review in a Functioning PSRO," *New England Journal of Medicine,* 292 (March 27, 1975): 671-675.

81. Clark Havighurst and James Blumstein, "Coping with Quality/Cost Tradeoffs in Medical Care: The Role of PSROs," *Northwestern Law Review,* 70, 1 (March/April, 1975): 60-68.

82. The regional basis of PSROs reinforces this. Each PSRO region establishes its own standards. Areas with many surgeons—and so many surgeries—could allow high surgery rates.

83. There are a number of different organizational arrangements under the general rubric of "HMO." In some forms, usually called "Medical Foundations," physicians are still paid on a fee-for-service basis. In "prepaid group practices," physicians are placed on salary and/or profit sharing. The literature has not settled the question of why HMOs are able to provide less costly health care (there is even some dispute over whether they do provide cheaper care, although the consensus is that prepaid group practices do). Analysts have suggested HMOs reduce expenses by only providing necessary services, by substituting cheaper forms of care (ambulatory for inpatient, preventive for treatment), and by undertreating. A recent review of the literature suggests that a key factor may simply be the elimination of fee-for-service payments and hence of physician incentives to overserve. Richard Foster, "HMOs: A Synthesis of the Evidence of Use," paper presented at the CHAS workshop, University of Chicago, April, 1977.

84. Bruce Spitz, "HMO Reimbursement and Regulation," in John Holahan, Bruce Spitz, William Polack, and Judy Feder (eds.), *Altering Medicaid Provider Reimbursement Methods* (Washington, D.C.: Urban Institute, 1977): 156.

85. J. Joel May, "Will Third Generation Planning Succeed?" *Hospital Progress* (March, 1976).

86. *Special Analyses, Budget 1978:* 228.

87. Victor Fuchs, *Who Shall Live?* (New York: Basic Books, 1975): 42.

88. Somers and Somers, "A Proposed Framework": 125.

89. Rick J. Carlson, *The End of Medicine* (New York: John Wiley & Sons, 1975): 2.

90. Ivan Illich, *Medical Nemesis: The Expropriation of Health* (New York: Pantheon Books, 1976).

91. In 1975. Highway deaths have decreased in the last few years, presumably because of the lower speed limit.

92. U.S. Department of Health, Education, and Welfare, Public Health Service, *Forward Plan for Health FY1978-82* (Washington, D.C.: U.S. Government Printing Office, August, 1976): 78; and *Fiscal Analyses Budget, 1978:* 224.

93. U.S. Department HEW, *Forward Plan for Health:* 77.

94. Somers and Somers, "Proposed Framework": 131.

Part III

THE SOCIAL FABRIC

CAN NATIONAL POLICIES PROMOTE THE MULTI-RACIAL SOCIETY?

10.

CIVIL RIGHTS POLICIES: MINIMIZING DISCRIMINATION BASED ON RACE AND SEX

ANTHONY CHAMPAGNE

Rutgers University

STUART NAGEL

University of Illinois

INTRODUCTION

The purpose of this chapter is to provide a general overview of the policies designed to ensure racial and sexual equality. In addition, an attempt will be made to suggest forthcoming policy developments in these two areas and to assess the implications of these developments. The paper will proceed by first examining major public policies related to race and then will examine those major policies related to sex.

Among the major policies related to race which will be discussed are policies related to education, public accommodations, voting, housing, and employment. Currently, the most controversial policies deal with schools, especially with the busing of children from "neighborhood" schools to other schools for the purpose of ending segregated school practices. Another policy area that has come to the fore of political controversy is the question of preferential admission of minorities to graduate and professional schools. The question of preferential admissions is related to the employment area, where affirmative action programs are aiming at eliminating segregated employment patterns through the preferential hiring of minorities. Many charge that such affirmative action programs have gone too far in attempting to enhance educational and employment opportunities for minorities. The result, it is argued, has been "reverse discrimination" where white males are discriminated against in order to improve conditions for minorities. In a rather contorted opinion, the Supreme Court has just ruled on a major reverse discrimination claim which provides support for both opponents and supporters of affirmative action. Another area which is quickly developing into a major political conflict involves housing. In particular, it is likely that attempts to break down the barriers of the ghetto and to expand housing opportunities for blacks will result in significant white reaction. One of the major areas of potential political controversy in this area involves the elimination of zoning restrictions. Such zoning restrictions, it is argued, may effectively prevent persons with low incomes (including, of course, minorities) from moving into a township.

The major policies to be examined in the area of eliminating sex discrimination involve employment, governmental benefits, family law, and personal rights. All of these areas are currently embroiled in major political controversy, though clearly the most controversial policy in the area of women's rights involves the right of a woman to obtain an abortion. The civil rights claims of blacks and women are quite similar in the employment area. Here again the policy debate is one of affirmative action versus reverse discrimination. Additionally, there has been a considerable amount of "protective" legislation based on sexual stereotypes which has perhaps lessened the toil of women compared to men, but has also lessened the total employment opportunities available to women. A serious questioning of the validity and value of this protective legislation is underway. A growing debate in the family law area has to do with the rights of women in marriage and the claims of women for alimony and child support payments after a divorce. Finally, the distribution of some governmental benefits, in particular Social Security payments, has been based on sexual classifications. There has been a growing tendency to remove these classifications in the making of government payments.

Obviously, there is no way to detail all policies relating to race or sex. To do so would entail volumes and would involve discussion of a variety of executive orders, administrative actions, statutory laws, and court decisions on various levels. In addition to discussing national level policies, a variety of state and local policies would have to be discussed. The purpose of this chapter is more modest. Major policies in controversial or potentially controversial areas will be discussed. In doing so, it is most useful to examine national level policies. Most of these policies can be discussed by examining Congressional statutes and Supreme Court decisions. However, from time to time in this analysis, it will also be necessary to discuss policies made primarily in the executive branch. It will also be useful to examine proposed amendments to the Constitution and sometimes to focus on state policies, especially state court policies, which may point the way for new developments in these areas.

RACE

Education

Brown v. Board of Education: Probably no decision of the U.S. Supreme Court in this century has aroused more political controversy than Brown v. Board of Education.[1] Quite rightly, former Chief Justice Earl Warren viewed this decision as one of the most important made during his tenure on the Court.[2]

> We conclude that in the field of public education the doctrine of "separate but equal" has no place. Separate educational facilities are inherently unequal. Therefore, we hold that the plaintiffs and others similarly situated for whom the actions have been brought are, by reason of the segregation complained of, deprived of the equal protection of the laws.

With these words, the Court set in motion a dramatic policy change which led to the outlawing of all forms of state supported segregation. Many years prior to Brown, Plessy v. Ferguson[3] had provided Constitutional support for the view that state facilities could be segregated, provided the facilities provided to both races were equal. In the field of education, this decision led to a tradition of segregated school systems in the South. These school systems, it might be pointed out, paid much more attention to separation than equality. In the South, black schools were funded at notoriously low levels.

The elimination of the "separate but equal" doctrine was much more gradual than is normally believed. Brown was not a dramatic shift in doctrine. Instead, over a period of 20 years, there was a gradual chipping away of the "separate but equal" doctrine. Decisions in a series of cases, involving higher education, strongly suggested that Plessy was a dying precedent.[4] Brown was simply a confirmation of that suspicion.

The Supreme Court felt it was incapable of supervising desegregation in every segregated school district in the country. Thus, it gave to the district courts the authority to carry out the principles of Brown "with all deliberate speed."[5] As Justice Black pointed out, desegregation proceeded with much more deliberation than speed.[6] Many district courts were most uncooperative in carrying out the mandate of Brown.[7] Where district courts were cooperative, public officials were not. Indeed, with very few exceptions, the elimination of segregated school systems in the South in the first decade after Brown was supported only by a handful of public officials, most of whom were federal judges. State officials were uncooperative and frequently, as in the case of Orval Faubas, aggressively hostile.[8] The Congress was at the time dominated by conservative

Southerners who had no desire to change the status quo. Even the President was most reluctant to lend his support to the Court's decision.[9]

Perhaps this kind of response is to be expected in any major policy change. That is, there will be disagreement among the various levels and branches of government as to the desirability of the change. Unfortunately, such disagreement can encourage a strong reaction to the policy. In the early days of the desegregation movement, violence was not uncommon. Violence occurred in such places as New Orleans, Louisiana; Clinton, Tennessee; Mansfield, Texas; and Little Rock, Arkansas. In other cases, the reaction to Brown led to attempts to close the public schools. Schools were actually closed in such places as Warren County, Charlottesville, and Norfolk, Virginia. Segregationists began to resort to private schools to escape the integration of public schools. In the heyday of the private school movement, as many as 500,000 children may have attended such privately run institutions.[10]

In the years immediately following Brown, there was little effort to comply with the decision. A handful of judges, it would seem, without intra- or inter-governmental support is incapable of imposing a major social policy. However, the courts did perform an important agenda-setting function. Brown established racial segregation as a national problem that had to be faced. Racial segregation was placed on the national agenda as a problem deserving discussion, examination, and solution. After Brown, racial segregation continued illegally, but it could no longer be ignored.[11]

The 1964 Civil Rights Act: It was not until the other branches began to develop mechanisms to attack segregation that integrated schools began to come into widespread existence in the South. Perhaps the most significant law aimed at bringing about the desegregation of public schools was the 1964 Civil Rights Act. Title VI of that act provides that race shall not be grounds for any exclusion from participation in any program receiving federal financial assistance. Any beneficiaries of federal financial assistance who practiced racial discrimination could have funds terminated. This law is a potent weapon. All public schools depend on substantial federal funding.[12]

It is generally agreed that Title VI was largely responsible for the dismantling of dual school systems. Between 1965 and 1970, the major focus of efforts to secure compliance with the law was in the South. The main effort was to eliminate dual school systems. As a result of both efforts by HEW and the courts the number of black students across the nation attending 100 percent minority schools dropped from 39.7 percent in 1968 to 10.9 percent in 1972. In the South results were more dramatic. The number of blacks in 100 percent minority schools declined from 68 percent in 1968 to 9.2 percent in 1972. In the South, enrollment in 90 to 100 percent minority schools decreased from 70.4 percent to 33 percent from 1968 to 1970. The South now has the most integrated schools in the country. Only 53.7 percent of schools in the South have more than one half minority enrollment. Seventy-one percent of public schools in the North have more than one-half minority enrollment.[13]

In large part, this progress toward integration in the South has been the result of fairly aggressive use of sanctions under Title VI. Between 1966 and 1968, 188 school districts had federal funds terminated.[14] There is, however, a growing recognition that desegregation of northern school districts needs attention. Though segregation by law is not as readily apparent in the North as in the South, a more careful examination of segregation in the North discloses that a considerable amount of it was facilitated by law. HEW has not, however, strongly pressed for metro-politan school desegregation in large cities. Full desegregation is far from reality. Thirty-nine percent of black students still attend schools that are 90 to 100 percent minority schools. In the nation's 26 largest cities, 75.5 percent of black students attend such schools.[15]

The efforts of the Nixon Administration to enforce Title VI were quite deficient when compared to those of the Johnson Administration. As previously mentioned, between 1966 and 1968, 188 schools districts had funds terminated. From 1968 to 1973, only 15 school districts had federal funds terminated.[16] A federal court has also found that the Nixon Administration inadequately enforced Title VI. The court in Adam v. Richardson especially emphasized that HEW had failed to terminate federal funds to schools which had continued to discriminate.[17]

How the Carter Administration will use Title VI remains to be seen. The success of Title VI under the Johnson Administration suggests that this law can be a powerful tool to bring about school desegregation if the executive is committed to that policy goal.

Busing: At this point, the busing of school children from one area to another occupies the center stage in the policy debate over desegregation. The busing controversy in Boston is an excellent example of the power of federal judges to fashion a remedy for the correction of segregation. It also illustrates the problems associated with obtaining compliance with a policy and even assuring general governmental support for the policy.

In 1974, a Federal District Court determined that the Boston School Committee's policies had maintained a segregated school system. Among the policies found to promote segregation were the selection of school sites in segregated neighborhoods where the school population would almost completely come from those neighborhoods. Segregation was also found to result from the way school district lines were drawn and from the way faculty and staff were assigned.[18]

Strong opposition to these findings was anticipated. That opposition immediately materialized. The federal court persisted, however, and ordered the parties to submit desegregation plans. Such desegregation plans can only meet constitutional requirements if they are effective by making every effort to achieve maximum actual desegregation.[19]

If an adequate plan is not developed, the federal court may then devise a remedy. The Supreme Court gives the federal courts broad discretion in fashioning a remedy.[20] The judge fashioned a two-phase remedy. Phase I used redistricting and busing to desegregate 80 of the city's 200 schools. Phase II involved almost all the remaining schools. Desegregation was to be achieved by revising attendance zones, changing grade structures, building new schools, and closing old ones.[21]

The implementation of Phase I brought with it violence and boycotts on such a scale that it can only be compared with the roughest days of school desegregation in the South in the late 1950s and early 1960s. Throughout the violence, the Boston School Committee remained opposed to the desegregation order. Indeed, the Committee was so belligerent that the federal court placed the school system in partial receivership in order to implement Phase II of the Plan.[22]

Though Boston is an extreme case of busing and the opposition it engenders, it is important to note the findings of the U.S. Commission on Civil Rights in their investigation of desegregation efforts in Boston. First, the Commission pointed out that there was almost a total lack of support for the order among Boston's public and private leadership. Additionally, both the Mayor of Boston and President Ford made statements about the court order which encouraged opposition to school desegregation. The Boston School Committee, the entity legally responsible for the operation of the schools, persisted in its opposition to the court order to an incredible degree. Indeed, its lack of compliance was so great that the court was forced to take almost full responsibility for the implementation of the decision. The court even had to assume responsibility for formulating educational policy and directing administration. Yet, one effect of the order—an effect which has widely been ignored—is that the overwhelming number of schools in Boston desegregated without difficulty.[23]

The hostility to busing, however, and its lack of support among political leaders, brings its utility as a remedy into question. In spite of these problems, busing is likely to remain a remedy. As the U.S. Supreme Court recently said:[24]

> If school authorities fail in their affirmative obligations judicial authority may be invoked. Once a right and a violation have been shown, the scope of

a district court's equitable powers to remedy past wrongs is broad, for breadth and flexibility are inherent in equitable remedies.

The importance of bus transportation as a normal and accepted tool of educational policy is readily discernible in this and the companion case.

The Carter Administration's position on busing is unclear. HEW Secretary Califano has stated that busing should be used in some circumstances, though his department was limited in its efforts to use busing because of Congressional appropriations riders that limited its use by the Department.[25] Assistant Attorney General Drew Days has stated that busing should not be used on an extensive basis in a school district unless extensive need for a remedy of that sort could be shown.[26] In the 1976 Presidential campaign, both Ford and Carter expressed opposition to busing. Carter argued that the "only kids who get bused are poor children" and Ford claimed busing was not "the right way to get quality education."[27]

Even if the Carter Administration was strongly supportive of busing, its utility as a remedy has been quite limited by a recent Supreme Court decision which holds that inter-district busing between cities and suburbs can only be ordered if proof of state action in segregation is established for both the city and the suburb.[28] This decision will likely prohibit a great deal of busing between the large minority populations in central cities and the large white suburban populations.

Private Schools: One of the major ways segregationists avoided Brown v. Board of Education was through creation of segregated private schools. The belief was that if a school was private, there was no violation of the equal protection clause because there was no state action. Of course, in many cases there was state action. Some private schools received supplies from public schools. In at least one case, for example, enough desks and books were either thrown away or declared surplus by the public school to furnish all the classrooms in the private school with desks and the private school library with books. Frequently, states paid supplemental salary benefits to the teachers in the segregated private schools.[27]

Until recently, there has been no broad legal attack on the legality of segregation in private schools. However, in Runyon v. McCrary (1976), the Supreme Court relied on the Civil Rights Act of 1866 to remedy the segregation of such private schools (commonly known as "segregation academies"). The Court held that segregation in private schools which were open to whites in general violated the rights of blacks to make and enforce contracts.[30]

At this point, it seems unlikely that the decision will bring about widespread desegregation of the segregation academies. However, the decision does remain the greatest threat to the exclusionary policies of these institutions.

Funding of Schools: An area of considerable importance, but one which is not directly related to racial discrimination in education, has to do with the funding of public schools. Actually, this issue is more related to wealth discrimination than discrimination based on race, but since race is strongly correlated with wealth, it deserves some mention. In general, schools are funded through local property taxes. As a result, the amount of money available for education in the community depends to a great extent on the value of the property in the community. The argument has been made before the Supreme Court that this is a violation of the equal protection clause of the 14th Amendment. The Supreme court has rejected this argument since, the Court argues, a reasonable basis exists for using local property taxes to support schools and since this is not strictly a matter of racial discrimination.[31] Thus, poorer black communities may have less money to spend on education than richer white communities.

Most interestingly, the funding issue shows that some state supreme courts are willing to be quite innovative and are willing to take from the U.S. Supreme Court its traditional role as protector of the underdog. The New Jersey Supreme Court, for example, interpreted its state constitution to ban highly localized funding of schools.[32] Indeed, one of the most interesting developments in constitutional law in recent years is the greater reliance on state constitutions and state bills of rights to secure individual rights. In large part, this tendency is the result of a belief that the current Supreme Court is unwilling to secure individual rights in many areas.[33]

Preferential Admissions for Minorities: More and more professional schools are adopting special procedures which are designed to increase the number of minority students in their programs. Currently nearly 130 law schools maintain some sort of special admissions procedure which is designed to admit more minority students than would be admitted under regular procedures. More than 100 medical schools extend preferential treatment to minority applicants. On one hand, it is argued that these preferential programs are necessary to remedy past injustices. On the other, these preferential admissions practices are viewed as violating the equal protection clause of the Constitution.[34]

The Supreme Court had the opportunity to decide this question in 1974 in Defunis v. Odegaard.[35] Defunis applied to the University of Washington Law School and was denied admission. Defunis was white and challenged his denial on the ground that giving preference to minority candidates discriminated against him on the basis of his race. He argued that such a racial classification was in violation of the 14th Amendment. But the Court refused to decide the case on its merits, instead holding that the controversy was moot since Defunis had in the meantime been accepted to law school and had nearly completed his legal education.

The California Supreme Court recently addressed itself to the question of preferential admissions and did find a violation of equal protection.[36] The Supreme Court has just decided an appeal from the California court's decision. In the California case, Bakke v. Regents of the University of California (1976), an unsuccessful white medical school applicant challenged the minority admissions program of the medical school. He challenged the constitutionality of the program on 14th Amendment grounds. The court, while acknowledging that the issue was both sensitive and complex, concluded:[37]

that the program, as administered by the University violates the constitutional rights of non-minority applicants because it affords preference on the basis of race to persons who by the University's own standards are not as qualified for the study of medicine as non-minority applicants denied admission.

In dissent, Justice Tobriner argued:[38]

To date, this court has always been at the forefront in protecting the rights of minorities to participate fully in integrated governmental institutions. It is anamalous that the Fourteenth Amendment that served as the basis for the requirement that elementary and secondary schools could be *compelled* to integrate, should now be turned around to *forbid* graduate schools from voluntarily seeking that very objective.

The Carter Administration's position on preferential admissions was at first waffling. HEW Secretary Califano first insisted that preferential admissions were necessary policies in higher education. He said:[39]

How am I, as Secretary of H.E.W., ever going to find first-class black doctors, first-class black lawyers, first-class black scientists, first-class women scientists, if these people don't have a chance to get into the best places in the country?

Shortly after the publication of these remarks, Califano was subjected to severe criticism. In the wake of the outcry, he repudiated the remarks.[40] Later, however, the Carter Administration filed a brief opposing Bakke in his brief before the Supreme Court. Both Attorney General Bell and Secretary Califano praised the Court's decision in the Bakke case. Bell stated that "he and President Carter regarded the decision as 'a great gain for affirmative action.' "[41] Califano said the decision "strongly supports this nation's continuing effort to live up to its historic promise—to bring minorities and other disadvantaged groups into the mainstream of American society through admissions policies that recognize the importance of diverse, integrated educational institutions."[42]

Actually, the 5-4 decision, which both admitted Bakke to medical school and upheld the constitutionality of affirmative action programs not based on rigid quotas, can only be seen as a strong statement in favor of affirmative action by the most incurable optimist. The rather confusing opinion does, however, provide guidance for schools to develop affirmative action programs and does allow race to be a factor in admissions decisions if the purpose is to overcome past injustices rather than discriminate.[43]

PUBLIC ACCOMMODATIONS

Only a few years ago, the desegregation of public accommodations was an issue that captured the headlines. It was the subject matter for sit-ins, boycotts, legislation, and countless court decisions. Today the desegregation of public accommodations is taken for granted. In the 1950s and early 1960s, however, virtually every public accommodation in the South was segregated. In fact, the first modern civil rights demonstration was a direct result of segregation in a public conveyance. The Birmingham bus boycott began with the arrest of Rosa Parks who refused to vacate her seat in the white section of a bus.

Brown paved the way for elimination of segregated facilities. The legal attack on segregated facilities was primarily twofold in the early post-Brown era. One approach involved the interstate commerce clause. The argument was made that segregation in interstate travel impeded the free flow of commerce among the states. Since the states cannot unduly burden interstate commerce, these segregation ordinances could be struck down. The other attack on segregation in public accommodations involved the argument made in Brown that segregated facilities violated the 14th Amendment equal protection clause. These arguments were useful in attacking segregation where state action was involved, but were of little use where private segregation such as restaurant or hotel segregation was involved.[45]

In spite of a large number of court decisions resting on these two grounds, there was little desegregation in public accommodations prior to

1964. The lack of desegregation was not only the result of an inability to attack private discrimination, but also the result of a need to rely to a great extent on the courts for a case-by-case declaration of the illegality of public accommodation segregation.

As was the case with education, the 1964 Civil Rights Act probably was the most important direct cause of desegregation in public accommodations. There were other earlier provisions that had been of limited applicability. For example, hotels and motels were bound by common law to serve any travelers requesting a room, but this requirement was unenforced.[46] In 1961, the Interstate Commerce Commission promulgated new rules prohibiting discrimination on interstate buses.[47] The Civil Rights Act of 1875 could have been an important public accommodations act, but it was found unconstitutional by the Supreme Court in 1883. The act would have protected persons denied services by businesses open to the public. In 1883, the Supreme Court decided that the 14th Amendment was insufficient authority for passing the act. The Court argued that the 14th Amendment prohibited discrimination by the state, but had no effect on private discrimination. Private owners were thus not even required to follow the separate but equal rule of *Plessy.*[48]

With the 1964 Civil Rights Act, Congress took the responsibility for determining rights of access to public accommodations. Under the statute, full access is guaranteed to all businesses with an involvement in interstate commerce. The commerce clause was the authority for the enactment of the law, so it was unnecessary to prove state action in the discrimination before it could be outlawed. Private business could be covered by the act provided the business was engaged in interstate commerce. The 1964 act made it illegal for a business to refuse service to blacks if the business served people who traveled from state to state or if a substantial portion of the products used by the business traveled in interstate commerce.[49]

Private clubs are of course not public accommodations, and they are not covered under the act. Since private clubs are purely private, they may continue to discriminate. For the most part, however, businesses may not discriminate. Justice Black pointed out how rare it would probably be to find a business not engaged in interstate commerce.[50]

> I recognize too that some isolated and remote lunch room which sells only to local people and buys almost all its supplies in the locality may possibly be beyond the reach of the power of Congress to regulate commerce, just as such an establishment is not covered by the present [1964 Civil Rights] act.

Unlike most other civil rights areas, there was widespread compliance. For the most part, it was unnecessary to go through lengthy negotation and litigation strategies to secure compliance with this provision. Voluntary compliance was made possible because it was to the economic advantage of businesses to comply. They could gain customers by complying and would no longer have to suffer the loss of white customers by serving blacks, because they could claim the government was forcing them to serve blacks. In addition, it would appear that segregationists do not perceive desegregation in public accommodations as terribly serious. Contact with blacks in public accommodations is only passing and does not raise the specter of miscegenation as does integration in education or housing.[51]

VOTING RIGHTS

Voting, as education, is an area where there has been a considerable amount of law and litigation. As public accommodations, it is an area which was the subject of intense controversy only a few years ago, but now seems to be rather noncontroversial. Black voting is now widely accepted. Southern politicians vie for black votes. In many southern states, the black vote is large enough to make blacks a significant interest group in state and local politics. It is hard to believe that only a few years ago, the black vote in many southern states was minimal in spite of large black populations. The reasons for the small black vote in the South had to do with a number of factors, not the least of which was intimidation. Such intimidation kept blacks from voting. In addition, a number of laws were developed to hinder the black vote. Among the most important of these legal encumbrances were: the poll tax, the white primary, and registration requirements, especially the literacy test. The expansion of black voting in the South is directly related to Court decisions and laws designed to curb the practices which hindered voting by blacks.[52]

Intimidation: For years, coercion was a common way of preventing blacks from obtaining access to the ballot. Such coercion was both private and public. Private individuals could be safe from arrest if they tried to prevent blacks from voting. Violence, threats, and loss of employment and credit were not uncommon ways of maintaining racial purity at the ballot box. The state was also frequently involved in using intimidation to keep blacks from the polls. Baseless arrests were frequently used against persons active in the voting rights movement. Police would also place voting activists under intensive surveillance in an effort to frighten them and other blacks in the community.

One example of intimidation of black voters should be sufficient in illustrating the problem. In Walthall County, Mississippi, two blacks accompanied by a civil rights worker attempted to register to vote. The registrar made them leave the office and hit one of them with a pistol. After the assaulted youth stopped the bleeding, he reported the incident to the sheriff. Rather than arresting the registrar, the victim was arrested for disturbing the peace.[53]

Federal laws had prohibited the intimidation of voters, but they had generally not been used for many years. Among the civil rights acts which were aimed at ending intimidation of blacks was the 1866 Civil Rights Act. The act provided that blacks would have full and equal benefit of all laws and proceedings. The act also provided for criminal penalties against any person who under color of law denied their rights. The 1870 Civil Rights Act provided criminal punishment for conspiracies to violate rights secured by the Constitution. The 1871 Civil Rights Act established civil remedies for the deprivation of civil rights.[54]

The real protection against intimidation of black voters, came with increased organization of the black community in the 1960s, and a greatly increased federal presence and surveillance of voting procedures in the South. This increased federal involvement was brought about by the Civil Rights Acts of 1957, 1960, and especially 1965. These acts will be discussed in later sections.

The poll tax: One way to discourage exercise of the franchise is to tax the exercise of that right. The poll tax was originally used in a number of Southern states as a way to discourage black participation. The idea was that blacks would either be unable or unwilling to pay the tax. Of course, the poll tax also affected voting by whites, especially poor whites. As soon as the white primary and other methods of prohibiting participation by blacks came into existence, the poll tax became obsolete as a method of disfranchising blacks. Instead, it became a tax on voting by whites.

The poll tax was specifically upheld by the Supreme Court in 1937[56] and 1951.[57] Nevertheless, there was continued strong opposition to the tax, not only because it was believed to discriminate against blacks, but also because it was believed undemocratic to charge a fee for the right to vote. By 1964, only Alabama, Arkansas, Mississippi, Texas, and Virginia had a poll tax. The 24th Amendment to the Constitution banned the poll tax in federal elections. In 1966, the Supreme Court declared the poll tax unconstitutional in state elections as well. Justice Douglas wrote: "To introduce wealth or payment of a fee as a measure of a voter's qualifications is to introduce a capricious or irrelevant factor."[58]

The White Primary: Until very recently, victory in the Democratic Party primary was tantamount to election in the South. Since the 14th and 15th Amendment clearly prevented an automatic exclusion of blacks from elections, the idea was to exclude them from the Democratic

Party primary. Such an exclusion would effectively foreclose black participation in the Southern political process.[59]

Either through state law, state party rules, county party rules, or informal practice, the white primary eventually prevailed over the entire South.[60] It took a long and tortuous process of litigation to have the white primary finally held unconstitutional by the Supreme Court in 1944.

Among the major cases was Nixon v. Herndon (1927).[61] This case had to do with the Texas White Primary Law of 1924 which prevented participation of blacks in any Democratic primary election in Texas. The Supreme Court held that there was an obvious violation of the 14th Amendment. In response, Texas repealed the law and passed another law allowing the executive committee of every party to determine the membership of the party. Of course, the Democratic Party then decided to allow only whites to be eligible to vote in its primaries. Again the Supreme Court struck down the statute as violating the 14th Amendment on the grounds that the Party was an agent of the state.[62] Incredibly, Texas then repealed the statute which allowed for the executive committee of every party to determine membership. The Democratic Party, acting on its own authority, resolved that it was a private group which allowed whites only. At first, the Supreme Court accepted this reasoning on the grounds that there was no state action and therefore no 14th Amendment violation.[63] Finally, the white primary was reconsidered by the Supreme Court, and it was held unconstitutional. The Court held that the character of the duties of the party made it an agent of the state.[64]

Literacy tests and other registration devices: The most recently used methods of preventing blacks from having the opportunity to vote have had to do with using a variety of discriminatory rules of registration. The most well-known and probably the most effective of these rules was the literacy test.

The literacy test was part of a requirement that the prospective voter be able to read and write. Whites were rarely found illiterate, but blacks frequently were. In Alabama, six blacks with doctorates failed the literacy test.[65] One favorite ploy used in rejecting blacks in Virginia was to give the blacks a blank piece of paper and tell them to fill in the information required by the state constitution. Whites were assisted in filling out the forms.[66] Blacks also had to be precise in proving literacy. Missed dots on i's or failure to cross t's could mean rejection.[67]

Frequently grafted onto the literacy test was a requirement that the applicant be able to understand a provision of the state constitution. Whites typically were given simple sections of the constitution to interpret, and virtually any answer was viewed as acceptable. One white Mississippian, for example, was asked to interpret a section of the state constitution stating, "There shall be no imprisonment for debt." His response was, "I thank that a Neorger should have 2 years in collage befor voting because he don't under stand." Needless to say, that person was registered to vote. Blacks, on the other hand, were asked to interpret the most complex sections of the state constitution, and virtually no answer was ever viewed as acceptable.[68]

A good character test was still another registration tactic used in preventing blacks from voting. In order to register, an applicant had to have the testimony of registered voters that the applicant was of good character. Such evidence was fairly easily obtained by whites, but in communities where few or no blacks were registered, it was very difficult for black applicants to prove good character.

The two most serious problems having to do with securing voting rights for blacks by the 1950s and early 1960s were intimidation and the use of such registration devices as the literacy test. A series of laws were passed to combat these abuses. The first, the 1957 Civil Rights Act, was not very successful in securing voting rights for blacks. Its major provisions involved the creation of the U.S. Commission on Civil Rights and the elevation of the Civil Rights section in the Department of Justice to full division status. In addition, the act authorized suits by black plaintiffs. The ineffectiveness of the 1957 act led to the passage of the 1960 Civil Rights Act. This act required local registrars to maintain their records for two years. They also had to make them available for inspection by federal officials. More significantly, the Department of Justice could sue local registrars if there was a pattern of voting discrimination. If the court found the charge was true, the court could appoint referees to register voters.

The 1960 act was much stronger than the 1957 act. However, showing a pattern of voting discrimination was very difficult, and the litigation process was very drawn out. In 1965, an extraordinarily effective voting rights act was passed. Based on a rather complicated formula, the act barred literacy and other tests for voting in six Southern states. It also set up new criminal penalties for attempting to keep qualified persons from voting. Additionally, federal examiners were used to register voters. This act was remarkably successful. In the first two months after passage of the act, 110,000 blacks were registered by local officials and 56,000 by federal examiners. In 1970, the act was amended. Among the amendments was a provision eliminating literacy tests as a precondition for voting in all states. Among the provisions in the 1975 amendments was a permanent prohibition of literacy tests in all states.[70]

The lengthy process to gain the franchise for blacks was finally successful after 1965. In part, this was because the last major tool of resistance, the literacy test, was eliminated. In large part, however, black progress in voting was the result of a clear commitment by the national government, especially after 1960, to end discrimination in voting. In no other area was this commitment stronger. In no other area was a firmness in assuring rights more likely to lead to success. Voting discrimination is much easier to eliminate than other areas of discrimination. This is because the official mechanisms of registration are relatively visible and easy to control and manipulate to achieve a policy goal.[71] Certainly, the problem of discrimination in voting is much more readily soluble than discrimination in housing.

HOUSING

The nation is rapidly becoming a nation of black cities and white suburbs. One of the most serious problems facing this country is the desegregation of housing. There have been a number of court decisions and several laws aimed at eliminating segregation in housing, but the success of these laws in bringing about an integrated housing market has been limited. Discussion of housing policy aimed at ending discrimination on the basis of race will proceed by examining some of the earlier Supreme Court decisions which attempted to secure fair housing rights for blacks. We will then discuss statutes aimed at ending discrimination. Finally, there will be an analysis of recent and possible future developments in this area. **Supreme Court initiative in ending housing discrimination:** For many years, the NAACP tried to outlaw the use of racially restrictive covenants in deeds. A racially restrictive covenant prevented the sale of a house to persons of a specified race, usually blacks. It was not until 1948 that the enforcement of these covenants was held unconstitutional. Prior to that time, the covenants were considered private discrimination which could not be voided by the 14th Amendment. Shelly v. Kraemer,[72] however, held that state action was involved through the enforcement of these private covenants. Such an interpretation effectively destroyed the restrictive covenant as a tool to maintain segregated housing, since the covenant was of little value if it could not be enforced.

Actually, it now seems that the 1866 Civil Rights Act outlawed racial covenants. The act had largely been ignored for many years because of doubts about its constitutionality. In 1968, the Supreme Court essentially resurrected the act, which among other things outlawed racial discrimination in any conveyance of real or personal property.[73] The decision is quite remarkable when viewed within the political environment in which it was decided. The 1966 civil rights bill had failed passage largely because it contained an open housing provision which outlawed discrimination in *all* housing. In 1967, open housing remained controversial, but President Johnson submitted such a provision to Congress, and it became law shortly after the King assassination in 1968. The Court in Jones v. Alfred H. Mayer Co., thus alleviated any fear as to the constitutionality of open housing legislation and provided still another law with which segregation in housing could be attacked. Indeed, since the 1968 act provided for a gradual opening of the housing market and since it only provided limited coverage to owner sales of housing, the 1866 act was a much stronger position in favor of open housing.[74]

Courts are rather limited, of course, in the policies they can develop to open the housing market. A litigation strategy is slow, incremental, and fragmented from jurisdiction to jurisdiction. Thus, significant changes away from segregated housing had to come from Congress.

Congressional open housing efforts: Perhaps the most significant recent Congressional attack on racial discrimination in housing was Title VIII of the Civil Rights Act of 1968. Title VIII prohibits discrimination in the sale or rental of most housing. It is estimated that more than 80 percent of the nation's housing is covered under Title VIII. The law prohibits discrimination in the advertising, financing, or provision of real estate brokerage services in housing. The Department of Housing and Urban Development has overall responsibility for the Title. One of the problems with the law is that HUD is limited in its power to require compliance with the law. If it finds discrimination, HUD can only use informal methods such as conference, conciliation, and persuasion to bring about compliance. If these methods fail, HUD can refer the case to the Department of Justice; HUD does not have the power to institute litigation against parties found to be discriminating.[75]

Another law of considerable importance in the housing discrimination area is Title VI of the 1964 Civil Rights Act. Title VI prohibits discrimination by recipients of Federal assistance. HUD can ensure compliance with Title VI by withholding or withdrawing funds from offenders. Since much housing does receive federal funding, the law is quite significant. Essentially, much of this law incorporates the 1962 Executive Order 11063 which required nondiscrimination in federally subsidized and insured housing. Under the Executive Order, HUD had the power to defer funds, retract funds, or cancel contracts with those who failed to comply.[76]

There have been real problems in the enforcement of desegregation laws in housing, however. The U.S. Commission on Civil Rights has found that a variety of governmental agencies,[77] have taken some positive steps, but the steps have not gone nearly far enough to have a major impact on racial, ethnic, and sex discrimination. The positive actions they have taken have generally been either superficial or incomplete and have had little impact on the country's serious housing discrimination problem.

In addition, the Commission found that HUD's efforts to provide guidance to other agencies regarding enforcement of Title VIII had been inadequate. Finally, the Commission found that the informal methods which must be used to bring about compliance with Title VIII have been inadequate in bringing about prompt compliance with the law.[78]

The Location of Housing Projects: One device that has been used to maintain segregation in spite of the law is to locate housing, including public housing, in such a way that it maintains racial segregation. Thus, a public housing project may be built and ostensibly have a nondiscriminatory admissions policy, but its location can bring about a segregated result. A housing project in center city Chicago, for example, is going to be black and bring about no change in segregated housing patterns. If such a project were built in the suburbs, it would desegregate housing patterns. Largely because it would desegregate housing patterns, there has been a tendency not to build this kind of housing in the white suburbs.

After a decade of litigation, the Supreme Court recently reached a decision which could have significant implications for site segregation in public housing. In response to a finding of site segregation, a lower court ordered that public housing should be constructed in scattered sites so that state action would not maintain segregated housing patterns. Hills v. Gautreaux (1976) confirmed the propriety of that order with a holding that a metropolitan area remedy was not necessarily impermissible.[79]

Gautreaux exposes the white suburbs to the possibility of integrated public housing. Unfortunately, such litigation can also produce a ban on the construction of public housing. Thus, if housing can not be built in such a way as to maintain segregated housing patterns, then it is possible that no public housing may be built.[80]

President Carter has waffled regarding programs for low-income, scatter-site housing. As a candidate, when Carter was asked about low-income, scatter-site housing, he responded:[81]

> I see nothing wrong with ethnic purity being maintained. I would not force a racial integration of a neighborhood by government action. But I would not permit discrimination against a family moving into a neighborhood.

The statement was, of course, frequently retracted. Subsequently Carter spoke approvingly of Gautreaux, saying that collusion between the community and HUD to exclude low-income housing could not be permitted.[82]

Zoning: Obviously, a zoning ordinance which said that no blacks could live in an area would be patently unconstitutional. Such an ordinance would be a clear violation of the 14th Amendment. It is doubtful, however, that an ordinance would be found unconstitutional if it essentially said that inexpensive housing could not be built in an area. Yet the effect of both ordinances is roughly the same. No blacks could move into the neighborhood under the first ordinance, and it is unlikely that many blacks could afford to move into a neighborhood with the second ordinance.

The U.S. Commission on Civil Rights believes that zoning is a major tool in efforts to perpetuate residential segregation. Fiscal zoning which is used to attract establishments that will pay large property taxes can prohibit low and moderate income housing. Large lot zoning limits housing construction to lots of several acres. This zoning can prevent persons, including minorities, from purchasing lots. Minimum house size requirements can raise the cost of housing to a point prohibitive to most minorities.[83]

The Supreme Court has generally been unwilling to consider the constitutionality of these land use practices. When the Court has considered such land use restrictions, it has generally upheld the ordinances as having no racially discriminatory purpose.[84]

The refusal of the Court to enter the zoning controversy has not been universally followed by other courts. One of the broadest attempts to eliminate zoning as a way to exclude poor people from a community occurred in New Jersey. The New Jersey Supreme Court in NAACP v. Mt. Laurel struck down municipal zoning ordinances that excluded poor or moderate income families through apartment prohibitions and large lot restrictions.[85] Though the court has recently backtracked,[86] in Mt. Laurel it did rule that every municipality in the state had to provide for a fair share of the surrounding region's housing requirements.

At this point, it is unclear exactly what Mt. Laurel and subsequent cases will really mean to minorities and lower income persons. Nor is it likely that most other states will undergo drastic zoning revisions. Thus, in most states zoning remains an effective minority exclusion mechanism.

EMPLOYMENT

The employment problems of blacks are vividly summed up in the expression, "Last hired and first fired." It has become an American tradition that blacks have greater difficulty in getting jobs than whites, that they are paid less than whites, and that they suffer more from dismissals and lay-offs than whites.[87] A number of policies are now being pursued to correct these abuses and thus to change the tradition of discrimination to one of equality. There are a number of laws and regulations that are important in ensuring racial equality in employment. Perhaps the most important of these efforts is the 1964 Civil Rights Act. **The 1964 Civil Rights Act:** The 1964 act makes if unlawful:[88]

> to fail or refuse to hire or discharge any individual, or otherwise to discriminate against any individual with respect to his compensation, terms, conditions, or privileges of employement, because of such individual's race.

The act created the Equal Employment Opportunity Commission as the agency responsible for the enforcement of this provision. The employers subject to the act and to the jurisdiction of EEOC are those with 15 or more employees who are in an industry affecting commerce. Thus, a substantial number of persons in the work force are covered under the act.[89]

EEOC's primary responsibilities are to investigate charges of discrimination, to attempt to resolve disputes through conciliation, and to file lawsuits where conciliatory efforts have failed. EEOC has other major responsibilities such as prescribing record keeping for those covered by the act, but its major responsibility remains the processing and resolution of charges of discrimination occurring under Title VII of the act.[90]

EEOC's enforcement of the 1964 Civil Rights Act has not been without problems. The major problems, according to the U.S. Commission on Civil Rights, include understaffing which has resulted in delays in filing lawsuits as well as a low overall number of lawsuits filed. EEOC has data on the racial, ethnic, and sex makeup of the work force, but it makes little use of this data. In addition, even though state and local governments are now covered by the act, EEOC has failed to attach any priority to the processing of complaints having to do with state and local government employment discrimination. There has been little effort made to enforce actions against employment agencies, in spite of these agencies being a major source of job applicants for many employers. Investigations conducted by EEOC have generally been inadequate for purposes of litigation. Its conciliation agreements may or may not be effective. Compliance with the agreements has not been systematically monitored. The commission has had problems with a backlog of cases. The result is a lengthy delay from receipt of a complaint until its resolution. Such problems as these have severely limited the effectiveness of the 1964 Act.[91]

Government Contracts: Executive orders issued by Presidents Kennedy and Johnson forbade employment discrimination by those businesses with which the government had contracts. The orders basically required that contractors make two commitments. One is that the employer will not discriminate on the basis of race, color, sex, religion, or national origin. The second requirement is that the employer must undertake affirmative action in order to ensure equal employment opportunities in all personnel practices in the company. There must be affirmative action even in those company facilities which are not working on federal contracts. Additionally, contractors must obtain similar commitments from subcontractors.[92]

The greatest problem in actually securing an end to discrimination in employment dealing with federal contracts is a lack of effort to secure compliance. One large problem is that the office responsible for enforcing these orders, the Office of Federal Contract Compliance, allocates only a small fraction of its budget and staff to compliance activities. The office has not seen to it that sanctions were imposed for violations of executive orders. Sanctions include termination of existing contracts, debarment from additional contracts, prohibition from being awarded a contract, or withholding contract payments. However, in the first 10 years of the contract compliance program, there has been minimal sanction enforcement. For example, only nine companies have been debarred from future contracts, and contract payments have never been stopped.[93]

Employment in the federal government: The federal government is the nation's largest employer. Thus, elimination of discrimination in federal employment opens up significant employment opportunities for blacks. In 1961, President Kennedy issued Executive Order 10925. The order established the Committee on Equal Employment Opportunity. It also announced an emphasis on affirmative action, an active effort to hire minorities, rather than simply a policy of nondiscrimination. In 1965 President Johnson reaffirmed this concern for eliminating discrimination in federal employment. He ordered the Civil Service Commission to "supervise and provide leadership and guidance in the conduct of equal employment opportunity progress . . . within the executive departments and agencies." In 1969, President Nixon ordered that each agency should be responsible for developing an affirmative action program.[94]

Taken at face value, these orders are most impressive. Yet there has been a problem in securing compliance. In 1971, Congressional committees found a lack of representation of minorities in the federal bureaucracy. The committees found two reasons for the lack of progress in this area. One reason was that the Civil Service Commission allowed federal agencies to judge themselves. The second reason was that the Civil

Service Commission's selection standards discriminated against minorities. Indeed, as a result of these findings, Congress extended Title VII to cover federal employment in 1972.[95]

Preferential employment: Much of what has already been mentioned in the discussion of preferential admissions in education is also relevant to a discussion of preferential employment practices. Though the Bakke decision specifically applies to education, its reasoning seems readily applicable to employment. Thus, the case will prove a major foundation for developing law in the area of preferential hiring practices.

There is considerable debate as to how employment discrimination can be eliminated. One argument is that the only way to assure employment of blacks is to develop quota systems. Quotas would require that the work force contain fixed numbers or percentages of minority members. Another way to ensure nondiscrimination is to establish goals and timetables for employing minorities. Such an effort would not be a quota, but it would ensure an aggressive effort by employers to recruit minorities. The third major argument is that there should be neither quotas nor aggressive minority hiring efforts. Instead, the effort should solely be directed at nondiscrimination. Believers in such a policy would argue that any position other than neutrality, any position other than one which allows all races to compete for jobs on the basis of ability alone, would establish race as a reason for employment. They would argue that if race were a governmentally approved reason for employment, the 14th Amendment equal protection clause would be violated.

Again, the Carter Administration showed indecision in this area early in the Administration. Secretary of Health, Education, and Welfare Califano has stated:[96]

I noticed in recruiting that if you press people hard enough to cast the net wide enough, you find [minority and female] people.

Mr. Califano also stated that though he had thought for a long time that quotas would not work, his experiences at *Newsweek* magazine and his work with employees at the El Paso Natural Gas Company had changed his mind. He apparently changed his mind a second time, since he later claimed he does not support preferential employment.[97]

SEX DISCRIMINATION

Employment

Rights of blacks compared to women: Many of the laws aimed at securing employment rights for blacks in employment are also applicable to women. The 1964 Civil Rights Act, for example, prohibits discrimination on the basis of sex as well as on the basis of race. Additionally, since preferential employment programs are relevant to women as well as to blacks, developments in this area which were previously discussed in relation to blacks are also applicable to women. The most significant difference between policies aimed at securing rights for blacks in employment and policies aimed at securing rights for women is a constitutional one. The 14th Amendment is a major protection for blacks in employment and other areas. Racial classifications as they relate to hiring are suspect. A racial classification is subject to special scrutiny by the courts, and it is most unusual for such a classification to survive that special scrutiny. Though some Justices on the Supreme Court also view sex as a suspect classification, this has never been shared by a majority of the Court. Thus, an equal protection attack on a sex classification has more difficulty being accepted by the Court. A sex classification is not presumed unconstitutional as a racial classification would be. One of the major effects of the proposed Equal Rights Amendment would be to make a sex classification as suspect as a racial one. Since the Equal Rights Amendment is a most significant attempt to remedy discrimination, though there is doubt it will be approved, it will be discussed in a separate section.

1964 Civil Rights Act: Overt discrimination on the basis of sex is outlawed by Title VII of the 1964 Civil Rights Act. Such discrimination includes such actions as restricting women from certain jobs or to certain jobs. Other forms of illegal overt discrimination include maintaining separate employment registers, seniority lists, or unions. There can be no difference in hiring or promotion qualifications for men and women, nor can there be different benefits or retirement conditions.[98]

Neutral criteria can also affect one sex disproportionately and disadvantageously. Many of these criteria are illegal under Title VII. For example, minimum height and weight requirements are not overtly discriminatory. In fact, however, they do discriminate against women, since women tend to be smaller and lighter than men. When there is no business necessity for height and weight requirements, these criteria have been held to violate the 1964 act. Similarly, restrictions of family medical coverage to "heads of household" is illegal under Title VII since it has a disadvantageous impact on women.[99]

In general, there are only two defenses under the 1964 Civil Rights Act to discriminate against women. A neutral practice that has discriminatory effect can be justified, if it can be demonstrated that the practice is a business necessity. That is, the practice must substantially contribute to the safe and efficient operation of the business. Essentially,

324 Nationalizing Government

the determination of what is a business necessity is a balancing process. A judgment is made about the strength of the business need balanced against the impact of that business practice on the affected class. The other defense against a charge of discrimination under the 1964 act is a claim that the discrimination is the result of a classification which is a bona fide occupational qualification reasonably necessary for the operation of the business. It seems unlikely that there will be many cases where sex is a characteristic necessary for normal operation of a business. Perhaps such a bona fide occupational qualification would be a requirement that an attendant in a men's room be a male.[100]

To a considerable extent, enforcement of the 1964 act has suffered the same problems, whether sex or racial discrimination is involved. There has been a problem with obtaining investigations sufficient for litigation, great delay, and lack of follow-up after settlement. Similar enforcement problems are found in federal employment and in federal contracts. That is, the laws governing sex discrimination are similar to laws regarding discrimination against blacks, and enforcement problems are just as serious.[101]

The Equal Pay Act: In 1963, the Equal Pay Act was signed by President Kennedy. Basically, the act requires that women and men receive equal pay for equal work. Salary differentials that are solely based on sex are prohibited by the act. The act is applicable to a large number of employees and covers at least 72 million workers.[102]

The Department of Labor has responsibility for enforcement of the Equal Pay Act. In enforcing the act, the Department has three major powers. (1) It may investigate possible violations of the law. (2) It may conciliate and negotiate a settlement. (3) It may litigate if the Department's efforts to secure compliance prove a failure.[103]

There have been some notable efforts related to enforcement of the Equal Pay Act. One of these cases involved AT&T. It was found that AT&T traditionally placed women in sex-segregated positions and gave women lower base salaries than men. When women were promoted to higher positions, their salaries remained lower than the salaries paid to men. To correct this disparity, AT&T agreed to pay $7.5 million in back wages to 3,000 female employees.[104]

The 1964 Civil Rights Act is, of course, closely related to the Equal Pay Act. The 1964 act is not limited to sex discrimination. In addition, the 1964 act applies to employers who refuse to hire a person because of sex. The Equal Pay Act only applies to those who are employed. Finally, whereas the Equal Pay Act requires only payment of back wages, the 1964 act requires actions to remedy past discrimination. Such remedies may include changing seniority systems or establishing goals for hiring or promoting employees who were discriminated against.[105]

"Protective" legislation: In the late 19th and early 20th century, a number of states passed laws designed to protect women from being exploited in the labor market. Basically, this legislation falls into four categories: (1) limitations on the number of hours women may work; (2) laws setting a minimum wage for women; (3) regulation of working conditions for women such as maximum weight lifting restrictions; and (4) occupational restrictions which excluded women from hazardous or "unladylike" occupations. It is true that much of this legislation prohibits the exploitation of female workers, but it does not prohibit the exploitation of male workers. The result is, of course, no real change in working conditions other than the exclusion of women from the labor market. Some of these laws, for example, prohibit women from working at night. The result is that women are excluded from employment that involves night work. Other legislation requires that women be paid a premium for overtime work. The result is that women are not given overtime work or are not given jobs that may require overtime work.[106]

The Equal Employment Opportunity Commission regulations are opposed to such protective legislation on the grounds that they have ceased to be relevant to our economy and are in violation of the 1964 Civil Rights Act. In spite of this ruling, much protective legislation remains. While such legislation is not allowed by Title VII, a considerable number of women employees are not covered by Title VII, and many states retain protective legislation for employees.[107]

Pregnancy and Employment: In recent years, there has been a considerable amount of litigation as to whether a woman can be forced to take a leave of absence because she is pregnant. The Supreme Court has addressed this question in Cleveland Board of Education v. LaFleur (1974). In LaFleur, the Supreme Court examined the constitutionality of a school board policy which required that pregnant teachers stop teaching five months before they were to give birth. The Supreme Court held that while this regulation was a good faith attempt to protect the teacher, it could not be constitutional because it "employ(ed) irrebuttable presumptions that unduly penalize a female teacher for deciding to bear a child."[108]

The Equal Employment Opportunity Commission has also established a policy that exclusion from employment on the basis of pregnancy violates Title VII. These policies are most useful in protecting the rights of pregnant women, but it is important to keep in mind Roxanne Conlin's statement, "This country is one of the very few nations that makes no provision for continued support to women who must cease employment temporarily because of pregnancy."[109]

Credit: At this point, it seems appropriate to briefly mention policies aimed at eliminating credit problems of women. Credit and employment are of course strongly related. It is difficult to go into business without credit. It is also difficult to enjoy a reasonable standard of living, if one relies only upon the immediate income from employment.

Women have had significant problems in obtaining credit. The National Commission on Consumer Finance found five credit problem areas. (1) Single women have had trouble obtaining credit—much more trouble than single men. (2) Upon marriage, women must frequently reapply for credit, often in their husband's name. (3) Married women have difficulty getting credit in their own name. (4) A wife's income frequently is not counted in a credit application. (5) Divorced, separated, or widowed women have trouble establishing credit.[110]

The most significant effort against credit discrimination is the Equal Credit Opportunity Act. It prohibits creditors from discriminating against any applicant on the basis of sex or marital status. In addition, in 1974 the Small Business Act was amended to prohibit discrimination on the basis of sex or marital status against an applicant or recipient of assistance from the Small Business Administration. Other agencies such as the Federal Home Loan Bank Board, the Federal Housing Administration, and the Veteran's Administration have also issued guidelines prohibiting credit discrimination.[111]

SEX AND GOVERNMENT BENEFITS

Supreme Court decisions: Governments have traditionally made sexual classifications in their distribution of governmental benefits. Beginning in 1971, the Supreme Court began to strike down these classifications. Among the earlier cases was Reed v. Reed (1971).[112] This case struck down a law which gave males preference in administering the estates of relatives. The Court decided the issue on 14th Amendment equal protection grounds, but the Court did not declare sex to be a "suspect" category. Such a declaration would make it very difficult for any sex-based classification to be constitutional. Instead, the court held that:[113]

> To give a mandatory preference to members of either sex over members of the other merely to accomplish the elimination of hearings on the merits is to make the very kind of arbitrary legislative choice forbidden by the equal protection clause of the Fourteenth Amendment.

The case is clearly a victory for women's rights, but since sex is not declared to be a suspect category, many sex-based classifications may have a reasonable legislative purpose and thus be constitutional.

Another case, Frontiero v. Richardson (1973) comes very close to a declaration that a sex-based classification is a suspect classification.[114] The question in Frontiero was whether a female member of the armed forces could claim her husband as a dependent in order to obtain increased quarters allowances and medical benefits. The law allowed a wife to be claimed as a dependent without reference to whether she was dependent on him for support. A husband could only be claimed as a dependent if he depended upon her for over one-half of his support.

In an opinion written by Justice Brennan and joined by Justices Douglas, White, and Marshall, this statement was made:[115]

> At the outset, appellants contend that classifications based upon sex, like classifications based upon race, alienage, and national origin, are inherently suspect and therefore be subjected to close judicial scrutiny. We agree.

Note, however, that only four of the justices agreed with this opinion. Thus, the theory that a sex-based classification is a suspect one was not established as precedent. In a brief concurring opinion, Justice Stewart argued that the statute worked an invidious discrimination which was in violation of the Constitution, but he used a less stringent test to make his determination.[116] Justice Rehnquist was the only justice to dissent,[117] but in their concurring opinion, Justices Powell, Burger, and Blackmun argued that Brennan's opinion showed no respect for legislative processes. This opinion argued that by declaring sex classifications suspect, Brennan was trying to make a major political decision through judicial action. Powell wrote:[118]

> The Equal Rights Amendment, which if adopted will resolve the substance of this precise question. . . . By acting prematurely and unnecessarily, as I view it, the Court has assumed a decisional responsibility at the very time when state legislatures, functioning within the traditional democratic process, are debating the proposed Amendment.

Other cases which illustrate Court action to strike down sex classifications include Stanley v. Illinois (1972).[119] In Stanley, the Court considered the constitutionality of an Illinois statute which presumed male parents of illegitimate children were unfit to obtain custody of their children. Such sex stereotyping was declared unconstitutional as violative of due process. In Stanton v. Stanton (1975), the Court considered the constitutionality of a Utah law that for purposes of child support extended the period of minority for males to age 21 and for females to age 18.[120] The Court found nothing rational in the statute which it considered was based on a sexual stereotype that women did not need the same degree of education as males. Similarly, in Weinberger v. Wiesenfeld (1975), the Court held that Social Security payments of benefits to the wife, but not the husband, of a deceased worker with minor children violated the Constitution.[121] The Court argued that the due process clause of the Fifth Amendment was violated because it "unjustifiably discriminated against women wage-earners."[122] However, in Geduldig v. Aiello (1974), the Court held that it was not an invidious discrimination for the California disability insurance system to exclude the disability accompanying normal pregnancy and childbirth.[123] Justices Brennan, Douglas, and Marshall argued that if the Court had used the proper equal protection test, the Court would have found the classification unconstitutional. They continued to argue, though remaining in the minority, that sex classifications must be considered suspect.

Disparities in Governmental benefits: There are a number of areas where governmental benefits are applied to men and women differently. Perhaps the most significant area of disparity involves the Social Security program. A major part of the Social Security system rests on a breadwinner-homemaker dichotomy. The Social Security program was, of course, primarily developed in the 1930s when the traditional family was more common. The system is not reflective of today's family relationships, however.[124]

It is possible for a retired couple who have both been employed to receive less in benefits than a family in which only the husband was employed. Such a disparity is possible, even if total family earnings are the same. Additionally, a disabled widow can only draw on her husband's account if she is over 50. A disabled worker can draw at any age. A woman who gets a divorce has no claim to Social Security benefits under her husband's account unless she was married to him for at least 20 years. A housewife can receive no Social Security benefits in her own account, even after a lifetime of housework. Such treatment of women in the Social Security program has led to calls for reforms in the program, reforms which will consider the claims of women.[125]

FAMILY LAW

Marriage: Historically, a married woman had no legal rights or remedies. Indeed, the condition of married women served as a model for the development of the legal system of slavery. Marriage under English Common Law was as follows: [126]

> By marriage, the husband and wife are one person in law: that is, the very being or legal existence of the woman is suspended during the marriage, or at least is incorporated and consolidated into that of the husband: under whose wing, protection, and *cover,* she performs every thing; and is therefore called in our law-french a *feme-covert* . . . or under the protection and influence of her husband, her *baron,* or lord; and her condition during her marriage is called her *coverture.* Upon this principle, of an union of person in husband and wife, depend almost all the legal rights, duties, and disabilities, that either of them acquire by the marriage. . . . For this reason, a man cannot grant any thing to his wife, or enter into covenant with her for the grant would be to suppose her separate existence; and to covenant with her, would be only to covenant with himself.

As might be expected, the struggle to secure rights for married women has been a struggle to escape from the common law heritage.

One policy aimed at securing rights for married women were the married women's property acts. The first was enacted in Mississippi in 1839. Such acts have been adopted in all American jurisdictions. Basically, these acts are efforts to redress the property and contract relations between wives and husbands. In general, the laws grant to women such rights as the right to contract, the right to sue and be sued, to manage and control property obtained prior to marriage, the right to work without a husband's permission, and the right to retain earnings from employment.[127]

The laws vary from state to state, and they have exemptions and exceptions which have limited their power to emancipate women. Additionally, court interpretations of the acts have sometimes been quite narrow.[128] For example, in some circumstances a woman may have trouble retaining her maiden name. Traditionally, the husband determines domicile. A wife must follow and live with her husband where ever he goes. Incredibly, not until 1971 did the Supreme Court strike down an Arizona law which revoked a woman's driver's license if her husband did not pay a judgment debt for negligent driving. Only in 1970 did Florida repeal a law that required a woman to prove "character, habits, education, and mental capacity for business" before she could do business in the state.[129]

Many states give major control over family property to the husband. Basically, 42 states are common law marital property states. In these states, property acquisitions during a marriage belong to the spouse who acquired the property. Frequently, the husband is a wage earner, while the wife's household work is uncompensated. Eight states are community property states. Roughly, this means that the marriage relationship is seen as a kind of partnership. Each spouse is seen as a contributor to the enterprise, and so theoretically each spouse shares equally in acquired property. Actually, community property states frequently give the husband the power to manage the property.[130]

Theoretically, in exchange for the control over the family wealth which the husband has, he has the obligation to support his wife. However, it is quite difficult to enforce this obligation. There is practically no remedy that can enforce a woman's right to support except personal persuasiveness. Essentially, the homemaker must rely on the husband's benevolence. Unfortunately, if a husband does fail to support his wife, appeals to his good nature may be of no avail.[131] McGuire v. McGuire (1953), a Nebraska Supreme Court case, shows the reluctance of the state to interfere with an ongoing marriage.[132] In McGuire, a lower court ordered the husband to provide support to his wife. That order included a requirement for repairs, appliances, a new car, travel expenses for his wife, and an allowance for her. Mrs. McGuire had lived with her husband for over 30 years and had contributed equally with Mr. McGuire to the operation of the family farm, but he controlled the assets. Mr. McGuire was, it seems, a remarkably frugal man, and age had possibly made him more frugal. In spite of being quite prosperous, he forced his wife to live with him in pitiful conditions. His wife had little money, little clothing, an ancient car, and a primitive home. Yet the Nebraska Supreme Court reversed the lower court order on the grounds of noninterference in an ongoing relationship. The Court said, "The living standards are a matter of concern to the household, and not for the courts to determine, even though the husband's attitude toward his wife, according to his wealth and circumstances, leaves little to be said in his behalf."[133].

The ending of marriage: One of the most controversial women's rights issues has to do with the ending of marriage. In particular, it is argued that alimony payments discriminate against men in that as the marriage is ended, the responsibilities of the husband to support the wife should also end. This may be an appealing argument, but it fails to consider that alimony is only awarded in a small number of cases. Indeed, some states do not provide for any permanent alimony. Other states allow for alimony to be paid to either the husband or the wife. Receipt of alimony is determined by the needs of the dependent spouse and the ability of the wage earning spouse to pay. Some states, however, do continue to limit alimony to the wife.[134]

Child support payments are also a serious problem area. A divorced woman with children is frequently in serious economic difficulty. One study indicates that one year after divorce, slightly more than one-third of fathers were in full compliance with child support orders. The degree of compliance with child support orders decreases with every year from the divorce. It may prove difficult for the divorced woman with children to obtain a job and adequately care for the children. Indeed, if she has been out of the job market while she was a housewife, she may find it impossible to obtain a job.[135]

Child custody is still another problem area in family law. The mother traditionally is given custody of the children because of a sex stereotype that the mother is more loving and that children need a mother's love. One court denied custody to a fit male parent saying, "(T)here is but a twilight zone between a mother's love and the atmosphere of heaven."[136]

At least, divorce policies are changing. It is becoming easier to obtain a divorce. Frequently, it is unnecessary to prove fault on the part of one of the parties in order to obtain a divorce. No longer is it necessary, in most cases, for one of the parties to be demeaned by being labeled the "guilty party." Less promising, more unchanging policies regarding ending of marriage continue in the other areas such as child support and custody, frequently to the detriment of women.

Personal Rights: A major controversy regarding women's rights has involved the degree to which one's rights of privacy outweigh the state's police power. The balancing of interests today is over abortion, but the right of a person to use birth control devices was, until recently, the major policy question. In Griswold v. Connecticut (1965), the Supreme Court held a Connecticut statute prohibiting the use or distribution of birth control devices unconstitutional.[137] The Court held such laws, at least insofar as they applied to married persons, interfere with Constitutionally protected privacy rights. In 1972, Eisenstadt v. Baird essentially extended Griswold to unmarried persons.[138] Justice Burger in dissent strongly argued as did Justices Black and Stewart in Griswold that such general rights to privacy had very tenuous constitutional moorings.[139]

In Roe v. Wade (1973), right to privacy arguments were again used, this time to strike down criminal abortion legislation.[140] The specific challenge in Roe involved a Texas abortion statute which made abortion a crime, except when it was done for the purpose of saving the life of the mother. The Supreme Court examined the reasons for the enactment of criminal abortion statutes and found them lacking. Basically, the Court found there were three possible reasons for criminal abortion laws. One was that such laws would discourage illicit sexual conduct. Texas did not use this argument, and it is clear the Court would not have seriously considered this reason. The second reason for such abortion laws was that abortion endangered the life of the mother. Such a reason was at one time a valid one, though current medical technology has advanced to the point that a first trimester abortion is safer than full-term delivery. The third reason for such legislation is the protection of prenatal life. Most of the Court's opinion was addressed to this point.

While the Court admitted that there was no explicit mention of any right to privacy in the Constitution, the Court argued that the Constitution did implicitly recognize a right of personal privacy. Further, the Court argued that the right was broad enough to encompass a woman's decision as to whether or not to terminate her pregnancy. The Court further argued that a fetus' right to life was not specifically guaranteed by the Constitution. Thus, as there was no absolute right of a fetus to life, it would not outweigh a woman's right of privacy.

The Court did hold, however, there was no absolute right to an abortion. Rather, the Court divided pregnancy into three stages. The point in pregnancy where the right to privacy is strongest and therefore more free from state control is the first trimester. During the second trimester, there can be stricter state regulation of abortion since the danger to the health of the mother is greater during this period. In the third trimester, the fetus is presumed viable, and the state may regulate abortion to protect human life.

The decision has been described at some length because it is probably the most controversial instance of policy-making by the Court in the women's right area. There was a very strong reaction to the decision. Such reaction even included a number of proposed constitutional amendments which are designed to reverse Roe v. Wade and return criminal abortion statutes to constitutional status. An example of these proposed constitutional amendments is one introduced by Senator Jesse Helms, an amendment which is the most complete repudiation of Roe. The Helms amendment provides that the moment of fertilization shall be the point that establishes constitutional status as a person and protects that person's right to life. Other proposed amendments would simply allow states to regulate or prohibit abortion if they so desire.[141]

The abortion issue was a troubling one for both major candidates in the 1976 election. Both Carter and Ford expressed personal opposition to abortion. President Ford supported a constitutional amendment which would give the states regulatory power over abortion. Carter opposed the amendment, but also opposed the use of federal funds to pay for abortion.[142] No doubt, the abortion issue will remain an important one, but there is little evidence that *Roe* will be completely changed or evaded by the executive, Congress, Court, or by the ratification of an anti-abortion amendment. At this point, it seems most unlikely that any of these anti-abortion proposals will become part of the Constitution. The most effective limitation on Roe may be a limited one, such as the prohibition of the use of federal funds for abortions, as is being debated in Congress as of this writing.

The Equal Rights Amendment: The previous discussion should indicate that policies designed to ensure equality for women have proved only partly effective. Nor is it likely that sex classifications will become suspect for purposes of equal protection analysis. The proposed Equal Rights Amendment may, however, prove to be an extremely powerful tool to end sex discrimination. Given a national commitment to equal rights for women, the Equal Rights Amendment could prove as useful to the cause of women's rights as the 14th Amendment was to black rights in the 1950s and 1960s.

The substance of the Amendment states quite simply "equality of rights under the law shall not be denied or abridged by the United States or by any state on account of sex." Behind that wording lies a long and arduous political controversy. Nevertheless, it is quite unclear whether the Equal Rights Amendment will finally become a constitutional amendment. Only three states are currently needed to approve the amendment. For the Equal Rights Amendment to become a part of the constitution, 38 states must ratify it; to date 35 have. Three states which have approved the amendment have voted to rescind that approval. However, this is of questionable legality. The amendment would rather dramatically change existing laws.[143] For example, protective labor laws which are still in effect and which are discriminatory or restrictive would be nullified. If possible, laws which extend a real benefit to women would also be extended to men, but if this would cause serious industrial disruption, the laws would be nullified. The basic principle would be that the sexes must be treated equally whether the equalization required extension or nullification of the laws. In family relationships, the amendment would require that state laws consider marriage an economic partnership. Laws such as those which give the husband management of community property would be invalidated.[144]

Obviously, the Equal Rights Amendment will not solve all problems relating to discrimination against women. Private sex discrimination, for example, is not covered. Yet the Amendment can broaden rights for women by providing "a simple, direct, and comprehensive method to assure permanent, enforceable, and complete equity for women."[145] Additionally, the Amendment can provide an impetus for further legislation to assure sexual equality. It can also provide security in preventing the return of sexist policies as law.[146] The Amendment should prove to be a valuable tool to be used to achieve rights for women.

SUMMARY AND CONCLUSIONS

This chapter has attempted to examine a variety of policies in many issue areas relating to the civil rights of blacks and women. For the most part, we have examined policies aimed at assuring racial and sexual equality, which we believe is a national goal. However, there has also been some discussion of policies which have now or have had discriminatory impact. There has also been an attempt to discuss some of the problems and limitations associated with each of these policies as well as an attempt to point to future policy developments.

At this point, perhaps, a few very general conclusions are in order. It seems clear that policy-making in the civil rights area is a very incremental process. Civil liberties are guaranteed by a gradual development of a variety of piecemeal laws aimed at various segments of perceived violations. "Freedom now" is a fine ideal, but it has little relevance in the actual policy process where freedom is obtained through a series of slow, halting, partial steps.

The gradual development of civil rights policies toward blacks and women is in part explained by the difficulty in solving the problems of discrimination in this society. In part, it is because of hostility to changing the status quo. Equality is not a concept without controversy. Changes interfere with human prejudices, traditions, and economic demands. Compliance with laws is a function of the benefits of noncompliance being outweighed by the benefits of compliance. It is thus important to note that a strong national commitment to the enforcement of laws promoting racial and sexual equality is needed before compliance occurs.

It is also important to note that the courts have played a central role in civil rights policy-making. In part, this is because the courts have become havens for oppresed groups in our society. The other branches are more responsive to established, more powerful groups who can influence elections and provide funds for campaigns. Protecting the rights of the weakest groups in society to a considerable degree has become the responsibility of the least politically responsive branch, the courts. It should be noted that even though courts have been quite innovative in civil rights policies, courts are rather weak institutions when it comes to securing widespread compliance with a policy. Generally, it is only when there is strong support for a court decision that the chances seem good for achieving a court-created policy goal. Courts are, of course, quite limited as policy makers. They cannot define the policy-making environment. Rather, they must wait for the case within which policy is to be made. Courts can not seek out cases. The case must be presented to them. Court decisions ultimately turn on the specific facts of the case, and the decision is limited to the parties in the case. Decisions are made only on a case-by-case basis. One could readily argue that there is no better mechanism than the courts for assuring avoidance and evasion of decisions as well as delay in implementing decisions. If that decision is to be effective, the other branches—legislatures through law-making authority and executives through enforcement authority—must support a court decision which promotes new civil rights policies. On the whole, executives and legislatures are better equipped to make broad policies since they suffer none of the institutional limitations of courts.

Finally, courts are nevertheless important as innovators and interpreters of policy. It may well be that the major significance of courts in the policy process is how they serve an agenda-setting function. That is, courts can take issues ignored or abused by other branches and frame those issues in ways that demand action and in ways that establish those issues as ones that are in need of immediate attention.

NOTES

1. Brown v. Board of Education, 347 U.S. 483 (1954).
2. Id. at 495.
3. Plessy v. Ferguson, 163 U.S. 537 (1896).
4. Henry Abraham, *Freedom and the Court* (New York: Oxford University Press, 1977): 362-368.
5. Brown v. Board of Education, 349 U.S. 294 (1955).
6. Alexander v. Holmes County Board of Education, 396 U.S. 19 (1969).
7. Jack Peltason, *Fifty-Eight Lonely Men* (New York: Harcourt, Brace, and World, 1961).
8. Abraham: 376-378.
9. President Eisenhower's views on southern segregationists were: "These are not bad people. All they are concerned about is to see that their sweet little girls are not required to sit in school alongside some big overgrown Negroes." See, "Ike's Private View of Desegregation," *Newsweek* (March 21, 1977): 14.
10. Anthony M. Champagne, "The Segregation Academy and the Law," *Journal of Negro Education* (Winter, 1973), pp. 58-60.
11. Perhaps the best discussion of agenda-setting by courts is Richard Lehne, "Complex Justice: Courts, Agenda-Setting and School Finance," paper presented at the 1976 annual meeting of the American Political Science Association, September 2-5, 1976.
12. U.S., Commission on Civil Rights, *The Federal Civil Rights Enforcement Effort—1974: To Ensure Equal Educational Opportunity* (U.S. Government, 1975) (Hereafter cited as *Equal Educational Opportunity*); Frederick M. Wirt, *Politics of Southern Equality* (Chicago: Aldine Publishing, 1970): 186-188; Harrell R. Rodgers and Charles S. Bullock, *Law and Social Change* (New York: McGraw-Hill, 1972):81-82.
13. These statistics are taken from *Equal Educational Opportunity*: 49-51.
14. Ibid., 128.
15. Ibid., 49-51.
16. Ibid., 128; Wirt, 189-194; Rodgers and Bullock, 88-97.

17. 480 F.2nd 1159 (D.C. Cir., 1973). See also, *Equal Educational Opportunity:* 4, 102-109.

18. U.S., Commission on Civil Rights, *Desegregating the Boston Public Schools: A Crisis in Civic Responsibility* (U.S. Government, 1975): xviii. (Hereafter cited as *Desegregating the Boston Public Schools.*)

19. Ibid., xx; Green v. New Kent County School Board, 391 U.S. 430 (1968).

20. See, Swann v. Charlotte Mecklenburg Board of Education, 402 U.S. 1 (1971).

21. *Desegregating the Boston Public Schools:* xxi; U.S., Commission on Civil Rights, *Fulfilling the Letter and Spirit of the Law* (U.S. Government, 1976): 17-23. (Hereafter cited as *Letter and Spirit of Law.*)

22. *Letter and Spirit of Law:* 18-19.

23. Ibid., 23.

24. Swann v. Charlotte Mecklenburg Board of Education, 402 U.S. (1971): at 15 and 29.

25. Nancy Hicks, "Califano Says Quotas Are Necessary to Reduce Bias in Jobs and Schools," *New York Times* (March 18, 1977): 1, 16.

26. "Carter's Rights Lawyer, a Black, Says He'll Limit Demand for Busing," *New York Times* (March 18, 1977): A17.

27. Henry A. Plotkin, "Issues in the 1976 Presidential Campaign" in Marlene M. Pomper (ed.), *The Election of 1976* (New York: David McKay, 1977): 44.

28. Milliken v. Bradley, 418 U.S. 717 (1974).

29. An extensive discussion of segregated private schools can be found in Champagne: 58-66.

30. Runyon v. McCrary, 96 S.Ct. 2586 (1976). See also, Craig S. Cooley, "Constitutional Law—Civil Rights—Private Schools Prohibited from Excluding Qualified Children Solely Because They are Black," *University of Richmond Law Review* (Fall, 1976): 221-228.

31. For example, San Antonio Independent School District v. Rodriguez, 411 U.S. 1 (1973).

32. Robinson v. Cahill, 62 N.J. 473 (1973).

33. Donald E. Wilkes, "The New Federalism in Criminal Procedure: State Court Evasion of the Burger Court," *Kentucky Law Journal* (1973-1974): 421-451; Donald E. Wilkes, "More on the New Federalism in Criminal Procedure," *Kentucky Law Journal* (1974-1975): 873-894.

34. John D. Peterson, "Constitutional Law: Affirmative Action—Does it Afford Equal Protection Under Law?", *Washburn Law Journal* (Fall, 1976): 190-196.

35. DeFunis v. Odegaard, 416 U.S. 312 (1974).

36. Bakke v. Regents of University of California, 553 P. 2d 1152 (1976).

37. Id. at 1155.

38. Id. at 1191.

39. Hicks, 1.

40. David Bird, "Califano Concedes Error in Advocating Job Quotas," *New York Times* (April, 1977) 1, 27.

41. Linda Greenhouse, "Bell Hails Decision," *New York Times* (June 29, 1978): 1.

42. Ibid., 23.

43. Warren Weaver, Jr., "High Court Backs Some Affirmative Action by Colleges, But Orders Bakke Admitted," *New York Times* (June 29, 1978) 1, 22.

44. Rodgers and Bullock, 56.

45. Ibid., 57-63.

46. Herman Pritchett, *The American Constitution* (New York: McGraw-Hill Book Company, 1977): 484-485.

47. Marion A. Wright, "Public Accommodations—The Sit-in Movement: Progress Report and Prognosis," in Donald B. King and Charles W. Quick (eds.), *Legal Aspects of the Civil Rights Movement* (Detroit: Wayne State University Press, 1965): 88.

48. Pritchett, 485-486 and see, *Civil Rights Cases,* 109 U.S. 3 (1883).

49. Rodgers and Bullock, 62.

50. *Heart of Atlanta Motel v. U.S.,* 379 U.S. 241 at 275 (1964).

51. Rodgers and Bullock, 63-66.

52. See generally, Ibid., 15-54; Wirt, 49-172; Abraham, 393-408; Charles V. Hamilton, *The Bench and the Ballot* (New York: Oxford University Press, 1973).

53. Rodgers and Bullock, 18-21.

54. William B. Lockhart, et al, *Constitutional Rights and Liberties* (St. Paul, West Publishing, 1975): 1166-1169.

55. V.O. Key, *Southern Politics* (New York: Vintage Books, 1949): 579.

56. Breedlove v. Suttles, 302 U.S. 277 (1937).

57. Butler v. Thompson, 341 U.S. 937 (1951).

58. Abraham, 400. See also, Harper v. Virginia State Board of Elections, 383 U.S. 668 (1966).

59. Key, 619-643; Abraham, 396-400; Hamilton, 23-31.

60. Key, 620.

61. Nixon v. Herndon, 273 U.S. 536 (1927).

62. Nixon v. Condon, 286 U.S. 73 (1932).

63. Grovey v. Townsend, 295 U.S. 45 (1935).

64. Smith v. Allwright, 321 U.S. 649 (1944).

65. Rodgers and Bullock, 21-23.

66. Key, 564 and see generally, 555-577.

67. Rodgers and Bullock, 21-23.

68. Ibid.

69. Ibid.

70. Excellent discussions of civil rights laws regarding voting are found in Ibid., 15-54; Abraham, 402-408; Wirt, 49-86; and Hamilton, 41-69 and 228-250.

71. Especially, Rodgers and Bullock, 15-54.

72. Shelley v. Kraemer, 334 U.S. 1 (1948). See also, Clement E. Vose, *Caucasians Only: The Supreme Court, the NAACP, and the Restrictive Covenant Cases* (Berkeley: University of California Press, 1959).

73. Jones v. Alfred H. Mayer Co., 392 U.S. 409 (1968).

74. Abraham, 392-393.

75. U.S., Commission on Civil Rights, *The Federal Civil Rights Enforcement Effort—1964: To Provide . . . for Fair Housing* (U.S. Government, 1975): 2-5. (Hereafter cited as *Fair Housing.*)

76. Ibid., 6.

77. Ibid., 238.

78. Ibid.

79. Hills v. Gautreaux, 96 S.Ct. 1538 (1976).

80. See, Henry W. McGee, "Illusion and Contradiction in the Quest for a Desegreagated Metropolis," *University of Illinois Law Forum* (Winter, 1976): 948-1011.

81. As quoted in McGee, 952.

82. Ibid.

83. *Fair Housing,* 7-8.

84. See generally, McGee, 948-1011.

85. NAACP v. Mount Laurel, 67 N.J. 151 (1975). See also, Jerome G. Rose, "Fair Share Housing Allocation Plancs: Which Formula Will Pacify the Contentious Suburbs,"

Urban Law Annual (1976): 3-20; Jerome G. Rose, "The Trickle Before the Deluge from Mount Laurel,," *Real Estate Law Journal* (Summer, 1976): 69-79.

86. Martin Waldron, "Court Reinforces Zoning Powers in New Jersey," *New York Times* (March 24, 1977): 1, B2.

87. Rodgers and Bullock, 113-117.

88. See, U.S., Commission on Civil Rights, *The Federal Civil Rights Enforcement Effort—1974: To Eliminate Employment Discrimination* (U.S. Government, 1975): 473 (Hereafter cited as *To Eliminate Employment Discrimination.*)

89. Ibid., 473-474.

90. Ibid., 474-476.

91. Ibid., 643-646.

92. Ibid., 230-240.

93. Ibid., 631-637 and 298-299.

94. Ibid., 11-12.

95. Ibid., 12-14.

96. Hicks, 1, 16.

97. Bird, 1, 27.

98. Roxanne Barton Conlin, "Equal Protection Versus Equal Rights Amendment— Where Are We Now?", *Drake Law Review* (Winter, 1975): 296-300.

99. Ibid.

100. Ibid.; Leo Kanowitz, *Sex Roles in Law and Society* (Albuquerque: University of New Mexico Press, 1973): 349-361.

101. *To Eliminate Employment Discrimination,* 617-673.

102. Ibid., 403-406.

103. Ibid., 407-417.

104. Ibid., 549-555.

105. Ibid., 416-417.

106. Conlin, 294-300; Kanowitz, 362-388.

107. Conlin, 298.

108. Cleveland Board of Education v. LaFleur, 414 U.S. 632, 647 (1974).

109. Conlin, 304.

110. Donna Dunkelburger Beck, "Equal Credit: You Can Get There From Here—The Equal Credit Opportunity Act," *North Dakota Law Review* (Winter, 1975): 382-383.

111. Ibid., 381.

112. Reed v. Reed, 404 U.S. 71 (1971).

113. Id. at 76.

114. Frontiero v. Richardson, 411 U.S. 677 (1973).

115. Id. at 682.

116. Id. at 691.

117. Id. at 691.

118. Id. at 692.

119. Stanley v. Illinois, 92 S. Ct. 1208 (1972).

120. Stanton v. Stanton, 421 U.S. 7 (1975).

121. Weinberger v. Wiesenfeld, 420 U.S. 636 (1975).

122. Id. at 636.

123. Geduldig v. Aiello, 417 U.S. 484 (1974).

124. Conlin, 280.

125. Ibid., 280-281.

126. Blackstone as quoted in Ibid., 261.

127. Kanowitz, 207-209.

128. Ibid.

129. Conlin, 270-275; and see, Perez v. Campbell, 402 U.S. 637 (1971).

130. Kanowitz, 210-220.

131. Ibid., 225-232.

132. McGuire v. McGuire, 157 Neb. 226 (1953).

133. Id. at 233.

134. Conlin, 285-289; Kanowitz, 267-283.

135. Ibid.

136. Conlin, 289-292; and see, Horst v. McLain, 466 S.W. 2d 187 (Mo. 1971) at 189.

137. Griswold v. Connecticut, 381 U.S. 479 (1965).

138. Eisenstadt v. Baird, 405 U.S. 438 (1972).

139. Id. at 472.

140. Roe v. Wade, 410 U.S. 113 (1973).

141. Jill Laurie Goodman and Alice M. Price, "Abortion and the Constitution: An Examination of the Proposed Anti-Abortion Amendments," *Rutgers-Camden Law Journal* (Summer, 1976): 671-697.

142. Plotkin, 45-46.

143. Lawrence Van Gelden, "After the Early Rush, the E.R.A. is Now at a Standstill," *New York Times* (April 1, 1977): A 16.

144. Conlin, 329-333.

145. Ibid., 330-331.

146. Ibid., 329-333.

11.

CONTROLLING CRIME:
THE LIMITS OF DETERRENCE

BENJAMIN GINSBERG

Cornell University

Since 1968, the federal government has invested several billion dollars in programs designed to reduce crime. With federal support, state and local officials have hired more police and prosecutors, purchased sophisticated crime-fighting equipment, and devised a variety of novel crime-control techniques.

Federal and state officials have generally conceived the control of crime to be a problem of social engineering rather than social theory. The theory is thought to be obvious. Criminals are deterred by fear of arrest and punishment. The capacity of the police to make arrests and of the courts to mete out punishments is in some measure a function of their manpower and technical and financial resources. It is assumed, therefore, that supplying the police and courts with more personnel, more money, and better hardware increases their ability to arrest and punish law breakers. In turn, an increased risk of arrest and punishment is expected to discourage more potential offenders and reduce the incidence of crime.

During the past several years, crime rates have shown considerable fluctuation but no substantial decline.[1] There is, moreover, no evidence to suggest that the changes in crime rates that have occurred have resulted from federal crime control policies. This outcome is not particularly surprising. Perhaps the reasons that this is not surprising are similar to those that seemed constantly to confound the strategists who sought to apply theories of deterrence in Vietnam. The theory is flawless, except when it is actually applied in practice. Its effectiveness in practice depends mainly upon conditions neither anticipated by the theory nor affected by its application.

There is little doubt that the risk of punishment can deter crime. At the same time, however, law enforcement agencies can do little to increase the average risk of punishment beyond some minimal level. However much money, manpower, and hardware are available to the police and courts, only a small proportion of all crimes are amenable to solution after the fact. However diligent the efforts of law enforcement agencies to prevent crimes before their commission, the number of opportunities for criminal activity is so large that police patrols almost literally would be required to be everywhere at once to significantly restrict the criminal's sphere of operation.

Selective law enforcement efforts *can* increase the chance of arrest and punishment associated with particular crimes or types of crime. By limiting investigative work to especially serious violations, as is indeed their practice, the police might discourage some forms of criminal activity. Extraordinarily heavy police patrols might protect a particular area.[2] But the major consequence of selective enforcement is probably to displace criminal activity from some potential targets to others. Indeed, in some circumstances, selective efforts to deter crime can have the paradoxical result of increasing the crime rate, as criminals attempt to compensate for the effects of law enforcement.

As we shall see, the consequences of deterrence in practice may depend less upon the resources available to the police than upon the alternatives available to potential criminals. For very good reasons, the only substantial reduction in crime rates in recent American history appears to have been associated with public policies which expanded the opportunity *not* to commit crimes rather than with programs aimed at the apprehension and punishment of more criminals.

Let us, first, briefly examine recent federal policies aimed at increasing the deterrence of crime. Second, let us consider the implications of deterrence in theory and practice. Then, let us consider the conditions under which crime rates might actually be reduced. The deterrence of crime, as we shall see, might well require programs which increase the "deterrability" of potential criminals.

CRIME CONTROL AS A NATIONAL POLICY

The primary responsibility for criminal law and its enforcement in the United States has historically been borne by states, municipalities, and other units of local government. During the 1960s, however, crime became an important national political issue. Civil disorder and dramatic increases in crime rates, especially in urban areas, precipitated considerable public alarm and seemed to suggest that local governments no longer had the capacity to control criminal activity.

The Crime Control and Safe Streets Act of 1968 represented a major expansion of federal involvement in law enforcement.[3] Secondary provisions of the act authorized the increased use of wiretaps in federal and state investigations, imposed some restrictions on the shipment and sale of firearms, and attempted to negate allegedly permissive Supreme Court decisions relating to the interrogation and arraignment of suspects, confessions, and the admissibility of identifications obtained in police lineups. The most important provisions of the Act, though, were contained in Title I. Finding that the "high incidence of crime" threatened the "peace, security and general welfare of the nation," Congress authorized the creation of the Law Enforcement Assistance Administration (LEAA) and allocated over $100 million to be used in fiscal 1968-1969 and $300 million for use in 1970 to help augment state and local law enforcement efforts. During each ensuing year, levels of funding were substantially increased so that, by 1976, LEAA had spent over $5 billion in support of crime control programs.

Neither the 1968 Act nor the subsequent pieces of federal crime control legislation passed in 1970 and 1973 were designed to reduce state and local primacy in the area of law enforcement. Rather, the federal government sought to supply resources and technical advice while states and localities continued to "establish their own priorities, devise specific action programs, and allocate LEAA funds according to their own plans."[4] Though LEAA directly administers a number of programs in law enforcement research, education, and statistical services, the bulk of its funds are awarded to the states in the form of block grants. The states, in turn, are responsible for distributing money to counties and municipalities. Additional funds are granted by LEAA to support specific state and local projects. On the whole, the advent of federal involvement in law enforcement has simply meant that more money is available to states and localities to pursue their own law enforcement aims.

Local governments have used federal funds to upgrade police manpower and equipment, to increase and streamline court facilities, and to improve correctional programs. Several states have expanded social services for prison inmates and developed new training programs for correctional personnel. A number of states and localities have introduced computerized administration and management systems to enable their courts to process cases more efficiently. One county in Nevada, for example, developed a computerized method of monitoring workload trends, juror usage rates, pre-trial detentions, and workflow bottlenecks.[5] Baltimore, Maryland introduced a "Criminal court status information system," designed to reduce case backlogs and delays in processing defendants and also, to prepare automatically subpoenas, summonses, and attorney notices.[6]

The principle beneficiaries of federal support have been local police departments. LEAA funds have not only enabled them to hire more officers, but have also given them the means with which to purchase sophisticated new equipment. For example, the Indianapolis, Indiana police force used LEAA funds to organize a "residential burglary tactical task force," a "business burglary tactical task force," a "tactical air patrol (helicopter)," an "electronic burglary control system," and an "automated burglary prediction management system."[7] The University City, Missouri, police force purchased a "police response early warning system" which, at a cost of only $3,400 federal dollars, was said to have the capacity to anticipate requirements for police services and, in addition, to be able to "predict and control crime by discovering its physical, social, and economic causes.[8] The New Orleans police department, apparently not as convinced as its counterparts of the merits of complex crime-fighting technology, used some of its federal money to buy a tank.[9]

DETERRENCE

State and local governments have obviously been quite innovative in attempting to apply computer technology and modern management techniques to the deterrence of crime. Yet, however exotic the technology used to implement it, the principle of deterrence is quite uncomplicated. To attempt to deter means simply to seek to increase the risk or effort involved in committing a crime (or any other act) in relation to the potential gain from its successful commission. Gain may take any form— an economist would use the term "utility income"—but in the vast majority of cases, crimes are undertaken for financial gain. Individuals may seek financial or other gain through criminal means for any number of reasons. Some criminals are presumably motivated purely by greed, some by necessity; some criminals may lack moral training, others possibly are oriented to norms other than those embodied in the criminal law.[10] There are many "causes" of crime, and not all are fully understood.

The possibility of deterring crime, however, does not require a full understanding of its causes. Deterrence requires only that individuals who contemplate the commission of criminal acts have the capacity to understand the risks involved. And there is every reason to believe that most individuals have this capacity. A large number of studies have indicated that as the risk of punishment associated with the commission of any given form of crime increases, the subsequent incidence of that form of crime diminishes.[11] If law enforcement agencies were able to increase the average certainty that the commission of any criminal act would lead to the arrest and punishment of its perpetrator, there is little doubt that the overall incidence of crime would be diminished. The problem is that, although the police and courts can, indeed, increase the risks associated with particular forms of crime, they cannot substantially increase the risk of punishment associated with crime *generally,* even with the help of modern technology and the support of LEAA's massive resources. Let us see why.

THE COURTS

It might seem plausible to assume that better staffed and more efficient courts would help to increase the certainty of punishment for law breakers and, thus, yield an increased measure of deterrence. No doubt, it is true that some criminals go free because of inefficient, overcrowded courts. But, there is still some question about the precise extent to which improvements in the courts can influence the deterrence of crime.

First, a sizable proportion of those individuals arrested by the police already receive some form of punishment from the courts.[12] Obviously, not every individual who is arrested is subsequently convicted and punished. But this is not entirely the result of poor court management techniques or lack of qualified prosecutors. Some individuals are not convicted because of lack of sufficient evidence. Some proportion of those individuals who are not convicted and punished may well be innocent. Unless the courts were willing to overlook the distinction between innocence and guilt or not worry overly much about evidence, it is not clear that the rate of conviction of those arrested by the police could be substantially increased. This is not "only" a question of legal ethics. For the purpose of deterrence, it is just as important that the innocent go free as it is that the guilty receive punishment. The reason is obvious—the greater the likelihood that an innocent person will be convicted and punished, the less the incentive to remain innocent. Overly zealous prosecutors and judges are as much in violation of the principle of deterrence as overly clement ones.

Whether or not they can increase conviction rates, courts, in conjunction with state legislatures, might presumably increase the average severity of sentence for those convicted. Most available evidence, however, suggests that merely increasing the severity of punishments has little deterrent effect in and of itself.[13] Harsh penalties can, in fact, diminish the certainty of punishment by making judges and juries more reluctant to convict. Longer prison terms do, of course, prevent convicted criminals from committing more crimes for a longer period of time, but there is considerable doubt about whether this has any substantial effect on the overall rate.[14]

Quite possibly, despite these difficulties, better staffed and better managed courts might have some impact on the likelihood of punishment for criminals arrested by the police. Unfortunately, however, court reforms cannot have much effect upon the more serious gap between crime and punishment in the United States—the rather minimal likelihood that the perpetrator of a crime will actually be arrested by the police.

THE POLICE

Only a small proportion of the crimes committed each year result in the arrest of a perpetrator.[15] The federal response to this problem has been to help states and localities increase police manpower and resources. However, there is little reason to believe that, even with increased manpower and "automated burglary prediction management systems," the police can solve a greater proportion of crimes or arrest a larger percentage of perpetrators. Though it is often charged that the police are hampered largely by permissive court decisions, the problem is much more fundamental.

To begin with, the police are not present during the commission of most crimes. Generally, solution of a crime and arrest of the perpetrator requires an investigation after the fact. Because of the huge number of crimes annually reported to the police, most investigations are cursory. With the exception of very serious or notorious crimes, the police seldom do more than go through the motions of interviewing the victim and filing a report.[16] Presumably, with increased manpower and resources, the police would have the capacity to mount serious; investigations of a larger proportion of the crimes reported to them. But two problems remain. First, full-scale investigations can be extremely costly. The search for Patricia Hearst, for example, is reported to have cost several million dollars. The efforts of the New York City police to apprehend the "44 caliber killer" cost many hundreds of thousands of dollars and occupied the attention of a special task force of 300 police officers over a period of many months.[17] Obviously, this much money and attention could not be devoted to more than a handful of investigations, no matter how large the resources of a police department. Second, few crimes *can* be solved by the police after the fact, unless a witness is willing to come forward and is able to identify the perpetrator. In the absence of a willing witness, the police seldom have sufficient evidence or information to justify undertaking a costly and probably futile investigation.[18] Since there is little reason to believe that increased police resources would have much effect upon witnesses' memories or sense of civic duty, more manpower and resources for the police do not necessarily translate into an increased rate of success for police investigations.

Even though the police may have considerable difficulty solving crimes after the fact, under most circumstances they are likely to arrest the perpetrator if they actually see the crime committed.[19] For this rather obvious reason, most individuals prefer to avoid committing crimes in the presence of the police. Since the risk presented by the presence of the police is a much more obvious and effective deterrent than the risk that a crime will be solved after the fact, the police devote the bulk of their resources to patrol activities, which are designed to maximize their presence. In principle, the greater the size of the police force and the more efficient its patrol routines, the greater the chance that the police will appear at a moment that is, to say the least, embarrassing to the criminal.[20]

Unfortunately, no matter how large and efficient a police force, the average chance that a police officer will be present at the commission of a crime is remote. The reason is simple. The number of opportunities for the commission of crimes is exceedingly large if, indeed, not infinite. Every item of property defines an opportunity for a property crime. The opportunity for auto theft, for example, is defined by the number of automobiles in service. The opportunity for house burglaries is defined by the number of private homes.[21] This conception of criminal opportunity should be especially familiar to residents of New York City who have always assumed, correctly as it turns out, that everything movable is available to be stolen. Given the exceedingly large number of criminal opportunities —indeed, more are produced in factories and made available in stores each day—the average chance that the police will be present at the commission of a crime must be remote, whatever the size and efficiency of the police force.

Obviously, just as the police do not attempt to investigate all crimes, they do not attempt to patrol all the sites that offer opportunities for the commission of crimes. Of necessity, they are selective in their allocation of patrol resources. The police may patrol some neighborhoods more heavily than others. They may concentrate on places of business relative to homes or vice versa. Since criminals presumably prefer to avoid police patrols, heavy concentrations of police resources in selected areas, or on selected types of crimes can displace criminal activity to other areas or other forms of crime. For example, if police officers ride every subway train, quite likely crimes that might have been committed on subways are instead committed elsewhere. Or, if one public park is very heavily patrolled, then presumably the availability of that park as a site for criminal activity is diminished and whatever crimes might have been committed there must be committed elsewhere.

Just as the police normally investigate only the most serious crimes, their patrol activities are normally focused upon the most important criminal opportunities—those which involve the greatest cost to society and potential gain to the criminal. Cost to society can, of course, be defined in any number of ways. Obviously political influence can yield more police protection. Sometimes cost to society is defined by the newspapers' concerns of the moment. On the whole, however, in both investigative and patrol activities, the police focus more on crimes against persons than on crimes against property. A murder, for example, is more likely to receive a serious investigation than a burglary. And, within the general category of property crimes, both the investigation and patrol efforts of the police are generally related to the value of the property in question. Not only are bank robberies more likely to be investigated than house burglaries, but banks are also more likely to receive the attention of police patrols than are private homes.[22]

On the whole, we might expect that the effect of such police efforts is to increase the risk associated with the most serious crimes and thus to diminish the average value to criminals of opportunities for crime. To take a simple example, the average value of criminal opportunities is reduced if the actions of the police increase the level of risk associated with bank robberies relative to the risk involved in the commission of house burglaries. The expected value to criminals of the more lucrative bank robbery is diminished by the increased risk, while the relatively safer house burglary is likely to be a less lucrative crime.

The availability of an almost infinite number of opportunities for crime means that the police cannot hope to deter law breakers by increasing the *average risk* associated with criminal opportunities, generally. But nevertheless, if the police can diminish the *average value* of criminal opportunities, then it might at least appear that federal and state efforts to augment police manpower and resources could have the effect of reducing crime. Presumably, any diminution of the average value of criminal opportunities also reduces the attractiveness of unlawful means of obtaining income relative to legitimate means. Thus, in principle, the lower the average reward that can be obtained through the commission of a crime, the more it is likely that potential criminals will seek legitimate alternatives. In short, crime will have been deterred. Unfortunately, however, there is one confounding factor.

WHO CAN DETERRENCE DETER?

Whether police activities which reduce the value of criminal opportunities can also reduce the incidence of crime depends largely upon the alternatives available to potential criminals. If the rewards that can be obtained from illicit activities are reduced and potential criminals have legitimate, alternative means of obtaining income available to them, then we might indeed expect crime to be deterred. If, on the other hand, legitimate alternatives are not available to potential criminals, then there is little reason to believe that diminution of the value of criminal opportunities can deter crime. Increased law enforcement efforts aimed at a criminal population with few or unattractive legitimate alternatives to crime may simply induce law breakers to minimize the risk of arrest by shifting from more to less lucrative crimes. Indeed, to compensate for their loss of income, criminals might even commit a larger number of crimes. This would be particularly true in the case of criminals whose income requirements were relatively fixed—heroin addicts, for example.

As a very preliminary test of these possibilities, I sought to determine the impact of changes in police manpower upon robbery rates in 56 American cities during one relatively short period of time. Though the results must be considered more illustrative than conclusive, they are still quite striking.

First, for each city, the amount of change in police strength between the 1958-1959 average and the 1960-1961 average was calculated.[23] Second, again for each city, the change in the number of robberies reported to the police was calculated for the ensuing time period; in this instance, the difference between the 1960-1961 and the 1962-1963 averages.[24] Third, we sought to compare changes in police strength with changes in robbery rates, controlling for the availability of legitimate alternative opportunities to potential criminals. Again, our suspicion was that increases in police strength could effectively reduce the crime rate only to the extent that legitimate alternative means of obtaining income were available to potential criminals.

Obviously, there is no easy way to measure and control for the distribution of legitimate opportunities in these 56 cities. One reasonable assumption, however, is that blacks are deprived, relative to whites, of access to legitimate means of obtaining income. Therefore, we used race as a surrogate for opportunity and controlled for the racial composition of the 56 cities in 1960.

Table 11.1 compares changes in the incidence of robbery among cities classified as more or less than 20 percent black and as having changed the size of their police forces more or less than the average of a four percent increase during this period.

Table 11.1. Deterrence and Opportunity in 56 American Cities.

Change in police strenth	Change in robberies reported during ensuing time period
Cities less than 20% black—police strength relatively increased	−.02 (16)*
Cities less than 20% black—police strength relatively decreased	+.22 (23)
Cities more than 20% black—police strength relatively increased	+.18 (9)
Cities more than 20% black—police strength relatively decreased	+.04 (8)

Mean change in robberies reported, all cities, +.12.
Mean change in police strength, all cities, +.04.

For cities less than 20% black, the correlation between change in police strength and change in robberies reported is −.44 (N = 39, the regression of change in police on change in robbery is significant at the .01 level, F = 8.72).

For cities more than 20% black, the correlation between change in police strength and change in robberies reported is +.73 (N = 17, the regression of change in police on change in robbery is significant at the .01 level, F = 16.66).

*The number of cases is given in parenthesis.

These data suggest, again assuming that race is a reasonable surrogate for opportunity, that the impact of changes in police strength upon the crime rate does vary with the availability of legitimate alternatives. In cities with only relatively small black populations, there is an inverse relationship between changes in the size of the police force and changes in the robbery rate. As the size of the police force increases, the robbery rate diminishes. This inverse relationship is certainly consistent with the principle of deterrence.

In cities with relatively large black populations, on the other hand, changes in police strength appear, if anything, to be directly associated with ensuing changes in the robbery rate. Not only does the incidence of robbery fail to diminish with increases in police manpower, but instead the robbery rate seems actually to increase as police strength is augmented.

This direct relationship between changes in police strength and ensuing changes in the incidence of robbery may, of course, be spurious. Obviously, a much more extensive and sophisticated analysis of the data over a considerably longer period of time would be necessary to even begin to confirm the validity of the finding.[25] But, at the same time, the finding is quite consistent with the argument that the effectiveness of deterrence depends upon the availability of legitimate alternatives for potential law breakers.

Assuming that such alternatives are more readily available to white than to black potential criminals, our data seem to suggest that those with few alternatives cannot easily be deterred. Indeed, the positive association between changes in police strength and the robbery rate in cities with large black populations could well support our earlier observation to the effect that, without legitimate alternatives, criminals might conceivably compensate for increased law enforcement efforts by committing more crimes. In any event, the data suggest that programs aimed at reducing the incidence of crime simply through increased law enforcement efforts are unlikely to deter a large group of potential criminals.

MAKING CRIMINALS "DETERRABLE"

Federal policies aimed merely at augmenting state and local law enforcement efforts are not likely, by themselves, to reduce crime rates markedly. One implication of our analysis, however, is that a different form of national policy could well have a significant impact upon the incidence of crime. Specifically, policies involving employment opportunities and the like, which have the effect of offering legitimate alternatives to those who presently lack them, might have the result of offering some potential criminals the opportunity *not* to engage in illicit activities.

The absence of legitimate opportunities is hardly the only cause of crime, and an increase in their availability would, by itself, certainly not prevent crime.[26] But, if our analysis is correct, legitimate alternatives may have the effect of making a greater number of potential criminals "deterrable." An increase in the availability of lawful alternatives might allow a larger number of potential criminals the option of responding to police and other law enforcement activities by refraining from the commission of crimes. Thus, again, while the availability of legitimate options may not, in and of itself, prevent crime, it may make crime prevention possible.

Interestingly enough, some bits of tantalizing evidence suggest that the public policies of one era of American political history—the period of the New Deal—may have had just such an effect.

CRIME AND OPPORTUNITY: THE NEW DEAL

Because crime data were not collected on a national basis until 1931, information concerning the extent and distribution of criminal activity prior to the New Deal is limited. The most reliable statistical evidence on crime rates before 1931 was compiled by the American Banker's

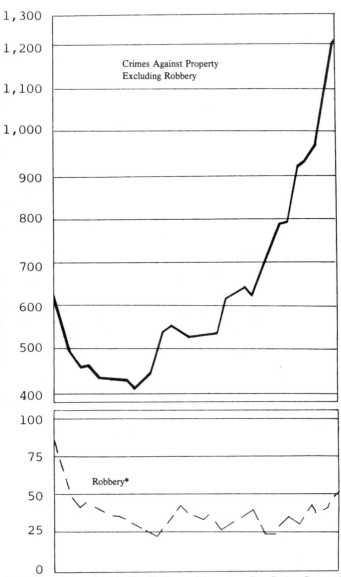

Adapted from data reported in *The Challenge of Crime in a Free Society,* Report of the President's Commission on Law Enforcement, 1965, p. 23.

*Scale for robbery enlarged to show trend.

Figure 11.1 Reported Crimes Against Property, 1933 to 1965

Association and is reported by Leroy Gould.[27] These data describe the incidence of bank robbery and burglary from 1921 and suggest an extremely high incidence of such crimes between 1921 and 1933, followed by a marked decline after 1933.

Other, more impressionistic accounts, suggest a "crime wave" during the 1920s and early 1930s which particularly affected the large cities. Public concern with the large number of crimes allegedly perpetrated by immigrants and their children in urban slums was one of the principle factors leading to the creation of the National Commission on Law Observance and Enforcement (Wickersham Commission) in 1930. And, indeed, the statistical evidence that does exist strongly suggests that urban ethnic minorities accounted for a disproportionate share of criminal activity from the turn of the century through the 1930s.[28]

These same groups were major beneficiaries of the policies of the Roosevelt era. While the New Deal acheived little in the way of immediate economic redistribution, its labor, social welfare, and work relief programs as well as significant increases in the political influence of urban groups did represent broad redistributions of opportunities. In turn, changes in the incidence and distribution of criminal activity in the United States after 1933 seem to exhibit a pattern suggesting that the New Deal had an important impact upon crime.

First, the national incidence of crime against property appears to have begun to decline markedly after 1933 and to have continued to diminish through the early 1940s. This decline, indicated by Figure 11.1, affected all categories of property crime. The reduced property crime rate, moreover, does not appear to have been simply a function of the diminished availability of property, and thus the opportunity for its theft, during a time of economic depression.[29]

Second, drops in the incidence of property crime during the New Deal era were most evident in the very largest cities. This is certainly consistent with the possibility that crime rates could have been affected by the New Deal's redistribution of opportunities in favor of urban groups (see Table 11.2).

Table 11.2. Changes in Robbery and Burglary Rates, 1933 to 1939

Size of city	Change in crime rates, 1933—1939	
	Robbery	Burglary
Cities over 250,000	−.50	−.12
Cities over 100,000 to 250,000	−.23	−.08
Cities over 50,000 to 100,000	−.32	+.01
Cities over 25,000 to 50,000	−.38	+.02
Cities over 10,000 to 25,000	−.29	−.02
Cities under 10,000	−.18	−.08

Source: F.B.I., *Uniform Crime Reports,* 1933-1939. Comparable rural data were not available.

Third, and most intriguing, the sharpest decline in property crime rates during the 1930s occurred in those cities which became most staunchly Democratic by the conclusion of the New Deal epoch. Table 11.3 compares changes in robbery rates during the 1930s with the voting pattern which had emerged by the 1940s.[30] The data suggest a relationship between changes in crime rates and popular voting. One plausible interpretation of this relationship is that property crime rates diminished most in those areas where the largest number of individuals also perceived themselves to have benefited from the policies of the Democratic party.

Table 11.3. Crime and the Democratic Vote

Cities above 100,000; Percent change in robberies reported	Mean percent Democratic
60% decline or greater	59.0 (7)*
40%-59% decline	58.0 (22)
20%-39% decline	51.2 (23)
0-19% decline	50.5 (14)
Increase	52.4 (10)

Mean percent Democratic, all cities, 54.2
Mean change in robberies reported, all cities, −.31

The correlation between percent change in robberies reported and mean percent Democratic is −.37 (N = 76, the regression of percent change in robberies on mean percent Democratic is significant at the .01 level, F = 11.84).

*The number of cases is given in parenthesis.

Obviously, none of these data prove that the New Deal reduced crime. Nevertheless, the pattern of findings viewed as a whole, is quite suggestive. A marked diminution in the incidence of crime was at least synchronous with the implementation of policies which could be said to have expanded the opportunity not to commit crimes. There is, moreover, at least some reason to suspect that it was, indeed the beneficiaries of those policies who contributed most to the reduction in crime rates of that period. If this is correct, then one effect of the New Deal may have been to help make at least one group of potential criminals deterrable.

DETERRENCE VERSUS REDISTRIBUTION

Discussions of crime control often lead to debates between advocates of increased deterrence and proponents of some form of redistributive social policy. Prior to the enactment of the Crime Control Act of 1968, for example, Congressional conservatives argued that more police and longer prison terms were the best responses to rising crime rates.

Congressional liberals, on the other hand, maintained that only policies aimed at the elimination of slums, discrimination, unemployment, and other factors they conceived to be "underlying causes" could have any substantial effect upon crime.[31]

Quite probably, deterrence and redistribution should be conceived as complementary rather than competing approaches to crime control. Whether or not discrimination and lack of opportunity are underlying causes of crime—and they are certainly not its only causes—they do inhibit the deterrence of crime. By diminshing alternatives, they also diminish the possibility that potential law breakers can be discouraged from committing crimes.[32] The ironic result is that "conservative" policies of deterrence are likely to be effective only if accompanied by "liberal" social policies. The new urban minorities that came to account for a large share of criminal activity after World War II are probably no more deterrable by the police and courts alone than were their predecessors in urban slums.

There have, of course, always been some policy makers who intuitively understood that a liberal social policy could complement police activities in combatting violence, disruption, and disorder. Piven and Cloward suggest a number of examples of this phenomenon.[33] Ultimately, however, the distribution of legitimate opportunities can have a zero-sum character. Gains for some groups can sometimes come only at the expense of others. Some of the very benefits that may have contributed to making members of urban ethnic groups more deterrable at the time of the New Deal also had the effect of foreclosing opportunities for the blacks and hispanics who migrated to American cities in subsequent years.[34] Redistribution of opportunities in favor of these groups may, in turn, come at the expense of others, perhaps reducing their susceptibility to deterrence. Whatever policies are adopted by the federal government, crime is likely to continue to be, as Durkheim observed long ago, one of the most normal features of collective life.[35]

NOTES

1. Overall crime rates increased only 0.4 percent between 1975 and 1976. Nevertheless, the 1976 overall crime rate was 37 percent above that in 1972 and 76.2 percent higher than in 1967.

2. Some experiments with intensive police patrols in selected urban neighborhoods, notably those conducted in Kansas City, Missouri, suggest that even these might have little impact.

3. 82 Stat. 197

4. United States Law Enforcement Assistance Administration, *Fifth Annual Report* (Washington, D.C.: U.S. Government Printing Office, 1973):1.

5. United States Law Enforcement Assistance Administration, *Sixth Annual Report* (Washington, D.C.: U.S Government Printing Office, 1974): 153.

6. Ibid., 142.

7. Ibid., 139.

8. Ibid., 150.

9. The tank, which cost more than $16 thousand, was eventually used against demonstrating black college students as well as to storm a Black Panther headquarters. An account is given in Joseph C. Golden, "The Cops Hit the Jackpot," *The Nation,* (November 23, 1970).

10. The notion that criminal behavior is a result of the internalization of norms different from those of the larger society is generally associated with the work of Sutherland. Edwin H. Sutherland, *Principles of Criminology,* 4th ed. (Philadelphia: Lippincott, 1947).

1. For example, Isaach Ehrlich, "Participation in Illegitimate Activity: A Theoretical and Empirical Investigation," *Journal of Political Economy,* 81 (May, 1973): 521. A useful bibliography of the literature in this area is presented in Gordon Tullock, "Does Punishment Deter Crime?" *The Public Interest,* 36 (Summer, 1974): 103.

12. Of approximately 467 thousand adults arrested for the commission of index crimes in 1965, 177 thousand were formally indicted. Of these,169 thousand, or over 95 percent, received some form of punishment. The data are reported in, "President's Commission on Law Enforcement and Administration of Justice," *The Challenge of Crime in a Free Society* (Washington, D.C.: U.S. Government Printing Office, 1967): 262.

13. See, for example, George Antunes and A. Lee Hunt, "The Deterrent Impact of Criminal Sanctions: Some Implications for Criminal Justice Policy," *Journal of Urban Law,* 51 (1973): 145.

14. Leroy C. Gould and J. Zvi Namenwirth, "Contrary Objectives: Crime Control and the Rehabilitation of Criminals," in Jack Douglas (ed.), *Crime and Justice in American Society* (Indianapolis: Bobbs-Merrill): 256.

15. In 1965, approximately 727,000 persons were arrested by the police in connection with the commission of index crimes. Almost 3 million index crimes were reported to the police in that year. At least an equal number of crimes probably went unreported.

16. The fact that the police do, "go through the motions," not only helps to comfort the victims, but quite likely also discourages victims from seeking private revenge.

17. An interesting account of New York City police efforts to apprehend the "44 caliber killer", is presented in Robert Daley, "The Search for 'Sam': Why it took so long," *New York Magazine* (August 22, 1977): 37.

18. This is why crimes against the person are more often solved than crimes against property committed in the absence of the victim. One exception is the crime of murder, which often involves a victim and offender with some form of prior relationship.

19. Riot situations are one set of obvious exceptions where the police cannot arrest all of the perpetrators they see.

20. If the chance of arrest for the commission of a crime in the presence of the police is 1.0, then the overall likelihood that the perpetrator of a crime will be arrested is equal to the probability that the police will be present, plus the probability that the police will solve the crime after the fact if they are not present at its commission.

21. This conception of "criminal opportunity" is discussed at some length by Gould. Leroy C. Gould, "Crime and Its Impact in an Affluent Society," in Douglas (ed.), *Crime and Justice.* Gould finds strong relationships between changes in the incidence of several crimes and changes in the availability of opportunities for their commission.

22. This could, indeed, be said to be the optimal strategy for law enforcement agencies.

23. Data on police strength were drawn from, Federal Bureau of Investigation, *Uniform Crime Reports* for 1958 through 1961. We have no way of knowing whether these are typical years. Obviously, the procedure should be repeated for all available years.

24. Robbery data were drawn from the F.B.I.'s *Uniform Crime Report* for 1960 through 1963. Again, the procedure should be repeated for all available combinations of years.

25. Obviously, there is an ecological problem, but no individual level data are available.

26. Cloward, of course, argues that lack of legitimate opportunity is a cause of crime. Richard A. Cloward and Lloyd E. Ohlin, *Delinquency and Opportunity* (New York: Free Press, 1960).

27. Gould, "Crime and its Impact," 93.

28. Clifford R. Shaw and Henry D. McKay, *Juvenile Delinquency and Urban Areas* (Chicago: University of Chicago Press, 1969 rev. ed.). Also interesting in this regard is Daniel Bell, "Crime as an American Way of Life," in Daniel Bell, *The End of Ideology* (New York: Free Press, 1962).

29. Gould, "Crime and its Impact," 104-196. Gould's explanation for this phenomenon has to do with changes in the character of criminals rather than any effects of the New Deal.

30. Voting data are for 1948. By this time, partisan attachments had stabilized following the New Deal realignment of the electorate.

31. This debate is discussed at length in Richard Harris, *The Fear of Crime* (New York: Praeger, 1968).

32. Though we have focused upon crime against property, an analogous argument might be made for crime against persons. It might, for example, be the case that alternate channels for the expression of violent impulses facilitate the deterrence of such crimes.

33. Frances Fox Piven and Richard A. Cloward, *Regulating the Poor* (New York: Patheon, 1971).

34. The minimum wage is one possible example.

35. Emile Durkheim, *The Rules of Sociological Method* (New York: Free Press, 1950).

12.

THE BURGER COURT AND CIVIL LIBERTIES: THE PROBLEM OF MOVING THE LAW BACKWARD

DARLENE WALKER

Cornell University

In the area of civil liberties, the Burger Court is not progressing toward a doctrine, but away from one. Questions of how far back it will move and in what areas keep the Court's docket crowded with cases designed to test the limits of its retreat. The exact position of the Court, and hence of the law, remains uncertain. This situation is exacerbated by the Court's reluctance or failure to define a rule of law. On criminal rights and on First Amendment freedoms, the Court has made repeated decisions occasioning many opinions, but has failed to define a rule or standard. Decisions are the bases of other decisions, leaving the state of the law a matter of constant judicial elaboration.

The Burger Court's philosophy on civil liberties markedly differs from that of the Warren Court. Through a gradual process of extending general and then specific consititutional guarantees, the Warren Court expanded and defined the dimensions of due process of law vis-à-vis the Bill of Rights. In the years between 1961 and 1969 alone, 10 of the specific guarantees of the Bill of Rights were made applicable to the states. The Warren Court period was also marked by increasingly absolute interpretations of the First Amendment and by a broadening of the issues protected under it. In both areas, the Court drew the line in favor of individual over community rights. And when the rights of the state were in conflict with the national government's rights, the Warren Court generally favored the power of the national government. Incorporation is a prime example of both the protection of individual rights and a reliance on the powers of the national government. However, civil liberties philosophy, which defends individual over community rights, is almost definitionally unpopular. The Warren Court's decisions delineating the rights of defendents required a revolution in the practices of law enforcement, crowded the dockets of state and federal appeals courts, and generated public demands for community protection. The Court's decisions on the First Amendment involving prayer and Bible reading in the schools were among the most unpopular in recent history. These decisions, coupled with the Court's civil rights decisions, combined to generate demands for a change in Supreme Court policy. The liberal Warren Court was charged with judicial lawmaking and chastised for its efforts to edge the law ahead. Politicians searched for "strict constructionists" and touted the virtues of judicial restraint.

The Nixon appointees were screened and selected to be ideological opponents of the Warren Court. Recruited for old virtues and sympathetic to new interests, the Burger Court has acquiesced to demands for community protection and has deferred to the powers of the long ignored states. The Burger Court has reversed the previous civil liberties trend by limiting or denying federal protection to a growing list of the specific guarantees of the Bill of Rights. And it has initiated a considerable change in the protection of First Amendment rights. The Burger Court's general preference for community over individual rights and for the state over national exercise of power mark the differences in constitutional philosophy between it and the Warren Court. But the philosophical principles have not been applied with consistency. As a result, one of the most significant characteristics of the Burger Court is ambiguity in the legal rules it will apply. This failure to provide clear guidelines and standards for applying and administering the law is a failure to provide a rule of law.

Difficulty in defining a rule of law derives from a number of sources. One such difficulty is inherent in the Burger Court's problem of "moving the law backward." An orientation to precedent is a strong norm in judicial decision-making. It has been particularly strong among conservative judges, who historically have found this dimension of restraint to facilitate their pursuit of policy objectives. Unhappily, the Burger Court has found its policy demands to be inconsistent with those for judicial restraint. In a desire to appear restrained, the Court has found it necessary to ignore relevant precedent or to distinguish the circumstances of the case in order to make the governing precedent irrelevant. Neither action is conducive to defining a rule of law. The Court has established conflicting precedents without adequate explanation. As a result, it has created ambiguity. Ironically, ambiguity increases demands on the Court by expanding the number of areas and issues requiring final adjudication. In its efforts to appear restrained, the Court has become more activist.

Another source of difficulty in establishing a rule of law is created by the Court's preference for balancing principles. Deciding to balance interests rather than to declare one interest dominant is one type of balancing. Similarly, any movement away from an absolute interpretation toward one which accommodates several interests or norms makes a single standard more difficult to define without carefully drawing the guidelines. Lacking such definition, any question raised under a balanced interest or principle requires continuing judicial supervision.

Perhaps the most significant difficulty the Burger Court has had in defining and pursuing consistent civil liberties policy has been internal divisiveness. Many of the significant and broad-ranging changes initiated by the Burger Court have been based on narrow majorities. To speak of the "Court" is almost inappropriate, because the Court itself seldom speaks as a single body. Despite Republican dominance, the Burger Court is at best very divided. In many cases, it has failed to produce even a majority opinion. The decision of the Court is badly weakened by the necessity of gleaning agreement across the multiple opinions for the majority. The divisions are made obvious in the often sharp and bitter disagreements which, unresolved in conference, reappear in the Court's opinions. The narrow and changing nature of the Burger Court's majority had handicapped its move to alter due process and First Amendment rights in any developmental or systematic fashion.

In nearly every area of civil liberties, there exists broad-ranging ambiguity regarding the rules of the law. While it is always true that peculiarities of any case yield uncertainties as to its resolution, the Burger Court is distinguished in the number of civil liberties issues left unresolved by recent decisions. The essence of the law is certainty. The failure to establish a clear rule of law in any political context is a serious problem for democratic government. Without some guiding element of clarity and certainty, the power and scope of government appear arbitrary. An examination of recent cases of the Burger Court on selected due process and First Amendment issues will illustrate both the nature of changes in civil liberties policy and the ambiguity produced by the change. Further, the analysis should provide insight into how these sources of difficulty inhibit establishing a new rule of law. The final section of this chapter will examine the consequences of the Burger changes and ambiguities on civil liberties policy, on the Court, and on the political system.

THE DEATH PENALTY

The Supreme Court's decisions on capital punishment are excellent examples of its failure to establish a rule of law. At the close of the 1971 term, the Supreme Court in Furman v. Georgia[1] effectively held most or all state statutes that prescribe the death penalty unconstitutional. The exact basis of the Furman decision was difficult to specify, for the Court was badly divided. Each member of the five-man majority wrote his own opinion; no one joined in the opinion of any other. Each opinion presented a different rationale for the holding and thus hinted at widely varying impacts. Daniel Polsby, in an analysis of the Furman decision, notes:[2]

> the way the *Furman* majority presented itself to the world—five separate opinions with none commanding the concurrence of any justice other than its author—seemed almost deliberately calculated to make this judgment of dubious value as a precedent.

Certainly, the years since Furman have demonstrated the difficulty of identifying and applying the precedent. Although the Furman decision strongly suggested that the Court would not hold the death penalty per se to be in violation of the Eighth Amendment, opinions only hinted at the nature of a state statute that might meet constitutional requirements. The result was a flurry of activity in state legislatures as 35 states considered and drafted new legislation aimed at meeting Supreme Court objections while retaining capital punishment. Since Furman failed to specify constitutional guidelines, legislative activity became judicial activity. In the 1976 term alone, the Court heard five cases brought to test the constitutionality of new capital laws. Again, the Court was badly divided in its judgment. In five separate sets of opinions, the Court considered each of the state cases. It was unable to muster a majority for any one view. In three 7:2 decisions, the Court upheld statutes of Georgia, Florida, and Texas. In two 5:4 votes, it overturned North Carolina and Louisiana statutes.[3]

The lead plurality opinion in each case was written jointly by Justices Stewart, Powell, and Stevens. These justices formed the core majority of the Court in all five cases. In upholding the state statutes they were joined by Justices White, Burger, and Rehnquist and in a separate but concurring opinion, by Justice Blackmun. These seven, on varying grounds, expressed the view that the death penalty, at least for murder, does not necessarily violate the constitution. Rejecting any static interpretation of the Eight Amendment, both plurality opinions relied heavily on public opinion and other objective indicators in determining the death penalty's constitutionality. Opinions cited the action by the states as evidence that the death penalty is a widespread and legitimate form of punishment.

It is significant to note that the plurality opinion used an essentially popular test in interpreting the constitutionality of the Amendment, not one which is based on the Constitution itself or on judicial precedent. Justices Marshall and Brennan, who dissented, held the death penalty inherently unconstitutional under Eight Amendment terms. Only this position would yield an absolute interpretation. But the decision could set rule of law standards, if, upon finding that the death penalty did not per se violate the Amendment, the court then enumerated a doctrine that specified the parameters of constitutional capital punishment. The opinions of the Court in these cases make it clear that the sentencing discretion criticized in Furman must be carefully controlled if state statutes are to meet constitutional approval. However, both the Court's positions and the majorities which established them are weak.

Specifically, in Gregg v. Georgia,[4] the Court ruled that the state statute imposing the death penalty for deliberate murder was constitutional. The Georgia statute limits sentencing discretion by providing for a bifurcated trial, by permitting informed sentencing by judge or jury based on a broad range of information about the defendant and the crime, and by defining an expedited appeals procedure if the death penalty is imposed. The statute sets 10 aggravating circumstances; the death penalty may not be imposed unless it is found beyond a reasonable doubt that one of these specified circumstances exists.

The Court approved a similar Florida death penalty statute,[5] though it differed slightly in that the judge was made solely responsible for sentencing and no particular form was given to the state Supreme Court review. The Court found nothing unconstitutional in the statute's "mitigating circumstances," though it noted that it might be difficult to determine whether there are sufficient aggravating circumstances to overcome mitigating ones.

A Texas statute allowing capital punishment for intentional murders committed in five specified circumstances was also declared constitutional by the same 7:2 vote.[6] The jury may be able to impose the death penalty if it can show beyond a reasonable doubt two or three of the following: that the defendant's homicidal conduct was deliberately committed with the reasonable expectation that death would result; "that there is a probability that the defendant would commit criminal acts of violence that would constitute a continuing threat to society," or that "the conduct of the defendant in killing the deceased was unreasonable in response to the provocation, if any, by the deceased." The Texas law also sets up a procedure for expedited review by the Texas Court of Criminal Appeals. The plurality opinion held "that, as in Georgia or in Florida, the Texas capital-sentencing procedure guides and focuses the jury's objective consideration of the particularized circumstances of the individual offense and the individual offender before it can impose a sentence of death."

Two state capital punishment statutes were overturned. In a 5:4 decision, the Court overturned a North Carolina statute making the death penalty mandatory for a broad range of homicides defined as first-degree murder.[7] Ironically, North Carolina had a discretionary death statute which the state Supreme Court severed in response to *Furman*. The Court's plurality (Stewart, Powell, Stevens) found that the statute failed to provide a "constitutionally tolerable response to Furman's rejection of unbridled jury discretion in the imposition of capital sentences." It also cited the statute's "failure to allow particularized consideration of relevant aspects of the character and record of each convicted defendant before the imposition upon him of a sentence of death." Rhenquist, in dissent, protested the inconsistencies in the Court's action. "It makes no sense to uphold a system requiring discretion while striking down one that merely permits it."

In Roberts v. Louisiana,[8] the same 5:4 majority struck down a mandatory death sentence. The Louisiana statute limited the sentence to five circumstances of murder. The state has a responsive verdict system which provides that a jury in a first degree murder case be instructed on first- and second-degree murder and manslaughter and must be provided with verdict forms for each. The plurality found these limitations insufficient to overcome the problems of a mandatory death penalty. It also held that the state's responsive verdict system failed to protect against arbitrary and capricious imposition of death sentences. White, Blackmun, Burger, and Rhenquist dissenting would have upheld the state's law. White, for the dissenters, argued that the Louisiana law was "indistinguishable constitutionally from the Texas law."

The Court's decision in Furman is an excellent example of its failure to define and pursue a rule of law. It also illustrates some of the factors which have made it difficult for the Court to establish a clear precedent.

(1) The narrow nature of the original Furman majority and the divided nature of the Court in subsequent cases have prevented it from stating and pursuing a single judicial rule.

(2) The Court rejected a per se interpretation of the Eighth Amendment vis-à-vis capital punishment without defining the standards for constitutional capital punishment.

(3) The Court's action in the three 1976 cases could have declared constitutional statutes that return to judges and juries discretion significant and unbridled enough to allow practices which could be considered unconstitutional under Furman standards. In Furman, the Court con-

demned discretion, in the later cases, the Court requires it. To abolish discretionary sentencing would have established a readily identifiable precedent; to require "controlled discretion" is to devise a standard that cannot be defined without further judicial elaboration.

MIRANDA RIGHTS—A COUNTER-REVOLUTION

Miranda v. Arizona[9] in 1966 was one of the most controversial decisions of the Warren Court. In Miranda, the Court established the now famous rules which affirm a criminal defendant's privileges against self-incrimination. Prior to the decision, the Court on a case-by-case basis judged the voluntariness of statements made during interrogation. Miranda fashioned Court-made guidelines to insure that admissions or confessions are reasonably trustworthy and not the mere fruits of fear or coercion. The Warren Court, freed from case-by-case deliberation of Fifth Amendment claims, applied the Miranda principles broadly and, as a result, required law enforcement practice changes that have been termed "revolutionary."[10]

Early in his term as Chief Justice, Burger expressed dissatisfaction with the Miranda rules. In Harris v. New York in 1971,[11] the Court held that statements taken without compliance with Miranda, while inadmissable as evidence, could be used to impeach the defendant's trial testimony. Criticized as lacking justification in precedent or stated rationale,[12] the Harris rule was the first serious attack on Miranda rights. The case foreshadowed a series of decisions which limited and weakened the Fifth Amendment rules. In a case initiated before Miranda was handed down, Michigan v. Tucker,[13] the Court held that the evidence obtained without safeguards of Miranda could be used in a post-Miranda trial. Rehnquist, for the plurality, said that Tucker had not been deprived of his Fifth Amendment privilege, since the warnings themselves are not the right. Rehnquist said the warnings were merely a prophylactic standard designed to safeguard the constitutional right. The police, said the Justice, acted in good faith, giving all warnings then required. Rehnquist argued that the deterrence rationale of Miranda had little force here. *Harvard Law Review's* summary of the 1973 term evaluates the decision this way:[14]

> Justice Rhenquist's analyses of the fifth amendment issue rejected the underlying premise of *Miranda:* he determined whether Tucker's testimony was compelled not by reference to the coercion inherent in custodial interrogation, but rather by "(a) comparison of the facts in this case with the historical circumstances underlying the privilege against compulsory self-

incrimination . . ." This mode of analyses effectively undercuts *Miranda's* efforts to provide clear Constitutional guidelines for police behavior and to expand the scope of the fifth amendment privilege.

The immediate implications of Tucker were unclear. "On the one hand it was possible to read Tucker as a broad repudiation of Miranda"; alternatively, it could be read narrowly as a reluctance to apply *Miranda's* full scope retroactively.[15] Distinguishing Miranda rules from the associated right, identifying the primary goal of the rules as deterrence, and balancing the benefits of Miranda rules against the cost suggest that, if not broadly repudiated, the Miranda rule had been both weakened and obscured. Subsequent cases supported that view.

In 1975, the Court again allowed incriminating statements obtained without full rights being afforded the defendant to be used for impeachment purposes. In Oregon v. Hass,[16] an arrestee who had been told of his right to see an attorney was questioned and made incriminating statements prior to consulting with an attorney. The Supreme Court of Oregon ruled the statements inadmissable for any purpose. The Burger court reversed that ruling, holding that the statements could be made available for impeachment purposes. Brennan, joined by Marshall, dissented, "After today's decision, if an individual states that he wants an attorney, police interrogation will doubtless now be vigorously pressed to obtain statements before the attorney arrives."

Another apparent attempt to narrow the application of Miranda has come by narrowing the period to which the rights apply. In Kirby v. Illinois (1972),[17] the Court declined to find unconstitutional the failure to advise an accused of his right to counsel at a pre-indictment police station line-up. The case is also an example of the Court's failure either to abide by or to overrule a governing precedent. In Wade v. U.S.,[18] the Warren Court ruled on the right to counsel at a line-up, but the Burger Court claimed Wade was not controlling since the line-up took place in a post-indictment period. As the *Akron Law Review* notes, this leaves Kirby to mean that Miranda rights need not apply if identification procedures are conducted before the indictment.[19] Clearly, the attempt to distinguish the cases was somewhat artificial. It is a good illustration of an attempt to depart from precedent without overruling.

In 1975 in Michigan v. Mosley,[20] the Court rejected a defendant's claim that the resumption of questioning after the initial invocation of silence was a per se violation of Miranda v. Arizona. The Court held that Miranda created no *"per se* proscription of indefinite duration upon any further questioning, by any officer on any subject." Hence, admission of statements made after the invocation of silence depends on whether the defendant's right to cut off questioning was honored. Brennan and Marshall dissented, holding that the majority had failed at the "easy task of establishing standards sufficient to assure with reasonable certainty that a confession is not obtained under the influence of the compulsion inherent in interrogation and detention." The dissenters called the decision a "distortion" of Miranda and noted that it was another step toward its ultimate overruling.

In Beckwith v. U.S.[21] (1976), the Court refused to extend Miranda rights to a taxpayer questioned in a non-custodial setting. Burger, for the Court, said that despite the fact that the taxpayer was later prosecuted, he was not entitled to Miranda warnings because the interview did not contain elements found inherently coercive in Miranda. Brennan dissented, arguing that Miranda warnings should have been given since the "taxpayer's practical compulsion to respond is comparable to the psychological pressures described in Miranda."

The Court in U.S. v. Mandujano[22] declined to extend Miranda protections to grand jury witnesses. In a plurality opinion by the Chief Justice, the Court held that no Miranda warnings need be given to witnesses testifying about criminal activities in which they may have been a part and that false statements made in the absence of warnings were admissible in a perjury trial based on them.

In Brown v. Illinois,[23] the Court found Miranda warnings given after an illegal arrest were alone insufficient to assure that a confession given to the police is voluntary and, hence, admissible. Justice Blackmun for the Court held that if Miranda warnings alone were sufficient, arrests made without probable cause would be encouraged by knowledge that the evidence could be made admissible at a trial by the simple expedient of giving warnings. "While we therefore reject the *per se* rule, we also decline to adopt any alternative or 'but for' rule. Whether a confession is the product of a free will under *Wong Sun* must be answered in the facts of each case." While this decision protects and even extends the Fourth and Fifth Amendment claims of the defendant, the decision, in a sense, strikes another blow at Miranda. Justice Blackmun is clearly noting that the "deterrent" purpose of Miranda rules would not be served by their application. And, although the situation is a narrow one, the Court returns not to a rule but to a case-by-case consideration of the degree to which confessions were made voluntarily.

(1) The Burger Court's opinions on confessions are good examples of the problems the Court has encountered in moving the law backward. Clearly, a sizable coalition on the Court would prefer to see the procedural protections of the Fifth Amendment given a lower priority than that afforded them by the Warren Court. The process of achieving

the policy change, however, has been both long and difficult. The new majority's first task was to undermine the constitutional status of the Miranda rules. Next, they sought to weaken the guidelines by emphasizing the goal of deterrence and by limiting the contexts in which guidelines applied. Finally, the court has introduced standards of voluntariness that Miranda rules were designed to replace.

(2) While failing to actually overrule Miranda, a sizable portion of the Court continues a direct assault—sometimes as the majority, other times in dissent. As a result, the status of Miranda is uncertain.

A similar pattern is apparent in the Court's opinions on the exclusionary rule.

THE EXCLUSIONARY RULE

The Fourth Amendment forbids unreasonable search and seizure; the landmark case of Mapp v. Ohio[24] applied the evidentiary exclusionary rule of Weeks v. U.S.[25] to state proceedings. Chief Justice Burger early expressed little enthusiasm for the rule; and as with the Miranda rights, the Burger Court has consistently narrowed its application. Under the exclusionary rule, evidence improperly obtained and all "fruits of the poisonous tree" (excepting those which would have been uncovered by lawful activity) must be excluded from court consideration. By federal standards, the rule means that an otherwise illegal search is not rendered legal simply by what it produces. Warrants, necessary for arrest and search, require "personal knowledge or probable cause"; warrants are not issuable for "general search." The admission of evidence that should have been excluded may be considered harmless error if the evidence does not contribute to the verdict. The Burger Court has weakened the exclusionary rule by limiting the scope of situations to which it applies, by broadening the context of "harmless error," and by eliminating the primary source of access to prisoners with Fourth Amendment claims.

The Burger Court early edged away from Warren Court precedent regarding the requirements and restrictions on arrests and searches. The watershed exclusionary rule case came in 1974; in U.S. v. Calandra,[26] the Court held that the rule does not apply to evidence sent to the grand jury. In Calandra, the Court said that using the unlawfully seized material as a basis for questioning worked "no new Fourth Amendment wrong," and presented a question "not of rights but of remedies." In Calandra, the Court concentrated almost solely on the rule's deterrent value. Justice Brennan, dissenting in Calandra, rejected the premise that an individual has no constitutional right to have unconstitutionally seized evidence excluded for governmental use. The Mapp majority would have agreed with Brennan. As Henry P. Monaghan notes, "The *Mapp* majority justified the exclusionary rule as a Fourth Amendment remedy on a number of grounds, but ultimately held the rule binding upon the states because it was 'an essential part of the right to privacy protected by the due process clause of the Fourteenth Amendment.'"[27] Justice Powell, for the majority, however, narrowed significantly the reasons for applying the rule and then developed a balancing cost/benefit method for deciding on the rule's application. Thus, the groundwork for the themes apparent in later exclusionary rule cases were laid in Calandra.[28]

In the U.S. v. Peltier[29] decided the same year, the Court again took the opportunity to discuss more broadly its shift in view toward the exclusionary rule. The case itself involved the issue of whether the Fourth Amendment doctrine narrowly defining broader searches (Almeida-Sanchez v. U.S.[30]) should be applied retroactively to exclude evidence seized in good faith prior to the decision. In deciding this issue, Rehnquist, for the majority, noted that the exclusionary rule should be required only if the cause of deterrence would be furthered or if required by the "imperative of judicial integrity." Brennan, joined by Marshall in dissenting, argued that the majority's emphasis on the deterrence rationale foreshadowed a modification of the exclusionary rule. Indeed, subsequent cases have confirmed the view.

The cases of the last term significantly limit the exclusionary rule's application. As *U.S. Law Week* notes, "The overall trend in fourth amendment law could also be measured quantitatively; in all eight of the search and seizure cases, the Court reversed a state or federal court decision supressing evidence."[31]

In U.S. v. Janis,[32] as in most of the recent search and seizure cases, the Court weighs the deterrent benefits of applying the exclusionary rule against the societal costs. In Janis, the Court held that evidence seized unconstitutionally but in good faith by state law enforcement officers is admissible in a federal civil proceeding. Blackmun, for the majority, called the exclusionary rule a judicial device primarily designed to deter unlawful police behavior. The majority declined to extend the rule to cases where this specific deterrent purpose would not be served. Brennan, Marshall, and Stewart dissented; Stewart, in a separate dissent, accused the majority of fashioning a "silver platter doctrine." "If state police officers can effectively crack down on . . . violators by the simple expedient of violating the constitutional rights and turning the illegally seized evidence over . . . on the proverbial silver platter, then the deterrent purpose of the exclusionary rule is wholly frustrated."

In U.S. v. Watson,[33] the Court upheld a public arrest made with probable cause to believe the suspect had committed a felony even though the arresting officer failed to obtain a warrent when he had ample time to do so. The warrant requirement is one of judicial preference, the Court said, not one of constitutional dimension. The Court also upheld the consent search of the defendant's car subsequent to the arrest, on the grounds that custody alone did not negate consent. In a concurring opinion, Justice Stewart noted that the decision did not address the question of arrest on private premises. Powell, concurring, justified a divergence in constitutional rules for arrest and searches. Marshall and Brennan in the dissent argued the majority not only decided the question wrongly but unnecessarily. They argued that warrants should apply with equal force to searches and arrests. They said a greater burden should be placed on the state in obtaining consent when a suspect is in custody. Marshall said the majority's decision adopts the partially overruled and thoroughly discredited rule of "whether the search was reasonable."[34]

In U.S. v. Santana,[35] the Court again upheld a warrantless arrest. In Watson, the Court upheld a probable cause arrest in a public place, specifically noting a distinction between public places and homes or other private places. In Santana, the Court made clear that public places is to be given broad definition. In upholding a warrantless arrest of a defendant who, while being pursued, fled to the home and was subsequently arrested in the doorway, the Court held that a private dwelling doorway open to view from the street is the functional equivalent of a public place for Fourth Amendment purposes. Mr. Rehnquist, for the majority, held that, though under property law concepts, the threshold of a dwelling may be private, it could be held public for Fourth Amendment purposes. Rehnquist also noted that once the suspect fled to the home, the "hot pursuit doctrine" established by the Court earlier[36] permitted officers to follow and arrest, thus extending the "hot pursuit" doctrine to warrantless entries for the purpose of apprehending felony suspects. Marshall and Brennan in dissent noted, "The Court declines today to settle the oft-reserved question of whether and under what circumstances a police officer may enter the home of a suspect in order to make a warrantless arrest." They adhered to their dissent in Watson holding that a warrant is required to effect arrest in the absence of exigent circumstances.

In U.S. v. Martinez-Fuerte,[37] the Court held that fixed check point border operations need not be authorized in advance by judicial warrant. They said that even a reasonable suspicion requirement would be impractical at fixed points with heavy traffic and would eliminate the deterrent effect of checkpoints. They held that intrusion on the Fourth Amendment interests of private citizens is "quite minimal" and outweighed by the public interest in making checkpoint stops. Brennan and Marshall dissented, noting that it was the ninth decision of the term "marking the continual evisceration of the Fourth Amendment safeguards." Permitting standardless seizures, they said, cannot be reconciled with previous precedent.[38]

In South Dakota v. Opperman,[39] the Court 5:4 held that the routine inventory search of an impounded automobile was not a Fourth Amendment search and seizure violation. The search, said the Court, was primarily for the purpose of safeguarding valuables and not ordinarily used for criminal investigation. Marshall, Brennan and Stewart dissenting, contended that the decision subordinates Fourth Amendment privacy and security interests to "the mere possibility of property interests."

In a per curium opinion reversing a decision of a Texas Court of Criminal Appeals, the Court 6:2 admitted into evidence checks seized in the warrantless search of a suspect's automobile at the police station. The Court held the search permissible if probable cause to search was present at the scene of arrest[40] (Chambers v. Molony[41] as precedent). Justice Marshall joined by Brennan claimed, "Only by misstating the holdings of Chambers can the Court make that case appear dispositive of this one." Chambers, they argued, provides for a search only where the car can be reasonably taken to the police station. To do so would have required independent justification in this case.

Three of last term's exclusionary rule cases involved the Fifth Amendment right of protection of private papers. In each, the Court limited protection against compelled production of books and papers for use at a trial. As early as 1886, the Court in Boyd v. U.S.[42] held that the Fifth Amendment's privilege against self-incrimination prohibits compelling the production of books and papers for use at a trial. In Fisher v. U.S.[43] last year, the Court held that the government can subpoena a taxpayer to produce an accountant's work papers relating to contested tax returns. In Andresen v. Maryland,[44] the Court held that Fifth Amendment protections do not prohibit for trial use written statements made by the defendant which were seized under a warrant containing questionably broad terminology. *The Harvard Law Review* notes:[45]

> Both decisions purported to distinguish *Boyd: Fisher* because papers prepared by an accountant are not a taxpayer's own "private papers," and *Andresen* on the grounds that the production of the papers had not been "compelled" since they were seized rather than subpoenaed. Nevertheless, the narrow theory of the fifth amendment articulated in *Fisher* and *Andresen* suggests that the reasoning of *Boyd* has been substantially undermined and that a defendant's privilege against producing documents containing his writings may no longer exist.

In a third case, U.S. v. Miller,[46] the Supreme Court reversed a fifth circuit ruling holding that the government's subpoena of bank records to establish criminal charges against a suspect was in violation of Boyd's prohibition of compelled production of personal papers under the Fourth Amendment. The Court 7:2 said the records were the bank's record of its negotiations with the defendant and as such did not constitute private papers. By revealing business affairs to the bank, the customer takes the same risks as the person who confides in another person.

In Stone v. Powell,[47] the Court effectively denied federal court authority to review state court search and seizure cases via *habeas corpus.* The Court, in a 6:3 decision, held that "where the state has provided an opportunity for full and fair litigation of a Fourth Amendment claim, a state prisoner may not be granted federal *habeas corpus* relief on the grounds that evidence obtained in an unconstitutional search or seizure was introduced at the trial." This case marked a distinctly different Court policy toward *habeas corpus* jurisdiction as one reviewer notes, "since *Brown v. Allen,* decided in 1953, most courts have assumed that all constitutional claims are reviewable on federal *habeas corpus.* "[48]

Powell, for the Court's majority, reiterated familiar themes. The exclusionary rule said the Court is a "judicial remedy," the primary purpose of which is the deterrent of unlawful police conduct. In using the rule, the Court should weigh the societal costs against the benefits. The rule, wrote Powell, causes defects in the fact-finding process, often frees the guilty, causes inefficient use of judicial resources, intrudes on the finality of criminal trials, causes friction between the state and federal courts, and upsets the balance of federalism. Deterrent benefits are insufficient to justify its use; "the additional contribution of the consideration of search and seizure claims of state prisoners on collateral review is small in relation to the costs." The Chief Justice would have gone further. In a concurring opinion, Burger argued for a modification of the exclusionary rule itself, retaining it "for a small and limited category of cases." Burger argued that the rule handicaps and penalizes the work of law enforcement and said that the Court had failed to build a satisfactory rationale "for the deliberate exclusion of truth from the fact-finding process."

Justices Brennan and Marshall, in dissent, disagreed both with the majority's treatment of the exclusionary rule and with the limitations on the scope of federal habeas corpus. Mapp v. Ohio, argued Brennan, describes the exclusionary rule as a constitutional imperative not one entitled to second class status. Brennan charged that the Stone opinion was not constitutionally based, "it is overruling the heretofore settled principle that *habeas* relief is available to redress any asserted denial of constitutional rights." He also noted the inconsistency in denying a state prisoner's habeas corpus while leaving intact his right to petition for certiorari.

The majority indicated that the Stone decision was confined to the Fourth Amendment. Justice Brennan, however, noted that the decision helped to lay the ground work for a broad ranging withdrawal of federal *habeas* jurisdiction. Indeed, *Harvard Law Review's* summary of the 1975 term notes that there is little in the opinion to suggest such a limitation.[49]

> While the court itself characterized *Stone* as a fourth amendment case, its opinion is not logically limited to this context—either by the supposed judge-made character of the exclusionary rule or by any explicit rationale delineating the proper scope of *habeas corpus* jurisdiction. A broad view of *Stone's* significance is also supported by other decisions of last Term that evidence the Burger Court's inclination to limit the jurisdiction of the federal courts in a manner consistent with its solicitude for federalism and the more efficient use of judicial resources.

The case illustrates the Burger Court's tendency to impose restrictions on access that reflect the same substantive preferences that are pursued in the Court's opinions—a preference for community or state interests in conflict with individual rights and preference for state action over national. Ambiguity concerning the status of the exclusionary rule increased demands on the federal courts for resolution of Fourth Amendments conflicts.

One of the Burger Court's most significant and systematic departures from the Warren Court has come in the area of the Fourth Amendment. In a recent issue of the *Harvard Law Review,* Justice Brennan in a discussion of state constitutions and the protection of individual rights, sums up the Fourth Amendment record of the Burger Court in the following way:[50]

> It has found that the warrant requirement plainly appearing on the face of the fourth amendment does not require the police to obtain a warrant before arrest, however easy it might have been to get an arrest warrant. It has declined to read the fourth amendment to prohibit searches of an individual by police officers following a stop for a traffic violation, though there exists no probable cause to believe the individual has committed any other legal infraction. The court has held permissible police searches grounded upon consent regardless of whether the consent was a knowing and intelligent one, and has found that none of us has a legitimate expectation of privacy in the contents of our bank records, thus permitting governmental seizure of those records without our knowledge or consent. Even when the court has

found searches to violate the fourth amendment rights, it has—on occasion—declared exceptions to the exclusionary rule and allowed the use of such evidence.

The Burger Court, in a somewhat more systematic trend than is evident in other civil liberties areas, has seriously restricted the exclusionary rules application and weakened the guarantees against unreasonable search and seizure. Despite a systematic move to limit the exclusionary rule, the court majority has fallen short of reversing Mapp. The Court leaves uncertain both the standards of constitutional search and the status of evidence collected in violation of Mapp's standards. The High Court's ambiguity leaves lower courts uncertain of constitutional standards—a situation that crowds the federal court dockets with cases awaiting a final judicial settlement. The Supreme Court itself heard nine such cases in 1976. In defining the exclusionary rule's purpose as one of deterrence, the Court identified a benefit easily exceeded by costs to society; in the cost-benefit analysis that the Court has consistently afforded it, the rule has not done well.

(1) The exclusionary rule cases demonstrate the movement away from rather than toward a rule of law in the area of the Fourth Amendment. Failure to support or overrule Mapp v. Ohio, in particular, makes the status of evidence taken in violation of the Fourth Amendment uncertain.

(2) Reliance on balancing the interests of the defendant with the interest of community protection and the resultant reliance on a cost-benefit formula in ascertaining the situations in which the rule will be applied have left lower courts without workable exclusionary rules.

(3) The failure to adopt easily identifiable standards has crowded the federal docket with cases awaiting final judicial review. Contrary to the Court's own stated preference, the lack of standards yields a situation of maximum intervention by the federal courts in lower court proceedings. In order to solve a problem which the Court itself was instrumental in creating, the Court significantly reduced federal jurisdiction over state court criminal proceedings.

OBSCENITY: THE PROBLEM OF DEFINING COMMUNITY STANDARDS

First Amendment questions were raised on many occasions during the Warren Court years, and they not only posed some of the most difficult questions faced by the Court, but also some of the most divisive.[51] Justices Douglas and Black took literal positions on this and other First Amendment issues, arguing that censorship constituted a *prima facie* violation of the freedom of expression. Other Warren Court Justices more moderately sought to draw the line between the right to freedom of expression and the right to limit it in the interests of the community. The incompatible nature of the views produced an uncharacteristically divided court. In 1957, in Roth v. U.S. and Alberts v. California,[52] the Warren Court set forth the "prurient interest" concept.

The test, described by Brennan for the majority, was "whether to the average person applying contemporary standards, the dominant theme of the material, taken as a whole, appeals to 'prurient' interests." Brennan made clear that to be obscene the material had to be utterly "without redeeming social importance." Although the decision was criticized for failing to define exactly what constituted obscenity, the Court set forth standards that it refined in subsequent decisions. The Court made clear that Roth's reference to "contemporary community standards" was intended to establish a *national* standard (Jacobellis v. Ohio)[53] and in 1967, the Court established identifiable rules to be applied which codified the obscenity standards that had been developing since Roth.[54] Despite a large and determined minority, the Warren Court in the 11-year period from 1957-1968 developed guidelines by which it adjudicated issues of obscenity raised under the First Amendment.[55].

The Burger Court is divided on the issue of obscenity. Despite the absence of Justices insisting on absolute interpretation, considerable conflicts remain. Brennan, who wrote many of the opinions outlining the Warren Court view, leads a large and consistent dissenting coalition. Unlike its predecessor, the Burger Court seems unable to build workable guidelines for First Amendment adjudication.

In 1973, the Burger Court in Miller v. California[56] set forth guidelines established to allow states and municipalities to ban materials offensive to *local* standards. The Court said, "It is neither realistic nor Constitutionally sound to read the First Amendment as requiring that the people of Maine or Mississippi accept public depiction of conduct found tolerable in Las Vegas or New York City." The Court thus moved away from Roth's *national* standard in favor of one which definitionally left obscenity without a national reference. And neither in Miller nor in the cases which followed has the Court made clear how local standards were to be defined or applied.

Ironically, having made the question of what is obscene a matter of community rather than national standards, the Supreme Court has not stopped hearing obscenity cases. In 1974, just a few months after Miller, the Court held unanimously that the film "Carnal Knowledge" did not show "patently offensive hard-core sexual conduct" and, under Miller, rules could not be banned by the State of Georgia.[57] The same day it announced a decision in which the Court 4:5 found an advertisement for an illustrated version of the *Report of the Presidential Commission on Obscenity and Pornography* to be hard-core pornography.[58] Both the Court's decision to hear the cases and the standards applied appear contradictory. The Court's actions in these cases alone demonstrate the theoretical and practical problems that community standards have presented for the Court. The Court leaves unanswered the question of how community standards are to be defined. Its continued review of such cases as these suggests that despite the rhetoric of community standards, it is still the Supreme Court which ultimately is the arbitor of obscenity standards.

In another case (1975), Erznoznik v. City of Jacksonville,[59] the Supreme Court found a local obscenity statute to be an unconstitutionally overbroad restraint of free expression and invalid on its face. Erznoznik, a theater manager was charged with a violation of city ordinance after showing a nonobscene motion picture containing nudity. In rejecting the City's claim that the ordinance protected minors from nudity, the Supreme Court held, "Speech that is neither obscene as to youth nor subject to some other legitimate proscription and cannot be suppressed solely to protect the young from ideas or images that a legislative body thinks unsuitable for them."

The case is again illustrative of the kinds of problems created and likely to be created by Miller's broad grant of power to the community. It also demonstrated the Court's continued reluctance to do anything to remedy the uncertainty. The Court's action in Erznoznik did not even clarify Jacksonville's problem. As one analyst notes, "Announcing a *per se* rule should generally be preferred, however, because facial invalidation deprives the state of the benefits of a law's permissible applications . . . . Over breadth review should therefore be employed only when the Court is unable to formulate a satisfactory, general rule of privilege."[60] This is precisely the Court's position. The Miller decision essentially leaves the Court without the ability to formulate guidelines, for to do so would undermine its own decision. As the *Harvard Law Review* notes, "its [The Supreme Court's] hesitation in defining obscenity as to minors suggests a belief that reentry into an area recently committed to states and localities would be inopportune and could indicate concern that the Court's own obscenity decisions have failed to provide workable standards."[61] In this position, the Court can make only case-by-case determinations of the constitutionality of state or local obscenity actions.

In the 1975 term, McKinney v. Alabama,[62] the court again reviewed the constitutionality of state actions. While yet approving of civil proceedings against obscenity, the Court limited the use a state may make of an obscenity declaration. A Birmingham bookseller was presented after the fact with a list of books found obscene in a Mobile case to which he was not a party. A few days later, he was charged with selling obscene material. Mr. Renhquist, for the Court, said that the interests of the parties to the Mobile adjudication could not be assumed to be those of the defendant. In a concurring opinion, Brennan and Marshall said that a defendant should be able to claim that community standards had evolved from the time of the proceedings to the time of the act. They also attempted to define procedural assurances that should be present in an obscenity hearing, including the use of a jury, though they noted that the Court had already rejected such a proposal.

The McKinney case indicates the Court's rejection not only of a national definition of obscenity but of state or community standards as well. In limiting the application of the judgment to defendants of the case, the Court essentially rejects the idea of any judicial standard, whatever the scope. What is obscene is situational, bound in place and time. The Court has not only failed to define obscenity but has refused to see it defined in the courts of the state or community. Communities have been given the power to define obscenity but are left without methods or procedures for ascertaining what is obscene.

In a second 1976 case, Young v. American Mini Theatres, Inc.[63] the Court upheld a Detroit zoning scheme regulating the location of adult theaters. In upholding the scheme the Court violated a general rule that the government does not regulate protected expressions on the basis of content. It also ignored the principle that "non-obscene expression, however sexually explicit, receives full First Amendment protection."[64] In a 5:4 decision, the majority presented two separate views. The lead opinion acknowledged the constitutional principle prohibiting content-based regulations but cited other contexts in which the Court had made such qualifications. It justified the move primarily on the basis that the type of expression regulated was "of a wholly different, and lesser, magnitude than the interest in untrammeled political debate." First Amendment interests were balanced with those of Detroit's interest in "attempting to preserve the quality of urban life." The concurring opinion by Powell expressed a varying view. Specifically rejecting the other majority's view, he held that the issue interfered only incidentally with First Amendment concerns and should be dealt with as a land-use case. Four Justices dissented: Justice Blackmun, Stewart, Brennan and Marshall would have held the statute unconstitutionally vague. They characterized the decision of the plurality as wholly alien to the First Amendment.

In the past, the Court dealt with speech as either protected or unprotected. In American Mini Theatres, the Court began to make distinctions within the category of protected speech. Doing so endangered the government's obligation to neutrality in the regulation of a protected interest, it moved the First Amendment farther from any absolute interpretation, and it signaled a rush of cases brought to determine the breadth of the activities that may not be fully protected under the Court's new terms. As in so many other cases, the lack of a single majority view made the interpretation of the case difficult and predictions of its impact speculative.

(1) The Burger Court's treatment of obscenity illustrates the difficulty of moving away from national guidelines toward community standards. Cases subsequent to Miller demonstrated both the Supreme Court's reluctance to provide substantive and procedural guidance to localities and its apparent inability to provide direction when it did intervene. In rejecting the procedural requirement for a jury in obscenity cases and in overturning local statutory and judicial pronouncements defining obscenity standards, the Court failed to provide a workable procedure to be used by local areas in defining community standards.

(2) Slim majorities and multiple opinions plague the Burger Court in obscenity cases as in other areas. The result of the division is inconsistent case law, a lack of developing standards, and Court holdings which are unnecessarily vague.

(3) In rejecting categorical determinations—"protected" and "unprotected speech"—in favor of a lesser protection option, the Court makes rule of law resolutions of First Amendment questions even more difficult. The Court suggests a willingness to consider issues long since closed and to consider them from a far less absolute perspective.

PRIOR RESTRAINT

In another First Amendment area, that of free press, the Court has been asked to specify the conditions under which prior restraint may be placed on publication. In Nebraska Press Association v. Stewart,[65] the Supreme Court considered the constitutionality of a prior restraint upon publication of information which might be prejudicial to a criminal trial. A rare, unanimous Court held to be unconstitutional a Nebraska court's pre-trial gag order restricting coverage of a highly publicized multiple murder trial. The case however, leaves unclear the principles which should govern future cases.

Burger, in his opinion for the Court, said that the Nebraska rule, which prohibited reporting the existence and nature of confessions or admissions made by the defendants to law enforcement officials or third parties (other than members of the press), and other "strongly implicative" facts, was in violation of the First Amendment. The Chief Justice outlined three factors considered by the Court: "(a) the nature and extent of pre-trial news coverage; (b) whether other measures would be likely to mitigate the effects of unrestrained pre-trial publicity; (c) how effectively a restraining order would operate to prevent the threatened danger." On this basis, he concluded that while publicity would be intense, other measures were available to protect the defendant's right to a fair trial. He also noted that it was unclear that the restraints would have protected the defendant's rights. In rejecting the restraints as unconstitutional, the Chief Justice concluded "that guarantees of freedom of expression are not an absolute prohibition under all circumstances, but the barriers to prior restraint remain high and the presumption against its use continues intact."

Brennan, concurring in an opinion joined by Stewart and Marshall, argued that the Court's decisions involving prior restraints on expression support an absolute rule protecting censorship. The balancing test proposed by the plurality, said Brennan, was both dangerous and unnecessary. Justices White and Stewart in separate opinions expressed doubt that orders like the one under consideration would ever be justifiable, but were reluctant to see a per se rule adopted. The Court, said White, "should go no further than absolutely necessary until federal courts, and ourselves have been exposed to a broad spectrum of cases presenting similar issues." Justice Powell, in a separate opinion, emphasized that use of prior restraint requires a showing that a clear threat to the fairness of a trial exists and evidence that no less restrictive alternatives are available.

The Court declined either to establish a ranking by which conflicts between the First Amendment free press guarantees and Sixth Amendment fair trial guarantees might be resolved or to establish an absolute rule protecting the press from prior restraint. Again, the Court comes short of establishing a rule-of-law. The balancing test put forward by the Chief Justice rejects a per se rule regarding prior restraints. Although he acknowledges that First Amendment interests are difficult to outweigh, Burger outlines the factors which could be used in determining whether a gag rule is justified. Brennan, on the other hand, adopts a per se rule and then notes that exceptions exist. In this case, the two views yield the same judgment. However, the two views are radically different in impact. One establishes a rule of law, while the other provides an outline around which a rule must be developed. Of course, the expression of both by sizable court coalitions produces further ambiguities. The precedent value of the case is diminished by the division, though it seems clear that the Court is, in general, ill disposed toward such First Amendment restrictions.

Burger's emphasis in the decision on other measures available to protect a defendant's fair trial rights may signal the development of First Amendment conflicts. Attempts to guard fair trial guarantees in a manner suggested as alternatives by the Court itself may generate restraints no less harmful to the guarantees of the First Amendment. *Harvard Law Review's* term analysis comments:[66]

> the Court appeared to hint—but stopped well short of asserting—that placing prohibitions on extrajudicial statements by lawyers, parties, witnesses, policemen, and court officials and closing preliminary hearings and other proceedings to the press and public might in some circumstances be permissible expedients to prevent prejudicial publicity. Judicial use of such measures is likely to become a focus of controversy as judges seek means of stifling publicity short of direct restraints on the press.

The decision in the Nebraska Press case is reminiscent of another Burger Court case that might have produced a landmark ruling on prior restraint, but did not.[67] In 1971, in New York Times v. U.S. and U.S. v. The Washington Post,[68] the Supreme Court rejected the government's contention that further publication of the Pentagon Papers should be enjoined on national security grounds; to do so would impose an unconstitutional prior restraint upon the press prohibited by the First Amendment. "The press," said Justices Black and Douglas, "was to serve the governed, not the governors. The government's power to censor the press was abolished so that the press would remain forever free to censure the government."

The 6:3 decision, however, occasioned *nine opinions* justifying the holding on varying grounds. As in the Nebraska Press case, some Justices (Black and Douglas) contended the First Amendment prohibited *any* judicial restraint on the press. Brennan, Stewart, White, and Marshall believed on varying grounds that the government failed to meet the burden it must in interfering with First Amendment rights. The remaining three judges in dissent felt that the government had made such a case.

The majority of the Court clearly used a balancing of First Amendment and national security interests in arriving at a decision. The use of a balance test in cases involving national security interests, however, had a broader basis of Court support than did a balance of First Amendment interests with fair trial claims. The number of varying opinions and the narrow basis of the decision made the case of little value as precedent and did little to define the dimensions of law in the area.

(1) These two First Amendment cases involving freedom of the press illustrate the Court's reluctance to adopt a per se rule. Despite the broad nature of the Court's decision, the balancing test deters the Court in developing any readily applied rule.

(2) A clear holding in the "Pentagon Papers" case might have provided a precedent for the Nebraska Press case, but a divided holding presented in nine opinions failed to produce a landmark ruling on prior restraint.

(3) The Nebraska Press case demonstrates the difficulty the Court has had even when its members are in substantial agreement in articulating an unambiguous statement of its position.

EXPANDING THE SCOPE OF THE FIRST AMENDMENT: PROTECTING COMMERCIAL SPEECH

Although the freedoms of expression protected under the First Amendment have always been broad, the Burger Court has moved beyond the Warren Court in the areas protected. In unprecedented decisions, the Burger Court extended freedom of expression to purely commerical speech.

In 1974, Bigelow v. Virginia[69] granted First Amendment protection to commercial advertising. The case involved a conviction of a Virginia newspaper editor under a Virginia statute for printing an advertisement for a New York abortion referral agency. The Supreme Court of Virginia sustained the conviction on the grounds that the ad was "purely commercial speech" and as such not constitutionally protected. The Supreme Court 7:2 reversed. Justice Blackmun, for the Court, proposed a balancing test to determine if the speech in Bigelow's case should be protected. Two factors—the "public interest" content of the advertisement and the legality of the commercial activity—would be important in determining the scope of First Amendment protection. The Bigelow advertisement was "covered," the Court said, since abortion was both of general public interest and legal in New York. The Court noted that constitutional claims were stronger since there was a constitutional right to abortion; additionally, the defendant's claims were strengthened by his status as a member of the press. Virginia's interest in regulation of the advertising, Blackmun said, was entitled to little weight. The balance of interests clearly drawn, the Court held the Virginia statute unconstitutional.

The Court's decision rejected but did not overrule the 1942 case of Valentine v. Christensen.[70] Blackmun acknowledged the departure, but, by confining Valentine to the facts, managed to distinguish Bigelow while leaving the precedent—"advertising is unprotected per se"—intact. To do so left the status of commercial speech without clear definition. As the *Harvard Law Review* notes,[71]

> The *Bigelow* opinion reflects the continuing unwillingness of the Supreme Court to confront the underlying rationale of the commercial speech doctrine . . . the Court never attempted to provide a definition of commercial speech nor did it provide any guidance . . . as to what forms of state regulation will be considered valid.

Perhaps the most serious problem presented was introduced by Blackmun's "public interest" test. Defining a rule of law based on the public interest is a task so difficult that it has prompted even judicial comment. Additionally, while such a determination, if practicable, might appropriate to statutory considerations, it seems far less relevant to constitutional ones. Certainly there is little "restrained," nor in this case, precedented, in defining the dimensions of the First Amendment on such an ill-defined and protean basis.

In consideration of Virginia's interest, the Court suggests a test weaker than the "compelling or substantial interest" usually required for First Amendment restrictions. In doing so, the Court suggests different and indeed lesser protection might be afforded the newly protected speech, but the dimensions and protections of the "lesser protection" category go undefined.

In a decision last term, the Supreme Court clarified at least some of the questions raised by Bigelow but left others awaiting resolution. In Virginia State Board of Pharmacy v. Virginia Citizens Consumer Council, Inc.,[72] the Supreme Court, in a 7:1 opinion, sustained a challenge by Consumers of Virginia to a law prohibiting the advertisement of prescription drug prices. In striking down the Virginia statute, the Court declared that tentative, nondeceptive commercial speech is protected by the First Amendment. Utilizing a balancing test typical of almost all its considerations, the Court weighed the interests of consumers, advertisers, and pharmacists and found the interests favoring the free flow of commercial information clearly outweighed those favoring the ban:

> Advertising, however tasteless and excessive it sometimes may seem, is nonetheless dissemination of information as to who is producing and selling what product, for what reason, and at what price. So long as we preserve a predominantly free enterprise economy, the allocation of our resources in large measure will be made through numerous public economic decisions. It is a matter of public interest that those decisions, in the aggregate, be intelligent and well formed. To this end, the free flow of commerical information is indispensable.

While concluding that the advertising bans at issue were unconstitutional, the Court pointed out that not all bans would necessarily be so. The Chief Justice, concurring, cautioned, "Quite different factors would govern were we faced with a law regulating or even prohibiting advertising by the traditional learned professions of medicine or law." Although the Court indicated that protections afforded commercial speech might be different (e.g. lesser) than those afforded other types of speech, the criteria for distinguishing among purely commerical speech, fully protected, and unprotected speech remain unresolved.[73] The Court will no doubt have ample opportunity to make such considerations. Expanding the First Amendment protections into broad commercial areas on the basis of ill-defined criteria may bring a large number of state regulations into question and many of them into court.

(1) The Court's decisions on commerical speech opens up a new dimenstion of First Amendment adjudication. In entering into the commercial field, the Court again interjects considerable uncertainty into the law.

(2) The Bigelow Court declined to overturn Valentine's precedent holding that "advertising is unprotected *per se.*" In Virginia State Board of

Pharmacy, Blackmun, for the Court, acknowledged that with Bigelow, "the notion of unprotected commercial speech all but passed from the scene." The action of the Court in these two cases is a good illustration of Court-created uncertainty resulting from a failure to relate to governing precedent.

(3) The Court's difficulty in defining the characteristics of protected commercial speech interests is complicated by its introduction of the concept "lesser protection." How the category might be defined and the scope of rights that might be afforded await judicial clarification.

(4) The Court actions suggest that it will be inundated with cases designed to explore its commitment to and perspective of commericial speech.

CONSEQUENCES

In nearly every civil liberties area examined, the Court is plagued by deep divisions. The ideological spectrum represented on the Court is large, but the divisons persist even when the justices are in substantial policy agreement. It is difficult to account for the large number of concurring and dissenting opinions on purely ideological grounds. The concurring opinions frequently cover much the same ground as do lead opinions. Impact considerations which have motivated other Courts to present united fronts seem to have little force on this Court. The Burger Court appears to lack leadership. Careful assignment of the opinion to the Justice most likely to appeal to the Court's largest majority might minimize the number of opinions—dissenting and concurring. Bitter comments exchanged by Justices in their formal opinions suggest that the Court might lack the amiable or even polite environment which facilitates easy and unified decision-making. Chief Justice Burger seems to be neither the Court's social nor its task leader.[74]

Compliance with the Court's decisions may be weakened by this decisiveness. Commenting on how compliance is affected by the kind of Court decision, Steven Wasby notes that the "relative unanimity of the vote in the case" and the "existence of an 'opinion of the court'instead of a plurality opinion" affect compliance with the decision.[75] Division indicates a variety of opinions on the Court itself. As a result, the potential impact is decreased "and the vultures who would pick over the bones of the Court also use split decisions, particularly those which are five to four, as a grounds for delay, claiming that all that is needed to reverse a decision is for one judge to change his mind or be replaced on the Court."[76]

Similarly, ambiguity or a lack of precision in the Court's opinion decreases the probability of compliance. As Thomas Barth suggests, "Ambiguity of a decision increases the likelihood that it will be misunderstood by other actors in the political process and that the policies of the other participants will not be adjusted to conform to the decision."[77] By these standards, the Burger Court's decisions in these areas of civil liberties are unlikely to generate uniform compliance. Lower federal court judges, trial court judges, law enforcement officers, district attorneys, or any actors who might be responsible for applying the rulings of the Court in the area of civil liberties have the difficulty of compliance increased when the law is unclear.

The failure of the Supreme Court to establish a clear rule or standard maximizes the activity of the federal courts in general and the Supreme Court in particular. Conflicts, uncertainties, and unresolved issues become the basis of legal appeal. As Wasby notes in his discussion of the impact of Supreme Court decisions, one "possible result of ambiguity is that it forces people to come back to the courts to ascertain what is meant."[78] Similarly, increasing demands are placed on the lower courts. "The ambiguous parts of Supreme Court opinions 'invited' contestants to turn to lower courts for explication and elucidation of the high court's rulings . . . Contestants . . . might . . . have felt they could persuade lower courts to adopt new interpretations of higher court rulings."[79]

The lack of a rule of law wastes not only judicial resources but the time and resources of lawyers and litigants who must repeatedly go to the bench in order to ascertain their position vis-a-vis the law. In moving into new, ill-defined areas or in moving the law backward without a careful judicial position, the Court encourages litigants who see new prospects for legal victory.

The use of balancing tests and other formulas which eschew rule making in favor of a case-by-case consideration encourages litigants to appeal cases to the federal courts. Despite the Court's stated concern for "comity" and "federalism," its general failure to establish unambiguous precedent maximizes rather than minimizes its intervention in state court proceedings. As a result, the Court is extraordinarily activist—virtually every issue is a potentially justiciable one. The Court maximizes the scope of its power by defining civil liberties law so that it requires continuing judicial overview. As Lowi notes:[80]

A strong clear rule is an act of centralization by the Supreme Court. Yet at the same time it leads to significant decentralization of the caseload and a good deal of self administration by lower courts and counsel. To look at it in a slightly different way, an area with good leading opinions is an area of "easy law" in which there are few appeals to the top; nonetheless the area is centralized too, in the sense that each decision in each lower judicial unit becomes more consistent with all other comparable decisions, because the clear rule is a good criterion, departures from which are easily detectable by higher courts and clients. In contrast, the Supreme Court can inundate itself in areas of "hard law" where it cannot or will not enunciate a leading opinion expressing good governing rules. In such an area there is even greater centralization; but in the worst sense of the word because responsibility can be maintained only through regular, bureaucratic supervision.

Not surprisingly, the federal dockets are crowded with cases awaiting a final court word. Burger's concern for the growing number of cases on the federal dockets has lead to a number of actions which indicate the resolve to limit access to the federal courts. At the request of the Chief Justice, Congress abolished the remaining category of three-judge Federal District Courts, eliminating the direct appeals from them to the Supreme Court. The Chief Justice's commitment to limiting federal court access is also illustrated by his support of the controversial Fraud Commission Report which proposed the creation of a National Court of Appeals, to which the Supreme Court would yield part of its caseload.

Concern for caseload is also reflected in the Court's moves to limit access to the Supreme Court and the other federal courts. Limits in *habeas corpus* review are one example of such limitations. In discussing the issues of access, political scientist Robert J. Steamer suggested recently that it is simply: "a substantive one of letting some people in while keeping others out." He continues:[81]

> One might suggest facetiously that it is all a matter of likes and dislikes. The Warren Court liked criminals, minorities, and people who wear sweatshirts with four letter words on them. It did not like police, prosecuting attorneys, or draft card burners. The Burger Court likes the police (although not enough to permit them to wear long hair), welfare people, Indians, women, and drugstores. The Burger Court also likes wild jackasses, prefers them in fact to people, on the basis of its ruling upholding the Wild Free-Roaming Horses and Burros Act against all human attacks. The Burger Court dislikes prisoners, shoplifters, pushcart dealers, homosexuals and human fetuses during the first three months of gestation.

Even a facetious look at the likes and dislikes of the two Courts suggests that it is something more than a matter of letting some people in while keeping others out. In the area of dependent rights for example, to dislike prisoners and shoplifters while liking the police is a change in preference which is neither random nor slight. Even a cursory examination suggests that by limiting access, the Court has achieved essentially the same type of result it would have achieved in hearing and deciding the cases.

The limits on access should thus not be viewed as reflections of a belief in judicial restraint. Action to limit the number of cases that come to the Court on mandatory review increases the time to be spent in cases selected at the discretion of the Court from other dockets. Decreasing the number of routine tasks frees the Court to devote its attention to cases especially selected for High Court review. Inevitably, the Court increases its importance as a policy-making body.

The Supreme Court's move in civil liberties toward a more restrictive position in individual rights has created a considerable problem for the state courts. The Warren Court doctrine of incorporation made federally guaranteed rights applicable to the states. Gradually, both through action of the state legislatures and state courts, state due process rights were modeled after Warren Court interpretations. The Burger Court's retrenchment had yielded substantial dissimilarity between the rights being applied in the state courts and those provided for under the Burger Court law. In many situations, the rights afforded the citizen of the state exceed those to which he would be entitled under new federal standards. In a recent article in the *Harvard Law Review,* [82] Justice Brennan called on the states to increase individual rights under state constitutions. Brennan argued that the substantial evisceration of rights at the hands of the Burger court necessitated state action to preserve fundamental liberties. He applauded the laws of several states that afforded citizens greater protection than provided by the federal courts, not as a vestiges of earlier action, but as actions of conscious choice. The fact, however, that both attitudes exist and continue to develop contributes to the atmosphere of uncertainty that surrounds civil liberties policy.

Court decisions which do not derive from a general rule or standard give an ex post facto character to the law. A defendant is convicted or a case is decided under legal terms that did not exist prior to the hearing. Lowi charges that decision-making on such a basis cannot yield justice:[83]

> Considerations of the justice in or achieved by an action cannot be made unless a deliberate conscious attempt was made by the actor to derive his action from a general rule or moral principle governing such a class of acts . . . The best rule is one which is relevant to the decision or action in question and is general in the sense that those involved with it have no direct control over its action. A general rule is hence *a priori*. Any governing regime that makes a virtue of avoiding such rules puts itself outside the context of justice. . . . In the question of whether justice is achieved, a government without good rules and without acts carefully derived therefrom is merely a big bull in an immense china shop.

Political scientists have recognized the influence of two subcultures on the federal judiciary. The legal subculture, steeped in the norms of rule of law, judicial restraint, and adversary justice, and the democratic subculture with its norms of representativeness, majority rule, and community rights, have both had a significant impact on the structure and functioning of the judiciary.[84] Although the Court sits in a distinctly political setting, the functions given to the federal courts—the impartial resolution of conflict based on the rule of law and the protection of individual rights against encroachment by the state—were deemed incompatible with the purely democratic norm of majority rule. Thus judges, constrained by statute and the Constitution and restrained by role and precedent, pursue not majority rule but the rule of law.

In the area of civil liberties, the Burger Court seems to be responding primarily to political stimulae and to majoritarian norms to the exclusion of the norms of the legal subculture. The Court has given a priority to community rights over individual ones and has subjugated national standards and power to those of the states. While these goals are well established positions in other areas, for the Supreme Court to pursue them in the area of civil liberties leaves individual and minority interests without national protection. It assists more majoritarian branches of government, while the protection of the individual or minority is relegated to second priority or to the states. In pursuing these goals, the Court has deviated from precedent and failed to define a new rule of law that can be applied consistently and without continuing judicial clarification. It maximizes its activity but minimizes its role.

The Supreme Court is "a big bull in an immense china shop"— pursuing justice without good rules and failing to provide a rule of law, without which the guarantees of individual and minority liberty are but empty rhetoric.

NOTES

1. 408 U.S. 328 (1972). Discussions of this case and cases which follow also rely on descriptive material presented in weekly and term reviews of *The United States Law Week* as well as *Harvard Law Review's* annual term summary. Descriptive material on the 1975 term is also drawn from William H. Erickson, "Pronouncements of the Supreme Court of the United States in the Criminal Law Field: 1975-1976." *The National Journal of Criminal Defense*, 2 (Fall, 1976): 157-236.

2. Daniel B. Polsby, "The Death of Capital Punishment? Furman V. Georgia" in Philip B. Kurland (ed.), The Supreme Court Review 1972 (Chicago: University of Chicago Press, 1962): 40.

3. For a discussion of these cases see "The Supreme Court, 1975 Term," *Harvard Law Review*, 90 (1976): 63-76. See also Erickson, 196-204; J. Harvie Wilkinson, III, "Mr. Justice Powell: An Overview," *University of Richmond Law Review*, 11 (Winter, 1977): 259-268.

4. 428 U.S. 153 (1976).

5. Proffitt v. Florida 428 U.S. 242 (1976).

6. Jurek v. Texas 428 U.S. 262 (1976).

7. Woodson v. North Carolina 428 U.S. 280 (1976).

8. 428 U.S. 325 (1976).

9. 384 U.S. 436 (1966).

10. For discussion of Miranda's development, see Henry J. Abraham, *Freedom and the Court* (New York: Oxford University Press, 1977): 144-155. See also Barbara Child,

"The Involuntary Confession and the Right to Due Process. Is a Criminal Defendant Better Protected in the Federal Courts than in Ohio?", *Akron Law Review,* 10 (Fall, 1976): 261-282.

11. 401 U.S. 222 (1971).

12. Janice Gui, "Civil Rights in the Burger Court Era," *Akron Law Review,* 10 (Fall, 1976): 333-334.

13. 417 U.S. 433 (1974).

14. "The Supreme Court 1973 Term," *Harvard Law Review,* 88 (November, 1974): 200-201.

15. S.C. 1973 Term, 201-202.

16. 420 U.S. 714 (1975).

17. 406 U.S. 682 (1972).

18. 338 U.S. 218 (1967).

19. ' Civil Rights in the Burger Court Era," 334 (note 40).

20. 423 U.S. 96 (1975).

21. 425 U.S. 341 (1976).

22. 425 U.S. 564 (1976).

23. 422 U.S. 590 (1975)

24. 367 U.S. 643 (1961)

25. 232 U.S. 383 (1914)

26. 414 U.S. 338 (1974)

27. Henry P. Monaghan, "Forword: Constitutional Common Law." *Harvard Law Review,* 89 (November, 1975): 3.

28. See also Schrock and Welsh, "Up From Calandra: The Exclusionary Rule as a Constitutional Requirement," *Minnesota Law Review,* 59 (1974): 251-309.

29. 422 U.S. 531.

30. 413 U.S. 266 (1973)

31. "Review of Supreme Court's Work: Decisions on Criminal Law," *The United States Law Week,* 45 (August, 1976): 3127. See also "Balanced Justice: Mr. Justice Powell and the Constitution," *University of Richmond Law Review,* 2 (Winter, 1977): 365-377.

32. 428 U.S. 433 (1976).

33. 423 U.S. 411 (1976).

34. Rabinowitz v. U.S. 339 U.S. 56 (1950)

35. 427 U.S. 38 (1976).

36. Warden v. Hayden, 387 U.S. 294 (1967)

37. 428 U.S. 543 (1976).

38. Almeida-Sanchez v. U.S. 413 U.S. 266 (1973).

39. 428 U.S. 364 (1976).

40. Texas v. White 423 U.S. 67

41. 399 U.S. 42 (1970)

42. 116 U.S. 616 (1886)

43. 425 U.S. 391 (1976).

44. 427 U.S. 463 (1976).

45. "The Supreme Court's 1975 Term," 78.

46. 425 U.S. 435 (1976).

47. 428 U.S. 465 (1976). For a discussion of Stone v. Powell see Sam Boyte, "Federal Habeas Corpus After *Stone v. Powell:* A Remedy Only for the Arguably Innocent?" *University of Richmond Law Review,* 11 (Winter, 1977): 291-331, Ronald S. Flagg, "*Stone v. Powell* and the New Federalism: A Challenge to Congress." *Harvard Journal on Legislation,* 14 (December, 1976): 152-171.

48. "The Supreme Court, 1975 Term," 214.

49. "The Supreme Court, 1975 Term," 220-221.

50. William J. Brennan, Jr., "State Constitutions and the Protection of Individual Rights," *Harvard Law Review,* 90 (Winter, 1976): 496-497.

51. The background for the obscenity discussion and other First Amendment case backgrounds rely heavily on Henry J. Abraham, *Freedom and The Court* (New York: Oxford University Press, 1977).

52. 354 U.S. 476 (1957)

53. 378 U.S. 184 (1964)

54. 354 U.S. 476 (1957)

55. Abraham, p. 220.

56. 413 U.S. 15 (1973)

57. Jenkins v. Georgia, 418 U.S. 153

58. Hamling v. United States 418 U.S. 87 (1974).

59. 419 U.S. 822 (1975)

60. "The Supreme Court, 1974 Term," *Harvard Law Review,* 89 (November, 1975): 131

61. "The Supreme Court, 1974 Term," 131

62. 424 U.S. 669 (1976).

63. 427 U.S. 50 (1976).

64. See "The Supreme Court, 1975 Term," *Harvard Law Review,* 90 (November, 1976): 196-205.

65. 427 U.S. 539 (1976). See "The Supreme Court, 1975 Term," 159-171.

66. "The Supreme Court, 1975 Term," 168.

67. See Abraham, 186-189

68. 403 U.S. 713 (1971); 403 U.S. 713 (1971).

69. 421 U.S. 809.

70. 316 U.S. 52 (1942)

71. "The Supreme Court, 1974 Term," 115.

72. 425 U.S. 748 (1976).

73. See "The Supreme Court, 1975 Term," 142-152.

74. For a discussion of leadership on the Court, see David J. Danelski, "The Influence of the Chief Justice in the Decisional Process of the Supreme Court," in *The Federal Judicial System.* Thomas P. Jahnige and Sheldon Goldman (eds.), (New York: Holt, Rinehart and Winston, 1968): 147-165.

75. Stephen L. Wasby, *The Impact of the United States Supreme Court: Some Perspectives* (Homewood, Ill: Dorsey Press, 1970): 44.

76. Wasby, 44.

77. Thomas E. Barth, "Perception and Acceptance of Supreme Court Decisions at State and Local Level," *Journal of Public Law,* 17, 2 (1968): 314, as cited in Wasby, p. 46.

78. Wasby, 46.

79. Wasby, 46.

80. Theodore, J. Lowi, *The End of Liberalism (New York: W. W. Norton, 1969): 302.*

81. Robert J. Steamer, "Contemporary Supreme Court Directions." Unpublished paper delivered at the Southern Political Science Association, Atlanta, Georgia, November 5, 1976: 5.

82. William J. Brennan, Jr. "State Constitutions and the Protection of Individual Rights," *Harvard Law Review* 90 (Winter, 1976): 489-504. See also Gui, 354-366; "Protecting Fundamental Rights in State Courts: Fitting a State Peg to a Federal Hole,

Harvard Civil Rights Civil Liberties Law Review, 12 (Winter, 1977): 63-112; A.E. Dick Howard, "State Courts and Constitutional Rights in the Day of the Burger Court," *Virginia Law Review,* 62 (1976): 891-906.

83. Lowi, 290-291.

84. Richard J. Richardson and Kenneth Vines, *The Policies of the Federal Courts* (Boston: Little Brown, 1970).

Part IV

THE INTERNATIONAL FABRIC

CAN NATIONAL POLICIES
PROMOTE WORLD PEACE?

13.

FOREIGN POLICY

GEORGE H. QUESTER

Cornell University

THE SPECIAL NATURE OF FOREIGN POLICY

One should introduce a few questions at the outset about the differences between foreign policy and the ordinary "public policy" we see in the domestic arena. When we look for the to-be-agreed-upon goals of domestic policy, we tend to talk of "the public interest." When we do the same for foreign policy, we tend rather to refer to "the national interest." Is this merely a slight difference in usage, or is it a signal of some bigger differences? Is there any reason why one should have all along expected foreign policy to be less rational or more rational? Why indeed have political science departments in American universities so long tended to have a separate course on foreign policy, and only recently begun to offer matching courses on public policy, agricultural policy, educational policy, mass transit policy, and other domestic policy areas?

One quick suggestion, of course, might simply be that foreign policy is much more important, involving such awe-inspiring questions as the prevention of nuclear war. A very opposite kind of explanation for the special treatment of foreign policy would note that the public's education and awareness in this area tends to be far more abysmally weak than in the other policy areas cited. The special courses of American universities might thus amount to a massive remedial education program.

Neither of these probably, however, explains what is special about foreign policy.[1] What is special is that it is generally seen to have an "enemy," a continuing need to deal with a rational adversary. This supposed need produces not only secrecy, but strategy and a sense of combative solidarity. And in the wake of this, it produces seemingly greater clarity about common goals, and seemingly greater opportunities for optimization and rational policy analysis. It is no accident, it will be argued here, that the most prominent "success stories" for rational public policy analysis in the United States were first written in areas of foreign policy, and also that the greatest disappointments then followed.

In the domestic sector, we do not find ourselves adopting the working assumption of having an adversary, a rational antagonist against whom we must close ranks. In the prevention of floods or epidemics, or the avoidance of unemployment, we do not steel ourselves to worry that "the enemy might be listening."

One can think of relatively few issues on the domestic side which impose a continuing need for secrecy. Advance information on the next location of new highways or the timing of currency devaluations must be held closely, of course, but these are the exception, rather than the rule. By contrast, secrecy is almost the rule in foreign policy, with openness the exception, because the foreign ministry of another state might exploit our openness. But the secrecy is indeed merely the symptom of a broader form of institutionalized hostility toward foreign governments, and institutionalized expectations of loyalty among one's own citizens. While American Congressmen on domestic issues are urged to have split loyalties, taking their constituents' wishes and needs into account, but also paying attention to national needs, no such diversity of goals is advocated for the foreign policy practitioner. As a working myth, foreign service academies still use something like "my country above all" as their first approximation of a goal.

The goals of foreign policy may include items very similar to those we might be discussing in public policy areas. We might want to stamp out a disease in the United States, and we might want to foster a regime in Ethiopia equally capable of stamping out disease there.

The fact that foreign regimes are involved, however, adds other categories of goals. The multiplicity of regimes produces the possibility of something called war. A set of accompanying concerns thus emerges, to reduce the likelihood of war, to reduce the costs of war if it comes, and to reduce the costs in peacetime of preparing for war. Another consideration which emerges from the multiplicity of regimes is simply concern for one's independence. Whatever else one may wish to achieve in foreign policy, an important ingredient will be maintaining the self-determination of one's own country. All this sets the stage for some of the special opportunities of foreign policy, along with some of the special problems.

In domestic policy, it is thus more difficult to judge what is to be maximized, and more difficult to discover what can be labelled Pareto Optimal solutions. If any one of the parties to a domestic dispute announces himself as having different preferences from the rest of the bargainers, the Pareto Optimality is upset. The bargainers hardly are dismayed by this, because the compromising of differences was the bulk of the process all the time.

In the foreign policy arena, it is easy to get to a stage where the remaining human conflict will no longer arise among Americans, but between Americans (as represented by their foreign policy apparatus) and another people's apparatus. It is at that point that clarification's breakthroughs, and victories will begin to seem possible. It is at that point that systems analysis may seem to promise greater and more unequivocal rewards. It is not so surprising that the "rational activist" would feel abundantly at home with foreign policy problems, at least at first blush. While this produced a sense of momentum and self-esteem for such advocates of rational policy analysis in the United States Defense Department, however, it did not produce anything like this in the Department of State.

THE CASE FOR POLICY OPTIMIZATION

The subject area of foreign policy has thus produced the most highly acclaimed applications of rational policy analysis in the U.S. government, and also the most generally endorsed findings of failure. The introduction of systems analysis and program budgeting into the Department of Defense in the Kennedy Administration became the model of what would later also be attempted for the rest of government. The Vietnam war by contrast has been the enbodiment of a general disillusionment with foreign policy and with activist government in general. The peaks and lows of the popular acclaim of rational analysis here in part reflect some idiosyncracies of foreign policy, which this article will attempt to explore. But another part of it may instead reflect a more general cycle of initial enthusiasm combined with hidden pitfalls, a cycle which can plague the application of rational public policy analysis anywhere.

In general terms, it is as hard to be against optimization, against rational budgeting, and rational policy analysis, as it is to be against motherhood. Why not now get all the facts and look at all the possibilities? Why not coordinate and manage the interactions of our government, so as to harness and to exploit the externalities and the spinoffs. By using rational programming and budgeting techniques, as taught by any good business school in 1960, one could avoid inadvertant pursuits of the wrong payoffs, one could relate governmental expenditures to end products rather than to line-item inputs.[2]

The general prescriptions here, as applied most interestingly to defense, were never to take the budget for granted as it stood, as Eisenhower apparently had done between 1952 and 1960, but to consider alternative higher and lower budgets, including budgets even going all the way down to zero. One similarly no longer was to take the functional boundaries of the armed services for granted, but rather was to be free to consider redefining the roles of the army and air force and navy. By extension, any ambassador in the future would be enjoined to consider and reconsider the role divisions between his cultural and commercial attaches.

Everything was to be related to final outputs, always asking the question of "what are we doing here?" Are we simply buying missiles? No, we are buying deterrence, while somewhere else we are buying the ability to fight local wars. Similarly, on other fronts, one might cease to be simply buying student-exchange, and instead see himself buying cultural closeness, and/or overseas governmental influence.

The battle-tested intuitions of the professional military were to be questioned at all levels. The new wisdom of the operations-analysis input was often illustrated with juicy examples from World War II, with cases where the enemy was clear, but where the intermediate object of pursuit in defeating him was misstated.

For example, one had the decisions on how to allocate antiaircraft guns to merchant ships running the gauntlet through the Mediterranean past the attacks of German dive bombers. Was it correct, as the military had conjectured, to assign such guns on the basis of how many Axis aircraft were being shot down, thus assuming that the guns were misplaced if they found no targets on a particular run? If this had indeed been the relevant object of maximization on this front, the advocates of more serious analysis would at least have been justified in insisting that the count of airplanes shot down be done carefully, rather than intuitively. But a rigorous analysis suggested that the count of airplanes shot down was not the appropriate maximand; rather it was the number of Allied merchant ships brought safely into port. An Allied antiaircraft gun which never found any German dive-bombers to shoot at might not have been misassigned, by this more refined analysis, but might have been making exactly the right contribution to the war effort, deterring German bomber attacks by its very presence.

Efforts to generalize the policy analysis propositions here basically amounted to applied economics. One should be clear about establishing the object of maximization, being careful to avoid settling for any seemingly appropriate yardsticks of success which in truth were not identical to the overall goal. One would not simply call this "utility," for this risked being a tautology. One instead hunted for something more concrete, which nonetheless in its own maximization would tend to maximize the national interest.

Having carefully thought through the object of pursuit, one would then also want to be careful about measuring real impact on that object, collecting objective data, in place of subjective impressions, wherever possible.

Some general rules could then be applied: the ratio of costs to returns for each venture should be equal, or else one would know that we were missing an opportunity for a Pareto Optimal improvement in shifting energy and resources from one sector to another. One should similarly pursue each project until the marginal cost had come to be equal to marginal returns. The logic would be remarkably close to what economists imputed to the profit-maximizing decisions of the firms of private enterprise, but the important difference would hold that the maximand was not business profits, but some aspect of the national interest (e.g., defeat of Nazi Germany, or the containment of expansionist Communism).

The entire drift of rational policy analysis here was thus framed as a counter to ignorance, or perhaps as a counter to what later might have been labelled "organizational process," the mindless turning out of program decisions without any real consideration of ends and means. Explicating the relationships of inputs and outputs, in this view, would improve the cost-effectiveness of the decisions reached. It would bring policies closer to what is normally called the "national interest" in foreign policy matters, or what is usually called the "public interest" in the domestic sector.

LIMITS TO ANALYTICAL ABILITY

Perhaps foreign policy might thus merit the claim of being the one area of policy most appropriate for national policy analysis, most lending itself to a search for Pareto Optimality. Yet, even the area most appropriate for rationality may display limits on how much rationality is possible.

But what could be wrong with such proposals for reform and improvement? Did the advocates of rational approaches to public policy in the area of defense, and more generally in foreign policy, not have an airtight case?

The first answer to this might have gone as follows: If all such assessments of impact could be done, fine; but if they could not be done, it was a mistake to try.[3]

Are all of life's opportunities expandible if one only studies them enough? Some might conclude yes, assuming that further analysis of the choices for government policy will always unearth some new opportunities, some new savings for the taxpayer, or new benefits in terms of policy output. A more realistic assessment might, however, counter that the returns here will often be far less than the energy invested in the analysis. It is either a tautology or a falsehood for one to assert that "additional information should always be brought to bear." It is a tautology if one defines "information" as the higher analysis that goes behind all questions (e.g., even on "should we study this further"). It is a falsehood if we think of information on the policy-choices themselves as an infinitely pursuable commodity.

Pessimism on the "can we do it any better" question can, of course, be a rationalization for quitting too early, a defense for those in government who are lazy or of below-average competence. But optimism on this question can be a rationalization also, a rationalization for playing too long with a particular opportunity, while in the meantime neglecting others which would be more productive.

The inherent tradeoffs here are well illustrated by some of the clichés which show up in the foreign policy process, and indeed in all the governmental process. Who is against coordination and analysis? Virtually no one. But everyone is against paperwork. The codewords are simply switched, as one shifts from the positive possibilities of "further study" to the negative.

One could of course trim the systems analysis proposal down to simply "measure what can be measured." If some things do not lend themselves so much to sharper calculation of inputs and outputs, let us limit the analysis to those other variables that do.

Yet this has risks also. There is a real danger here of a subtle tendency to overweigh such precisely calculated variables in the overall mix. Perhaps this is because of the extra effort in the calculation of these particular variables, with an implication that one will expect to find some overall decisions that were changed, thus justifying the human and computer time that went into the calculations. Perhaps it will be simply because precise numerical answers will look more powerful and important than the fuzzier answers of other categories.

One can cite homely university examples to demonstrate the tendency. A department will every so often attempt to apply operations research methods to take stock of what it is achieving as an educational output. Along with all the other mushier considerations of output, one may unearth some crisper data on total courses taught, total improvement in test scores, or whatever. When any committee then takes all such considerations into account for the evaluation of various policy choices, there is clear tendency to let the crisper numerical differences dominate choices, even when the data did not apply to categories which anyone would have rated as most important.

HIDDEN PRICES FOR ANALYSIS

But a second kind of problem with the application of rational analysis emerges even when the information-management work can be done. The problem relates to the rationing and allocation of the credit for the perceptions of opportunity. How does one reward a superior technocrat, for example, Secretary of Defense McNamara, without mistakenly thereby also allocating authority to undertake decisions on values?

There is a real risk here of confusing someone's "rationality on opportunities" with a "rationality on preferences," of deciding that wisdom on showing how more can be done for less, in the field of defense policy or foreign policy, is connected logically with wisdom and authority on which "more" should be pursued in terms of foreign-policy outputs.

Good systems analysis, as applied to public policy, in effect offers something free. It identifies Pareto Optimal moves in which waste and redundancy are eliminated. As is evident from the reading of any of the literature extolling and defending the McNamara innovations after 1961, it brooks little or no criticism, because it replaces some prior arrangements which are clearly dominated by the newer solutions. The phrase "rational activism" captures a lot of the spirit of the position here, a general dissatisfaction with the wasteful prior arrangements which were non-Pareto Optimal, which could basically be improved upon at zero-cost. Yet in the political world, does anyone ever give something for free? Or is there a subtle price exacted in the case of such free-good operations-research innovations, a price which might have been quite injurious to the overall public interest also?

The technocrats who took over part of foreign policy in the rational-ization of defense could be accused of grabbing various kinds of payoff here. Some of it came in "use decisions," as suggested just above (for example, as McNamana pushed his own ideas on the development of conventional defenses for Europe, ideas which most Europeans and perhaps a majority of Americans never endorsed).

Another form of payoff, less directly linked to policy substance, is the accumulation of an image of infallibility, a stockpiling of reputation which became clearly evident in the case of Secretary McNamara and then, in a somewhat modified form, became a problem also with Henry Kissinger. If policy analysis allows policy practitioners to offer no-cost,

Pareto Optimal improvements, the kind of improvement where everyone comes out ahead and no one suffers, this may develop a vested interest which blocks the serious handling of decisions where someone has to lose.

The correct handling of this problem for the technocrat might seem easy to describe; pay him in cash rather than in reputation. Yet doing this in practice may be much more difficult, or indeed impossible, in a world of public curiosity and the press's search for heroes. Someone who has collected a reputation for taking up slack may have escaped criticism, and may have become very used to escaping it, but when the issues become those of rationing scarcity, rather than eliminating waste, criticism may come soon enough. The worry, of course, will be that the issues of allocating scarcity will then somehow be mishandled, as part of an effort to prolong the escape from criticism.

THE SPECIAL SUCCESSES OF DEFENSE

One can hardly deny that the accomplishments of program-budgeting within the Department of Defense were quite substantial. A great deal of money was saved in the identification of obvious irrationalities and redundancies, in the elimination of simple waste. Perhaps even more significant, a substantially greater military potential was achieved in the process of asking the right questions and taking the time to compute the right answers. Traditional categories of military function were no longer taken for granted, and traditional seat-of-the-pants estimates of military value were no longer accepted. Practical experience and intuition were challenged by more scientific approaches, with a substantial amount of grumbling directed against the new whiz kids by the old professionals.

Yet the success of the McNamara innovations then sets the stage for the question of whether the Defense Department might not have been a special case. Could it be that extraordinary factors made Defense especially ripe for the introduction of "rational policy analysis," in ways which could not be duplicated for the rest of foreign policy, or indeed for the rest of government? Could it be that even the impact of such improvements within Defense could be overstated or misinterpreted, as a sudden taking-up of slack misled observers into assuming that similar gains could be extracted year after year?

One can think of several reasons why Defense was especially prone to reform at this point.[4] We will look at these first, and then turn to the "comparative pathology" of the State Department, and of all of foreign policy, to see whether one should have expected very parallel developments, or very different.

At the beginning of the Kennedy administration, the United States was perceiving that a fundamental shift had occurred within the military-industrial complex, as to which side of it would be called upon to conceptualize the military hardware of the future. While the army or the navy would have done this in earlier days, and then directed industry to the task, a sharp reversal was underway, where industry would now have to be the first to identify weapons possibilities as they come onto the horizon. The shift here to civilian weapons planners inevitably would upgrade the civilian management side of the Department of Defense, while downgrading the uniformed officers.

Second, the revolution in the availability of computers meant that it would be possible to calculate numerical estimates which previously would perforce have had to be left to the intuitions of experienced officers. This capability clearly required that it be used where it could, but it meant a shift in policy-making procedures.

Third, the change in forms of warfare had eroded the clarity of inter-service distinctions, as the army and navy would have to cooperate more than ever before in amphibious operations, since each would have to integrate more than before with the air force. Blatant discrepancies between the numbers of paratroopers trained by the army and the numbers of troop carrier aircraft supplied by the air force were examplary of the generally growing need for coordination.

Fourth, related to this, was the Kennedy Administration's assumption that the functionality of military forces would generally have to be restored. What was irrational in the force preparations of the army or navy might have made less difference when all wars were going to escalate immediately into World War III, anyway. But now less reliance would be placed on using such forces merely as tripwires to bring massive nuclear retaliation into play, and more stress would be directed to preparing for limited conventional wars.

Rational budgeting thus developed a certain momentum and track record and public reputation, on what were perhaps the special kinds of slack and waste which had existed in Defense, or the special new opportunities and changes of role which hit Defense in the early 1960s. After 1965, an effort was made under President Lyndon Johnson to extend program budgeting and systems-analysis to all of government, as part of a "learn from the Defense Department" campaign (not quite the same as the Chinese "learn from the People's Liberation Army").[5] The years from 1961 to 1965 had seen Defense largely exempted from the scrutiny of the Budget Bureau, as the superior internal methods of Defense seemed to suggest only the most perfunctory review by the budget analysts who were so carefully monitoring all the civilian-sector departments.

But the introduction of program-budgeting to the rest of the government can hardly be said to have produced the enthusiasm or aura of success that was achieved in Defense. If there is anything to the idea that a foreign "enemy" produces the clearest arrangements for the application of theories of optimization, then it would not be surprising that the Defense area would exemplify this. Foreigners are never quite so "foreign," never quite so much the object of a "united national effort" to thwart their purposes, as when one is contemplating the possibility of fighting a war against them.

Compared to this, a domestic debate on how to handle a natural gas shortage is simply a cacophony of explicitly competing interests. Compared to this, the more "peaceful" foreign policy decisions of the State Department may have similarly produced less objective agreement on what was to be maximized, and less of a single common goal.

THE SPECIAL FAILURES OF STATE

Why did the high morale of the policy analysis approach not transplant to State? Why is there a general consensus in the American foreign policy process that State suffers from chronically low morale, from extreme pessimism about whether rational policy analysis can be achieved?[6]

Some of the low morale of State must simply be traced to confusions about its function. Is the State Department to be the grand coordinator of all foreign policy, or just the executor of a special part of it? Some of the grand coordinator role is suggested by the ways in which it was founded, indeed even by its title. Why a "State" Department rather than a "Department of Foreign Affairs?" Why is the Secretary of State given the decidedly domestic chore of proclaiming the enactment of Amendments to the Constitution?

Yet the State Department has inexorably lost most of such central coordination function to the staffs of the White House, even while it has been faced also with rivals in a vastly expanded day-to-day practice of active diplomacy. Having in effect been demoted from the general staff of the entire army of the foreign policy battle, to become just one of its combat divisions, the Department of State has thus been burdened by the morale problems of a shrinking role.

As the growth of the foreign policy problem has dictated the minting of staffs closer to the President than the State Department, since 1945 it has also introduced a greater role for the Departments of Defense and of the Treasury, both generally to be viewed as "high-morale" departments. To grow in function in the federal bureaucracy is to convince oneself that one is doing a good job, that "rational policy" is indeed being made. Thus, the mere shift in burdens can explain some of the optimism of Defense and the pessimism of State on foreign policy analysis. It can also suggest that all such optimism was badly taken, as the inherent confusion of an increasingly divided foreign policy task would exact a price soon enough.

The reality of State's coordination role has thus been preempted by the White House and diluted by the growth of importance in other department's operations. But the American myth is still nonetheless that foreign policy *needs* to be coordinated, and the State is responsible for doing it. Periodic announcements are made that the U.S. Ambassador to each foreign country is to be head of the "country-team" (i.e., that all U.S. government operations in that country are to be overseen and coordinated by the representative of State). Whether such coordination is needed goes almost unquestioned. How can the United States be operating in London without coordination among its agencies? One might note in contrast that various agencies of the U.S. Federal Government seem to operate separately in Elmira without coordination, without periodic meetings of the "Elmira team."

Whether such coordination is actually achieved by a weekly meeting in the Ambassador's office is a different question, less frequently addressed, with the result typically being negative.

If State's need to share labor with Defense and Treasury occasioned some confusion before 1960 (and some lowered morale in State), this confusion can only be growing worse with the much more manifold division we are finding necessary in the 1970s. It has been suggested that every cabinet department except Housing and Urban Development (HUD) now must have a substantial foreign operation, and now plays an unignorable role in American foreign policy.

By the scorecards to be applied by systems analysis, the State Department thus could have been expected to come out badly. In terms of national mythology, it was still made to feel accountable for any lack of coordination in American foreign policy, even as coordination was becoming harder to achieve, even as its power to control and coordinate other departments has been declining. Failures of coordination look a lot like inefficiency and waste, like slack to be taken up. But taking up the slack among parallel foreign policy agencies may require more power than State has.

Some of State's performance will, of course, pertain not to any overall coordination of other agencies or the totality of American foreign policy, but rather to the efficiency and rationality with which it executes policy in the domains that are still exclusively its own. But here, too, State has consistently brought poor grades down upon itself. As the American public was congratulating McNamara for technocratic genius and rational efficiency in the day-to-day operations of the military structure, the parallel front-line structures of State showed no signs of cost-benefit analysis or operations research. Indeed, State showed a great reluctance to accept the procedures of program-budgeting, and responded with general criticisms of the utility and practicality of all such efforts. "How can one measure the output of foreign policy operations in numbers?" was a typical response. How can one assess the impact of a cultural exchange program by which American jazz musicians go to Moscow, and the Bolshoi Ballet comes to New York? How should we then interpret such a clear division about foreign policy analysis, whereby the civilian leaders of Defense are calling for full use of operations research and the civilians of State are denouncing it? One possibility, implicitly suggested above, might simply be that the two departments had been sorted into handling the most tangible, and least tangible, parts of policy. If one can be crisp and didactic about the operations of antisubmarine warfare, one has to be mushy about a cultural exchange program.

A considerably different view, however, traced the disputes to weaknesses and self-serving defensiveness in State. The bulk of the problem, as seen by the rational-activists, was no longer simple ignorance or organizational process, but rather the conscious pursuit of narrow career interests before the national interest; the conscious moves of less competent people protecting themselves against the unemployment they would face if the American public were ever to become aware of their inefficiencies.[7] The supporters of the civilian echelon in Defense had often noticed subtle alliances and agreements between the professional, uniformed soldiers, whose judgments were being overridden in the Pentagon, and the career, Foreign Service officers, who had been around for the same length of time across the Potomac.

A third point of view, of course, to which we have to return, is that the traditionalists in State were correct all along, not only about the pitfalls of "rational policy analysis" in the nonmilitary sides of foreign policy, but about similar pitfalls within the alleged areas of success in McNamara's Pentagon.

SECOND THOUGHTS ABOUT DEFENSE

It is a fair generalization that many of McNamara's "clear successes" of 1965 looked far less impressive by 1975. Even within the terms of straightforward weapons procurement, the cases where objective rational analysis was inherently most likely to show Pareto Optimal successes, serious second thoughts were in order. The TFX became the F-111 and basically proved a failure. The C-5A transport was similarly a non-success for the methods of operations research.

One of the alleged advantages of program-budgeting was that it allowed Congressmen and Presidents and taxpayers to know the end-use for which line-item weapons were intended. Yet even here the boundary between the "program-packages" of strategic warfare and general-purpose forces turned out to be a fuzzy one. The B-52 was obviously an original part of the strategic warfare package, but by 1966 was in continual use for dropping non-nuclear bombs on supposed Viet Cong positions in South Vietnam. The latter use may or may not have been a worthwhile return for the money which had been spent five years earlier in maintaining such bombers, but the new budget format in any event would not have shown this, and in its own terms would only have been misleading.

The cases cited tended to support both of the originally cited qualms about the advantages of rational analysis. What if it cannot be done? What if the exact functions of a weapons system cannot be accurately measured and predicted? Is it not a mistake to pretend accuracy and prediction where one does not in truth have it? And if predictions can be made well on some things, if slack can be taken up, is there not the risk that infallibility here can become addictive, as may have been the problem in the TFX procurement?

But more serious problems, besides these first two, may have been coupled to the phenomenon of rational activism. The risk was inevitable that confidence that one "could take up the slack" would produce a more general confidence through all of foreign policy that "more could be done." It may be no accident that all of this came to the surface in the early 1960s, the "days of Camelot," in the Kennedy Administration, which saw a general upsurge of optimism engulf considerations of American governmental policy on many different questions.[8]

The Republican Eisenhower Administration had come across as a great respecter of limitations, both at home and abroad. In domestic policy, the Republicans preached that there was a limit to what government could do. On foreign policy, there was a general apprehension that the U.S. should not try to do more than it could.

The Kennedy Democrats, by contrast, brought in thoughts of "new frontiers" and Keynesian economics; an expectation that economic growth and full employment and more effective defense of threatened states of the Free World could all be undertaken and achieved. It is in those Kennedy years that public opinion polls for the first and only time saw Americans rejecting the pessimistic prediction that "we are losing the Cold War." It was thus a period that saw a general sense of Pareto Optimal possibilities all across the board, illustrated perhaps by the insights that operations research methods had brought to defense, but reaching well beyond; improvements could be made by which everyone would be ahead.

There was seemingly no need yet to acknowledge any inherent limits, by which to do better in one category was always to do worse in another. Such limitationist arguments were what one expected of Eisenhower and the Republicans, of career Foreign Service Officers, and of career uniformed officers. But the limitationist arguments were to be brushed aside.

In retrospect, of course, all of this optimism and enthusiasm for the days of Camelot looks bad. Altogether appropriate to our topic, one must note the disillusionment about the entire spectrum of political and economic possibilities which followed in foreign policy's wake. The war in Vietnam began as an example of "can do" attitudes in the McNamara Pentagon, and in the end was seen as a prime "can't be done" exemplar. Similar disillusionments ensued about the possibilities of reconciling political democracy with economic equality ("economic democracy") all around the underdeveloped world.

At home, the disillusionment then arose with regard to the War on Poverty and the Great Society and even, after a time, to such purely technological developments as the BART rapid transit system. Where computers and computation had, a little earlier, seemed a great liberating breakthrough, they now came to seem untrustworthy sources of foul-ups in what had previously been well-managed human processes. The worst examples of the American problems in the Vietnam War came to be illustrated by the "body counts"—an attempt to be precise and scientific about the trends toward or away from American victory—by "measuring what previously had been estimated by intuition," or "counting what can be counted." Apart from its sheer grotesque nature, it predictably enough became an exercise in deliberate deception and inadvertant self-deception, with guesses being rephrased as reliable data; with decisions coming to be framed around such data more than they rationally should have been.

IS CAPABILITY SOMETIMES UNDESIRABLE?

There is yet a fourth problem with the "successes" of rational policy-planning in defense that may seem bizarre. Could it be that in the early 1960s we made the military services more functional than they needed to be, or indeed more functional than they should have been?

This draws us fairly directly into theories of military strategy and nuclear deterrence. As noted, the army and navy in the Eisenhower years were widely seen as having become mere tripwires for the massive retaliation which might be inflicted by the U.S. Air Force. It made little difference, in the view, whether the army could really be effective in conventional war battles defending Berlin or West Germany, since the mere presence of American soldiers in a future combat situation would be likely to trigger a full American nuclear commitment, and thus would deter such combat from ever breaking out.

The Kennedy and McNamara tendency was, as noted above, to criticize this, and to seek more real combat options for the professional military. The supposed result of serious operations research about conventional forces was thus to be that a meaningful non-nuclear defense of Germany and Vietnam and other marginal areas could be achieved.

What could be the costs of such a conversion? The gains seemed obvious, offering an American President options other than World War III for the defense of Germany, keeping Vietnam from falling to salami tactics if the American bluff on nuclear retaliation were called. Why would anyone be against having an army that could really fight as an army, when the status quo amounted only to a military plaything for generals or bureaucrats who were unwilling to question their own traditions and experiences?

In retrospect, several kinds of cost can be identified. First, the massive retaliation deterrence of attacks on places like West Berlin and West Germany may already have been credible and adequate, so that additional infantry power and effectiveness were simply redundant. No matter how efficiently the Defense Department was administered, the addition of substantial amounts of conventional warfare capability was likely to cost money, and the Defense budget rose from about $45 billion in the last of the Eisenhower years to something over $50 billion under Kennedy.

There were additional reasons to expect an increase in cost. The very process that brought greater rationality and effectiveness to the conventional army, navy, and air force brought a reduction in reputation and status for the uniformed admirals and generals whose judgment had been displaced. Bureaucrats, like other people, can be paid in money or in reputation. Given the blows inflicted on their reputations by McNamara's whiz kids, it is doubtful that these officers would have stood for this, but for the accompanying substantial increases in the amounts of appropriations they were given to spend. By accident, rather than by design, the new civilian leadership in Defense thus had bought the right to allocate money rationally, but had bought it only by allocating more money. One

wonders what would have happened if the operations research practitioners had tried to implement rational policy in Defense without having
this extra money to disburse; one suspects that their efforts would have
brought a wave of press leaks and complaints far in excess of what was
encountered, a wave which might have made it much harder for Kennedy
and McNamara to retain the political support they needed.

Efficiency does not directly relate to how much is spent. How much to
spend, in fact, is more a value question than an efficiency question. Yet
the reality of 1961 was that greater efficiency needed more than the
systems-analysis insights that were brought to bear, it also needed more
money to spend.

Would the U.S. public want to spend less money, with inefficiencies, or
have more efficiency at producing military power, by spending more
money? Such may have been the real choice, because of the inherent
power of career professionals to fight back when their personal interests
come into conflict with someone's view of the national interest. In a world
of selfless men, interested only in the country's welfare, this would not
have been a problem. But it is politically naive to assume such a world. As
noted above, even the advocates of rationality can be suspected of being
not altogether selfless men.

Yet the problem here may come to be remembered as worse than one of
unnecessary or redundant expenditures. Could it be that military forces
that are functional are actually worse than redundant, worse than a
meaningless "improvement," as they set up a hunt for their own use?
When asked where the projected enhancement of conventional warfare
capabilities could make any significant difference, the spokesmen of the
Kennedy Administration at the start had typically talked of the threats to
West Berlin and to Western Europe. When the threats here abated after
the Cuban missile crisis, the focus shifted typically to countries like
Vietnam.

There are at least two separate versions of the "ability leads to trouble"
argument to be considered here. One would be illustrated by reference to
the "prisoners' dilemma" problem of game theory, whereby certain kinds
of political capability or military capability will inherently frighten two
sides into lunging at each other, in conflicts or wars which neither side
truly wanted. Each side is tempted to strike when it has offensive
capabilities, on land, or sea, or in the air. Each, moreover, is deeply
concerned about whether the other side may not use similar capabilities
in a preemptive attack. In a crisis, the rule than becomes "shoot first, and
ask questions later."

Such reasoning helps to explain the outbreak of World War I. It was
also typically the model of how World War III could break out, in the
days of vulnerable bomber forces or first-generation missiles on each

side. On the conventional war front, similar preemptive temptations might thus have been generated by the Kennedy-McNamara investment in counterinsurgency forces, which would try to preempt the guerrilla offensives of the other side, or by the investment in expanded air transport and naval transport capacities to bring troops forward rapidly into crisis areas.

A second, simpler, version of the "capability leads to trouble" argument addresses itself only to the domestic political processes of the countries acquiring such capabilities. Sooner or later, one is going to have to justify the expenses of counterinsurgency preparations, or any other rational military expenses to the taxpayers, showing exactly what was the threat that required such expenses. Political publics are notoriously unimpressed by hypothetical menaces that are never realized in any tangible form. As the threat of Soviet conventional attack against Berlin faded, one could almost sense a sigh of relief among the defense planners of the Kennedy Administration that Vietnam was next to become the test-case, the clear example of what the threat had been. This is hardly to argue that anyone sensed this very consciously, or that anyone looked forward to repeated uses of American conventional forces in active combat situations. Yet it suggests that at least one Communist guerrilla challenge, if decisively rebuffed, would have been somehow more satisfying than if no challenge had been delivered at all, for the lessons it taught the Communist leadership, and for the lessons it taught the American public.

The hunt for a mission here may be endemic to all forms of public investment, as much on the civilian side as on the military. Woe be it to a fire department that purchases expensive new equipment and then never has to fight a fire. Yet the supply of fires may take care of itself without any pyromania, while political processes involving human adversaries are harder to sort out for cause.

The process may be well illustrated by the expansion of the "Green Beret" Special Forces. These units were originally created with a view to *conducting* guerrilla operations behind Soviet lines in the event of a ground war in Europe, with the result that they had a heavy population of Ruthenians, Ukrainians, and other Eastern Europeans. By the third year of the Kennedy Administration, such units had undergone a sizable expansion, and had been shifted to the role of *countering* guerrilla operations in Vietnam.

An earlier example of the logic that "expensive weapons must be used" comes, of course, with the decision to use the first atomic bombs in combat against Japanese cities. While it may be easy to refute the charge that such use was consciously directed at intimidating the Russians, it would be far harder to deny the fact that some executive decision makers by 1945 favored their use simply in the fear that the Manhattan Project would otherwise be viewed as some sort of collossal boondoggle with the close of World War II, a scandalous waste of the taxpayers' money by selfish scientists, while the rest of the country was painfully defeating the Germans and Japanese by conventional means.

A last, and broader, version of the "ability means trouble" position would emerge if one accepted a general indictment of American foreign policy purposes as criminal and warlike, serving interests such as predatory capitalism. If such were the situation, any increase in the efficiency of defense or other foreign policy management would ipso facto be undesirable, since it was an efficiency in pursuit of bad purposes. Given that this author does not share any part of this interpretation, he is confined to some of the more specialized and limited versions of "efficiency is not always desirable" cases listed above. Even in a good foreign policy, even in a just society, there may be hidden costs to efficiency and rationality, hidden incentives away from what was an entirely desirable central norm.

Despite the alleged clarity of an adversary relationship confronting the outside world, it is hardly clear that foreign policy has been seen to produce better results, closer to optimal results, than the more conflictual domestic policy areas. Indeed, foreign policy seems now more generally to be a "bad news" area, an area in which administrations are more likely to lose reputations than to enhance them. Could it be that the costs of having to contend with a rational enemy, equipped with foreign policy instruments and military instruments of his own, more than outweigh the alleged simplifying advantages we have been discussing?

We may disagree among ourselves about how to handle the problems of overweight, versus the risks that saccharine may produce cancer. But at least the forces of overweight and cancer cannot scheme against us. We pretend to disagree less about how to stop the spread of totalitarian regimes, but such regimes have all the planning capacities of sentient beings.

A point was made at the outset about the seemingly necessary prevalence of secrecy in foreign policy as opposed to domestic policy. This secrecy may indeed be a weapon against external adversaries, an accessory to "united, rational goal-pursuit," but it becomes a barrier to full confidence in the values of governmental actors, and it becomes a barrier to full communication among all these actors.

The discussion so far suggests at least a few pessimistic preliminary conclusions on the basis of the McNamara experience. Even when the area, as in the case of foreign policy, produces an explicit outside adversary, and generates "common interests" and "Pareto optimalities," the implementation of policy faces numerous pitfalls.

A few of these relate to a genuine difficulty in obtaining the correct information upon which to base policy choices. A number of pitfalls emerge from some subtle and disguised conflicts of interest, conflicts which may be all the more difficult to handle because the analytical framework does not tend to recognize their legitimacy.

THE TENDENCIES SINCE 1968

But what, then, of the further career of "rational activism" for the making of foreign policy, in the eight years since the Democrats lost the Presidency in 1968?[9] Have State and Defense learned any clear lessons from the experiences of the Kennedy and Johnson years, or do the lessons fractionate in complicated ways? We might do well again to begin with some observations about Defense, from which the "clearest lessons" were allegedly abstracted, and then to turn again to State.

Melvin Laird as Secretary of Defense was clearly inclined to move in different directions from what had characterized Robert McNamara, substantially deemphasizing the visible operations of the Systems Analysis office, while retaining an important part of its operations at a low-ley. The hard findings of the Systems Analysis operations researchers were now to be used to head off the very worst of the weapons projects sent up the line for approval by the services, thus driving them to do such elementary analysis themselves, rather than having their recommendations embarrassingly rejected. At the same time, Laird made a point to avoid flaunting this analytical competence in the face of the military professionals, and discouraged the kinds of "gee whiz" media reporting that had been so abundant in the McNamara years, thus restoring to the uniformed military officers some of the psychological status remuneration which they had missed.

Among other things, this showed that Laird had superb political sense, being willing to avoid advertising what he was aiming for, and avoiding taking public credit for achieving it when it came. It was clearly the case, for example, that Laird was more anxious to terminate the Vietnam War during the Nixon Administration than either National Security Council Director Henry Kissinger or Secretary of State Rogers, and was at the same time willing to let the public believe entirely the opposite. A policy of failing to specify one's goals is very sensible in politics and in poker, but it is totally against one of the rules of rational policy analysis.

When comparing the accomplishments of Laird with McNamara, one was surprised to see the professional military seemingly happier (as in the

Eisenhower days), even while actually having a smaller defense budget to play with in real dollar values. If the rational-activists inadvertantly or otherwise had bought themselves their ability to apply reforms by increasing the budget, Laird reversed this—achieving a real budget cut— by letting the military play more of a visible role again in the determination of policy.

This is hardly to conclude that Laird's Defense Department had returned to the bad old days of unrationalized policy choice. One can never turn back the clock totally, and many options are never recoverable. Some of the reforms of policy analysis introduced in the early 1960s were bound to persist, as one would never abandon the use of computers for the analysis of complicated problems, or let some of the more blatantly wasteful practices of Defense return. While Eisenhower had been able to point to his own military experience as a counter to the claims of the Joint Chiefs of Staff, Laird did not have five stars to point to, and thus needed some of the threat of systems analysis to keep military budgets down.

Some of the coordination and oversight mechanisms of the McNamara years had indeed been captured by the professional military and converted into vehicles for their positions. In the Eisenhower Administrations, it had been common to see the navy openly criticizing programs of the air force, and vice versa, giving Eisenhower and his Secretaries of Defense another bit of leverage for holding down budgets. Having then been ridiculed by the rational activists for the "interservice bickering" this allegedly represented, the services had learned under McNamara never to let their disputes show in public, and this was a piece of leverage that the Nixon Administration thus would not again have at its disposal.

Where Laird did more explictly revert to the pre-1960 method was in explicitly or implicitly moving back to a "predetermined budget" model, whereby the budget limit was set first, and each service then told to divide it as it thought best. This has been made to seem blatantly irrational in the operations analysis literature, but it clearly had an important political punch for the holding back of service budgetary demands.

If Melvin Laird thus seemed in many ways a pale copy of Eisenhower in his approach to defense policy decisions, we might conversely find a pale copy of McNamara in James Schlesinger, who served as Secretary of Defense from 1973 to 1975.

Schlesinger, as a professional economist, came into office openly articulating much of the rational activist tone, looking for options and explanations, looking for explication and clarity where Laird had and Eisenhower had been the models of muddiness and poor articulation. While some other academics have had the failing or the advantage of forgetting what they have written upon assuming office, Schlesinger seemed instead to be altogether faithful to policy options he had recommended in published articles over the past decade. Some of these made a great deal of sense, for example with regard to tightening up procedures for the command and control of nuclear weapons. Others were much more controversial in their arms control implications, for example the advocacy of counterforce targeting options for strategic nuclear weapons, with target choices other than the Soviet civilian population (an idea that not so coincidentally had also won some approving clarification by McNamara).

Whether the clarification of policy was good or bad on substance, a predictable result in light of what has been said above, it set the stage for increases again in defense spending. Rather than let generals and admirals plan their own strategy, Schlesinger (albeit in a milder way than McNamara) proposed to do it for them. But the generals and admirals were to get some compensation for this, for by endorsing various of Schlesinger's projects, they would get approval for expensive new weapons systems.

Before returning to State, some words must be said about the style and self-description of Henry Kissinger, who began as Director of the National Security Council under President Nixon and then became Secretary of State. There was also a substantial rational-activist tone about Kissinger, advertising himself as constantly looking for options, surveying the landscape on behalf of the President, rather than letting policy be determined by short-run and pragmatic considerations. Kissinger did not share the enthusiasm of McNamara and his associates for numerical analysis of problems, having held all along a humanist's distrust of such precise calculations, and placing a greater trust on an educated intuition. Kissinger, supposedly sharing the distrust of badly thought-out decisions, clearly shared the rational activists' distrust of the motives of the rank-and-file bureaucracy of the State Department and the professional military.

When looking at Kissinger's performance in office, however, it becomes difficult to identify what the tangible difference was between his methods and the pragmatism he was criticizing. Kissinger may have been more intelligent than some of his predecessors, but he was no more prone to ignore the short-run and watch the long-term. The systems-analysts' fixations with objective data had at least provided one sure difference in analytical method, with all kinds of gains and losses. Kissinger, despite all his advocacy of a different method and a broad-ranging overview, really provided only a different (and possibly superior) intellect.

Kissinger's two adversaries were thus allegedly the lack of pre-planning, and the self-service of the mediocre bureaucrat. It is very debatable whether the first was ever seriously engaged or defeated (a pragmatist of course would question whether it even needed to be engaged or defeated). The second was much more continually engaged, as Kissinger used the ploy of personal and secrt diplomacy, recruiting a very small cadre of career State Department professionals whose motives and talents and energies he trusted, leaving the rest of the department typically in ignorance of what was happening.

Drastically reducing the number of governmental actors involved in any particular task is one way to alleviate the problems of coordination, and to assure that the policy positions adopted will serve the nation instead of the narrow agency. Yet the costs are obvious, too, in that some very knowledgeable experts on each subject will be passed by uninformed and unconsulted, and in that the limited time and energy of the Secretary and his intimates will limit and reduce the number of issues on which attention can ever be focused.

If the SALT negotiations thus drew a great deal of Kissinger's attention, almost none of it was available before 1974 for the topic of halting nuclear proliferation. With the rest of the State Department enjoined from undertaking serious action where the Secretary could not control things directly, a number of such issues were allowed to drift.

And what of the efforts of the regular Department of State to maintain any part of its reputation and prerogatives, as the general area of foreign policy came to look less and less like a success story in the later 1960s and then the 1970s? As noted, there was already the problem that State looked like the agency responsible for coordination, when lack of coordination had seemed the problem. As the rational activists of the Kennedy Administration had felt cheated of total success, the villains had then come to be identified as self-protecting bureaucrats: the uniformed officers of the military, and the career diplomatic specialists of State. Henry Kissinger had, as National Security Council Director, expressed himself quite often as sharing this distrust of the bureaucracies, albeit that his own "rational activism" was of a form quite different from that of McNamara or a Charles Hitch or an Alain Enthoven. When Kissinger then was asked to replace William Rogers as Secretary of State in 1973, this could hardly have cheered the State Department rank and file with any new hopes that their reputation and ways of doing things would be more assiduously protected.

Making matters all the worse over these last 10 years was, of course, the compounding of the objective coordination problem, as more and more agencies of the U.S. federal government were drawn into having some form of foreign policy participation. To have lack of success at coordinating Treasury and Defense was hardly to suggest much for

State's ability to coordinate another seven or eight cabinet-level departments in their overseas operations.

The state of the bidding as the Carter Administration came into office was thus that foreign policy continued to be regarded as a "bad news" area (a characterization which had applied ever since 1945, with the possible exception noted of the first two years of the Kennedy Administration), and that the specific reputation of the State Department continued to be quite low.

Some of the low esteem held for State may be a function of how the department has recruited its people, and of bad practices that have been encrusted into its standard operating procedures. It would be foolhardy to deny all the criticisms made of the Foreign Service, just as it would be foolhardy to question all the objective Pareto Optimal improvements introduced into the military's standard operating procedures by McNamara's operations analysts. Yet the charges can easily be overstated, as generalizations become stereotypes, as criticisms of responses to a situation begin to mask problems with the original objective situation itself.

To repeat some points made at the outset, there may be ways in which the very subject matter of international politics lends itself to more disappointment and fewer positive surprises than the domestic matters of politics. There may also be a pattern by which the more specialized and subject-matter-specific agencies such as Defense and Treasury in effect get to skim off the success stories of diplomacy, leaving the residue of seeming failure to the generalists of the system.

FOREIGN COMPARISONS?

Before leaping to overall generalizations about the extent to which American foreign policy had done well or badly by the standards of rational policy process, one might consider a broad-brush survey of what other societies credit for or against their equivalents of the State Department. There are indeed countries in which the professional diplomatic corps come out better, on the report cards composed by rational-activist critics of ineffectiveness in government. The foreign ministries of West Germany and Brazil, for example, are characterized by the same high internal morale, and external reputation for toughness and effectiveness, that we find in Treasury in the United States. Yet it is also easy to find a number of foreign ministries that are under a cloud every bit as much as our own State Department, accused of being incapable of imaginative thinking or the discovery of Pareto Optimalities, of being bound by archaic methods which mainly serve to protect incompetence and to hide waste. Such may well be the case in Japan and in Britain, and in the USSR and in China. If Kissinger took pride in cutting most of the State Department out of his most sensitive dealings with the USSR, there was indeed a fair amount of symmetry here, as the Soviet Foreign Ministry has not been seen as a center of great political clout or technocratic reputation.

Where foreign ministries succeed in maintaining high relative reputations, as in West Germany or Brazil (the two salient cases cited), it is often by wrapping themselves in the mantle of the legal profession, making a law degree almost a prerequisite for appointment or advancement. This fosters an image of their portion of foreign policy as being just as subject-matter-specific as that of the bankers and economists of Treasury, or the battalion-designers of Defense.

SOME CONCLUSIONS

One senses today a general disillusionment in the United States with the workings of the policy process. General feelings of malaise tend to make one look for some unifying source, and there is thus a tendency to lump together criticisms of the domestic and foreign policy outcomes. Yet, as has been a general theme of this article, there are some important differences in the style and the implications of the criticism.

On the domestic side, the disillusionment with rational policy analysis is more open and above board, typically coming in an explicitly pessimistic discovery that proponents of an improvement scheme often do not have the Pareto Optimal case they claim, but are rather proposing something that would make themselves better off, while leaving others worse off. The disillusionment here goes straightforwardly at the heart of optimistic beliefs in liberalism or the welfare state, the beliefs that the opportunities of governmental intervention could be managed so as to place everyone ahead of the game.

In foreign policy, however, the disillusionment has not taken this form yet, for it is rather still phrased more typically in terms of incompetence, or of stupidity, or of some other form or pathology. One can thus expect a debate running long into the future as to whether the primary analytical problem in foreign policy is excessive optimism or excessive pessimism, whether our problem is the foolhardy assumption of the rational-activist that "there has to be a way," or the selfish, cautioning words of the professional that "sometimes there's nothing more that can be done." It is suggested here that a side-by-side comparison of the achievements and failures of domestic and foreign policy, and of our implicit assumptions about such policy, will tend within limits to lend weight to the latter view.

Is this entire discussion to be seen simply as an argument for leaving well enough alone, for avoiding rational analysis in the area of foreign policy? Not really.

There is no doubt that information is power in politics, just as in the other areas of human endeavor, and that information can often be developed and extracted at costs that are bearable. If one wants better policy results, it will be important to get such information into the hands of those whose motives we trust, because they will be able to make wiser decisions, and also because they will be able to use good information as a weapon in the political struggle against those whose motives we do not trust.[9]

Yet it is also desirable to avoid wasting efforts where such information can not so readily be obtained, where the costs of obtaining it would be prohibitive. Program budgeting and systems analysis are desirable and necessary, when used in moderation, when the pitfalls noted above are compensated for. But when unnoticed biases and tendencies creep in to alter the rationally designed policies away from the optimum, something clearly has been lost in the process.

We have noted that the country as a whole clearly has not come to remember the 1960s as the time when everything was done correctly, as the model of policy-making for the future. Has this led the proponents of policy analysis to abandon their model? Not very much.

Rather, the failures of policy, most especially the war in Vietnam, have led these people to look even more closely at the nonoptimization they had sought to correct, and to blame bad foreign policy results largely on such failings of the prior system. A substantial change of indictment has nonetheless occurred. The evil to be corrected earlier had largely been portrayed as *mistakes* of analysis, the failure to think through the most intelligent results for the general problem. Rather, the principle villain was to be painted as the *selfishness* of bureaucratic actors, pursuing the interests of their narrow career domains ahead of the broader nation-serving policies developed by the President and the Secretary of Defense. Explaining the failures of systems analysis thus became instead an enormous venture in elaborating and amplifying the evils of bureaucratic self-interest. Defeat is always an orphan, and the American defeat in Vietnam did not find the rational activists in the mood to claim paternity.

What general lessons should we then want to extract, if any, from this review of the applicability of policy analysis to foreign policy? Our first observation has been that foreign policy, even if it were for Americans to prove the best and most conflict-free policy areas for rational analysis, has demonstrated clearly many difficulties that have nothing to do with a conflict of interest. However much one is tempted to turn to bureaucratic politics models as the explanation of foreign policy failures, or the particular failings of the Department of State, one must concede that the general problems of dispelling ignorance, and of generating correct answers on factual questions about such policy, have become more difficult.

The operations researcher is entirely correct in contending that more information would facilitate better results in foreign policy, as in any area of governmental activity. But the question of the how to get correct answers more often is crucial, for the development of information is never free, and may now, in the complications of foreign policy, have indeed become more and more expensive. The elementary cynicism of predicting that "where you stand depends on where you sit" is indeed an antidote to a great deal of naiveté or disappointment, but it can mask the fact that one is incapable of standing correctly, no matter where one has been sitting, if the clues on how to stand for the national interest have become very hard to find.

There is then much more to be said about the problems of insufficient information, drawing on fields ranging from psychology to operations research. While the implications of some of the bureaucratic politics analysis are that this is a problem particularly exacerbated by the workings of such bureaus (organizational process), a broader analysis might find it spread across all decision process, group or individual. This indeed is much of what the field of cybernetics is about. Allison's threefold model of foreign policy decision-making might thus well be regrouped into at least four categories. Foreign policy can indeed be pulled away from the national interest by misperceptions of possiblity, or by differences of motive, or by both (Figure 13.1).

	motives: national	parochial
accurate	"national interest"	"bureaucratic politics"
perceptions:		
ignorant	"cybernetics"	"organizational process"

Figure 13.1. Foreign Policy and National Interest

Where there are distortions of motive or of perception, moreover, these may come because of bureaucratic affiliation or because of individual quirks, thus perhaps expanding our necessary typology to seven categories, as each of the deviations from the ideal can be of two different kinds of causes (Figure 13.2).

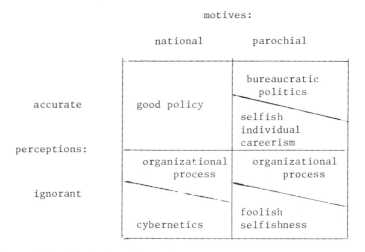

Figure 13.2. Deviations from the Ideal

But the second observation of course is that there are many conflicts of interest remaining in the foreign policy area, even when the style of foreign policy analysis has been to deprecate these. The handling of the conflict-of-interest possibility thus produces some of the most interesting comparisons of domestic public policy and foreign policy analyses. The conflicts of interest acknowledged on the foreign policy side are still less direct, and more complicated. They are portrayed in more involved and cumbersome forms, and there is almost a certain joy of discovery in the literature now addressing such conflicts. Along with this joy of discovery, however, there is evidence also of a general contempt for such conflicts, in part because their legitimacy is still much in question, in part because they are seem more narrowly and specifically as the special interests of incompetence. The opponents of good policy have been portrayed as people with something to lose, but with rare exceptions, with something to lose only because of their own lack of wisdom and imagination.

There are some ordinary kinds of parochial interests in foreign policy. Legislators may fight to get defense contracts for their own districts, the commercial interests of competing regions may affect American preferences in a European war, ethnic ties to Germany or Britain or Israel may make a difference. Yet the dominance of the particular policy focus of foreign policy tends to suppress these special interests, and to replace them with others which look more weak and contemptible.

The literature's discovery of conflict of interest in foreign policy has thus been quite incomplete. Bureaucratic politics models identify the selfishness and the foibles of the parochial defenders of career interests, but overlook the different kind of selfishness and foibles of the technocrat. The models tend to ssume that a rational-activist better policy is possible, that no real interests of any significant and legitimate part of the population would need to be sacrificed to attain the assumed goals. For a bureaucrat to counter that "the country is not united; that you can't serve one interest without hurting another," is viewed simply as a lazy rationalization minted up to protect that bureau, a pretense that no Pareto Optimal moves will be possible.

SOME COMPLICATIONS: THE CHANGING GOALS OF FOREIGN POLICY

There will be at least a few reservations that will have to be expressed about all our conclusions here, on any side of the issues, if one takes more seriously the possibility that in truth the country is not united on foreign policy. Could some of our difficulties and disappointments with foreign policy now be appearing, not because of any excessive optimism and energy, or excessive pessimism and laziness, in procedures, but instead because the United States is at length passing through a major crisis in the sorting out of its preferences for foreign policy outcomes? Could it be that we have indeed *succeeded* at establishing the regimes we wanted in Italy or South Korea, and then have discovered that we hate what we created?

This all relates heavily to issues of public policy at home, and how we view parallel issues of public policy abroad. As we care more and more about activist government at home, and have less and less respect for laissez-faire market-economy methods, has this at last thrown us into division and confusion about what we are defending abroad, about whether political democracy and freedom of the press are worth defending, if they conflict with economic democracy and land reform?

When discussing the general expansion of governmental activity in most countries on most subject matters, one might at the outset be tempted to guess that foreign policy was all along some sort of exception, in that such policy had always had a great deal of governmental activity, and a great deal of substance. If Prussia was an "army with a state," rather than a "state with an army," this was only typical of how engrossed states in an earlier stage must have been with their military and political dealings with other countries. A paramount consideration in the days of the balance of power system was simply retaining one's existance as an independent government.

The laissez-faire advocates of "anarchy plus a constable" would have always hastened to amend this to "anarchy plus a constable plus some ambassadors and armed forces." While the role of the state in every other area surely has grown in the transition from laissez-faire to the welfare state, is there any inherent reason why the foreign policy activity pattern should also have grown?

We are largely focusing on the American pattern in this collection, and we must confront the fascinating historical accident that America's endorsement of laissez-faire and Lockeian views of limited government coincided in time with the possibility of having a foreign policy of isolation.[10] This may have simply been an accident. But there may also have even some causal relationships in both directions. Able to stay at long remove from the power struggles of Europe, Americans also missed the revolutionary struggles by which liberal capitalism replaced traditional remnants of feudal landlord authority. If isolation made Lockeian systems more workable in the U.S., the love of this liberal environment may in turn have stimulated a desire to maintain and renew this isolation. One might then have great difficulty in determining which faded first, the American commitment to foreign policy isolationism, or the American inhibitions against governmental activity on domestic fronts, for the two more or less faded together as they had earlier persisted together.

Perhaps the fading of isolation, the "growth of foreign policy," came first.[11] The immediate driving forces for the change in foreign policy might straightforwardly enough be viewed as a change in the external objective situation, rather than a change in philosophy. The Germans in World War I developed the submarine, and destroyed commerce in a manner unknown to the previous century. The Germans in World War II were led by Hitler, a dictator with unprecedented capacities for conquest and evil. The introduction of airplanes and missiles and nuclear weapons changed many of the technological presumptions of an earlier isolation. The appearance of a globally influential Stalinist ideology, espousing political dictatorship, among other things, moreover seemed to be replication of the Hitlerian threat.

Such changes in the objective situation might thus make Americans feel they had to participate in global politics now, even without rejecting any of their earlier political-philosophical character. Defending American political-democracy had earlier suggested a foreign policy of non-involvement. Now it required involvement. The goals might be the same, but the means might have to be drastically different.

The shift to an activist foreign policy was thus debated as much in instrumental as in philosophical terms, and for its earlier stages produced less ideological heat and light than the debate about changes on the domestic scene. What was being defended could be seen as a constant; only the methods of defense were to be different.

There was a consensus, entirely parallel to our analysis above, that foreign policy should be left largely to the executive branch, that a bipartisan foreign policy, largely planned and executed by the President and by the professionals of the military and foreign service, would be needed to stop totalitarian enemies from reaching in to upset the American way of life.[12] While a separation of powers at home would still seem essential to that way of life, exceptions might be altogether necessary for the conduct of hot wars and cold wars. New to the daily practice of foreign policy, Americans were quite ready to conclude that it might have to be played by different rules from domestic policy.

This could be rationalized somehow as "Presidential leadership abroad to preserve a checks-and-balances government at home," or even as elitism in external affairs to protect political democracy at home (after all, one typically surrenders some parts of freedom of speech, and acquires the obligation to salute, for the period one is called into the armed forces). If there were internal contradictions in such a formulation, they could be addressed simply as the "difference between foreign policy and public policy," or "politics stops at the shoreline."

But the broader problem may have come with the ongoing progress of governmental activity at home, which over time might even begin to upset the national consensus about "what was being defended" in this newly active foreign policy. Some Americans might become disenchanted by the Lockeian status quo at home, and feel far less "threatened" by alternative philosophies being proposed from abroad. Others would feel quite content with that status quo at home, but dreadfully confused about how this was to be compared and related to conflicts abroad.

This all relates to some fundamental changes in how the United States as a political-economic system related to the outside world. There were many years (1848 was a prime example) in which the United States, because of its advanced political democracy and economic liberalism, could have been seen as an inadvertant (or at times somewhat deliberate) "exporter of revolution." Being quite content with its own arrangements, it served as a model and a catalyst for those European states still beset by older and less rationalized systems.

As the United States however remained content with a relatively laissez-faire system in the latter nineteenth century, other nations reached this system too, and then went on past it. Driven by greater economic deprivations, the outside world was then to become a source of puzzlement and disappointment for many Americans. Having achieved political democracy, foreign nations seemed intent on more, on something that might be called "economic democracy." Worse than this, many such nations then became willing to sacrifice the elections and free press of political democracy for the greater economic promise or economic equality of the latter economic democracy.

As the successes or failures of efforts to achieve rational decisions in foreign policy have been discussed, the reader will have to bear in mind the possibility that some of the failures are due instead to confusions and changes in the preferences of Americans about the world, changes in preference which could make the most rational implementation process deliver very confusing outputs.

Our frustration with foreign policy was displayed nowhere better than in American attitudes toward the Vietnam war. A great number of people were appalled at the cost. Another slice was appalled at the overoptimism and the headlines with power with which we had entered that contest. Another slice of Americans, albeit perhaps smaller, was appalled that we had entered, in their view, on the wrong side.

Some of the Americans now opposed to defending the perimeters of the "free world" will tend to phrase their objections in procedural terms. They claim, as above, to be appalled at the excessive "can do" spirit of the Kennedy years, and will claim that bureaucratic and organizational imperfections are bound to upset whatever efforts we make for useful intervention in the world. Regardless of the proper outcome for any overseas political conflict, they will argue, the United States has no business intervening to try to affect that outcome.

Yet this alleged procedural generalization will, in many cases, actually be a mask for changed preferences about those very outcomes. Many of the Americans who have spoken against intervention in Korea would welcome it if it came in the form of a turning against President Park. Similarly, they would not mind sending American boys to fight abroad, if the fight were to depose the white South African regime. Such people may pretend to share the isolationist sentiments of others who would simply want to do without so much foreign policy, but their real preference is not far a lack of foreign policy, but rather for a drastically different activist foreign policy.

It is not easy to predict where these tendencies are all headed. At the least, they confuse American foreign policy, and thereby make it more difficult for us to be certain that the process is the cause of our disappointments. At the least, they also tend to eliminate that consensus and apparent unanimity about the goals of foreign policy which made rational activism seem so appropriate.

The entire public policy literature is a function of America's ceasing to be content with its earlier nature, and moving leftward at home. Governmental activity changes what previously had seemed a satisfactory status quo; it was because that status quo had no longer seemed satisfactory that we brought government into the problem. But what then when parts of our public ceases to find satisfactory the status quo of America's foreign commitments, a set of commitments which previously had looked satisfactory to virtually everyone?

NOTES

1. Some of the inherent nature of foreign policy, as it differs from public policy in domestic arenas, can be found well dissected in Hans J. Morgenthau, "Another 'Great Debate': The National Interest of the United States," *American Political Science Review,* 46, 4 (December, 1952): 961-988; Arnold Wolfers, " 'National Security' as an Ambiguous Symbol," *Political Science Quarterly,* 67, 4 (December, 1952): 481-502; and James Rosenau, *Domestic Sources of Foreign Policy* (New York: Free Press, 1967).

2. For optimistic and straightforward discussions of the application of rational analysis to foreign policy and to all policy, see Alain C. Enthoven and Henry S. Rowen, *Defense Planning and Organization* RAND Paper P-1640 (Santa Monica, Cal.: Rand, 1959); Charles J. Hitch and Roland N. McKean, *The Economics of Defense in the Nuclear Age* (Cambridge, Mass.: Harvard University Press, 1960); William W. Kaufmann, *Methods and Models of Operations Research* (New York: Prentice-Hall, 1962); James Schlesinger, "Quantitative Analysis and National Security," *World Politics,* 15, 2 (January, 1963): 295-315; Edward S. Quade, *Analysis for Military Decisions* (Chicago: Rand McNally, 1964); and William W. Kaufmann, *The McNamara Strategy* (New York: Harper & Row, 1964).

3. Various kinds of analysis have been presented on the limits of rational policy analysis. Among those stressing the simple limits of *capability* here are Aaron Wildavsky, *The Politics of the Budgetary Process* (Boston: Little, Brown, 1964); Karl Deutsch, *The Nerves of Government* (New York: Free Press, 1966); Leonard Merewitz and Stephen H. Sosnick, *The Budget's New Clothes* (Chicago: Markham, 1971); Irving Janis, *Victims of Groupthink* (Boston: Houghton Mifflin, 1972); and John D. Steinbruner, *The Cybernetic Theory of Decision: New Dimensions of Political Analysis* (Princeton, N.J.: Princeton University Press, 1974).

4. For discussions of the special problems and opportunities of management in the Defense portion of foreign policy, see John P. Crecine and Gregory W. Fischer, "On Resource Allocation Processes in the U.S. Department of Defense," *Political Science Annual,* 9 (1972): 181-236; Keith C. Clark and Laurence J. Legere, *The President and the Management of National Security* (New York: Praeger, 1969); and Ralph Sanders, *The Politics of Defense Analysis* (New York: Dunellen, 1973).

5. The efforts to project the "success story" of Defense program-budgeting out to other portions of the government are presented in David Novick (ed.), *Program Budgeting: Program Analysis and the Federal Government* (Cambridge, Mass.: Harvard University Press, 1965); and Fremont J. Lyden and Ernest G. Miller, *Planning, Programming, Budgeting: A System Approach to Management* (Chicago: Markham, 1967).

6. The generally low morale and self-image of State has been discussed from many perspectives. Among the written accounts are Charles Frankel, *High on Foggy Bottom* (New York: Harper & Row, 1969); Richard Holbrooke, "The Machine That Fails," *Foreign Policy,* 1 (Winter, 1970-1971): 65-77; John Franklin Campbell, *The Foreign*

Affairs Fudge Factory (New York: Basic Books, 1971); William N. Turpin, "Foreign Relations, Yes; Foreign Policy, No," *Foreign Policy,* 8 (Fall, 1972): 50-61; John W. Tuthill, "Operation Topsy," *Foreign Policy,* 8 (Fall, 1972): 62-85; and Monteagle Stearns, "Making American Diplomacy Relevant," *Foreign Affairs,* 52, 1 (October, 1973): 153-167.

7. Clear statements of the now fashionable "bureaucratic politics" perspective are to be found in Graham T. Allison, *The Essence of Decision* (Boston: Little, Brown, 1971); Roger Hilsman, *The Politics of Policy-Making in Defense and Foreign Affairs* (New York: Harper & Row, 1971); and Morton H. Halperin,*Bureaucratic Politics and Foreign Policy* (Washington, D.C.: Brookings Institution, 1974). For a provocative statement of the counterview see Stephen D. Krasner, "Are Bureaucracies Important? (Or Allison Wonderland)," *Foreign Policy,* 7 (Summer, 1972): 159-179; and Robert J. Art, "Bureaucratic Politics and American Foreign Policy: A Critique," *Policy Sciences,* 4 (December, 1973): 467-490.

8. The "second wave" of criticism of McNamara's accomplishments in Defense, and of the impact of rational policy processes on foreign policy in general, shows up in Richard J. Walton: *Cold War and Counterrevolution: The Foreign Policy of John F. Kennedy* (New York: Viking, 1972); Ronald Steel, *Pax Americana* (New York: Viking, 1967); J. William Fulbright, *The Arrogance of Power* (New York: Random House, 1966). The general over-optimism of the Kennedy years on all fronts has been drawn together in Phillip Green, *Deadly Logic* (Columbus: Ohio State University Press, 1966); Robert W. Tucker, *Nation or Empire?* (Baltimore: John Hopkins Press, 1968); and Anthony Hartley, "JFK's Foreign Policy," *Foreign Policy,* 4 (Fall, 1971): 77-100.

9. For discussions of the further evolution of the foreign policy process debate since 1968, see John P. Leacacos, "Kissinger Apparat," *Foreign Policy,* 5 (Winter, 1971-1972): 3-27; I. M. Destler, "Can One Man Do?," *Foreign Policy,* 5 (Winter, 1971-1972): 28-40; and Graham Allison and Charles L. Schultze (eds.), *Setting National Priorities: The Next Ten Years* (Washington, D.C.: Brookings Institution, 1976): 227-270.

10. Valuable discussions of the special relationship of American domestic society to the issues of foreign policy can be found in Herbert C. Butterfield, "The Scientific versus the Moralistic Approach in International Affairs," *International Affairs,* 28 (October, 1951): 411-422; Foster Rhea Dulles, *America's Rise to World Power* (New York: Harper & Row, 1954); Louis Hartz, *The Liberal Tradition in America* (New York: Harcourt Brace, 1955); Henry A. Kissinger, "Domestic Structures and Foreign Policy," *Daedalus,* 95 (Spring, 1966): 503-529; and Stanley Hoffman, *Gulliver's Troubles: or the Setting of United States Foreign Policy* (New York: McGraw-Hill, 1968).

11. The exact nature of the changes in America's relationship to foreign societies are of course debatable and hardly easy to determine. For conflicting interpretations, see Julius Pratt, *A History of United States Foreign Policy* (Englewood Cliffs, N.J.: Prentice Hall, 1955); William Appleman Williams, *The Tragedy of American Diplomacy* (New York: World, 1959); Walter LeFeber, *The New Empire: An Interpretation of American Expansion 1860-1898* (Ithaca, N.Y.: Cornell University Press, 1963); and Alexander DeConde,*A History of American Foreign Policy,* 2nd ed., (New York: Charles Scribners, 1971).

12. For glowing accounts of the desirability of Presidential predominance in foreign policy, see Richard E. Neustadt, *Presidential Power: The Politics of Leadership* (New York: Wiley, 1960); Arthur Schlesinger,*A Thousand Days: John F. Kennedy in the White House* (Boston: Houghton Mifflin, 1965); and Theodore Sorenson, *Kennedy* (New York: Harper & Row, 1965). For more disillusioned interpretations, see Arthur Schlesinger, *The Imperial Presidency* (Boston: Houghton Mifflin, 1973); and Les Aspin, "Why Doesn't Congress Do Something?," *Foreign Policy,* 15 (Summer, 1974): 70-82.

14.

PLANNING, PUBLIC POLICY AND CAPITALISM

ALAN STONE

University of Houston

When one examines the papers collected in this volume together, rather than singly, several strong impressions come to mind. First, the amount and extent of government intervention has increased dramatically in the recent past and portends to increase still more in the near future. Regardless of the ideological perspectives of the writers—and the reader will have noted that they are diverse— the anticipated prospect in each examined policy area is that government will undertake expanded programs in the future. The second major impression with which the reader is left is that new programs devised and implemented by government will be undertaken without any overview of the relationship of that program to the range of others. Reinforcing the narrowness of policy-making is the fact that, as Theodore Lowi has demonstrated, agencies and not legislators have made (and will probably continue to make) most real policy, with Congress offering little more than the general guidelines required by Supreme Court decisions.[1]

The term planning may become the new cliché of the 1980s—as several of the papers suggest—joining, or perhaps, supplanting such other terms as pollution, liberty, and racism. But planning will most likely mean nothing more than a hopeful projection of results anticipated by some new or revised public policy.

Although planning is apt to become a leading word in future public policy discussions, as it has among large corporation executives as well as economic officials of several Western European nations, I am going to argue that the kind of planning envisioned is, at best, only a mite better than no planning at all—and perhaps even worse as some of the proponents of the free market solution advise. In any event, such planning as is envisioned is a far cry from the kind of planning which a centrally directed economy can undertake, where planning can be both *comprehensive* over many issue areas, and *controlling* over most of the particulars in each issue area. (I do not suggest that central planning is equivalent to omnipotence—but merely that, as a system, it is much better equipped to deal with a modern complex political-economy than one without planning). And just as General Motors, for example, did not "plan"—notwithstanding its "planning"—for the sharp drop in automobile sales which occurred during some recent years, so planning in the future by both private firms and governmental units is destined to fall short of intended results. Let us look at the nature of planning and place it in the perspective of the American political economy in order to understand the hypothesis that policy planning is more necessary in the future than ever before, and that it is virtually impossible to do in a capitalist society. The best that policy-makers can do is balance competing interests, but this is a far cry from planning.

Planning is often conceived as nothing more than goal oriented behavior, and thus corresponds to what Max Weber defined as instrumentally rational social action. "Action is instrumentally rational when the end, the means, and the secondary results are all taken into account and weighed. This involves rational consideration of alternative means to the end and . . . of the relative importance of different possible ends."[2] Instrumentally rational action thus takes into account means, ends, and secondary results. But planning is something more than instrumentally rational action in two respects. First, while instrumentally rational action has *an* end in contemplation, planning has a large number of specific ends in mind. Thus, the administrator of a program engaging in instrumentally rational action might seek to institute programs to clean up Lake Michigan and will, accordingly, order certain firms discharging pollutants into that body of water to cease that activity pursuant to some schedule. The planner, on the other hand, is concerned not only with that end, but, in addition, with other ends involving energy use, economic development, employment dislocations, and changeover costs. The planner has the far more difficult and unenviable task of balancing competing and often conflicting ends in accordance with an overriding structure of values. The administrator, in contrast, is concerned with the fulfillment of *his* program, and the corporate "planner" is concerned, even more narrowly, with the profit and sales results of *his* corporation.

This leads to the second major difference between instrumentally rational action and planning—control. Let us take as one pole the capability to alter every factor which may affect a desired goal. Such factors may exist at the time a policy course is set in motion, or they arise—unforeseen at the inception— after the policy has been adopted and is in the process of implementation. But in either event, the model at this pole posits the abilities either to control the factor, modify the means or modify the goal. At the other pole is what I call the racetrack tout model. The tout accumulates a great deal of information about the relative merits of horses entered in a race, and then places a bet on the one that he adjudges will be the probable winner. But, in no event does he control the event or the desired outcome. The latter pole is instrumentally rational action, while action which comes close to the former model is planning. Planning, in a word, is distinguished from the misuse of the word by the two attributes of *comprehensiveness* and *control.* [3]

The hypothesis that emerges from these distinctions will now be stated: capitalism is inconsistent with planning, and yet as the gamut of public policies adopted by the capitalist state become more and more inter-related, the need for planning becomes more manifest. Moreover, the substitutes for planning, particularly (1) the allocation of resources on the basis of market relationships without government intervention and (2) automatic stabilizers, are not adequate substitutes for planning. Conse-quently, public policy in each of the areas examined in this book will continue to be narrowly focused on instrumentally rational action. Policy-making and implementation will, at best, be examples of "blun-dering through," often meeting hidden surprises along the way, clashing with policies undertaken in other areas, and, more often than not, destined for outright failure, falling far short of desired ends or—if ruthlessly pursued—leading to unacceptable or undesirable side effects. Changes in direction and emphasis will surely occur, but the patterns described above will persist, even granting the highest idealism and level of competence in policy-makers and administrators. Let us look at a sketch of the argument supporting the hypothesis.

PLANNING AND POLICY INTERRELATEDNESS

As James Anderson makes eminently clear, the amount of govern-ment regulation in both the economic and noneconomic spheres has been growing rapidly in recent years and shows every promise of continuing its advance. Yet, while the state continues to limit the decision-making discretion available to both individuals and corporate bodies, this dramatic movement sometimes makes us forget the wide amount of discretion, which can have substantial public impact, still left in private hands. An automobile manufacturer may be precluded from making one kind of false and misleading statement by the Federal Trade Commission, but it still has available the power to make a vast number of other statements. A firm may be precluded from acquiring a competitor or supplier because of the Clayton Act, but it still has vast discretion in investment opportunities available to it. Indeed, part of the essential foundation of capitalism is the vast amount of discretion available to a large number of individual units, even after restrictions on parts of this discretion through government intervention.[4] Even public utilities, whose discretion is more inhibited than other firms, still have vast discretion to make choices. Now, if planning requires comprehensiveness, it is obvious that the vast amount of decision-making discretion available in numerous private hands precludes such comprehensiveness. Nor can we assume that there is an unconscious consensus of goals among both public and private decision makers; the numerous conflicts between government and private groups attest to that.

But the problem is even greater for quite often the policies pursued by governmental actors are at odds with those pursued by actors in the private sector. And, again, the crucial problem is not mean-spiritedness but rather the exercise of discretion in pursuit of different ends. Let us take two recent examples to illustrate. The vigorous Federal Power Commission (FPC) effort to restrain the upward movement of natural gas prices has led to a reluctance on the part of firms in the business to explore for additional supplies, leading to a severe shortage of the product. The underlying reason for this unhappy result is the dissonance between the FPC's goal of restraining prices for the consumers' benefit, and the producers' goal of profit maximization. When expected returns fall below a certain rate, capital which would have been used for natural gas exploration flows to another economic activity. Probably of even greater consequence is the sharp drop in capital spending for new plant and equipment which has persisted through the 1970s. Surveys conducted by business periodicals of business managers responsible for expansion activities reveal that the predominant reason for their reluctance to engage in such spending is the fear that the labyrinth of government regulations can render a costly new facility inoperative at the beginning of its effective life. Business executives nominate the plethora of municipal, country, state, and federal environmental regulations as the worst of these burdens. Again, we can observe the sharp conflict not only between the private goal of profit maximization and the public goal of environmental protection, but also between the latter and the equally important goal of economic growth. And, it is again the discretion vested in private decision makers employed, not in a venal manner, but simply pursuant to "reasonable" business criteria that can defeat a public effort or impose unacceptable costs on the accomplishment of the other public effort.

The second example also illustrates a point which, though obvious, still requires elaboration: the interrelatedness of policy areas. Very clearly, energy policy affects macroeconomic policy, particularly an economy's capacity for growth. As energy becomes scarcer or more expensive, there is a clear effect on an economy's growth potential as well as upon the standard of living enjoyed by its citizens. Equally clear is the restraining influence of overly zealous environmental policy on economic growth, and nowhere is this clearer than in EPA's trade-off policy, which precludes the operation of major new sources of pollution (such as industrial plants) in a "nonattainment" area unless emissions are reduced by more than offsetting amounts at other facilities in the area.[5] Less obvious, although the connections are far from thoroughly understood, are the relationships between crime and criminal justice policy, on the one hand, and the state of the economy on the other hand, as Benjamin Ginsberg points out. Eminently clear is that only a political economy in good economic condition can permit the extensive government spending required to finance the elaborate, and sometimes grandiose, schemes of government planners in such diverse policy areas as health, urban reconstruction, and defense.

In short, planning to be effective must be comprehensive; it must embrace the interrelatedness of diverse policy areas since the failure of expectations in one policy area may adversely affect outcomes in other areas seemingly remote from the one under consideration. Can this be done under capitalism? Notwithstanding attempts at centralized budgeting such as the work of the Office of Management and Budget (OMB), even economists and business analysts dedicated to the economic system readily concede that planning cannot be effective under capitalism. A 1974 survey of a large number of such people concluded that "the chances of serious error in forecasting have increased alarmingly. . . . Even the best forecasts are now out of date shortly after they are constructed."[6] One principal political reason for the failure of interrelated sector planning is sharply revealed in both Don Hadwiger's analysis of agriculture policy and Howard Sherman's analysis of macroeconomic policy. Notwithstanding the sharp divergence in theoretical orientation between Hadwiger's apparent pluralism and Sherman's sophisticated variant of Marxism, both conclude that policy in various areas is in large degree shaped by the self-interest of affected groups. Whether one accepts Hadwiger's group framework or Sherman's analysis based upon class and class fractions, the conclusion which emerges here is the same. This is not a society based upon a perceived integrated national interest, but one in which specialized interests are at odds with each other. In seeking to bend legislation or administrative outputs to their ends, such interests are concerned almost exclusively with maximizing their payoffs and do not give a hoot for other interests (except insofar as they are obliged to engage in compromising or logrolling processes) or that elusive thing called the national interest. The underlying reason is, of course, that capitalist society is built upon class and intra-class divisions, and public policy historically has been and will continue to be the product of interests seeking self-benefit. Obviously, planning for the interrelatedness of policy areas cannot take place in such an environment.

Couple this with the widespread discretion available for decision-making which resides in private hands, and the best intentions of a would-be planner in our society must be thwarted. "Planning" in the private sector consists of nothing more than each firm singe-mindedly seeking to achieve its private ends which are often at variance with public ends. Thus, automobile manufacturers were indifferent to the safety of their product until compelled to do something about the problem. Moreover, notwithstanding the fact that firms will sometimes collude, imitate each other, or that a leadership pattern will occur in an industry, each enterprise's planning is in-firm to the exclusion of the industry as a whole. Ford's planning, for example, is structured around the benefits it desires for itself, not General Motors or the automobile industry generally. In the public sector, agencies and private groups focus on specific programs and desired ends, again largely inattentive to any broader goals, although the pursuit of private goals is invariably clothed in the laudatory language of the public interest. Thus, the EPA and environmental purity middle-class groups which form the agency's clientele may demand "in the public interest" that economic growth in Texas should be sacrificed to the goal of cleaner air. But the equally voluble voices of Texas officials and businessmen call for air quality to be sacrificed to rapid economic growth, again "in the public interest." When one adds together the vast amount of private discretion and the operations of large numbers of public agencies and interest groups seeking to influence them, the net result more closely approaches chaos than planning.

Although public policy in these respects promises to be a continuation of the past, there is one fact which *may* be causing a qualitative change in the relationship of government and the private sector—the sheer weight of contemporary government intervention and the likelihood of additional layers and layers of future intervention. While conclusions about the direction of public intervention and its impact must necessarily be tentative, the importance of the topic requires it to be examined. And I am going to suggest that while the planlessness described above will continue as before, it will do so in a new framework with important consequences.

GOVERNMENT INTERVENTION AND CAPITALISM

One of the important debates during the classical period of political economy concerned the distinction between productive and unproductive labor. Every observer sensed that the labor of a clown or prostitute was somehow different from that of a clothworker or steelmill hand.[7] Although it is often ignored today, the most elementary common sense tells us that the employment of an advertising executive, whose principal account is a steel manufacturer, depends, ultimately, for his income upon the labor of steel workers, yet the converse is not true. I wish to begin with the distinction between the categories of productive and unproductive labor articulated by Karl Marx, following Adam Smith, and then develop another distinction mentioned by Marx, but not developed. To Marx and Smith, productive labor produces commodities (goods produced for sale), while unproductive labor produces personal services. "The former includes . . . all material and intellectual wealth— meat as well as books—that exist in the form of things."[8]

Now one must not assume from the distinction between productive and unproductive labor that the term unproductive is equivalent to unnecessary or wasteful. Indeed, much unproductive labor is necessary for the operation of the capitalist system. In Marx's time, for example, a lawyer's services were needed to consummate transactions for the exchange and sale of commodities, while the priest was useful to the system by helping to socialize the working class in the habits of obedience. But these and similar occupations were only the foetal beginnings of what now constitutes a veritable army of persons not engaged in productive labor. However, as David Ricardo observed, a nation need not be ashamed of having a large number of unproductive citizens. Indeed, if a relatively small percentage of persons engaged in agriculture and industry can support the rest of us in reasonably comfortable style, this is an index of great national productivity.[9] And if unproductive sectors such as the military assist, as Howard Sherman urges, in creating markets for commodities, so much the better for capitalism. But—and this is the question to be raised in the context of contemporary capitalism—suppose some part of the unproductive labor impedes the development of capitalism?

And this is precisely the sort of distinction I wish to make; as Marx observed, some labor is not only unproductive, but destructive of capitalism. Let us start with a simple, but brilliant, argument set forth by Joan Robinson in order to understand the argument I wish to make.[10] We take for granted the widely held view that capitalism's overriding characteristic is growth; businessmen must undertake investment in new plants and equipment, which in turn is dependent upon anticipated profits. These profits must be realized in order for the system to grow. Conversely, anything which either erodes profits or makes investment more hazardous will lead to slower growth or stagnation. While wage increases, which cannot be passed on to purchasers of industries' products, would consitute one such impedimemt to profits and invest-ment, the ones I wish to look at here are: (1) high levels of both corporate and upper income bracket taxation and other costs sufficient to retard significant capital formation and (2) government interventions, the effects of which are to destroy investment incentives. Let us begin with the former.

Costs imposed upon corporations and the upper income groups which are apt to constitute most of the individual investors in future economic growth are of two types: taxes and costs involved in complying with government interventionist programs. The former category is relatively easy to compute, while the latter category is extremely difficult to quantify. Nevertheless, some recent estimates have been made of the costs of government intervention which, at least, indicate its current magnitude. Dow Chemical estimated in 1975 that federal regulations cost it $147 million a year,while Goodyear Tire and Rubber Company calculated in 1974 that its regulatory costs amounted to $30 million.[11] Taking into account the differing regulatory requirements affecting various industries, a researcher concluded in *Physics Today* that "the costs of compliance efforts for industry as a whole when passed on to the consumer amount to an estimated $2000 per family annually."[12] What is glibly assumed by many observers of this phenomenon is that these costs can simply be passed along to consumers. But it is far from obvious that all, or even most, of such costs can readily be passed onward, and not even the continuous intonation of the Naderite chant, "market power," makes this clear. Certainly the sharp decline of profits as a percentage of corporate income from 20 to 22 percent in the early 1950s to 10 to 12 percent inthe early 1970s, as reported in one important paper, would tend to show that industry absorbs much of the dead-weight loss of complying with government intervention.[13]

One, then,can do no more than be watchful about the current and long-term effects on capital formation resulting from government intervention.

But if the expansion of intervention continues at anything like the dizzying pace of the 1970s, it should not surprise us to see a serious effect on capital formation. Thus, programs from affirmative action to antitrust and pollution controls (et al.) aggregated together could unwittingly be contributing to a chronic and, perhaps, worsening crisis of capitalism. But intervention is hardly the only impedance to profit-making. Another cost which bears close watching in the next few years is taxation. At the moment, the problem is not very significant in the United States; federal taxes have remained relatively stable while state and local taxes have increased from about $260 per capita in 1966 to $731 per capita in 1976—hardly a jump sufficient to remotely approach the confiscatory stage.[14] Nevertheless, a look at the experience of several Western European capitalist nations and the strong posibility that sharply increased taxes will be imposed on business firms and upper income individuals in the name of "tax reform," "closing up loopholes," or "equity," requires us to look at the problem a bit more closely.

Reporting on a number of studies, *Business Week* found that the Western capitalist nations with the largest public sectors experienced the lowest annual growth rate between 1962 and 1971. Expanded public spending programs are viewed as the short-run answer to recession, but in order to curb an excessive amount of deficit spending and to help finance such programs, taxes are increased, expecially on the groups which traditionally finance capital investment. Because of their popularity, these programs, of course, are not abandoned when the recession ends. Nor are the taxes decreased. But during the next recession, both programs and taxes increase again. And the cycle repeats. Variations from country to country determine each's programs and tax structures, but the more influential the social-democrats are in the government (West Germany excepted), the more likely it is for economic development to stagnate under capitalism with funds for investment drying up.[15] The result is that unemployment rises, products become too expensive since unit costs are not reduced through innovation or more efficient production facilities, and living standards decline.[16] While the American working class is considerably less class conscious and militant than those in England or the Netherlands, the same scenario *could* develop here. Enactment of a bill which would make the government an employer of last resort, radical reform of welfare or a vast expansion of a public medical care system financed through general revenues coupled with increased taxes at the top levels could shrink funds for capital expansion—already in short supply.[17] And since in a capitalist society, private entrepreneurs and not the government are charged with industrial expansion decisions, we could confront the stagnation represented by the United Kingdom. This suggests, in a general sense, the upper limits of welfare-state capitalism.

But a reading of American public policy does not suggest that the kind of tax and welfare policies characteristic of some western European countries is likely to occur here. At best we may confidently expect enactment of symbolic legislation like the Employment Act of 1946 which declared that unemployment was a monumental evil—but took no steps to correct the problem. Rather, in a nation with low working-class consciousness and no social-democratic party, segments of the upper and middle classes which are not involved in problems of industrial growth will wield considerable influence in support of their comforts (such as clean air) at the expense of other ends. And only in this country has this strata attained center stage in the policy-making and administration processes, resulting in a plethora of government agencies, laws, and regulations. Beginning in the late 1960s, these strata have succeeded in securing the enactment of a large number of regulatory laws in the environmental and consumer protection areas which are quite different in support patterns, purpose and effect from many older regulatory laws. Whereas the older regulatory laws drew considerable support from affected business interests, the regulatory policies of the late 1960s and the 1970s form an entirely different pattern and have usually been opposed by the affected business interests.[18] A meticulously researched article in *Harper's* illustrates the dynamic of the new forms of government intervention and the class nature of its supporters. In brief, the author traced the Consolidated Edison Company's failure to deliver adequate and cheap power to New York residents to the company's inability to construct needed power facilities. And this inability, in turn, was attributable to the legal and political maneuvers of the few wealthy residents of a rural area chosen by Consolidated Edison for new facilities. These residents desired to maintain the area in its rustic purity, free of industry. In a word, the author found in this case and others examined in a more cursory manner that the interests of the low-income user of power in New York City was being sacrificed to the interests of upper income groups in the name of a then new slogan—environmentalism.[19] And these groups energetically employed every legal, political, and legislative tactic they could in order to thwart the development of new power facilities.

One case, or several, does not prove the point. What I am setting forth as a plausible hypothesis here is that mounting evidence indicates that certain powerful upper and middle strata in our society have discovered the merits of conspicuous consumption and are intent on preserving their life styles, even at the cost of deterring crucial economic development. Persons involved in the production of commodities, both workers and managers, are almost never involved in the various holy crusades for environmental, health, or product purity. Instead the spokesmen for such crusades tend to be such professionals as educators, lawyers, health and governmental professionals, as well as persons engaged in such service enterprises as recreation, amusement, communications, and miscellaneous services—all far-removed from the process of commodity production.[20] Briefly, the Smith-Marx distinction, based upon the commodity, between productive and unproductive labor has taken a new important dimension for the analysis of American public policy. Specifically, the policies advocated and advanced by the unproductive sector may be a crucial deterrent to investment and thus, unwittingly, may be contributing to American capitalism's stagnation—and perhaps,demise.

While I have singled out environmental intervention, it must be remembered that the effects discussed are attributable to the cumulative impact of regulations at the federal, state and local levels. To gauge the *qualitative* leap in government intervention, consider that from 1970 to 1975 alone spending by major economic and social regulatory agencies leaped from $1.566 billion to $4.728 billion, and the number of pages in the *Code of Federal Regulations* covered by rules of these agencies jumped from 54,105 to 72,200.[21] Tying together two important economic trends of the 1970s: sluggish capital investment and an accelerating merger wave, a *Wall Street Journal* survey of business executives leaves little doubt that one of the crucial factors accounting for both trends is the extent of government intervention. The remarks of the chief financial officer of a large corporation are worth quoting in this respect:[22]

"With the difficulty of obtaining various permits and the environmental-impact studies that must be submitted, it takes years to get a major project off the ground . . . . For heavy industry, the environmental restrictions have almost reached the point of being ridiculous. And corporate executives dont't know what the business environment will be like when the project is completed. All the difficulty and uncertainty tend to make companies purchase existing facilities rather than build new ones."

Accordingly, it is easier to acquire an existing facility than to build a new one.

The impact of government over-intervention can be seen not only upon industry as a whole, but upon many industries specifically, as well as upon such activities as research, productivity and innovation. In the energy field, we have already noted that FPC regulation is, at least, one of the principal reasons for shortages of natural gas upon which economic growth is so dependent.[23] Less well-known is that while the federal government's rhetoric favors increased use of coal, the tough regulatory restrictions, on both its mining and burning, act as a strong disincentive for both supply and consumption.[24] Similarly, price and profit controls imposed on petroleum refiners have acted as a disincentive to the construction of additional and modernized refining capacity—notwithstanding the almost uniform belief in its need.[25] Disincentives to research because of stringent government regulation have been seen most dramatically in the pharmaceutical industry, but the problem is not limited to that industry.[26] Fewer patents are granted to Americans now than 10 years ago, while relative sums expended by corporations on basic product and process research dwindles. Again, the conclusion of a *Washington Post* survey is in order:[27]

> Many companies put the blame for the research downturn on federal regulations. These companies say the money they would normally spend on exploratory research is being spent to satisfy new regulations. . . . DuPont says it now spends 10 percent of its research dollars satisfying federal safety and environmental regulations. RCA and Alcoa say they divert more research money into people and machinery doing nothing more than meeting new federal regulation. . . . General Motors Corp. said that as much as half of its research dollars is now spent to meet regulation.

Thus, disincentives are double: not only do regulations perceived as onerous deter new facilities; but, in addition, increasingly large sums must be diverted by corporations from research into the nonprofit-making activity of complying with government regulations. In turn, both of these incentive deterring factors translate into obsolescent or inefficient facilities and a decline in productivity which, in some critical industries, such as steel, has reached crisis proportions.[28] Given such obsolescence and the failure to install more modern machinery, it is not surprising if constant prices rise.

It would be foolhardy to hold that the sluggishness of capital investment and formation is *entirely* attributable to the cumulative mix of government intervention and taxes on income which could be employed for expansion and modernization, but the case that such policies are a major factor is overwhelming—unless we adopt the paranoid posture that the testimony of most businessmen is a conspiratorial lie. I prefer not to accept the latter outlandish formulation, and suggest that what we are witnessing is a manifestation of a capitalist society's contradictions. Because of the class nature of the society and the widespread discretion vested in the owners of the means of production which is oriented by profit maximization, the government cannot plan, and well intentioned public policies are either doomed to defeat or to imposition of unacceptable costs. The cumulative effect of the government intervention discussed and its probable expansion in the near future is to retard private investment in productive facilities and development, which in turn has other serious consequences of which low profit rates is one of the most important. Most observers (including government officials) concede that business investment in productive facilities must be the key to driving the economy; yet it is limping along at unacceptably low rates of 3 percent to 4 percent, leading to continued (and chronic) high rates of unemployment.[29] And, as jobs remain scarce—and perhaps get scarcer—there will likely be important consequences even in such remote policy areas as civil rights and crime.

But is there no way out? Clearly the conservative proponents of allocating resources without government intervention as well as the liberal and social-democratic proponents of government intervention both think that an acceptable equilibrium can be reached if only policy formulations follow their respective recommendations.

PLANLESSNESS AND AUTOMATIC ADJUSTMENTS

To summarize the argument thus far, the underlying structure of our economy—based upon widespread private discretion and antagonistic divisions between classes and fractions of classes, each eager to pursue its interests at the expense of others and of a "national interest"—precludes effective planning, defeats and frustrates many public policies, and often results in the effective cancellation of competing policies. In addition, contemporary trends in public policy threaten the effectiveness of the private economy. Yet there are many observers who would concede all, or most, of this argument, but theorize that the economic system will more or less adjust because of its internal dynamics. The search for automatic adjustments within our political economy is, of course, not new, stretching back to such famous formulations as Say's Law or Adam Smith's invisible hand. But in comtemporary terms, the policy prescriptions seem to be founded either upon a return to a political economy based largely upon the free market with a minimum amount of government intervention—a renewal of the invisible hand idea—or the more widely held view of liberals and social-democrats that macroeconomic government intervention can adequately substitute for central planning.

The superficially attractive merits of the conservative view are: (1) the widespread range of choice available within the society, free of government's capability to limit individual discretion, and (2) the enormous cost savings which would accrue from a more limited government role. Most government labor is, after all not productive (in the sense employed in this paper). The conservative prescription is based upon the centrality of the free contract—X and Y *voluntarily* entering into agreements, free of restraint. Yet, every first-year law student learns about contracts of adhesion in which there is no effective bargaining between the parties. One who purchases a railroad ticket, for example, or the provision of natural gas or medical services, does not bargain. He takes it or leaves it, and usually must take it for compelling reasons. One of the major difficulties with the free-market view is that contracts of adhesion are rather widespread in this society, and instead of being subject to the dictates of government, we are effectively subject to the dictates of private individuals possessing vastly superior bargaining power. For this reason and, as James Anderson observes, because the market does not work effectively or according to the model in many different situations for a variety of specific reasons, we have and will continue to have a vast public interventionist apparatus. But the conservative perspective has also been rejected because the numerous individual decisions made by private entrepreneurs do not aggregate to something congruent to public needs. Mass education and public transportation are only two illustrations of the widespread gap. Finally, the unaided free-market system is, as analysts from Marx to Keynes have pointed out, inherently unstable with boom and bust cycles latent within it.[30]

For these reasons, liberals and social-democrats have advocated a mixed system involving considerable government regulation, some public enterprise, and above all, a mix of macroeconomic policies as the appropriate substitute for planning. All of this takes place within a central capitalist context in which many critical decisions are made by private entrepreneurs. I have already commented on the regulatory set of policies and its impact upon the political economy as a whole, and will not repeat myself here. But it is particularly macroeconomic policy which has been the pride of the policy-making establishment in Western countries. Based upon Keynesian programs and the implications of the famous Phillips Curve, these policies have been credited with the unprecedented growth of the Western economies (and Japan) since the end of World War II. But as Howard Sherman has shown in his essay in this volume and elsewhere, the policies which worked relatively well during much of the post-war era no longer do. Space precludes any extensive comment on why macro-economic policies no longer work as they once did, but clearly one major problem is the declining rates of investment and return in the productive sector of the economy.[31] Government spending programs which do not trigger profits and expansion in the industrial sector can only produce an Argentine-style economy of rampant inflation, no real growth, stagnant or declining living standards, and high unemployment.

It would be rash in the extreme to describe the American (and other western) economy as being in shambles. But clearly the smug confidence of the forecasters is gone. And they readily admit their frustration and confusion.[32] Confidence in automatic stabilizers, such as unemployment compensation, to right the economy has dwindled.[33] Price controls have failed to stop either inflation or unemployment. Big deficits in the federal budget have failed to stimulate economic growth, while panaceas like the Humphrey-Hawkins Bill for job creation (in whatever form it ultimately is enacted) are generally viewed as both very inflationary and extremely costly.[34] Even the policy proscriptions based upon the famous Phillip's Curve trade-off between inflation and unemployment—true for 100 years—no longer hold. Inflation and unemployment rise together during this period of stagflation, leading even Professor Paish, one of the foremost economic policy formulators, to concede that his theoretical notions of an automatic regulator governing the trade-off between inflation and unemployment are no longer true.[35] In a word, the traditional liberal and social-democratic methods for handling the economy no longer work. The range of effective public policy choices available to a society ultimately depends upon its system of production. And, unless radical changes are undertaken in American capitalism, that range will narrow rather than widen.

NOTES

1. Theodore J. Lowi, *The End of Liberalism* (New York: W.W. Norton, 1969).

2. Max Weber, *Economy and Society* (New York: Bedminster Press, 1968): 26.

3. That even the most comprehensive attempt at planning within a capitalist context falls far short of comprehensiveness and control is clear from Stephen S. Cohen, *Modern Capitalist Planning: The French Model* (1969, Berkely: University of California Press, 1977).

4. The argument is developed more fully in Alan Stone, *Economic Regulation and the Public Interest* (Ithaca, N.Y.: Cornell University Press, 1977): Chapter 11.

5. See, for example, "The Texas Rebellion Over EPA's Air Rules," *Business Week* (December 6,1976): 97,98.

6. "Theory Deserts the Forecasters", *Business Week* (June 29, 1974): 50.

7. See the historical discussion in Karl Marx, *Theories of Surplus Value,* Part 1 (Moscow: Progress Publishers, 1963).

9. David Ricardo, *Principles of Political Economy and Taxation* (London: G. Bell & Sons, 1929): 336. The reference in other editions is to Chapter XXVI.

10. Joan Robinson, "Full Employment and Inflation" in *Collected Economic Papers,* vol. 2 (Oxford: Basil Blackwell, 1964): 271-279.

11. "Dow Chemical's Catalog of Regulatory Horrors," *Business Week* (April 4, 1977): 50, and "Goodyear Chief Hits Regulation," *New York Times* (November 11, 1975): 45.

12. Harold L. Davis, "Overregulation—A Problem for Research," *Physics Today* (January, 1977): 112.

13. William D. Nordhaus, "The Falling Share of Profits," *Brookings Papers on Economic Activity,* 1 (1974): 169-208. For a less dramatic estimate of profit decline see Martin Feldstein and Lawrence Summers, "Is the Profit Rate Falling?", *Brooking Papers on Economic Activity,* 1 (1977): 211-228.

14. "State, Local Taxes Still Heading Up," *U.S. News & World Report* (November 14,1977): 82.

15. "Government Growth Crowds out Investment," *Business Week* (October 18, 1976): 138-145.

16. On the current capital shortage see, among other reports, "Can U.S. Industry Find the Money It Needs," *Business Week* (September 22, 1973): 42-54, and "Where Will the Growth Capital Come From?", *Business Week* (December 14, 1974): 70,71. For a critical analysis of the capital shortage hypothesis, see Paul Sweezy and Harry Magdoff, "Capital Shortage: Fact and Fancy," *Monthly Review* (April, 1976): 1-19..

18. For further analysis of this difference see Stone, chapters 2, 7, 9, and 10.

19. William Tucker, "Environmentalism and the Leisure Class," *Harper's* (December, 1977): 49-56, 73-80.

20. A similar argument, although applicable to a different era, may be found in Thorstein Veblen, *The Theory of the Leisure Class* (1899, New York: Random House Modern Library, 1931), chapter 3.

21. "Regulatory Reform is A Political Necessity," *Business Week* (April 4, 1977): 47.

22. Ralph E. Winter, "A Desire to Acquire," *Wall Street Journal,* LIX, 35 (1977): 1. On the recent merger wave, see "The Great Takeover Binge," *Business Week* (November 14,1977): 176-183.

23. See, for example, Paul MacAvoy, "The Regulation Induced Shortage of Natural Gas," *Journal of Law and Economics,* XIV (April, 1971): 167-199.

24. "The Gloom in Coal," *Business Week* (November 28,1977): 76-93.

25. "Why the Big Refiners Aren't Expanding", *Business Week* (Sept. 12, 1977), pp. 69-72.

26. On the pharmaceutical industry see Sam Peltzman, "An Evaluation of Consumer Protection Legislation: the 1962 Drug Amendments," *Journal of Political Economy* (September/October, 1973): 1049-1091.

27. Thomas A. O'Toole, "U.S. Industry Cutting Basic Research," *Washington Post* (November 28, 1977): 1.

28. See, for example, "Spotlight on 'Productivity'—Why It's A Key to U.S. Problems," *U.S. News & World Report* (October 4, 1971): 25-28, on productivity.

29. Hyman Solomon, "Prime Engine of U.S. Recovery May Need A Kick," *Financial Post* (November 18,1977): 1. On the relationship between economic growth and unemployment, see Julius Shiskin's estimates reprinted in James L. Rowe, Jr., "Carter May to Have Top Growth Target to Meet Goal for Unemployment," *Washington Post* (January 23, 1977).

30. For a brilliant exposition of Keynes' views on the inherent instability of capitalism, see Hyman P. Minsky, *John Maynard Keynes* (New York: Columbia University Press, 19750.

31. "The Slow Investment Economy", *Business Week* (October 17, 1977): 60-114.

32. See footnote 6.

33. "The Flaws in Relying on Lower Prices to Help the Economy," *Business Week* (March 17, 1975): 74.

34. See, for example, "Why the Big Deficits Fail to Stimulate," *Business Week* (March 4, 1972): 66-68, and Art Pine, "Cost of Jobs Bill," *Washington Post* (November 15, 1977): A-2.

35. The Phillips Curve hypothesis is empirically developed in A.W. Phillips, 'The Relationship Between Unemployment and Rate of Change of Money Wage Rates in the U.K., 1861-1957," *Economica,* 25, 100 (1958): 283-299. Paish's formulations are contained in F.W. Paish, *Studies In An Inflationary Economy* (London: MacMillan, 1962). See also "Is the Phillips Curve Losing its Allure," *Business Week* (April 18, 1973).

SUBJECT INDEX

NAME INDEX

ABOUT THE EDITORS

Theodore J. Lowi is the John L. Senior Professor of American Institutions at Cornell University. Before coming to Cornell in 1972 he was Professor of Political Science at the University of Chicago. He spent 1967-1968 on a Guggenheim in Paris and another year in Paris in 1973-1974. During 1977-1978 he was a Fellow at the Center for Advanced Study in the Behavioral Sciences. His major publications include *At the Pleasure of the Mayor* (1962), *The End of Liberalism* (1969), *The Politics of Disorder* (1971), and *American Government: Incomplete Conquest* (1976). He is co-author of *Poliscide* (1976), a study of science policy. *Arena: of Power,* a book in preparation for 1978-1979, is a study of public policy of which the contribution in this volume will be a part.

Alan Stone is currently Associate Professor of Political Science at the University of Houston. He previously taught at Rutgers University and prior to that time was an attorney with the Federal Trade Commission. He is author of *Economic Regulation and the Public Interest,* co-author of *The Ruling Elites,* and has published articles in scholarly and popular journals. His current interests include the relationships between private law, public policy, and the economic system, and his new work, *Structure and Superstructure,* is a study of private law and public policy.

DATE DUE

GAYLORD			PRINTED IN U.S.A.